BLOOD, SWEAT
& THEORY

BLOOD, SWEAT & THEORY

John Freeman

First published in 2010 by Libri Publishing

ISBN 978 1 907471 04 9

Cover design by Helen Taylor
Cover image of Helen Paris by Hugo Glendinning
Typesetting by Carnegie Book Production
Printed in the UK by Ashford Colour Press

Acknowledgements

In the first instance, thanks to Paul Jervis, Celia Cozens and Matt Skipper for their commitment and continued professionalism in the face of more problems than this page could contain.

This book would be no book at all without the expert contributions of Hala Al-Yamani, Annette Arlander, Johannes Birringer, Elena Cologni, Robert Germay, Helka-Maria Kinnunen, Yves Knockaert, Lee Miller, Felix Nobis, Allan Owens, Helen Paris, Yoni Prior, Leena Rouhiainen and Joanne 'Bob' Whalley. Their generosity in the sharing of views, experiences and insights is greatly appreciated.

Any acknowledgements would be incomplete without thanking my colleagues and students for the conversations, performances and assorted creative energies that make working at Brunel University the experience that it is. Similarly, work seen during the writing of this book, up to and including the incredible 'Isabella's Room' by Jan Lauwers and Needcompany, has served as a reminder that when it all comes together, performance can still stir the blood, the spirit and the brain like nothing else on earth.

Contents

Preface

> Writing about art is like dancing about architecture:
> it's a really stupid thing to want to do.
> **Elvis Costello**

When it comes to art, Clement Greenberg cautioned, we should all watch out for thinking. (Greenberg, 1981: 42) We hear echoes of this in William Rubin's argument that only a small number of practitioners are conscious enough of process to recognise the ways in which their work might transcend its own moment in time. (Rubin, 1977: 189) This translates into a performance context through Andrew Quick's description of 'the conventional refusal of the experimental artist to explain their work'; a state Quick links to a pragmatic emphasis on the 'experience of negotiation, rather than explication'. (Quick, 2007: 269–270) It is at the point where the negotiations of practice meet research demands for explication that this book explores the relationship between academic research and an evolving field of performance. In doing so it reports on the constructive tensions wrought by an increasingly complex collapsing of distinctions in the worlds of performance, research and practice.

The emergence of 'practice as research' as a catch-all term for many methodologies and outcomes that sit outside text-based research has brought new challenges to our understandings of research. More pertinently, it has forced us to question the roles of (academic) practitioners and (practising) academics. The fresh categorisations that stem from this provide a useful jumping-off point in considering the written text's historical authority in terms of both thesis and dissemination.

Practice occupies a unique place in academic research, encountered simultaneously as inert and active and often sidelined by its dual need to be studied and interpreted through reading as well as through spectating upon what are still most usually live experiences. Research generally concludes with the written word, yet performance can only be fully discussed when the multiplicity of factors determining the *experienced* product have been taken into account. Accordingly, links between research theory (and theory-speak) and performance run through this book, primarily through focusing on the role of practice as research in performance-related PhD registration, investigation and submission. Drawing on established theory models from art and design and fusing these with more nascent dialogues concerning performative interventions, something of the zeitgeist is captured: a zeitgeist that is provoking students, supervisors and examiners into innovative areas of debate and discovery.

There is a substantial early caveat here. The sense of this as in key ways being linked to the drive towards the new, alongside the institutional urge towards postgraduate registration and retention and the students' need for the professional validation and entry that the qualification is seen to bring, carries with it the risk of leading – or *appearing* to lead – subject-specific research into short-term and sometimes solipsistic discovery.

Making reference to this carries implications of circumspection that are currently unfashionable in academic performance circles and which kick against the canonicity of practice as research activity. Circumspection does not amount to negativity and in its review of a boom period in research that is both carried and created by cultural shifts in the constituent nature of PhD submissions this book offers a critique that is supportive without being easily swayed by hyperbole. Accordingly, where claims for practice-based research are made subject to questioning in the pages to come, they are challenged in ways that see doubt as an epistemological tool, as well as forming a somewhat fatigued response to the widespread application of trends in academia: trends which seem at times to do no more than take the art-ness out of art, the essentially performative out of performance and the critical out of reflection.

This book's critique is carried out in tandem with an identification of the qualities most often required for successful practice-as-research PhD registration, research and completion, providing a series of useful steps for consideration. These include:

- Exploration of what is at stake in adopting and working through practice-based research methodologies

- Identification of the features, attitudes, principles and skills involved in practice-based work

- Articulation of effective and persuasive ways of communicating the advantages of practice-based research

- Provision of models for PhD proposals and research procedures

- Analysis of Mode 2 Knowledge, Heuristic Research and Autoethnography

- Definitions of stages in the creative process

- Foregrounding a series of key questions for prospective researchers

- Challenging received ideas of practice as thesis

- Distinguishing research from reflection and feelings from findings

- Addressing originality, multivalence, tacit knowledge and dissemination

- Locating practice-based research within an arts and educational continuum.

Through its inclusion of a series of case studies, this book contains more than a passing focus on the role of ongoing practice undertaken by full-time university lecturers as part of their assessable research outcomes. This creates an intrinsic examination of the academic and professional questions raised when performance practice identifies itself as an ipso facto research outcome. Within the university sector, performance making has become rightly synonymous with performance development, bringing with it the critical implication of practice turning a microscope on itself, challenging the elastic boundaries of its own forms and applications in ways that published writing can often echo but rarely outdo. Contemporary approaches to performance research are multifaceted, paradoxical and constantly evolving; and the new theories and often generative processes that stem from and through practice and its role within university research are having a profound impact on the ways in which our subject develops.

Within *Blood, Sweat & Theory* some readings, interpretations and suggestions are likely to be a little more potentially controversial than others, and I have no doubt there will be plentiful evidence of that which may well read as internal contradiction. Where this evidence occurs, readers are invited to consider these contradictions as something positive, fluid and even organic; reflective of a process (not unlike the processes involved in performance making) where yesterday's certainties serve to fill us with doubt when we view them anew. Rather than settling on an unswerving perspective at the point of commencement and seeing it through I am acknowledging that both the text and my convictions will be swayed in part by some of the arguments encountered along the way.

In this way the construction of this book is a developmental echo of an earlier writing project and publication: a thesis and subsequent book that investigated the possibilities of and for acts of critical written reflection taking place in the moment of creative performance making; (Freeman, 2003) whilst the writing for this book is markedly different to those exercises in near-immediate response, a little of that flavour remains. Its incorporation here is intended to afford the writing some of that sense of process, addition and reiteration that is an identifiable feature of the rehearsal room. The writing here clings then to the capacity for infinite revision, rethinking and reconsideration so that the book aspires to something of Brecht's ideal of a mode of presentation that reserves the right to review positions taken and to adjust them in full sight. It is, ultimately, a small attempt at fusing *this* critical work with *those* creative impulses and in this it owes much to the Italian term *pentimento*, where an underlying image in a painting shows through as the top layer of paint, the finished article, becomes transparent with age. This idea of an early draft being somehow made visible, of half-thoughts and potential changes of mind being exposed rather than edited out is my continued concession to *pentimento* as an act of seeing once and then of seeing again.

Abstracts of Case Studies

Everything I know, I write about. My research is what I did.

Mort Walker

For a playwright such as Valère Novarina a performance text is nothing but footprints on the ground left by performers who have subsequently disappeared. (Novarina, 1993: 102) For Maurice Merleau-Ponty a performer is always already possessed of innate and immediate knowledge, an understanding of the world by and through the body, (Merleau-Ponty, 1968) whilst for Hélène Cixous the task of writing is to create sites of possibility, where the performing body can make itself heard. (Cixous, 1993) If a certain *jouissance* exists in the act of reading then the case studies in this book also allow for that which (with a nod to my colleagues Josephine Machon and Janet Free) Julia Kristeva sees as a sense of *J'ouis sens*: an enjoyment in the activity of making sense: a hearing and reading of meaning as it unfolds. (Kristeva, 1980)

Writing about one's own practice is an act of critical reflection that is becoming increasingly established as a key aspect of experiential knowledge across a range of subject areas. Within the fields of medicine and clinical psychology, for example, reflective practice is commonly regarded as one of the means by which practitioners are able to extend their knowledge and skills in order to maintain competence throughout their professional lives. Within the study of theatre, drama and performance we are seeing researchers paying focused attention to the knowledge of their own creative and cognitive processes, to the extent that metacognitive practitioner awareness is now widely accepted as providing invaluable links between 'knowing about' and 'knowing how', between inspirational acts of creativity and the conscious ability performance makers possess to talk rationally and well about their work. It is this fusing of the creative and the cognitive that is at the heart of practice-based research developments, marking as it does a shift from seemingly objective reporting to the more overtly perspective-acknowledging *reportage*, and from observations of others to reflections of self. It is a process that makes description experiential and experience available, allowing us to make some small sense of our time through the words of those who practise what they write. In this sense, this book's case studies also function as a way of reminding readers that in performance it is the work – the *practice* – that comes first... and that where it doesn't, it should.

Contemporary performance remains at the forefront of developments in current art, crossing, dissolving and exposing as false many of the boundaries between seemingly discrete disciplines. In this fashion, performance is able to offer a range of aesthetic, applied, conceptual, critical and experiential possibilities. It is in this spirit that the case studies included here stand as a sample of the wide range of performance-related practices currently made within the shared contexts of art houses and universities, galleries and theatres, claimed spaces and social gatherings. For Gay McAuley, the type of work included here has often been created 'below the radar of official culture, unfunded or underfunded, ignored by the mainstream press, and occupying marginal spaces in the community, but this stream of work, while it has not transformed mainstream theatre and dance, has certainly transformed dominant ideas of what constitutes theatre.' (McAuley, 2002)

Certainly the case studies offer here the much-needed noetic sense of the immediate, the intuitive and the bodily that my own more distanced writings will be less likely to provide and I am as indebted to contributors in advance as readers will be when they move through the pages of this book.

Despite their writings here and elsewhere, the practitioners contributing case studies share an innate belief that, alongside the context for the work, the bodies of performers and participants create expressions of ideas that leave their own cultural, aesthetic and social traces of significance and signification. That performance does more than function as a means to the end of authorial ink. Some of the case studies focus on the specifics of particular projects, whilst others articulate the concerns of work across a range of years and contexts. In all cases the writers have made their own choices and have written about the types of practice they felt most appropriate within the parameters of this publication. There were no suggestions of any house style, either in terms of the types of work to be discussed or of the manner of that discussion. If, for once, a claim can be made that a book such as this contains something for everyone then that claim is premised on the diversity and quality of the case studies.

The abstracts and biographies that follow are in the contributors' own words: any variance in style, approach and articulation is consistent with the independent nature of their choosing.

Hala Al-Yamani and Allan Owens

Hala Al-Yamani PhD is Assistant Professor at the Faculty of Education at Bethlehem University, Bethlehem, West Bank, Occupied Palestinian Territory. Long-term research interests focus on the role of drama in teacher education. Current work includes the use of forum theatre to highlight issues of gender at student political representation level, school drop-out and community awareness of the Convention of Children's Rights. She worked with the Palestinian Ministry of Education in evaluating the drama curriculum and has extensive experience with international foundations such as Save the Children and UNICEF.

Allan Owens PhD is Professor of Drama Education and Distinguished Teaching Fellow of the University of Chester. He is a UK National Teaching Fellow and in addition to teaching at undergraduate and postgraduate levels works in a wide range of fields including education, theatre, health, community, business and justice. His extensive range of international work includes long-term collaborative projects in Finland, Palestine and Japan. Current practice, teaching and research interests centre on intercultural applied drama work and in particular the use of process drama form.

Returning to Haifa: Using Pre-text Based Drama to Understand Self and Other

This case study identifies the origins and briefly traces the evolution of the series of encounters between two applied drama practitioners working in two different countries over a period of six years (2003–2009). The on-going intercultural applied drama project of which this is a part moves between two universities and their communities in the UK and Palestine. The focus of this case study is on the ways in which research questions are embedded in and arise from practice. Particular attention is paid to the shifting imperatives and motivations, or in Arabic 'Dawafe', for doing this work. It is the particular dynamic of the restructuring of practice as a result of the shifting research questions asked that has encouraged us to consider it as an example of practice as research.

Mindful that any attempt to 'simply describe' this series of encounters would be an attempt to pass interpretation off as fact, we try to present the case as 'a specific, complex, functioning thing' in some detail, messy though it might be. (Stake, 1995: 2) It is intrinsic in the sense that we want to use the writing of this study to learn more about our particular case. It is instrumental as in doing this we also want to try and make explicit our tacit understandings of the ways in which practice, research and ethics continually interface in this project. Our intention is not to burden the reader unduly with understandings that may result from this attempt to present practice-as-research in a traditional written format. It is rather an exercise in identifying what we thought was happening at particular points in time, a gathering of human experience more as 'a matter of chronologies than of causes and effects'. (Ibid.: 12)

Case studies conventionally surface prominent issues, which the reader reasonably expects the researcher/s to develop. As Stake argues, 'Issues are not simple and clean, but intricately wired to political, social, historical and especially personal contexts'. (1995: 17) This is particularly true of the issues surfacing from the context of this project, focusing as it does on the Palestinian situation. We do identify issues but resist developing them. Whilst the reader may find this frustrating, we do so in the attempt to lay open the overall shape of this practice-as-research project to the reader in the clearest way possible.

In summary, the presentation of this case study in chronological form is not an attempt to pass off interpretation as fact, nor is it an excuse to duck the responsibility of constructing an original conceptual organising structure. It is instead an attempt to provide a concrete example of the messiness of the journey of two practitioner-researchers as they grapple with the practice and research questions and the ethics of these in the attempt to get them 'right' in order to allow the next shift to occur.

Helka-Maria Kinnunen

Helka-Maria Kinnunen graduated with an MA in Acting from the Theatre Academy of Finland in 1982. She has worked as an actor in several Finnish theatres and for the Finnish Broadcasting Company. She has an interest in making manuscripts and directing, as well as carrying out artistic work in different environments. Kinnunen works as teacher at the Theatre Academy, where her doctoral thesis, *Stories in the artistic process of theatre-making*, was successfully completed in 2008.

Towards Collaborativity in Theatre-making

The starting point for my dissertation, *Stories in the artistic process of theatre-making*, was a production, where storytelling was used as a means of producing material for the manuscript and also of delving into collective theatre-making.

Having started my doctoral studies I was filled with experimental ideas. I was very much affected by and feeling invited to the possibilities of narrative means in theatre practices. When reflecting on the artistic work afterwards, several questions arose, the main problem having occurred during the process: instead of a free and playful collaboration the process became dim and complicated.

In this case study I ask those questions again: what kind of abilities or preparation would the group need to have in order to share a practice where storytelling and bodily action alternate? How could I lead this kind of process whilst at the same time avoiding a traditional director's authoritarian role in the group? Where does the borderline go between artistic and other communication, when and how should the storytelling be conducted, and who would have the right to conduct it?

By answering these questions I discuss the target of the artistic work and how it changed during the process. As a conclusion I characterise artistic processes as collective and transformative journeys containing breaks or jumps that always tend to guide to an unknown result. As a conclusion on utilising narrative means in researching my own artistic practices, I describe narrative perspective as a strategy of confessions that constantly breaks through. This works as a fruitful medium for inviting material from practice into writing.

Helen Paris

Helen Paris received her PhD from the University of Surrey and specialises in live art, solo and one-to-one performance and new media. She has been making performance for over 15 years and is co director of Curious with Leslie Hill. Curious was formed in 1996 and has produced over 30 projects which have been shown and exhibited widely by such venues as the Sydney Opera House, the British Council Showcase at the Edinburgh Festival and Artist Links, Shanghai. The work includes performance, installation video and film and the company is know for its edgy, humorous interrogations of contemporary culture and politics, work which has been called 'as smart as it is seductive'. Recent publications include DVDs *Essences of London, Lost & Found*, and the 35 mm film *(Be)longing*.

Hill and Paris' book, *The Guerilla Guide to Performance Art: How to Make a Living as an Artist* is published by Continuum. Their second book, *Performance and Place* is published by Palgrave Macmillan. Curious is represented by Artsadmin: see www.placelessness.com for details.

The Smell of It

This case study will chart the research for and creation of *On the Scent*, a live-art, site-specific piece which explores the elusive connections between smell and memory. This project was created by Helen Paris and Leslie Hill and scientific research was undertaken in collaboration with biological scientist Dr Upinder Bhalla, at the National Centre for Biological Sciences, Bangalore, India. The project has been supported by a Wellcome Trust Science on Stage and Screen Award, an AHRB Innovation Award and Arts Council England. *On the Scent* has toured to North and South America, throughout Europe and the UK, China and Australia, with over 450 performances to date.

On the Scent takes place in a home through which audience members are invited on intimate and distinctly aromatic journeys.

An archive of over 3,000 smell memories has been collected from the project, which have been shared with Dr Bhalla thus establishing a reciprocal relationship between science and art.

Robert Germay

Robert Germay holds a Licence in Germanic Philology (ULg). He was awarded a Doctor of Philosophy and Letters in 1972 with a dissertation that explored the influence of Bertolt Brecht on German theatre. Germay was Senior Lecturer in the Department of Information and Communication of the ULg (Theory and Practice in the Theatre) and director of the Théâtres Universitaires Liégeois (University Theater and Theater of Germanists), renamed the 'Théâtre Universitaire Royal de Liège' in 2002. Between 1977 and 1983 he was Instructor in Dramatic Arts at the Conservatoire Royal of Liège and between 1976 and 1980 at the Volkshochschule of Aachen.

The founder/director of the Rencontres Internationales de Théâtre Universitaire, Liège (since 1983); president and founder of the International Association of University Theaters (AITU/IUTA), 1994–2008 and member of the administrative council of the ITI – French-speaking Community of Belgium, Germay has worked as a director with numerous professional stage companies (Rideau de Bruxelles, Nouveau Gymnase de Liège, Kobold d'Aachen, l'Etuve à Liège…), as well as with amateur companies (Liège, Visé, Heyd, Haïfa…), and above all, at the Théâtre Universitaire Royal de Liège, for whom he has directed more than 80 plays in French, German, English and Walloon. Professor Germay has directed workshops in Germany, Israel, Canada, Morocco and Brazil and has editorial input to *Coulisses* and *Performance Practice*.

Robert Germay retired from teaching in October 2006. He remains President of the TURLg.

The Relationship between University Theatre and Professional Theatre: A Question of Method

The choice of a play is always a challenge, for every director. Questions of which play... and why... and how... and for whom... and with whom?

This problem is even more acute for directors of university amateur theatres where the performers are generally not theatre students, and where they are far away from wishing to become professionals.

This is certainly true for the Royal University Theatre of Liège, which was founded in 1941. Robert Germay's case study provides examples of a number of Liège-made touring productions in which he had to deal with the challenges (and sometimes the problems) of casting, in terms of overall group size, age and ability of performers. These issues, alongside the necessity for portable stage sets, highly transferable scenography, limited rehearsal time, small budget and the imperative to make work accessible to international audiences with different language needs are articulated in Germay's description of work that is fuelled in equal parts by ideology and pragmatics, aesthetic philosophy and creative pedagogy, group-loyalty and inclusivity.

Elena Cologni

Elena Cologni is a practitioner whose work is developed in the academic and artistic contexts. Currently Research Fellow at York St John University, and studio artist at Wysing Arts Centre, Cambridge, she studied at the Academy of Art Brera in Milan, Bretton Hall College, Leeds University, and her PhD 'The Artist's Performative Practice within the Anti-Ocularcentric Discourse' is from Central St Martins College of Art and Design (CSM), London. After the post-doc AHRC and CSM awarded project 'Present Memory and Liveness in delivery and reception of video documentation during performance art events', she is developing 'Experiential' a project funded by York St John University and the Arts Council of England, focusing on questions of memory, remoteness and transmission of information over time and space. She is active in the debate on practice-as-research methodologies (PARIP 2001–2005), and she contributes to the teaching team of the MPhil course Arts Education and Culture at Cambridge University, Faculty of Education. She also looks at the relationship between performance and new media (TAPRA, PSinternational), on which she has presented extensively. Her artwork has been supported internationally, by Galleria Neon and Galleria d'Arte Moderna, Bologna; Gennazzano Museum, Rome; GAMeC Museum, Bergamo; Venice Biennale, Venice, Italy; Oslo Kunstforening, Norway; Garanti Platform and Karsi Sanat, Istanbul; Brown University, RI; Artists Space, New York; Watershed Media Centre, Bristol; Tate Modern, National Portrait Gallery, Gallery 291, Whitechapel Art Gallery, ICA, London; Wysing Arts Centre, Cambridge.

Cologni's artistic practice as research involves studio and academic work, with outlets in both the academic and the art/museum environments. Its outcomes are mainly mediatised performances, with specific interest in perceptual/ psychological dynamics between artist (artwork/environment) and audience. In particular, Merleau-Ponty's concept of chiasm/intertwining is expressed by adopting various systems to stimulate a continuous communication shift between artist and audience. Cologni's PhD thesis placed the evolution from sculptural and photographic work to performance in relation to the critique of the ocularcentric Western philosophical tradition, developed by twentieth-century French thought, as referred to by Martin Jay and Amelia Jones.

The issue of documentation of Cologni's performative work has been embedded in the work itself, thus becoming both research methodological tool and meta-linguistic art practice, and avoiding the schizophrenic scenario often brought about by the artist–academic overlapping roles. Since 2001 Cologni's conference presentations have been practice based whereas the written analytical material is usually published as contextualisation or documentation of the practice.

That Spot in the 'Moving Picture' is You

> You define the present as that which is, when it is simply what is
> happening. [ce qui se fait.] Nothing is less than the present moment,
> if you mean by that the indivisible limit that separates the past from
> the future. When we think of this present as what ought to be [devant
> etre], it is no longer, and when we think of it as existing, it is already
> past... all perception is already memory.
>
> (Bergson, 1994)

As I am reading it, I realize I am experiencing the meaning in this very moment... always a bit later, rather.

For recent mediatised performances like *Mnemonic Present, Un-Folding Series* (MP) in 2005–2006 (the outcome of an AHRC-funded project), the use of the document as 'live-recording' and 'pre-recording' opened up questions on the involvement of the audience and their perception of what is present and represented, generating a form of 'present memory' of the event from which the notion of 'mnemonic present' takes shape.

With this strand of investigation I contribute to the debate on the ontological value of performance documentation. Embedding the document (e.g. a video recording) in the event allows an audience to witness its very production, thus emphasising the document's 'performativity' aspect. The *Mnemonic Present* project has led me to conceive a more complex set of issues around time perception which are being explored and developed in 'Experiential' (outcomes include Re-Moved Gi08, Centre for Contemporary Arts Glasgow and Apnea, Museum of Manchester, 2008). These are: time in fruition of mediatised performances for construction of performative self; distinction between reality and forms of its representation due to our perception of time; the reception of archival material in relation to live video; self-awareness generated by use of forms of dystonia (unbalance), i.e. between sound and vision.

The written account will be an example of research-based practice (on the page), whereby the shaping of knowledge is achieved in a balance between the 'making' and its contextualisation. Hence I shall organise the text so that it will follow a certain pattern/shape. This will be in tune with my recently used strategies including: scotoma (gap in visual field), apnea (gap in breathing activity), amnesia (and scotomisation as gap in mnemonic archive).

Yoni Prior

Currently Convenor of Creative Arts, and Head of the Drama Strand in the School of Communication and Creative Arts, Deakin University, Yoni Prior was a member of the Theatre Board of the Australia Council, and the National Multicultural Arts Advisory Committee between 1999 and 2004. She is on the board of Back To Back Theatre Company, and Chair of the Big West Arts Festival.

A founding member of Gilgul Theatre, Prior holds a Bachelor of Education degree (Rusden State College, 1981) and a Masters Degree in Theatre Studies (Monash University, 1998). She has published on contemporary performance practice, practice as research, dramaturgy in dance and theatre, rehearsal practice and repertoire development, as well as working as a performer, animateur, director, dramaturg, translator and writer with many major theatre and dance companies in Australia.

Bleeding Narratives: *Levad*, 1993

This case study reflects on the nexus between real and performed effort in a work about suffering.

The monodrama *Levad* was created as part of *The Exile Trilogy*, a sequence of performance works devised by Gilgul Theatre reflecting upon Jewish history and experience through the prism of the concerns and disintegration of the Yiddish theatre. This third part of the trilogy attempted to represent the fractured, tragic and peripatetic life of an actress from the Yiddish theatre through a series of remembered fragments visited upon her in a 'Blakean memory mill'.

Written from the perspective of the devisor–performer–researcher, the study attempts to unravel a complex reticulation of narratives – real and fictional – which coalesced to reframe the performance event, and to condition critical and audience responses to the work.

Leena Rouhiainen

Dr Leena Rouhiainen is a dancer–choreographer and dance scholar who has worked as a professional contemporary dance artist since 1990. Her doctoral dissertation, published in 2003, addresses the issue of being a freelance dance artist through a phenomenological perspective. She held a post-doctoral researcher position at the Theatre Academy in Finland between 2005 and 2008. She was the head of the research project called *Challenging the Notion of Knowledge* between 2005 and 2007 at the same institution. Rouhiainen currently holds a position as associate professor in dance and physical education at the Norwegian School of Sport Sciences in Oslo and runs a research project entitled *Intuition in Creative Processes* at the Media Lab of the University of Art and Design in Helsinki. She is the chair of the board of Nordic Forum for Research in Dance (NOFOD). Her current research interests are in artistic research, somatics and bodily knowledge as well as a phenomenological understanding of the dancer's space.

A Mono-trilogy on a Collaborative Process in the Performing Arts

This case study introduces an artistic collaboration between a dance artist, a sound designer and an architect. While the paper discusses themes that emerged from the artistic process, it mainly exemplifies an approach to conducting artistic research. It attempts to offer an evocative view on the challenges of articulating shared and open-ended artistic practice in writing. It does so by creating an artistic–scholarly tale that combines reflections on artistic research, writing and some theoretical sources with poetic images and journal notes on the artistic process.

Annette Arlander

Annette Arlander is a Doctor of Arts and Professor of Performance Art and Theory at the Theatre Academy, Helsinki (www.teak.fi/annette_arlander). Her art work is focused on performing landscape by means of video or recorded voice (www.harakka.fi/arlander). Arlander's research interests include performance as research, performance studies, site specificity, landscape, and the environment.

Performing with Trees: Landscape and Artistic Research

In performing landscape, I try to show time taking place. While performing a still-act in front of a video camera, the events taking place in the background, in the landscape, can come to the fore.[1] By repeating this at regular intervals over long periods of time, and condensing the material by editing, the slow happenings not discernible in real time can be seen and shown. Could this working method and/or method of presentation be developed into a research method? The answer is, probably, yes. However, the question is for what: a research method for what exactly?

I am using a three-stage working method for performing landscape on video. First, I am repeating a still-act or a simple action in the same place in front of a video camera with the same camera positioning, at regular intervals over long periods of time. Secondly, I am condensing the material by editing, preserving the chronological order, but choosing only a fragment of the action and using various durations. Thirdly, I combine several video works to form an installation or exhibition in a specific space. For the fourth stage (the research part?), I describe the work and reflect upon some aspect of the material (the videos, the working notes and the documentation from the exhibition) in relationship to some concept from another field and write about it for a research context. The still-act, for instance, borrowed from anthropology and dance studies.[2]

The above working method is in itself quasi-systematic. The data gathered by video documentation could be used as research for a study in weather and climate changes, for instance. But they do not really tell about performing landscape, except as a form of demonstration, an example: 'perhaps in this way'. However, I prefer to use my art work as research data, rather than as demonstration of research outcomes, perhaps because I want to go on 'singing'. 'In the artistic research experience studies experience, producing new experiences'.[3] Producing material and choosing what to do with it depending on what you get, resembles approaches in qualitative research. Still, there is something unsatisfactory in considering the artistic process as a tool for producing research data only, and regarding the critical reflection on the working process afterwards as the 'real' research outcome and knowledge production. And, although theorising, like methods, preferably evolves out of the work itself, most artist researchers need some theory to challenge or support reflection.

Notes

1   Andé Lepecki uses the notion in his 2006 book *Exhausting Dance – performance and the politics of movement* (New York and London: Routledge).
2   'The "still-act" is a concept proposed by anthropologist Nadia Seremitakis to describe moments when a subject interrupts historical flow and *practises* historical interrogation. Thus, while the still-act does not entail rigidity or morbidity it requires a performance of suspension, a corporeally based interruption of modes of imposing flow. The still *acts* because it interrogates economies of time, because it reveals the possibility of one's agency within controlling regimes of capital, subjectivity, labor and mobility.' (Lepecki, op. cit.: 15) See also Seremitakis, C. Nadia, 'The Memory of the Senses, Part I: Marks of the Transitory' and 'The Memory of the Senses, Part II: Still Acts' in *The Senses Still – Perception and Memory as Material Culture in Modernity*, 1994 (pp.1–18 and 23–43) C. Nadia Seremitakis (ed.) (Chicago: University of Chicago Press).
3   Hannula et al., 2005: 59.

Felix Nobis

Felix Nobis is a Teaching-Research Fellow with the Centre for Drama and Theatre Studies at Monash University. He has worked as a professional actor for many years, performing with theatre companies such as Sydney Theatre Company, Belvoir St, Q Theatre and Red Stitch. He is the creator of two one-person shows which have toured Australia and internationally, and was Affiliate Writer with Melbourne Theatre Company in 2007. He holds an MA in Old and Middle English from University College Cork, and is in the process of writing his PhD in Medieval Storytelling. Currently Nobis is a commissioned writer with the Melbourne Theatre Company.

Nobis has toured his one-person adaptation of *Beowulf* throughout Australia, Europe and the United States. He also adapted the work for ABC Radio National's *Poetica* programme. His one-person show *Once Upon a Barstool* has toured extensively throughout regional Victoria and Ireland. In 2007, Felix played Huxley, the narrator of the arena spectacular *Walking with Dinosaurs: The Live Experience* for both the Australian and North American tours. He has written, and presented academic papers on all of these experiences.

Un-telling Myself: Performance (Preparation) as Research

In this case study I focus on the performing body in preparation. I reflect on my work as professional storyteller – with specific focus on my adaptation and performance of the medieval epic *Beowulf* – in an international career that has spanned ten years. In this time I have devised routines of physical and vocal warm-up as well as a series of exercises in spatial and sensory awareness. In privately enacting these routines I perform myself into a storyteller. In this discussion I ask what these exercises mean. I ask how they have become part of my practice, and what purpose they serve in performance. The writing interrogates my preparatory processes from traditional stretching to the evolution of exercises devised to address specific needs of storytelling. As storyteller, I highlight and give shape to a particular narrative amidst a complex web of narratives that clutter the storytelling event. In preparation I not only tune voice and body to tell a story, but enact techniques that help un-tell other stories. Of particular concern in this case study are the exercises that I perform to un-tell myself.

Yves Knockaert

Yves Knockaert has been Director of the Institute for Practice Based Research in the Arts at the K.U. Leuven Association since May 2006, and Chair of the preparatory board of that institute since 2002. Until 2006 Knockaert was Professor of Music History, Philosophy of Music and Contemporary Music at the Lemmens Institute in Leuven. Since 1997 he has been linked with the Orpheus Institute for Advanced Studies & Research in Music (Ghent, Belgium).

Knockaert is the author of *Wendingen* (Turns), which addresses changes in twentieth-century music, and of 'Systemlessness in Music' in *Order and Disorder*, Collected Writings of the Orpheus Institute (2004).

In Tränen unendlicher Lust: **An Artistic Inquiry into an Innovating Audiovisual Lied Project**

The Lied is a musical-theatrical genre which reached its peak in the nineteenth century. The aim of this research project is to remove the Lied from its ivory tower of classical performance and the academic and to translate it into a contemporary form. This process will take place through an inquiry into the possibilities of score and poem, in a collaboration of singers, performers, and visual artists (video). This will lead to an inquiry into the artistic processes which arise from collaboration between these various disciplines.

The project is a co-operation between singers from a conservatoire (Lemmensinstituut) and a videomaker (Fine Art Department Sint-Lucas Ghent).

Lee Miller and Joanne 'Bob' Whalley

Joanne 'Bob' Whalley and Lee Miller have collaborated on various performance projects since they met in 1992. In 2004 they completed the first joint PhD to be undertaken within a UK Higher Education Institution. Bob is Senior Lecturer in Devised Theatre at University College Falmouth, incorporating Dartington College of Art, and Lee leads the MA in Performance Practice at the University of Plymouth. They continue to research through practice with their company, the fictional dogshelf theatre company.

Partly Cloudy, Chance of Rain

This case study focuses upon the first jointly authored practice-as-research PhD project to be undertaken in a UK Higher Education Institution. The thesis consisted of *Partly Cloudy, Chance of Rain*, an originally devised, site-specific performance centred on Whalley and Miller renewing their wedding vows and a complementary written thesis. The entire project, processes and products, were collaborative and the case study will include an overt reflection upon the joint creation of knowledge, drawing on Deleuze and Guattari's concept of 'two-fold thinking', primarily articulated in *A Thousand Plateaus*. When writing about their collaborative research, Gilles Deleuze commented on his work with Félix Guattari thus: '[s]ince each of us is several, there was already quite a crowd'. (Deleuze and Guattari, 1988: 3) This sentiment accurately articulates Whalley and Miller's collaborative research and practice, because the research in which they were engaged throughout the course of the PhD lay in the interstitial gaps, a product of manifold conversations, arguments, and dialogues.

This account will also debate the concept of practice as a 'supplement'; a concern that informed the development of Whalley and Miller's PhD, as well as some of the wider discussions in relation to practice as research. This case study will thus consider the implications for a PhD project if practice is considered as 'supplement', reinforcing as it does the position that knowledge must be located within the Academy. The inference being that practical work in the form of documentation (which becomes a literal supplement to the thesis/written account) ultimately needs to be situated within the library in order to attain the 'status' of research, and become research/PhD 'worthy'. This suggests that it is not until its location within the Academy that practice can become research, which in turn suggests a hierarchy of knowledge production.

Johannes Birringer

Johannes Birringer is a choreographer and media artist. As artistic director of the Houston-based AlienNation Co. (www.aliennationcompany.com), he has created numerous dance-theatre works, video installations and digital projects in collaboration with artists in Europe, the Americas and China. He is founder of Interaktionslabor Göttelborn in Germany (http://interaktionslabor. de) and director of DAP-Lab at Brunel University West London, where he is a Professor of Performance Technologies in the School of Arts. He is also co-founder of a collaborative research group in telematics and online performance (ADAPT). He has authored numerous books, including *Media and Performance: along the border* (1998), *Performance on the Edge: transformations of culture* (2000), *Performance, Technology and Science* (2008), alongside many articles on contemporary art, performance, and media.

Corpo, Carne e Espírito: Musical Visuality of the Body

In this case study, Johannes Birringer introduces compositional ideas relating to emerging digital performances in the twenty-first century, offering as a case study his recent production, *Corpo, Carne e Espírito* (2008), an oratorio inspired by the paintings of Francis Bacon with music written by Paulo C. Chagas. For this project Birringer was commissioned to create the visual film projections and real-time processing of animations/motion graphics.

Contextualising his interest in wearable technologies and the hypersensorial (a concept derived from Brazilian artist Hélio Oiticica and his construction of the Parangolés and Quasi-Cinema), Birringer will begin to theorise some research approaches and methods to composition with movement, music, and

real-time digital animation within the context of contemporary interaction design, i.e. the design of real-time environments or computational systems for embodied processes that were once understood through theatrical action dramaturgies or choreographies in the older conventions of performance.

Underlying the new design process is Birringer's preoccupation with Bacon's contorted/decomposed bodies, the manipulability of the images of human or not human (avatar) body, the music of digital flesh and the pornography of sensation.

SECTION 1

Ineffability; Illustration and the Intentional Action Model

> I can't tell you what art is and how it does it…
> **John Berger**

Notwithstanding the vagaries of any of our personal views regarding the grand narratives of history, none of us could easily miss the heady proliferation of smaller, emotive and more localised narratives. These have led to a series of publications and performances where subjectivity, autobiography and autoethnography have been placed at the core of documented and disseminated versions of experience; where the incorporation of a researcher's self has demanded from academies a value that is imbued with methodological and epistemological weight. We have seen in recent years the inclusivity of multiple research voices, each reflecting its own peculiarities of perspective, each illustrating something of the variety of freedoms and limitations, expansions and reductions of contemporary investigations.

Taken as a whole these do more than demonstrate a shift in research-thinking and thinking about research; they form a collective address to historical tensions in the academic exploration of performance. It is from these tensions that research into practice has led to practice-based research and it is this phenomenon that this book will address.

We can be a little more specific as well as ambitious and state that the chief aim of this book is to provide a critical overview of practice-led research within the generic field of performance. As many readers will already know, the terms 'practice-led', 'practice-based', 'practice-as', 'practice for' and 'practice through' (research) are used to describe a growing diversity of approaches. Explanation of the ways in which these terms are used to suggest different foci will be given as we move through the book; for the moment, however, it is fair to say that 'practice as' and 'practice-based' are being used relatively interchangeably and without prejudice. The terms have given rise to seemingly unstoppable conference and symposia debate, bringing to mind the plethora of semiotics think tanks many of us saw and/or participated in during the 1980s.

At the time of writing, a call for papers has just been issued by the Central School of Speech and Drama, University of London for a short conference entitled 'The Ends of Practice-as-Research'. The solicitation is worded playfully by Broderick Chow, who likens practice-based researchers to zombies, moving slowly and with single-minded purpose towards their aims. (SCUDD, 2009) Whilst single-mindedness is possibly appropriate, the idea of practice as research moving slowly is not a notion that stands up to any scrutiny at all. Certainly, if the significance of an area is measured by the strength of debate generated in its direction then the relatively new (or newly articulated) field of practice as research is among the most pressing and fast-moving concerns in early-twenty-first-century thinking about performance. Simultaneous 2009 publications by Palgrave Macmillan bear witness to this: Shannon Rose Riley and Lynette Hunter's *Mapping Landscapes for Performance as Research: Scholarly Acts and Creative Cartographies* and *Practice-as-Research in Performance and Screen*, edited by Ludivine Alleque, Simon Jones, Baz Kershaw and Angela Piccini. At nearly 600 collective pages, a considerable force of argument is created, and it is one that augurs against any ideas of slow motion.

Like these two publications, *Blood, Sweat & Theory* is intrinsically concerned with approaches to research, knowledge and dissemination. Through its various sections it will address the implications and some of the claims of practice-based research in performance as an effective and viable method of communicating experiential content. It is here that the concerns of this book take their own specific turn.... And it is here that our first area of serious contestation occurs. It does so as a direct consequence of experienced content being widely regarded as tacit, explicit or ineffable. No particular problems with that. But it follows from this that explicit content is capable of being expressed linguistically, whilst tacit content contains elements that stretch and challenge the limitations of this linguistic expression. This leaves ineffable content as that which can only be utterly beyond the capabilities of speech and words. The term ineffable is commonly used to describe feelings, concepts or elements of existence that are too great to be adequately described in words and which can only be known internally by individuals, and this is the belief that most commonly underpins the idea that practical work has value as part of a PhD submission.

Common examples of the ineffable are sensory experiences or *qualia*, the nature of love, the certainty some people possess of a thing called the soul, musical composition etc. Indeed, the literal meaning of ineffable is 'not comparable to', 'defying expression or description'. In the context of practice-based research, ineffability is premised on the notion of embodiment as an existential condition: one in which the researcher's performing (doing) body is the subjective source for experience, and it is from this conceptual platform that arguments in favour of practice as research are often launched.

And yet, if it is the case that we can only imagine that which we first remember, then many of these ineffable aspects are already communicated to us perfectly comfortably in words. When Clark Moustakis undertook the experience of being lonely in order to understand better and then communicate the way it felt, he did so in such a way that we came to know a little more of what it is to be lonely without necessarily being lonely ourselves and, crucially, without witnessing the (assumed) authenticity of the writer's solitary life. (Moustakis, 1961 and 1972) When a poet writes about love we are moved by the power of the words and, unfashionable though the suggestion might seem in the reality-saturation of 24-hour television and the twin cults of autobiography and celebrity, bearing witness to the various stages of love might tell us less that matters than the purpose and power of the poet's words. When the poet speaks to us of love s/he makes the seemingly ineffable clear and we do not need to see the same poet locked in a fevered embrace to be moved by the impact of words. The act of floating in space is presumably regarded as ineffable and yet the demands of contributory knowledge are such that it is the duty of science to describe, analyse and assess the worth of this experience to those of us who will never be astronauts.

It is at this early point that my own gnawing caution emerges into the light, for the fact that experiential practice is an undeniably valuable aspect of research does not necessarily make it a particularly useful way of articulating what it is that the researcher discovered. This reveals my unashamed starting position as one of 'if we can see it, we can say it'; and in an academic climate where the idea of ineffability is increasingly ruling the roost it is hard to make a statement like this without inviting charges of philistinism and a naïve misunderstanding of the ephemeral nuances of performance. The introductory 'Lay of the Landscape' in Riley and Hunter's book gets the practice-as-research defence in first when Kershaw describes those who resist as 'academic traditionalists' whose desire for criteria of value is a 'fool's illusion'. (Riley and Hunter, 2009: 4–5)

Small wonder that the idea of written language as something almost pejorative has put down the roots that it has when a journal with the international standing of *PAJ* chooses to conclude its issue 91 (January 2009) with Alison Knowles' *Fluxus Long Weekend Drawings*. In Knowles' paper, six photographs and four line drawings frame a brief six-paragraph description of work undertaken at the Tate Modern, London, during the period 24–27 May 2008. (Knowles, 2009: 139–148) What is most interesting about Knowles' description is not what she describes so much as the form she uses. Performance photographs, as RoseLee Goldberg's *Performance: Live Art Since the 60s* reminded us and as some of this book's case studies confirm, can be extremely useful ways of providing visual information to supplement our extant conceptual understanding, and inasmuch as they illustrate and support a written thesis they add clarity and insight. As a journal of performance *and* art rather than performance art, *PAJ* has a logical commitment to non-literary forms. This is some way short of saying that either performance photographs or drawings are able to function comfortably when it comes to communicating the fine detail and detailing the rationale of any given performance.

To say after Peggy Phelan that linguistic description, like all representation, inevitably conveys more than it intends is one thing, (Phelan, 1993) but we could say the same about any descriptive form. The shift we have witnessed towards the recognition of theatre first and foremost as a nonverbal medium does not mean that we need to throw the baby of written dissemination out with the bath water of a *French's Acting Edition* play script, where each i is dotted and every t is crossed in advance, turning rehearsal into reproduction and creative production into rehearsal by rote.

The question might usefully be asked that if PhD students can write 40,000 words about their research, as is common with practice-based research approaches, then why not write 80,000? The issue is not, it seems, most often one of ineffability so much as it is about the emerging status of practice as a method and means of research rather than as its potential subject, and the pioneering zeal of people such as Alleque, Jones, Kershaw, Hunter, Piccini and Riley, accompanied by the likes of Katy Macleod, Caroline Rye, Robin Nelson, Henk Borgdorff, Graeme Sullivan and Yves Knockaert, lends considerable academic weight and energy to this cause. With this paragraph, this book's focus starts to narrow to the subject of practice as research within PhDs, and despite inevitable detours this focus will remain throughout.

The idea of practice as research in performance hinges on the extent to which aesthetic practices produce knowledge of any kind. And if so, what types of knowledge are contained in a work of performance? But answering the question of imbedded or embodied knowledge is only part of the challenge. What is of an equally pressing concern is whether knowledge that resides in the body (either the body of the performer or the body of work) is so dense and impenetrable, so complex and sophisticated, so innate and as we have seen so *ineffable*, that its expression cannot be distilled into words: the 'I know it, but I can't explain it' argument that Stanley Fish sees as a route to inevitable failure. (Gill, 2008: 35) Despite the subtleties of varying arguments this is the crux of the matter. If we believe that the primary function of a thesis is to explain, and that academically viable explanation is at its most effective when it is written, then the value of practical demonstration lies most significantly in its illustrative function: i.e. it illustrates the written thesis without ever standing for it. If on the other hand we believe that the expressivity of art is its own (or only) articulation and that sense and knowledge can be best communicated through practice then demonstration becomes more than illustration: it becomes the thesis itself.

Whilst producing a performance work of some quality and subsequently reflecting on the processes involved in its creation is undoubtedly a useful string to a university's bow this is not always the same thing as research, where post-practice reflection needs usually to be harnessed to pre-practice questions. This is what Anne Pakes refers to as the Intentional Action Model, where value stems from the researching practitioner's intentions and creative processes rather than residing in the produced event as the embodiment of knowledge. (Pakes, 2004) For Pakes, evidence of intentional action requires the articulation of intentions, the documentation of process, the presentation of an art-product and critical reflection that locates the work and its processes in a context that is academically as well as aesthetically appropriate. When Pakes describes the epistemological value of the art-product as something that dissolves in this act of critical intentionality, (Ibid.) she articulates something that fits fairly neatly within the increasingly accepted idea of practice-as-research PhD theses consisting of equal parts practice and written text.

An alternative to Pakes' model is one where the art product functions as the complete embodiment of knowledge: where any written elements of the thesis serve at best to illustrate the practice rather than *vice versa*. A common and commonly encouraged feeling amongst students of performance at undergraduate and postgraduate level is that their research can only be explored and investigated in and through practice and that this puts any practical work produced at the heart of the thesis, essay or submission. This ties in with (and buys into) the belief that art research is only possessed of meaning when one's work is immersed in art practice. According to this view art practice functions within its own terms and these neither include nor rely on the addition of discursive rhetorical text-based analysis. The work and one's working processes thus stand at once as research, evidence of research and findings.

This insistence upon the primacy and sanctity of embodied knowledge draws on the ancient *ars* and *scienta* binary which sees the *ars dimension* as practical, creative and open and the *scienta dimension* as something word-bound, intellectually self-serving and rigid. As a consequence of this we find that the range of established methodologies is rapidly expanding in order to accommodate the newly conceptualised fields of experiential, autoethnographical, autobiographical and distinctly practice-based research... as durational investigations that explore the politics of dissemination in addition to the specifics of one's research topic. Along the way something of the assumed academic imperative of a thesis is swapped for the interdependence of ontology and epistemology.

This ambivalence towards and refusal to be bound by the restraints of convention is leading to submissions where the written thesis and the practice experience no compartmentalised privacy. Rather, each element circles the other in a restless/relentless choreography of mutuality and co-operation that is concerned with undertaking a substantial examination of the persuasive powers of practice. As we shall see, this is not an approach that is easily reducible to the values and value systems of the types of dissemination encountered in traditional research approaches. The corporeity of one is part of the other's existence as typeface on a page, with each pursuing a relational counterpoint: as relational as Linda Montano seeing her life/practice relationship as something that could be dissolved into post-Duchampian living sculpture. Within the practice-based research concept of co-operation discussed here, certain types of exploratory activity are asking to be regarded similarly as forms of living thesis, foregrounding along the way the notion that the interrogative drive of contemporary research is as concerned with the processes of discovery and articulation as it is with what it is that is being discovered and articulated.

Some small pockets of resistance to the fulsome embrace of practice-based research remain. As Marcel Cobussen sees it, practice-based research is a potentially disastrous initiative, one that has been invited into a strategically important site and which has the potential then to punish the very people who brought it in. In Cobussen's words, 'Though not quite as disastrous – perhaps even the converse (it depends on whose side you are on) – I tend to regard Practice-based Research (PBR) in the arts as a Trojan horse, brought within the firm walls of the academic community or university kingdom.' (Cobussen, 2007) Despite these words, Cobussen's stance is not one of anti-art or anti-practice: a trained musician long before he entered Leiden University, his practitioner pedigree is strong enough to lend coal-face credibility to his views. The fact that Cobussen's views seem somewhat alarming says much about the ways in which practice-based submissions have moved from the periphery to the core of performance research: to the extent that a word of caution has come to be read as dissent. Another cautionary voice is Lawrence Grossberg's who suspects that dangers lie in the collapsing of a field of study's borders. Grossberg asks us to consider the extent to which descriptions of certain bodies of work have become 'increasingly content-free'. (Grossberg, 1993: 2) Grossberg develops his theme by wondering whether we will increasingly 'need to ask what is being lost? What specific bodies of work have no name?' (Ibid.)

Practice-based research offers a clear challenge to conventional thinking in its premise that the practice of performance can be at once a method of investigative research and the process through which that research is disseminated. In *Blood, Sweat & Theory* readers will be introduced to and/or reminded of a series of issues in the field and to some of the key methodologies underpinning, and sometimes undermining, practice-based research. The book encourages, if not quite demands, an open and inquisitive response to the benefits, possibilities and problems of innovative research practices. It is a response which acknowledges the inevitability of change alongside the probable need for some consensus in terms of qualitative assessment: one which is no less (and no more) cognisant of creative processes than it is of the rigours of research.

In its picking out of a path through practice as research in performance this book is also at times an exercise in quasi-schizophrenia. Ideas that seem watertight in one section have their leaks exposed on subsequent pages and any of the linguistic certainties that creep unwittingly into the territory of authorship exist to be challenged by readers' own experiences, agendas and beliefs. I can see, from the perspective of a final draft, that the process of writing this book has been one of reflection in action, a process wherein one is never fully sure of what it is that one thinks until those thoughts are transposed into words on a page... with all of the dread calcification that brings. Bertrand Russell's ideal for education was of a moving from inarticulate certainty towards articulate doubt. The journey this book has taken me on has been from one set of doubts to another, with precious few certainties at all. The only constant has been a nagging concern that practice-based research suffers as much from a celebration of its newness by some as it does elsewhere from its dismissal as something fashionable and ultimately insubstantial.

The truth may not lie in the middle ground of this binary of old versus new, but that possibility does not dilute the need for a series of debates around the function and academic assessment of creativity within educational research contexts. The sections that follow these introductory words add a series of voices to those debates. Whilst the notion of research is increasingly used to refer to a wide range of activities, the term is used here to indicate investigation based on a systematic methodological approach linked to an appropriate subject understanding. Within that frame, research is considered in this book in a way that is inclusive enough to accommodate a series of activities. Where any potentially negative tension exists it does so at those points where inclusivity impacts on rigour and it is in the pursuit of an address to this concern that this book is written.

Where my own background is UK–European with experience of predominantly non-mainstream theatre and performance in a primarily British university sector, it is almost inevitable that these givens will shape the way the book proceeds, and many of the regulations, procedures and guidelines referred to will be UK-based. The relative localisation of my own experiences is tempered by the fact that our case studies come from many countries and cultures and whilst the limited number of these augur against any wild claims of universality their inclusion here does more than provide a snapshot of practice-based research in a number of contexts. The case studies articulate culturally divergent approaches and a range of interests, to be sure, but these cultural and applicatory differences are matched by differences in thinking about the relationships between practice and reflection, reflection and research, research and dissemination... and these are the issues that make or break practice-based investigations in performance.

The book then is constructed as a series of sections. These are separated and sliced into by a dozen case studies from fourteen international practitioner–researchers. My own writing thus exists as the string on which the pearls of practice-as-research case studies are hung. As with a necklace, the string creates a form and imposes a certain length but almost all that counts and has lasting value are the pearls.

CASE STUDY 1

Returning to Haifa: Using Pre-text Based Drama to Understand Self and Other

Allan Owens and Hala Al-Yamani

> In everyone's life at some time, our inner fire goes out. It is then burst
> into flame by an encounter with another human being.
> (Albert Schweitzer in Brabazon, 2005)

To encounter is to come against, to meet face to face as we did at an academic conference in 2003. Our initial meeting was not characterised by 'the euphoria of initial contact' as some theorists of intercultural communication would have it (Bennett, 1998) but it was positive; positive in the sense of encountering an other, travelling along the same road, engaging in conversation for what we thought would be a few days. Our subsequent encounters over a period of six years have been deliberate and increasingly systematic as has the way in which we have sought to engage participants using pre-texts arising from the Palestinian–Israeli conflict to explore the concept of the Other and the forms of drama we use to generate these.

This study focuses on two pre-texts run over the last three of these six years. A total of 20 performances for 520 participants including young people, students, teachers, local politicians, national and international drama practitioners, academics and other communities both in the UK and Palestine. The average length of the pre-text has been two hours but in this study we focus on the nature of our encounters in particular cultural contexts as much as the applied drama events we stage. We use the term 'event' in Sauter's sense as a holistic concept in theatre and performance studies. In his theoretical model of the theatrical event, 'cultural context' is taken to be one of the 'simultaneous factors of a theatrical event'. (Sauter, 2009)

This acknowledgement is intended to alert the reader to the fact that s/he can expect to hear as much about the way our perceptions of our encounters with each other inform the practice and research process as the interactions within the theatrical event itself. The participants' voices remain intentionally silent in this study as we deliberately focus on the dialogue between us, including extracts from our reflective writings and e-mail correspondence. We view this as a recursive process where the present is guided and given meaning by the past and in which the present can alter the interpretation of the past so that a variety of possibilities can be considered.

In doing this we have taken a consensual and 'communicative approach to validity' where the 'validity of an interpretation is worked out in dialogue' (Kvale, in Denzin and Lincoln, 2000: 315); in this case between two university applied drama practitioners, one in Palestine and the other in the UK.

Rather than viewing discourse as a game between adversaries, (Lyotard, 1991) we position ourselves with Eisner (1991) who argues for qualitative research as art, where the aim is for 'consensual validation' which 'is, at base, agreement among competent others that the description, interpretation, evaluation and thematics of an educational situation are right'. (p.112) The messiness of getting this 'right' is very much part of our practice and research process.

We make it clear at the start of the pre-text that we are telling the narrative of the Palestinian–Israeli conflict from a Palestinian perspective. We do not ask participants to side with this, but to question it in the light of other narratives they hear, their own reason and their own common sense. The ethics of this work constantly trouble us and we reflect specifically on this in the last section of this study.

The text presented in boxes at regular intervals throughout the study is intended to provide a window on the political situation for readers who are unfamiliar with the Palestinian–Israeli conflict. The windows frame events from a Palestinian perspective with the onus placed on the reader to decide if she or he believes what is being shown and told. This mirrors the work of the participant in practice who is urged to interrogate all that is presented.

First Encounter

> Go back where you started, or as far back as you can, examine all of it,
> travel your road again and tell the truth about it.
> (Baldwin, 1955: 7)

At our initial meeting in June 2003 we were each presenting a conventional 20-minute academic paper at the University of Northampton, UK. Our initial conversations centred on the Palestinian–Israeli conflict and our own practice of drama education, a mix primarily of the educational and the political informed by our approach to participatory forms of drama in the communal and oral tradition.

> Israel began constructing the Wall in the West Bank in 2002 following a decision by the Government of Israel, on 23rd July 2001, to construct a 'security fence'... The wall has a precedent. Since 1994 the Gaza Strip has been surrounded by a wall which cuts off Palestinians living there from the rest of the world. (Feron, 2009)

(Hala, written reflection, November 2008) I was keen to tell our story as Palestinians. Not to force people to see what I see, but to encourage them to ask questions about what they are being shown about the conflict. I saw that you had had a rich experience in Palestine. It was obvious to me that the Palestinian political aspect was so strong for you. It was as though someone had seen something that others didn't know about and felt the responsibility to open it up for others to see. You wanted to share it with everyone and your tool was 'The Bird in the Cage' pre-text. But my thoughts were that... maybe there are times when we can not tell the narratives we have seen.

(Allan, written reflection, November 2008) I had lost contact with Palestinian colleagues I had been working with prior to the start of the second intifada in 2000 and sought you out at the conference. You were extremely direct in your critique of the paper that I presented on translation and vulnerability. I told you about 'The Bird in the Cage' pre-text I had created with practitioners in Gaza and West Bank in 1995–97 and which I had subsequently run in the UK and other countries. I thought it was a Palestinian story that still needed telling in the UK to counter the dominant Israeli narrative, but wondered if you agreed.

On reflection, the main motivations/Dawef informing our individual work at this point were the political and pedagogical informed by artistic and research imperatives. We both viewed ourselves as educators using the aesthetic of drama form to generate dialogue but acknowledged our distinctive and different cultural backgrounds in the West Bank and North West of England. Neither of us had seen each other's practice. We were connecting through the spoken and written word, theorising our practice not engaging in practice together – through what we said we were doing, not necessarily what we were actually doing. There were possibilities for co-operation but a sense of the difficulties that intercultural collaboration invariably entails.

(Hala, written reflection, November 2008) I felt for the first time when we met and you talked about your experience in Palestine that you are a familiar person to me. You were one of the dramatists who would understand our situation and what was going on there. On the other hand I was not sure how much you were interested in Palestine and for what reasons? What were your intentions and motivations? There was this mixture of being familiar and unfamiliar at the same time. I noticed the difference between my Eastern understanding to the 'Other' and your Western understanding. I was a bit concerned but curious to know how you were dealing with our stories.

(Allan, written reflection, November 2008) I felt that we were making contact in some ways but not in many others. There was awkwardness on my behalf that seemed to come from a presumption that you would be interested in collaborating just because I had worked in your country and because that experience had been important for me.

These thoughts and our initial conversations marked the start of our exploration of the Other through collaborative practice as we came to ask 'How does each of us "look", how does each of us deal with the Other?' In focusing on this concept we are continuing a pre-occupation of qualitative research, which was originally 'born out of concern to understand the Other'. (Vidich and Lyman in Denzin and Lincoln, 2000: 2) We use the concept in the well-established social sense to suggest that self requires the Other to define itself. (Hooks, 1990) In the course of our encounters the Other is used to refer to anyone familiar or unfamiliar to a person, relative or stranger, close or far away. (Gioultsis, 2005)

For the purposes of our project, 'Othering' also implies practices of integration and segregation in the construction of national identity and can be used as shorthand for the process whereby certain peoples are dehumanized as they are exploited by those who say they are 'civilizing inferior beings'. Our key reference here is the Palestinian scholar Edward Said who critiques the skewed understanding that he believes many in the 'West' have of Arab culture. He argues that this is a result of unquestioned assumptions held by the 'West' about the 'East' denoted by the pejorative term 'Orientalism'.

Said argues that very little of what he calls 'the detail, the human density, the passion of Arab-Moslem life has entered the awareness of even those people whose profession it is to report the Arab world'. (1978: 12) Our collaborative practice is driven by political, educational, artistic and research imperatives to move beyond what Said calls the 'crude, essentialized caricatures' to consider the potential and limitations of pre-text-based process drama form in doing this. Said wrote extensively on Palestine (1994, 2000) and was internationalist in perspective. We also have made it increasingly clear that our work does not begin and end with the Palestinian–Israeli conflict.

Whilst the pre-texts we create aim to bring the complexity of this specific conflict simply and sharply into focus, we encourage participants to identify situations in their own experience that resonate for them in the drama. This may be in terms of the themes and subtexts embedded in the pre-text such as home, loss and return and can be on personal and national political levels. No knowledge of the Middle East is needed to engage in the work but in the Freirian (2001) tradition the experiences that participants bring with them into the room are valued.

This study does not focus on participants' voices but the reader should know that references have shifted at times within the pre-texts to Afghanistan, South Africa, Korea, Lithuania, Finland, Spain, Serbia, and focused on many aspects of separation in family life. Our task has been to create work that challenges dominant narratives, not as propaganda, but in the form of a quiet instilling of curiosity and generation of dialogue with the potential to disrupt, disturb and extend horizons.

Second Encounter

After the first encounter we kept in contact for around six months and messages came and went between us and included our concerns and news related to the main political subject of Palestine and our own projects. The intifada continued and Bethlehem fell quiet as tourists stayed away. Allan initiated the next encounter by inviting Hala in March 2004 to the UK to give an open lecture entitled 'Life as a Higher Education Lecturer in Palestine', and to look more closely at practice as embodied in 'The Bird in the Cage' pre-text.

We use the term 'pre-text' here in O'Neill's (1995) sense to refer to the text which launches an unfolding collective drama and, in doing so, acts as 'an excuse' to hear the individual voices of those taking part in it. The participants perform, watch and reflect in response to their own and the lead-practitioners' provocations.

> On 9th July 2004, at the request of the UN General Assembly, the International Court of Justice – the most distinguished legal body in the world – rendered an advisory opinion on the legal consequences of constructing the wall in the Occupied Palestinian Territory, stating that the construction of the wall and the settlements on West Bank land, including East Jerusalem, were illegal under international humanitarian and human rights law. (Feron, 2009)

The first opening-up of practice took the form of a solo run-through, and commentary on, 'The Bird in the Cage' by Allan for Hala. The pre-text had originally been created during a pilot project in Gaza with Hanan Hasan and colleagues in the Gaza Drama Project Group in Gaza City. This was part of a Pilot Project funded by the British Council (Owens, June 1997) intended to improve the learning experiences of young people. Two curriculum focus groups of practitioners were pulled together, one in Gaza and one in West Bank. The pre-text was based on a traditional Palestinian story and the key questions that surfaced in the project were: 'What stories do we tell our children, young people and educators in the times of occupation?' and 'How do we tell these stories in ways that allow the participants' voices to be heard?'

> ## 'The Bird in the Cage' Pre-text Narrative
>
> A boy lives with his father. The boy does not have any friends or family nearby but loves his father and the relatives that he has all over the world. His father has to leave on a business trip on the eve of his birthday, but leaves his son a large wrapped present to open the next day.
>
> Having opened the presents that have arrived from his relatives, he turns to the present from his father. Inside the wrapping is a cage in which sits a wonderful bird, the same sort he last saw when his mother was alive and he had visited the zoo. As the bird sings he sits enraptured and the day passes. He finally covers the cage and falls into a deep sleep.

In terms of practice, this narrative is opened up to participants through drama in education conventions, (Goode and Neelands, 2001) for example the participants become the boy's relatives and decide what presents they have sent him this year and last for his birthday. This oblique approach to the eventual confrontation between the boy and the bird brings into focus the totally unequal power balance between them, hugely stacked as it is on the boy's side. 'What would they do if they were in the bird's position?' 'Can words, dialogue, lead to change in this situation?' 'Do actions have to be taken and if so what actions would participants be prepared to take?'

> ## Narrative Continued...
>
> The next day just before lunch, the bird stops singing and the boy demands that it start again and begins to lose his temper. He can't contact his father so phones his relatives for advice. Having tried their ideas with no success his anger grows. When he finally opens the cage door to tell the bird that it can fly around the room and sing he adds, 'Don't try and escape. If you do I will break both of your wings.'

The driving force of the pre-text, based on the metaphorical dimension of this story, lies in the way the metaphor 'is' and 'is not' like the Palestinian–Israeli conflict. (Ricouer, 2003: 293) A boy has a bird locked in a cage behind bars, a state has a people imprisoned behind walls; a boy wants compliance, a people want freedom; bird's wings and young men's arms get broken and much worse. In this situation what are a boy, a bird and a people to do?

> (Allan, written reflection, November 2008) I was nervous about running the pre-text, wondering if it spoke to the current situation. Your immediate response was positive but you were also critical about the way I had restricted the focus to Palestine, saying that participants should be encouraged to bring their own frames of reference and experiences to the fore to place the work in an internationalist context. For me, part of the resonance in doing it were the autobiographical incidents I could weave into the work from my experience in Palestine. I reflected on my stance, wondering about the relationship between the educational, political, ethical, moral, social and where the balance lay, or if it had to keep shifting.

> (Hala, written reflection, November 2008) It was so interesting seeing an English drama practitioner using a Palestinian story. I did not expect that the work would be so strongly related to our narrative as Palestinians. I felt that I was dealing with a Palestinian person who believes in the notion of Palestine as his main cause... I was so glad to discover this, but at the same time I noticed other things that needed to be spoken about but I did not know if it was good to talk about these honestly. For example, I felt it was not fair for others who are living imprisoned in all different sorts of oppressive contexts to focus only on our situation. At this moment I became acutely aware of my understanding and attitude towards the Other as a concept and as an approach and discussed this openly with you in relation to the main points in the pre-text.

In the process of this drama we encourage participants to start the journey of investigation, defining, translating and interpreting roles with one eye fixed firmly on perceptions of self. The process starts by looking for reasons for action and leads deliberately to interactions of the self and the Other. This sort of investigation is called the 'dialogue' by Carasso (1996) or 'negotiation' by Heathcote et al. (1984) Participants act and watch, but also reflect on the meanings of actions as they evaluate the actions of others and, critically for the development of an ethical self, evaluate their own actions.

After the visit Hala wrote, 'My visit to Chester allowed me to see all those friends who know us and believe in our story and they tell the right story to others just as you do. I felt that as people we are not isolated or alone, but there are friends here and everywhere'. (E-mail, April 2004) But we both subsequently asked as we began to collaborate in practice, 'What is "the right" story' and 'What are "the right" questions?'

Third Encounter

There were no opportunities for further encounters from summer 2004 to Winter 2006 as Hala returned to Bethlehem and Allan worked in Chester on a project he was already committed to. But our project did not fall silent as a continuous stream of e-mails passed between us, and continues today, about the political situation in Palestine, continuous communication and a way for us to participate in the telling and sharing of narrations related to the conflict.

> Once completed, the length of the wall's route will be between 726 and 790 km in total. About 57 per cent of the construction has already been completed. When completed, 125,000 Palestinians will be surrounded on three sides, 35,000 Palestinians will live in closed areas – enclaves. (Feron, 2009)

Hala's return to Bethlehem involved facing a new reality, not only in professional terms of returning with new knowledge to the University she had been on study leave from for over four years, but politically, symbolised by the wall which now cut into Bethlehem, clearly visible to anyone entering or leaving the University.

> (E-mail, Hala, May 2005) Regarding the wall, it is one of my difficulties after I came home... It is an obstacle in the way of my re-adaptation... wherever I stand in our campus I see it there standing in front of me. In addition, there are other big settlements.... I cannot imagine how this world is working... how governments cannot recognize their crimes against us... In all news they are talking about peace and negotiations between our Palestinian authority and the Israeli government. However, they do not focus on what is going on on the ground, of actions of confiscating our lands, creating all sorts of actions in making our prison smaller... and smaller.

If we were to develop our collaborative practice, Hala felt that we needed to move on from 'The Bird in the Cage' and the questions it asks about present imprisonment.

(E-mail, Hala, August 2006) It does not tell the whole story, the real story, it tells part of the story, the latest part of the story... We could do some work related to the issues raised in it by dealing with part of Kanafani's 'Returning to Haifa'... [it] tells the story from the beginning. I know it's not fair to focus only on our situation. However, sometimes I feel it is so difficult and dangerous. Keeping a whole nation imprisoned in small ghettos by using the excuse of security is a big crime and the world is doing nothing about this... Our situation is becoming worse and worse and none are taking an action to stop this.

Ghassan Kanafani, the Palestinian writer and political activist, was assassinated by Israeli Special Forces in Beirut in 1972. In the novella 'Returning to Haifa' he considers the right of return for Palestinians to their homeland, but in doing so asks hard universal questions about the need to, and possibilities of, recovering the past through action. Hala had tried one run of an initial draft of a pre-text based on 'Returning to Haifa' at the Hellenic Drama Conference in Athens (Spring 2006). Some parts worked, others did not. We started to look for funding to develop and sustain our practice and clarify, shape and sharpen the research focus.

Fourth Encounter

Nakba, Arabic for 'catastrophe', is the term used by Palestinians to refer to the first round of population transfer undertaken by the Zionist movement... between 1947 and 1949. More than 750,000 Palestinians were forcibly displaced from their homes and lands, and approximately 500 Palestinian villages were depopulated. The establishment of the state of Israel in 1948 was, amongst other things, the result of ongoing racism and the persecution of Jewish citizens in Europe, in particular the Holocaust. (Feron, 2009)

The first draft of the 'Returning to Haifa' pre-text was produced in June 2007 in Chester in just two days and then taken out to be run and shaped over a two-week period. Hala brought two of her students from Bethlehem to Chester, Laura Zidan and Shireen Basil. Workshops took place in a range of venues including: with young people in Cheshire and Warrington schools and Chester Cathedral; with experienced drama practitioners at the 'Thinking through Practice' North West Drama Education Symposium; and with City Councillors in Chester Town Hall chambers.

'Returning to Haifa'

The pre-text focuses on Palestinian husband and wife Sofia and Said who were forcibly displaced from their home in Haifa in spring 1948. In the turmoil of that day their baby son is left behind. They try many times to return but it is not possible until after the 1967 war when Israel, confident in its occupation, finally allows Palestinians to return briefly and see the places where they used to live.

Three key sections provide the main framework of the pre-text. The first focuses on a discussion between Sofia and Said in their house in Ramallah about the opportunity to visit Haifa after nineteen years. The second shows their arrival in front of their former home in Haifa. Sofia decides she will not go in and Said fails to convince her. She gives him the key, which like many Palestinians she has kept through the years.

The third and final section focuses on the entrance of Said to the house, his memories and traumatic meeting with Miriam the Israeli woman who moved into his home the very week he and Sofia were forced out. Miriam tells Said that his lost son David is about to come home at any moment. David enters wearing an Israeli Army uniform.

In a similar devising process to that employed in the creation of 'The Bird in the Cage', we aimed to embed questions in a strong unfolding narrative. We stood back from the text in order to allow participants to interrogate it. Key moments of narration were spoken in English and Arabic to allow for slow looking and listening. We were working again in the playful and ironic pre-text-based process drama tradition with its careful use of distance to frame events simply but surprisingly. In terms of the aesthetics of representation we created a series of moments where Hala, Laura and Shireen could be interrogated in relation to the words they spoke on behalf of the Palestinian and Israeli characters in the drama, of self and Other.

We also created opportunities for casual conversation between participants and ourselves. For example, when the image of Sofia handing the key to Said is finally broken at the close of the second section, participants are asked to work in small groups, each to make one key, any size, any shape using newspaper and masking tape. We make it clear that this is a chance for talk, to give opinions and ask any questions about Kanafani's story, about Palestine, about Hala, Laura and Shireen's life there. As we ran the pre-text we began to be more deliberate in creating such opportunities. This was driven by the experience we had of some participants holding back, saying that it is hard to find the right language to ask questions, to make mistakes about what might hurt those present or that might sound foolish to others.

We had doubts about this activity initially, but as we ran the pre-text we began to see that it was one way of switching the work from the level of narrative involvement to personal and political engagement. Participants could ask questions in this informal context that they might not otherwise have asked, for example: 'Why did people leave their homes in 1948 rather than fight to keep them?' 'Where does this wall run to and from?' 'Could Said and Sofia really not have got back to their home to find their child?'

The questions we asked were embedded in the pre-text and centred on notions of home, loss, return, self, other and identity. To quote Edward Said (1978) again, they were intended to provide something of 'detail and human density' of Palestinian life and challenge the 'essentialised caricatures' of 'a people' portrayed as being prepared to simply walk away from their homes and children. For example, the initial activity leading into the pre-text is based on the question 'What is your ideal home?' Participants are invited to quickly draw their ideal home and then share this with a couple of other participants. After discussion and exchange, the drawings are used to demarcate what will become Miriam's home. These act as a visual reminder of this early question when others surface later in the pre-text such as 'Can the right to return ever be wrong?'

Fifth Encounter

> We had become temporary residents of Greater Israel, living on Israel's sufferance, subject to the most abusive treatment at the hands of its young male and female soldiers, controlling the checkpoints, deciding on a whim whether to keep us waiting for hours or to allow us passage. But worse than all this was the nagging feeling that our days in Palestine were numbered and one day we were going to be victims of another mass expulsion. (Shehadeh, 2008: 185)

We presented 'Returning to Haifa' at the Researching Applied Drama and Theatre 6th International Conference at the University of Exeter as an important step in the early validation by peers of this pre-text-based research project. We were apprehensive about this and felt the force of Schratz and Walker's statement that, 'in qualitative research we are all beginners every time we start a new project'.

(1995: 4) The 20 participants in our two-hour session were from a range of continents and included internationally recognised applied drama practitioners. We were particularly interested in feedback on the research dimension and ethics of the practice.

The overall response was that that the 'description, interpretation, evaluation and thematics of [the] educational situation are right'. (Eisner, 1991: 112) There was strong support for the notion of 'Telling the situation the way you see it' and framing the event in the way we had done in terms of declaring the Palestinian perspective from the outset. In terms of consensual validation we felt that there had been sufficient 'agreement among competent others to suggest that the encounters we allowed for were "right"'. Following Exeter we took the pre-text in November 2008 to Palestine (**Sixth Encounter**) working with Palestinian students and teachers in Bethlehem, and back to the UK in June 2009 (**Seventh Encounter**) working with adults returning to education. In the 2009 encounter we also shared our latest research dilemma and questions with another gathering of internationally recognised 'competent others' at the International ARROW Symposium 'Citizen Artist in a Fractured World', Plymouth. These questions are concerned with the political imperative of 'building silence' through an academic, arts and cultural boycott and the ethics of falling silent.

During our Fifth, Sixth and Seventh Encounters, the phase of consensual validation of practice, we began to realise that whereas we had documented the research questions embedded in and driving the drama, we had not given sufficient attention to interrogating the drama form itself. Our next two encounters (Autumn 2009 and Spring 2010) will mark a shift into a phase of more conventional, social-science-based research. This will take the form of a prescribed study in the UK and Palestine, 2009–2011, with four different groups, two in each country. The focus will shift to the participants and we aim to get further insight into their understanding, acceptance or rejection of our motivations in using this form of drama in their context as well as the potential and limitations of the form itself.

The 'Returning to Haifa' pre-text will be used to study the interaction, reaction, thoughts and understanding of participants during and after their engagement with it. The purpose of the study is to focus on the uses of drama as intercultural tool and its potential to provide better understanding of self and the Other; it aims to achieve the following objectives:

- Studying the various possibilities, strengths, difficulties and limitations of using pre-text-based drama with groups in different contexts

- Developing better understanding of the use of pre-text based drama as intercultural tool and the role of the practitioner in this form of work

- Studying the effectiveness of pre-text-based drama in developing better understanding of self and Other

- Developing the knowledge in the world of drama and how to research it.

The study questions are:

- What is the range of possibilities of being the Other in this drama?

- What are the mind-sets of the participants and practitioners being challenged, reinforced, changed, shifted and in which ways?

- What sort of understandings and learning arise from and are generated by this drama event?

- How do the participants and practitioners deal with the questions and concepts embedded in the pre-text?

The sample will comprise two groups. The first consists of 20 teachers and educators selected according to the interest and commitment they have in using participatory drama approaches in their own contexts. The second will include 20 other professionals interested in the approach including NGO and social workers, journalists, dramatists, academics and university students. We will co-ordinate this with the relevant social and civilian institutions. We are planning to use three conventional tools for collecting data: firstly, observations and audio recordings by an assistant in the session who will document participants' interactions and reactions; secondly, interviews with participants and ourselves, one immediately after the event and a second three months later; thirdly, participant and practitioner reflective sketchbooks kept for three months in which there will be an invitation to look beneath surfaces, to ask questions and raise issues.

The ethics of our praxis have quite rightly troubled us from the outset and will no doubt continue to do so as we move into the next phase. We side with Nicholson's argument that 'Becoming ethical is an on-going process – a continual journey of action, reflection and evaluation – in which values and beliefs may be challenged and tested over time and in response to new situations and different people'. (2005: 166) Nicholson identifies key questions that have informed our thinking such as 'whose stories are told in drama, about the context and ownership of autobiographical stories... about the relationships of trust and reciprocity between practitioners and participants'. (Ibid.: 157) Where matters get stickier is the argument advanced against 'seeking to discriminate against a plurality of perspectives and multiple ways of living'. As Nicholson points out, encouraging participants to see things from multiple perspectives reveals a specific set of (Western European) ethical values which 'seems inappropriate and hollow in a context where the participants had their cultural identities systematically denied by a brutal occupying force'. (Nicholson, 2005: 70) Thompson touches this directly when he talks about 'the single-minded sense of direction that a community in struggle needs if it is to overcome virulent oppression'. (Thompson, 2003: 183)

The narrative structures of the pre-texts considered in this case study are intentionally not innocent, presented as they are through a Palestinian frame. However, what might be hugely unethical for an ethics committee might be highly ethical in an applied drama setting where a wider, artistic and political imperative has a place. We stress that we are telling the story of the Palestinian–Israeli conflict 'as we see it', a story that a Palestinian audience will greet in one way – often with laughter – but which may be seen differently by a non-Palestinian audience. We continue to ask ourselves about our motivations/Dawefe, in particular: the reason we are doing this; and secondly, who we are doing this for. We see these as part of a continuous dynamic process which, as long as it is moving, will open up new horizons rich with many other questions, fears, concerns and thoughts; a process that needs to dialogue on different levels internally within oneself and externally with another and the Other to create better understanding.

SECTION 2

Paradigms and Trojan Horses

> We know more than we can tell.
> **Michael Polanyi**

N
o performance is an entire abstraction and our case studies reveal the fact that performance projects are the results of specific events and intentions, even when these intentions might appear to be the pursuit of obfuscation. Obfuscation is a useful word to consider, not least because it reminds us of our collective predilection, which almost amounts to a subject-specific curse, to engage, particularly in print, in an overly complicated theorising of what is in effect a performing mainly in the light for spectators seated mainly in the dark. The implications of ignorance and knowledge wrapped up in the imagery of darkness and light are too well-rehearsed to re-articulate here. What is worth pointing out however is that the majority of our case study contributors are chronicling work that challenges, erodes and/or subverts this idea of art with a secret to tell to an unknowing spectator.

The deadlines given for the case studies meant that they arrived after the book's main sections were completed, although abstracts were submitted and agreed some time earlier. The case studies arriving when they did amounted to an act of deliberate intent. The intention was that the case studies would form a chain of stories: stories of experience. That these experiences are re-told by same accomplished academics that were responsible for the work invites the type of inevitable theorising that many of the case studies contain. So be it. But no additionally theoretical explanations of the work are offered.

The case studies included are in many ways examples rather than paradigms. The distinction is based on the notion of the paradigm as a pattern, model or exemplar, as a set of practices that define a discipline during a particular period of time, as opposed to an example, which is more commonly used to refer to a representative of a group or concept. It is important to stress that I am making no claims for the work described in this book's pages to stand as intrinsically paradigmatic. The description of examples as paradigms would suggest a value-system that I am in this book and elsewhere at some pains to resist. The case studies used here are not necessarily better than any others: just in key ways different. Mattei Dogan and Robert Pahre argue that unlike hard science the social sciences are made up of intrinsically polysemic concepts, making paradigms redundant. (Dogan and Pahre, 1990) Inasmuch as performance, like all art, flirts shamelessly with subjectivity the connotation of hard science objectivity that gets linked to the idea of paradigmatic practice is something that is probably best avoided. What it is that can take the place of these assumedly objective analyses is at the core of practice-based research in terms of both activity and acceptance.

It is inevitable that the case studies engage in certain types of dialogue with the sections they follow and/or precede, suggesting an element of semi-systematic placing. Nothing could be further from the truth. Case studies occupy the places that they do in this book based <u>solely</u> on the order I jotted names on an early note to the publisher. However things appear, the truth is as arbitrary here as that. Like a watered-down version of the 27 unbound chapters in a box that make up B.S. Johnson's novel *The Unfortunates*, the sections of this book can be read in any order. Likewise, reading case studies one after the other would be as logical an approach to this book as any other; conversely, picking the order in which to read case studies based on the information contained in the practitioners' abstracts would be the most suitable way forward for some. Perhaps the permanence of typeface and page numbering creates a sense of order and instruction that these words can do little to offset. Nevertheless, they serve here, or at least are intended to serve, as a means of encouraging alternative readings and re-orderings.

My relationship with contributors has been based partly on the fact that this book is authored rather than edited. My role therefore has not been the usual editorial one of solicitation based on advice, encouragement and the issuing of specific instructions. It was premised instead on a handful of briefly written invitational e-mails. In terms of prior knowledge, I knew to a greater or lesser extent Johannes Birringer, Robert Germay, Lee Miller, Allan Owens, Helen Paris and Joanne 'Bob' Whalley before starting work on this book. The remaining contributors were invited based on a more distanced knowledge of their work and a number of justifiably persuasive recommendations. In addition to the experience, integrity and academic–artistic credibility that contributors have in common, what matters most is that they are able to articulate a wide range of practices in ways that seek always to broaden the book's scope without diluting its focus. To honour the spirit of the standard comment in instances such as these I should point out that the contributors' views are not necessarily reflective of my own... which is not to say that reading them has not resulted, in many cases, in acts of envy on my part. Practice can make true that which dry theorising might make false and perhaps the greatest value of the case studies used here is that they reveal some of the ways in which art-making and academic research can be woven together in investigative intent.

CASE STUDY 2

Towards Collaborativity in Theatre-making: Reflections on an Artistic Research Case

Helka-Maria Kinnunen

Stories as Means and Mediators

As always, the work tells about the maker. Having started my doctoral studies – and jumped out of actors' routines – I was filled with experimental ideas. Narrative means urged me and invited me to discover new possibilities in theatre practice. I also felt a collective pressure for finding ways of deconstructing and rebuilding theatre-makers' – especially actors' – comprehension of work. More precisely: I wanted to know more about the activities, layers and phases of artistic processes.

The starting point for my doctoral dissertation (*Stories in the artistic process of theatre-making*, 2008) was an experimental theatre production. In the creation process, *storytelling* was used as a means of producing material for the manuscript and also as a mediator for delving into collective theatre-making. The production was called *Sadetarinoita* (*Rainstories*). It was produced and performed in Helsinki in 2002.

I had found some preliminary understanding for my interests in dialogical philosophy.[1] I also had a personal, professional task: it was time for me to jump out of the conventional system, which I had been a part of; to recognise my artist's quality and thinking, to choose otherwise than presumed. Much later I recognised in this personal storyline *a vagabond* – a characteristic quality to many artists; to those who feel that being constantly renewed must be a part of their profession.[2]

Afterwards, when reflecting on the first artistic work, several questions were aroused. An acute problem occurred already during the process: after a promising beginning, instead of a free and playful collaboration, the process got dim and complicated. In this contribution, I ask the questions once more, following the spirals or loops of a hermeneutic process.[3] Despite problems, narrative means proved to be interesting alternatives in theatre-making. This makes me wonder what happened, how did the process develop what it became in good and bad, and what is there to be learnt from it?

The Experiment: *Sadetarinoita*

My desire was to realise a *collective* artistic process. It would go through various phases and lead to a performance, which would contain our views on contemporary life and its phenomena. Would the piece of art become talkative or wordless, physical or philosophical, dramatic, visual, lyrical, minimalist or something else? That was all to be solved in *collaboration*, and in *communication* with our environments. I wanted to invite an expansion of possibilities and working methods to a process, where action and discussion would come together.[4]

I invited five talented actors, a sound and light designer and a producer, to start an experiment together with me, a director for the beginning.[5] We had no text, almost no money, and no time limits. Together we agreed on creating a piece of art on stage in a collaborative process. We decided to divide the process into three phases, and we agreed to have our premiere next June – almost a year later. My own idealistic thought was to begin a process led by each or any member of the team; the starting point included the idea that everyone is capable of acting in several roles in the process, that everyone is creative and productive, and that everyone is willing to share their hidden skills and ideas.

The first rehearsals took place in a playful, joyful atmosphere. The group improvised eagerly, as I gave subjects and hints. Storytelling made them curious. We had sessions where everyone recalled private memoirs, sessions for spontaneous monologues spoken by improvised characters, reflections over improvised scenic events and storytelling along given headlines or the latest news. We tried storytelling without words, by movement and acting. My job was to encourage people to freely talk, tell, show and play, and to collect the material into notepads and on videotapes.

I had suggested *rain* for a preliminary theme, for something to start with; to be used as an example of a narrator's focus. I encouraged the group to cross the so-called reality–fiction borderline; to question in action its conventional limits. Shyness seemed to fall off the work quite soon, after rehearsing for a while with a carefree attitude, which allowed us to forget spontaneous self-criticising and evaluating.

First rehearsals went well. After two weeks' daily work there was a break, and we continued after two months had passed. The agreement was that people would keep their eyes open, collect anecdotes from everyday life, and bring them to the rehearsals. In the meantime, I was working with the stories collected in the first meetings: I wrote some scenes out from my notes, and I wrote some characters out, too. In my mind the process was developing into a mosaic or into a collage, a fragmentary piece of art on stage. We were all surprised, when we met in the beginning of the second period of rehearsals.

It proved that the actors had unconsciously waited for a traditional Aristotelian storyline, whereas I had expected them to develop new ideas for a collage, from the working basis we had started together. First marks of frustration showed up, as rehearsals continued. Since we all were still very optimistic and willing to work together, we tried to hide our disappointments and to find compromises; a comprehension of a common focus to help us back to process.

Here, according to my research, lies the beginning of a complicated, sticky work. Instead of facing the emerging confusion and taking seriously the challenge of changing our working methods, we tried to shrink the problem. We led ourselves astray together by turning, little by little, to conventional, familiar manners; we had a lack of recognition of the situation and a lack of attitude towards the developing process. It created a nice and polite atmosphere, where people felt safe but participated passively compared to the joyful first period of rehearsals. Storytelling went on merely verbally; activities on stage became on-demand-acting; careful and reserved.

Where Stories Act

When reflecting on *Sadetarinoita*, I have faced attempts to pass by my emerging emotions. Also some colleagues have criticised me for digging into something that gets only worse when analysed. The pains of artistic work are almost taboos. But as Anne Bogart puts it, theatre-making is violent, and I consider this quality of it also worth reflecting and learning. (Bogart, 2001)

For the research and its results, it has been more than valuable to delve into a case like *Sadetarinoita*, and into its network of narratives. After a profound analysis it has been pleasurable to see *how* stories, or *narrativity*, act both as spaces for artistic work and collaboration and as paths for individual and collective reflection. At first sight, of course, narratives can be considered as obstacles, which is one of their strong features. But to form a profound interpretation of their qualities and possibilities, the tacit, emotional, collective layers have to be taken into account. Narrative thinking is an essential way of being a human person in connection with environments. It can be utilised in many kinds of human processes, if it is recognised as a whole.

The thought of a freely forming collaboration may seem naïve. Nevertheless, it was based on my former experience of collaborations in theatre. Several productions during my two professional decades had included spontaneous, passionate individual activities and sacrifices for the process. They had aroused from the capacity of the participants; actors, musicians, stage designers... Often those activities emerged, when there was a crisis in the process, and the group stayed stuck in a frustrating situation, until someone brought an idea, which solved the problem or at least opened it up and brought it back to practice.

On the other hand, from an actor's angle, Finnish theatre rehearsals are typically physical, action-based and hierarchic, with very little conversation or shared reflection. It is seldom that spontaneous activities are welcome. If the leader of the process does not see the team as a group of artists, but only a group of those who carry out his or her plans, there may not be space for that kind of pleasant surprise. The need for an experiment on stage came from this background: from the hierarchic and seldom collaborative, strictly guided tradition of theatre-making. Behind there was the experience of being one of the quiet majorities in a group.

Those were the first *stories acting in our process* – and since they were partly hidden and only partly discussed together, they were powerful partners, in good and bad. In the research process of this work I learned, what it really means to the collaboration, that actors are educated and taught to be creative only in a flexible way, while directors are taught to be leaders, even dictators. Actors' creativity is often on-demand-creativity. They are not supposed to perform their own ideas or interpretations of the piece of art that is being made. In other words: they are not often heard in the process. And that is impossible to change at once; there is no recognition of one's own position and importance. Nevertheless those who stand near may notice the capacity left over. I had a strong sense of collaborative possibilities. I knew there was a store of seeds hiding beyond routines. I thought they were only waiting for use – as positive means of the process, not only as a first aid for panic. And I thought the others saw it as I did.

One of the problems of our beginning was that I was not conscious of my projections on the others. However, projections took forms of expectations, some of which I discussed with the group, and everybody seemed to understand and to want to take their responsibility. Later I noticed that the roles were already typical: since I was the leader, the others listened to me nicely. They did not make personal agreements; actors often think of themselves as a collective organised by the director. This theme, which consists of a system of projections and traditions, had a significant meaning in my auto-ethnographical research process.[6] It was a source of narratives. It showed views and connected dimensions: It told *stories about the starting point* and *stories of how the process was constructed*. It gave me a vivid, painful example of how stories act as means and mediators, and it made a turn in my understanding of theatre-making.

How did the aims in process change during the work? How did my expectation change from the beginning? There are numerous ways to answer the first question. The participants can be considered as characters of the collaboration story; they constructed the phases of the process. The performance – a more or less Aristotelian drama – came true through their action. From the result of the collaboration it can be seen that the aim of creating something new and uncommon did not lead to an experimental performance. As we already know, the process faced difficulties. Difficult moments during work attracted the participants to lean on conservative *ways of acting for the collaboration*. That caused a turn, where the original aims shrunk – they became messy and complicated. That already answers the second question, as well: during the process I became aware of my projection on the others. I also became aware of their desire of making a drama with a complete plot, and since I had started a democratic process (which could be led by any member of the group) I adjusted to the situation, more or less.[7]

What Did the Process Teach?

Narrativity is like art – it is a space for relations more than a vehicle, and it is an expanding space.[8] *Narrative means* were a part of the artistic process *Sadetarinoita*. *Narrativity* formed the subjective perspective and methodological basis of my research. The layers of narrativity showed never-ending networks – the learning of it goes on. *Narrative analysis* proved to be a powerful way for deconstructing and discovering the constructions of human activities in artistic processes.[9] *Narrative means* proved to give strong new possibilities and dimensions for artistic work, and to be a challenging field of learning.

Answering the questions arising from the artistic process means new ones appearing: where does the borderline go between artistic work and other communication? When and how should the storytelling in a theatrical process be conducted? Who would have the right to conduct it – who is the author? Who puts limits and aims in a collaborative practice? Narrativity brought these questions with it, and they bring us to a very basic question of the line between fiction and reality, and the many meanings the question has in an artistic process. They also bring us to face the possibilities of change in theatrical practices, and to face the fear of change. In my understanding, searching for unknown paths – following the passion and curiosity for change – means seeking for the essentials of artistic collaboration, and that means more than technical virtuosity or a strict hierarchy between different professional skills. Theatre has its origins deep in a lively, communicating artistic event, between artists and their audiences, in gathering together – a shared moment, an intangible whole. Denis Guénoun claims that *a stage* can appear only there, where an audience answers to the invitation of the performance.[10]

Artistic processes (at least those ending up in communicative events) show up as collective and transformative journeys containing breaks or jumps, collective and individual, that tend to lead to an unknown result.

As a conclusion on utilising narrative means in researching my own artistic practices, I describe it as a strategy of confessions that constantly break through. It works as a fruitful medium for inviting material from practice into writing.

Dimensions of a Process – Networks of Narratives

Preparing for theatre rehearsals means taking into account at least three different layers: the *circumstances* under which the production is made (schedules, economies and other practical limits); then the *tasks* and *responsibilities* of the participants (agreements, contracts and negotiations); and finally, the *contents* and *aims* of the work (including all of what is usually considered artistic planning).

Normally the so-called artistic group plans the process together.[11] Actors come along when the rehearsals start. But what if they joined the pre-work? There is no doubt that the artistic process would develop differently, if responsibilities and aims were shared. A noteworthy side of sharing the whole of the process is that a lot more becomes shared than what is told and discussed. Even more important than stories told are untold narratives, the tacit knowledge that every culture has as collective resource, but which is often forgotten and hidden beyond practices, since it is intangible.

A group of artists brings more creative ideas for a piece of art than any individual artist can develop, *when* they start to recognise the space waiting there for their actions. But it demands a new working manner – a new attitude towards artistic work and the relation between art and everyday hierarchies. A narrative process demands emancipatory preparation, and a collaboration demands open, mutual communication.

A new method of group work needs to be introduced more profoundly than I had thought, and it needs time. Questions appear: how to lead this kind of a process and avoid the authoritarian role in the group? What is the difference between balance and compromise in an artistic process? How to have an open artistic aim, but not lose the focus? All the questions affect the three layers of the process: the producing, the individual tasks and the artistic aims. They each form their own narrative entirety, an entirety including habits, manners, wisdom, practical advice, attitudes, ideas and fears – experience and knowledge. Those narratives open a medium to a complexity; they show a landscape of possibilities and obstacles. And they show how important it is that the borderline between artistic and something else sometimes seems to disappear in a process of theatre-making.

Notes

1   *I and Thou* by Martin Buber (1996/1923, translated into Finnish in 1993)
    became a companion for my research journey. In the beginning Buber's thinking
    had a strong effect on the change happening in my mind as a theatre-maker.
    It started by questioning the working practices and hierarchies in theatre, and
    by asking the possibility of a dialogical, mutual encounter between those who
    participate.

2   See Zygmunt Bauman, 1997. Bauman describes human, postmodern ways
    of being in the world through different characters. A *Vagabond* is a character
    who constantly constructs his or her identity in a nomadic movement, pushed
    forwards to unknown places by a power that prevents him or her from settling
    down. Also a *Tourist* is travelling a lot, but the character is attracted by changing
    interests and he or she is mostly wandering to gain enjoyment. A vagabond does
    not have a home place, like a tourist always has. The difference between the
    action of those two is a vagabond lives in constant change instead of returning
    back and staying the same.

3   Gadamer's (2004) dialogical hermeneutics was a methodological background of my
    narrative research journey. According to Gadamer, a researcher who wants to form
    new understanding returns to a viewpoint round after round. Every glance gives
    him or her new views from a slightly new position – the construction of knowledge
    happens in a dialogical process. My figure of reflection became like a loop or a bow,
    consisting of two different dimensions, practice and theory or theatre-making and
    writing, and the reflecting movement in between.

4   In this contribution, 'action' is used in the meaning which Hannah Arendt (1958)
    gives to it. Arendt separates *work*, *labor* and *action* from each other and claims that
    action makes us human beings. "To act, in its most general sense, means to take an
    initiative, to begin… to set something into motion". (1958: 177)

5   The invited artists were actors and dancers, a trained sound-and-light designer and
    a trained producer. One of the actors had a twenty years' career; all the others were
    less experienced. They all had various skills in physical theatre-making, pedagogy,
    music, etc.

6   Autoethnography, see Ellis, 2004; Sparkes, 2002; Tierney, 2000.

7   In my analysis, I came to the conclusion that the actors' desire for a traditional
    drama was based on a conventional attitude towards acting a role: they wanted to
    have psychologically developing, believable characters and dramatic key scenes for
    expressing the inner feelings and qualities of the roles. According to convention, a
    good part (and a good actor) seems to cover the scale needed for those qualities.

8   See Gergen and Gergen, 2002.

9   Narrative analysis, see Polkinghorne, 1995: 12; Denzin, 1997: 234.

10   The French philosopher Denis Guénoun (2007) considers *stage* the focus of a
      theatrical event. According to him, a stage can be set up anywhere. He sees that
      communication and community makes theatre a living art form, and suggests that
      theatre buildings should be abandoned, since inside the institutions the need of
      gathering together is faded away.

11   In Finnish theatre-making the artistic group members are usually a director, a
      dramaturge, a stage designer, a costume designer, probably also a composer and a
      sound and light designer.

SECTION 3

Origins of the PhD and the Current Educational Climate

> What is research but a blind date with knowledge?
> **Will Harvey**

I t should be reasonably clear by now that this book's function is as a resource for researching performance, drama and theatre practitioners including postgraduate students, supervisors, mentors and examiners. In this sense the book takes as its premise the idea – call that a *starting belief* – that a number of key features need to be in place before investigations, no matter how of-the-moment and critical, can be accurately regarded as academically viable research. In this regard *Blood, Sweat & Theory* adopts a position which may appear somewhat at odds with the situation we find ourselves in currently. This is a situation where practice as research has become something of a methodological law unto itself; an activity that in its subversion of traditional research procedures and protocols is becoming creative arts researchers' new tradition of choice.

Even the most cursory trawl through an internet search engine shows this to be the case. The following examples are indicative of a much wider picture, as readers can determine for themselves with the click of a mouse. Keying in 'University Theatre Drama Research' with a UK filter produced these sites and statements, in the following order. Firstly, Lancaster University's subject page for Theatre (http://www.lancs.ac.uk/fass/lica/theatrestudies/ba_theatre. htm) claims at the very outset that they have a number of registered students undertaking higher postgraduate study, several of whom are engaged in one of the variety of currently available approaches they offer in support of practice-based research. Next in line, the Drama Department at Goldsmiths, London, lists four main research clusters, the first of which, we are immediately informed, is practice-based. (http://www.goldsmiths.ac.uk/drama/research/) Manchester Metropolitan University states on its welcome page that it 'has a reputation for pioneering Practice as Research PhDs', (http://www.cheshire.mmu.ac.uk/dca/) whilst Dartington College of Art's opening sentence flags their ability to offer postgraduate degrees which are attainable 'through distinctive practice-led learning methods'. (http://creativesteps.org.uk/Colleges/DartingtonInfo) The University of Chester is next with its Centre for Practice as Research in the Arts, followed by Leeds University's Centre for Practice Led Research in the Arts (CePRA). The first five hits then concentrate almost exclusively on practice-based research, and this significance is heightened by the fact that the word 'practice' was not keyed in at all. Removing the UK filter allowed the University of New South Wales to stress the fact that within Performing Arts they are able to offer 'places to graduate students wishing to undertake a PhD by means of Practice-Based Research, (e.g. theatre direction, film direction, dance choreography and the production of media artefacts).' (http://empa. arts.unsw.edu.au/) And the list goes on. The names of institutions might be different on the first page of a search undertaken today but the focus will almost certainly be the same.

In Bruegel's *Landscape with the Fall of Icarus* the titular figure we care about most falls into the sea without meriting so much as a glance from shepherds, sailors or ploughmen: a literal drop in a canvas ocean. It is worth mentioning that practice as research as it is being discussed here is, whilst engrossing to some, similarly unremarkable to a great many others. Indeed the term has a considerably reduced currency within the realms of professional theatre that exist outside of the university or academy. Patrice Pavis goes so far as to suggest that 'only in the university do we have a relationship between theory and practice, even if it is polemical and undecided.' (Pavis, 2000: 68) Because of this, it is worth noting some information that will remind readers of the educational climate within which this book is being created (and probably being read), as well as providing some sense of scale.

A recent report entitled *Doctoral Futures* set out to investigate the career destinations of PhD students in the Arts and Humanities. What emerged in the findings was that over 70 per cent of those PhD graduates who took part in the investigation had commenced their studies after having worked, often in career-oriented situations, and having successfully completed a related or subject-sympathetic Masters programme. This information correlates to age, with a significant proportion of Arts and Humanities PhD students coming to university-based research in their 30s, 40s and beyond. The report refers to these researchers more economically as 'mature students', a term which at the time of *this* writing rather than *that* has found its way onto the incrementally odd banned list at numerous UK universities. We can compare this with information collated by the Wellcome Trust, which in its report on *The Student Perspective*, determined that slightly more than three quarters of Biomedical and Science researchers and more than half of all physical scientists and engineers start their PhDs immediately after graduating with their first degree. Chemistry and Physics are consistently regarded as the most popular of the 'Direct Entry' subjects. (Wellcome Trust, 2000)

A PhD is awarded for an original research project that makes a significant contribution to the field of study and it remains, alongside its derivatives, the highest degree awarded by universities. The PhD has over the years become the highest degree one can earn. Its detailed requirements for award vary throughout the world; there are, however, a number of common factors. In all but the rarest cases a candidate is expected to submit a thesis consisting of a suitable body of original academic research which is, in ideas if not always in form, considered worthy of publication in a peer-refereed context. The thesis is subsequently examined by a panel of experts in the field who decide whether the work is in principle passable and/or the extent to which any issues arising from or contained within the thesis need to be addressed before the award of PhD can be given. There is usually a prescribed minimum period of study. In the UK this is typically three years for full-time registrations and this has to be completed before submission of the thesis. This requirement is sometimes waived in the case of experienced academics or theorists who are invited to submit a portfolio of peer-reviewed published work. This differs from an Honorary Doctorate, similarly offered in recognition of a body of work but lacking the pass/fail element of an academically 'earned' award.

In terms of historical origins we can trace the PhD back to the ninth-century licence to teach and issue legal opinions: a licence which had sole application through Islamic law. In the Middle Ages, the degree of Doctor of Philosophy was generally granted as an honorary degree to a small number of select and extremely well-established scholars. History is somewhat hazy on the matter, but the first PhD was probably awarded in Paris in or around 1150. It was not until the early nineteenth century that the term began to acquire its modern meaning, thanks primarily to emergent university practice in Germany.

Like the PhD, the study of theatre has a long history. James Arnott suggests that we can trace the tradition of theatre study from the Indian Sanskrit tradition, essays on dramatic theory by Zeami and Aristotle's *Poetics*, each of which he feels formed the basis for our academic embrace of theatre studies. Arnott sees links between ancient study and recent scholarship, citing the establishment of the Berlin Gesellschaft für Theatergeschichte in 1902, the Gesellschaft für Schweizerische Theaterkultur in 1927 and the Société d'Histoire du Théâtre in 1933 as key moments in the transition from the long-past to the near-present. (Arnott, 1981: p.37) Prior to the nineteenth century, professional doctoral degrees could only be awarded in Theology (ThD.), Law (J.D.), or Medicine (M.D.). In 1861 Yale University adopted the German practice of awarding the degree to students who had completed a prescribed course of graduate study and successfully defended a thesis containing original research in Science or in the Humanities. In 1900 the PhD emerged in Canada and from there to the UK in 1917, where the award largely replaced the existing Doctor of Philosophy (DPhil).

The academic study of Drama in the UK began at Bristol University in 1947. There are at the moment a seemingly endless number of UK institutions offering Higher Education programmes in Drama, Theatre and Performance: 1,103 Drama courses at 121 institutions; 685 Theatre courses at 102 institutions; 423 Performance Art courses at 90 institutions. Added to the 156 courses in Performance Studies, 40 in Performance Practice, 41 in Performance Art Studies, 50 in Directing and 24 in Performance Writing, and even accounting for the statistical overlap that occurs when an institution offers programmes in Drama and Theatre Studies (Aberystwyth University) or Drama and Performance Studies (London South Bank University), the numbers and range of options are staggering. (UCAS, 2009)

Whilst in the years since 2005 numbers on UK undergraduate Drama programmes have remained relatively stable, with between 10,000 and 11,000 applicants for close to 7,000 places, (HESA, 2008) during the last fifteen years there has been rapid growth in the number of PhDs awarded in the UK, and statistical evidence suggests general parity across Canada, the US, Australia and much of Europe. In the ten years leading up to 2009 there has been a substantial increase in the number of UK-registered PhD researchers expected to graduate during a calendar year. The vast majority of this growth has come from large increases in non-UK domiciled overseas and European Union (EU) full-time researchers (a 75% increase) and part-time UK researchers (an increase of 62%). The growth of full-time UK domiciled researchers has been relatively low at 41%, but this is relative only to the increase in full-time overseas and part-time domestic students: by any other measure a 41% increase is huge. Non-UK domiciled students now account for approximately half of all registered PhD researchers. So far, so statistically interesting – but how does this evidence relate to practice-based research in performance?

It relates on at least two levels. Firstly, being somewhat older than postgraduate students in other fields, those within the arts are commensurately more likely to bring a body of prior practice and experience to bear on their research towards PhD and significantly they may have the maturity and confidence to look for ways of building explorations of their own practice into their formal research strategies. Secondly, we can see the drive to accommodate and indeed often prioritise practice-as-research students within drama and arts departments as a way of keeping pace with national and international trends as well as with achieving domestically defined targets. Often these institutional targets are sold to lecturers as staff development and/or necessary prerequisites for promotion: evidence of successful PhD supervision, for example, is increasingly regarded by promotion and interview panels as something of a *sine qua non*, with prolific supervision alongside the ability to attract and retain PhD students as the new fast track to accessing keys to professorial washrooms.

Many of this book's readers will be working in or on the fringes of education, and those who are do so at a time when every academic qualification from secondary school to university is made subject to claims of inflation. And maybe this view, made common through regularity, is in some ways correct. This is not quite tantamount to biting the hand that reads me and it is not yet saying the unsayable but I am aware that in the context of non-retractable print it comes perilously close. To contextualise things slightly we need do no more than look at the ways in which we have gone meekly to the state where just about anything is able to constitute an object of assessable study. This is not a narrowly held view: in June 2008 the UK House of Commons Select Committee on Innovation, Universities, Science and Skills announced an evidence session to investigate standards in universities. In response to this news, Roger Brown and Geoffrey Alderman writing in the *Times Higher Education* note that 'there is prima facie evidence to suggest that all may not be well with the process through which the quality of degrees is safeguarded'. (Brown and Alderman, 2008: 24) The writers, co-director of the Centre for Research and Development in Higher Education and former Chairman of the Academic Council of the University of London respectively, go on to suggest that the various competitive pressures of league table success combined with increased consumerism and commercialisation 'lie behind the evidence of cheating and apparent grade inflation'. (Ibid.: 25)

Whilst the recent rapid growth in the types of work offered for assessment has much to answer for, most of us would agree, I suspect, that at its best the type of learning engendered through work experience, professional development and/or work-based learning has made a huge and positive impact on dragging academia forward into application, and only the most conservative among us would deny its qualitative worth. However, in the same way that movement is not the same thing as action we know that change is not always progressive and that assessable outcomes ranging from composing a curriculum vitae or webpage to reflecting on what might appear to be fairly meaningless work experience have resulted at certain institutions and in some cases to what amounts to a retention-led lack of regard for the idea that it is a student's knowledge that will most often constitute the object of academic assessment within a subject-based system of learning. Whilst we will rarely admit this about our own work it is a fact of academic life that for every university that sees work experience as a means of encouraging students and staff to be proactive in the development of transferable skills there is another that will see it as a cynical opportunity to tick the box labelled 'External Collaboration'; for every tutor who sees professional placement as a vital, and vitally supervised, stage in a student's progression there is another who will see it as time off from teaching alongside the freeing up of an otherwise heavily timetabled space.

A number of us will have experienced the ways in which the pressures to compete for student numbers has had a profound bearing on the forms of assessment and examination, transforming students into customers to the extent that a good degree is increasingly seen as the outcome of a primarily commercial and client-driven transaction. Certainly, the time when most prospective students had to compete hard to gain their university places has long gone, with all but a handful of universities now having to compete for the same type of students they once attracted with ease.

What has happened as a result of raising numbers and making programmes ever more attractive to potential as well as existing students is that forms of assessment that are widely perceived to be lacking in intellectual merit in either delivery or learning have assumed an elevated role in the university sector. A consequence of this is that what is being graded often has little in common with assessments that are consistent with the measuring of academic standards. We take this alongside suggestions that external examiners are sometimes putting pressures on internal assessors to be lenient in their marking, with certain externals going so far as to suggest that lecturers have to 'work harder to find the excellence' in students' work. (Newman, 2008: 11) An immediate consequence of this is that universities move a couple of rungs up the value-added league ladder. An equally immediate consequence is that many lecturers believe that standards have changed for the worse but feel disempowered to talk publicly about this. (Ibid.)

Allegations of grade inflation are in no way limited to the UK system. After the disclosure in 2002 that Harvard University had been awarding Honors grades to more than 90 per cent of its students, the Washington University School of Law adjusted its grading scale accordingly. For no more reason than a desire to keep pace with assumed inflation elsewhere, the Law School moderated all of its internally agreed B- grades to B+. This is not intended to isolate Washington and/or Harvard for criticism. In fact the proportion of top grades across all US universities has quadrupled in the past three decades with institutions such as Northwestern University awarding more than half of all its grades at A. (Marcus, 2002) When this is regarded alongside a UK practice that has seen the generic pass grade drop without fuss or full consultation at some universities from 40 to 30 per cent, it is hard to mount a serious argument against allegations of falling standards.

In 2009, 400,000 UK students are about to graduate with Bachelors degrees, moving into an employment field that boasts fewer than 80,000 jobs each year that genuinely require graduates. (Graduate Jobs, 2009) At A Level and AS Level (taken typically by 16-to-18-year-old students in further education or the sixth form of secondary schools), results have improved dramatically to the point where we are informed that in the last twenty years 'A Levels have got nearly 40% easier.' (Davies, 2008: 20) The Office of National Statistics concurs, conceding recently that 'A level grades... certainly do correspond to a lower level of general academic ability than the same grades would have done in previous years. Whether or not they are better taught makes no difference to this interpretation – the same grade corresponds to a lower level of general ability.' (Office of National Statistics, 2007) In 2003, *BBC News* reported that the pass rate for A levels was creeping closer to the 100 per cent mark, increasing by an average of 1.1 percentage points per year, (*BBC News*, 2003) and this trend has continued with Laura Clark's 2007 report that 'The scale of "grade inflation" in schools and universities... is laid bare in official figures.... The number of A grades at A-level and top honours degrees has soared more than 50 per cent since 1997'. (Clark, 2007) My own experience of examining and moderating at A Level has revealed the high number of candidates who receive maximum grades (very common with practical work) and the huge numbers that are awarded marks of 80 per cent and above for combinations of written and practical elements.

At the level of GCSE (General Certificate of Secondary Education) in 2007 more than 600,000 students achieved GCSE passes of which more than one in five exam scripts were awarded a top grade pass, with an overall pass rate of 98.2 per cent. (Garner, 2008) Lies, lies and damned statistics perhaps, and yet

BLOOD, SWEAT & THEORY

the figures come thick and fast and they come from all angles: even infant and primary school teachers are being offered incentives at some UK schools with performance-related pay that is dependent upon a certain numbers of pupils in each class meeting pre-determined sets of achievements. These achievement tests or SATS (Standard Assessment Tests) are taken by children at the end of year 2, year 6 and year 9. Whilst they are ostensibly used to monitor a child's progress compared with other children of the same age, there is little doubt that their prime purpose is to place schools rather than pupils at their appropriately measured levels. These are subsequently published on league tables; and being seen to move one's school further up these tables is connected to various financial rewards as well as an increase in one's professional standing.

A recent statement from the Higher Education Statistics Agency (HESA) shows that arts and humanities students in the UK have a considerably better chance of gaining a good degree (i.e. a First or Upper Second) than students in other areas. By 2001 over 68 per cent of arts and humanities students were graduating with these degrees, compared with the 52.3 per cent national average. As Tony Mooney ponders, 'Perhaps this is because, on average, humanities students are a brighter bunch than the rest.... Or has it something to do with the fact that their work is much more open to interpretation and therefore more susceptible to lenient marking?' (Mooney, 2003: 19) Chief executive of the Quality Assurance Agency, Peter Williams, is concerned enough to suggest that the 2008 figures 'intensify the questions that must be asked about degree classification. Each year, they show an upwards march.' (Atwood, 2008)

In her paper, 'British Doctorates in the Dock', Ann Mroz addresses the issue of students completing undergraduate degrees at a lower standard than at any time in the past and that as a consequence 'the road of travel' to a PhD is longer and more strained than it should otherwise be, resulting in a 'weaker PhD at the end of the process.' (Mroz, 2008: 23) In the same paper, and citing the Bologna Process, Chris Park suggests that the international view of UK PhD awards is that they are less vigorous than elsewhere and that, potentially at least, the value of the UK doctorate is being diminished on the world stage. (Ibid.)

These concerns over process, alongside issues of evidence, truth, evaluation, dissemination, rigour, representation and reliability weave their way through many of our questions about practice-based research and they form the basis of the ways in which new performance understandings are able to develop in the light of new possibilities.

The words contained in this book offer no panacea, if indeed such is required, only a series of connected suggestions and statements that might serve to further already ongoing debate; debate which in its own turn can only ever be concerned with the maintenance and raising of standards. And these standards are not raised by the type of resistant response that regards any and all remotely adversarial comments as indicative of arch conservatism aligned to a fearful resistance to innovation. Terrible is the temptation to do well, as Brecht warned us, and they do most harm who believe they know most emphatically what is best for the rest of us… and that includes those of us who see ourselves as proponents of practice as research as well as those we might identify as antagonists. Heeding Brecht, it is not then important that readers agree with every statement made in these pages so much as that the statements offered help to focus our attention on matters of consequence to practice-based research. In this sense all debate is good debate. Stated in this way, the opposite also applies.

In recognising that contemporary performance knows few if any boundaries it is logical that performance research is similarly unfettered. That research is a broad enough church to accommodate the creation of spaces for dynamic practice-led learning means also that assumptions of standardised expectations and correctness are being challenged, and it would be hard to see this as something other than a force for good.

CASE STUDY 3

The Smell of It: Case Study of Curious' Live Art Performance *On the Scent*

Helen Paris

Lilac. The smell of lilac. It's not the earliest smell I can recall from childhood but it is one of the most potent. This spring the trees are full of lilac, packed with white, lavender and purple coloured cones of heavily scented flowers. I am pushing my nephew Jem in his pram. There has just been a heavy spring shower and the leaves above my head are dripping. A bough of lilac hangs over the neighbour's fence. I reach up and break myself a stem. I shake the droplets of water from it and I show it to Jem. 'Fower,' he says knowingly – happy to show off one of his first words, along with the rest of his repertoire: Bib, Apple and All Aboard! I lift the stem to my nose, sink my face into it and breathe in our back garden in Kent. I am six-years old wearing an egg-yolk-yellow scratchy nylon dress. I am playing house under the low-slung branches of a lilac tree. My mother is sitting on the porch step peeling potatoes into an orange bowl. My father is mowing the lawn with a noisy green metal lawn mower. The experience is intensely physical. I can see my mother, I can hear the loud hum of the mowing machine, feel the fabric of the dress against my legs. I am right there. This is olfactory time travel.

Smell has a unique relationship to memory. This relationship has been a catalyst for creating text and movement throughout my performance practice. My first solo performance *Sniffing the Marigolds* (1994), which explored identity and sexuality, was written and created using olfactory memories to choreograph movement and generate text. One of the first works I made with Curious, co-founded in 1996 with Leslie Hill, was a live performance called *Random Acts of Memory* (1998). *Random Acts of Memory* juxtaposed digital memory with body memory and explicitly used smell within the performance. Scenes in the show were triggered by sudden smell memories experienced by the performers. Smell acted as a sort of 'starter motor' activating the performance. (See Vroon, 1997: 103) The audience were also included in the olfactory experiences of the piece. After reading a scientific study which claimed to identify the smells 'most arousing' to American men and women (measured by blood flow to the genitals), we decided to infuse the auditorium with these two smells: women were given a handful of liquorice as they entered the theatre and for the men, we baked a pumpkin pie under the seating rostrum. We felt sure it added a certain *je ne sais quoi* to the atmosphere.

Smell permeates the everyday, triggering memories, transporting us through space and time even though we are mostly unaware of it. Piet Vroon writes that:

> A person who lost his sense of smell was amazed by how much he lost. 'Sense of smell,' he said. 'I never gave it a thought. You don't normally give it a thought. But when I lost it – it was like being struck blind... You *smell* people, you *smell* the city, you *smell* the spring – maybe not consciously, but as a rich unconscious background to everything else. My world was suddenly radically poorer.'
>
> (Vroon, 1997: 168)

The extraordinary power of smell to evoke memory inspired me to want to try and create a performance that not only used smell as one of the elements but wherein smell had a leading role. I wanted to discover how to utilise smell fully in live performance and also explore the mutual elements of smell and live performance. Both are ephemeral, transitory, they have a shared ontology. Compare these two quotes, one about smell, the other about performance, but each almost interchangeable with the other:

> Smell, like taste, is a sensation of the moment, it cannot be preserved. We do not know what the past smelled like, and in the future our own odour will be lost.'
>
> (Classen et al., 1995: 204)

> Performance's only life is in the present. Performance cannot be saved, recorded, documented, or otherwise participate in the circulation of representation of representations: once it does so, it becomes something other than performance. To the degree that performance attempts to enter the economy of reproduction, it betrays and lessens the promise of its own ontology.
>
> (Phelan, 1993: 46)

I wanted to create a live performance where the shared ephemeralities of live performance and smell worked together to create an experience of the moment. An experience when you didn't just have to *be* there, you had to *breathe* there. The piece would be called *On the Scent*.

As an initial part of our research for creating *On the Scent*, Leslie and I wanted to work with a biomedical scientist whose research focus was on the olfactory. To be honest, we didn't know how easy it was going to be to find such a scientist, let alone one who wanted to collaborate with artists. After some research on the web, I approached Dr Upinder Bhalla, a leading expert on the neurological connections between smell and memory, at the National Centre for Biological

Sciences, Bangalore, India. I wanted to know how smell affects memory and emotion, to ask whether he felt that in a commercialised, digitised and sanitised world the sense of smell was being 'downgraded'. He e-mailed back with this reply:

> [The research] gives a glimpse of human reactions to smell. There have been plenty of psychophysics experiments on the subject measuring things like detection thresholds and the like, but much fewer studies looking simply at what people think and how they react to smell. Although this is less quantifiable, it is in some ways more important now that the field is moving towards looking at the cognitive aspects of sensory responses.
>
> Humans themselves seem to be conditioned by society to ignore smell, especially in the sanitized modern world. It is interesting to see what happens when they are asked to pay specific attention to it. For myself, I am most interested in seeing how an artist approaches the topic of smell.
>
> My training has given me a particular line of thinking and this could always do with some new perspectives. I view science as an expression of creativity. It would be great to complement this with an altogether different form of expression coming from a different world of creativity.
>
> (Bhalla, U., e-mail, 1st March 2002)

From the outset, the collaboration with Dr Bhalla positioned itself as a reciprocal relationship where both science and art would benefit from the dialogue and exploration. The next part of the research was to secure the funding to enable it to happen. The Wellcome Trust had recently launched their Science on Stage and Screen fund, the criteria of which was apposite for the collaborative research on smell. Other funding included an Arts and Humanities Research Board Innovation award and Arts Council England funding.

Not only did Dr Bhalla seem the ideal collaborator for this project, but where better than India as a location for smell research? Arriving in Bangalore, Leslie and I were both overcome by the smell of the city. It was evening and the smells from the day were heavy in the air; the petrol fumes from the auto rickshaws; the sultry jasmine, the sharp smell of spices and scent of warm garbage collided.

Smell is a transgressor, 'smells resist containment in discrete units, whether physical or linguistic; they cross boundary lines'. (Classen et al., 1995: 204) Like live performance, smell is ephemeral, transitory and elusive. Through observing their experiments in the lab, we quickly realised that the scientists working with smell encounter many of the same problems that we face in trying to control smell in art spaces. Because smell is a chemical sense, every smell concocted from a complex cocktail of odorant molecules, it is almost impossible to deliver odour stimulus with any sort of precision or regularity, much less to smell the same smell twice. For the same reasons, it is extremely difficult to eliminate one odour in order to make way for another or to mask the background odours of an environment.

In George Orwell's *Nineteen Eighty-Four*, olfactory concerts are piped through a 'scent organ' with smells rising and falling effortlessly into and away from one another. Through the application of science, we had imagined, it might be possible for us to achieve highly orchestrated olfactory engineering in an installational environment. Far from having mastered control over smell molecules, however, scientists have struggled with the problems of odorant delivery for years, prototyping various devices in an attempt to do for the olfactory what the slide projector or tape player do for sight and hearing. A few days after our arrival, for example, the third generation in the prototype referred to at the NCBS as an 'olfactometer' was ready for its first trial. Comprised of a series of eight flasks and tubes connecting each of them to a pure airstream, the olfactometer didn't look terribly complicated or high tech at first glance, though it was connected to a computer which could be programmed to deliver smells from the different flasks randomly or in specified sequences. In the olfactometer room great care was taken to ensure an odourless environment so as not to interfere with the accuracy of the experiments, including a giant vacuum tube descending from the roof, sucking smell molecules out of the room. The scientists constantly checked the ventilation system, cleaned the equipment and rebuilt the olfactometer in an attempt to exert olfactory authority over the space. If a smell 'leaked' or 'stuck', the entire olfactometer had to be dismantled and washed down repeatedly with alcohol in

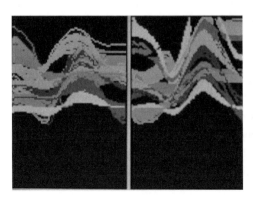 

order to remove the 'sticky' odorant molecules. Thus we learned that some smells are stickier and harder to control at a molecular level than others, illustrating the truth of the statement that 'odours cannot be readily contained, they escape and cross boundaries, blending different entities into olfactory wholes'. (Classen et al., 1995: 4)

Curiously enough, working with Dr Bhalla led us away from qualitative concerns for methods of delivery and recording back to our original fascination with the unquantifiable, personal, emotive aspects of the olfactory. Though we were fundamentally asking the same questions as the scientists, i.e. how does smell impact memory and emotion, as artists we were operating in a different world with different freedoms and limitations. Scientists have a burden of proof; performers have a burden of entertainment, the methodologies are going to be different. Our time in the lab opened up a whole new appreciation of the complexities of smell at the molecular and neurological levels. In contrast to the design of the scientific experiments, we decided to make *On the Scent* as subjective an experience as possible to try and tap into the rich veins of personal associations our audience members would bring with them.

Firsthand experience of the difficulties that scientists experience in their efforts to control odour even in laboratory environments gave us even more respect for smell as the most enigmatic of senses. Back in London we devised several potential plans for gallery installations or theatre spaces but with each new draft idea it became more clear to us that we needed to work with smell in a 'natural habitat' rather than in an art space in order to allow it really to have the impact we wanted it to, particularly in terms of audience reaction. We decided to site *On the Scent* in real homes rather than in art spaces and in a way this was the key breakthrough in designing the performance. Working in homes seemed to provide the ideal combination of a space small enough to effectively broadcast smells by means of simple everyday actions as well as providing a meaningful and familiar setting for the work, laden with personal memories and a sense of place. We developed 'home sick' as our overarching theme for the creation of the piece.

In designing the experience for an audience, we decided to work in the rooms of a house where visitors are received, working in from the semi-public nature of the living room to the cosy familiarity of sitting round the kitchen table to the intimate inner sanctum of the bedside for visitors to the sick room. We decided that one performer would occupy each of the three rooms, creating a smell-scape and a related narrative of personal memories and emotions for their room. We felt that the audience should experience the piece in small groups of no more than four at a time, to preserve the intimacy of the design and the feel of being guests in the home. Leslie took the kitchen, I took the bedroom and we invited the artist Lois Weaver to create the performance for the living room. Each performer created a smell-scape, installation and performance for their room. Texts were written using body memory and smell memory to create three very different autobiographical pieces. As stated earlier, we wanted the piece to have an emotional and experiential arch, starting with a nostalgic, romantic texture and moving, as the audience went deeper into the house, into darker more troublesome smell-scapes.

The performance is very intimate due to the small audience numbers and the very 'up close and personal' nature of the performances. The audience is given the key to the house and let themselves in. They hear a voice coming from the living room. Whether they are expected or are intruding is not quite clear. They follow the voice and enter the room. A glamorous woman in black evening dress, Lois, is in mid-flow speaking to a camera set on record. Her impossible, compulsive project is to capture the 'essences' of moments and save them to enjoy over and over again. The audience have interrupted this ritual and Lois takes a moment out of her talks to tell them to, 'wait a moment, I have to finish this,' before returning to the camera to finish recording her smell memory. This scene directly relates to the impossibility of recording and capturing smell. Weaver tries to recollect exact fragrances and record them digitally, but playback will always be odourless. Yet the room in which she sits is pungent, overloaded with scent. It is heady with the scent of 'Evening in Paris' perfume, rose and violet cream chocolates, and vases dripping with heavy stems of lilies. In the live, smell persists. When Lois completes her recording she turns and gives her full attention to her guests. She goes up close to the audience and sniffs them. If they were on edge before, thinking they have interrupted something, now the stakes are definitely raised. Because of the intensely personal nature of smell, a sniff can be more intimate than a kiss; it goes beyond the skin. It is animal, instinctive and decidedly primitive.

> Sniffing and smelling, a predilection for powerful animal odours, the erotic effect of sexual odours all become objects of suspicion. Such interests, thought to be essentially savage, attest to a proximity to animals, a lack of refinement, and ignorance of good manners.
>
> (Corbin, 1994: 7)

Lois seems to be a woman addicted to scent. She blames her addiction on formative experiences…

Lois Weaver: I blame it on the Avon lady. What got to me was her bag. It was so compact, so organized and so full of bottles shaped just to make you want to hold them, stroke them and explore the miracles of their cures. But you could not have them right away. You had to order them and she couldn't tell you exactly how long it would take to get them. Then the space between that immediate craving and the possibility of satisfaction was packed up inside her bag and carried down the sidewalk to her car and driven home to a place I didn't know and couldn't imagine. What would she do at night with all those bottles and jars? I had to get my hands on that case. But she stopped coming. They never last, Avon ladies. They are temporary. Itinerant. Door to door.

With her 'door to door' Lois directs the audience into the Kitchen. Leslie invites the audience to join her round the kitchen table. At first her olfactory reminiscences seem innocent enough as she cooks up smells of her family:

Leslie Hill: [*Lights up a Lucky Strike cigarette*] I don't smoke, me. And I'm a vegetarian. [*Throws a pork chop on the grill*] But sometimes I just have to light up a Lucky Strike and throw a pork chop on the grill. It's like my Granny Parker is right there in the room with me. [*Sprays hairspray into the air*]. A little touch of Aquanet Extra Super Hold rounds it out nicely. God only knows how she kept herself from going up in flames with all that hairspray and the constant flicker of the cigarette lighter around her head. And if I am missing Mom, why I just turn on the popcorn popper. [*Loads popcorn popper with kernels*]. Popcorn was the only food my mother really enjoyed cooking. I like having them around together.

The cosy setting becomes imbued with danger as she starts to talk about her native New Mexico, home of the atomic bomb, while all around the temperature begins to rise. The comforting smells of home cooking begin to mix and mingle with the dangerous smells of burning.

Leslie Hill: They made the bomb in New Mexico and then, to see if it worked, they dropped it on New Mexico. That's the kind of place I come from. After they detonated it, blind birds rained down for miles all over the state. You know, there was absolutely no military need for the American government to drop the bomb on the Japanese. But they dropped it anyway for three reasons: [*popcorn erupts – Leslie tries to ignore it*] 1) Money: more money was spent developing the bomb than the entire American car industry cost. They were terrified of what the taxpayers would do when they found out they'd spent that much money on a weapon that was never used. 2) Revenge: the US never got over the wound to its pride from the 'unprovoked attack' on Pearl Harbor. They wanted to punish the enemy for all the world to see. 3) Curiosity: thousands of scientists had been working on two different prototypes down in the tunnels – one bomb, little boy, was uranium; the other, fat man, was plutonium. They just wanted to know… which one worked better. [*Plunges grill pan under cold tap, producing large cloud of steam and turns off popcorn popper. Returns to table and razors off a lock of hair*]. Little boy: 200,000. Fat man: 140,000. [*Holds hair between fingers and set on fire – keeps holding until it melts*]. White House Press release: the greatest achievement of organized science in history. [*Pours tequila shots for everyone in the room*]. Here's to home. Sickness.

From the kitchen, the audience makes their way into the most intimate room, the bedroom. I lie in bed and the theme of homesickness is further played out as I am 'home sick', in a room steeped in the aroma of Dettol and Pepto Bismol. This is a place of limbo, where faintly unpleasant odours permeate and linger despite every attempt to freshen, to heal, and to fend off aging and death.

> **Helen Paris:** What are the days that mark the change? That firmly shut the doors on the soft silk frocks and talcum-powdered indulgences and instead open the way for the parcels of upper-arm under hangs to flop down, falling in a sheave to the elbow, in raffia folds. What happens to make sane the choice to pull on elasticated trousers and more senile than sensible shoes? When is the exact moment that Chanel # 5 is replaced by three-for-the-price-of-two anonymous 'family' soap which no-one in the family claims ownership for? There should be signs to let you know what lies ahead. Government Health Warnings to let you know when her bags full of perfume and lipstick change and become full of safety pins and chewable Gaviscon indigestion tablets. And that is why the quest of the Roget Gallet Sandalwood Body Lotion was so important…

This space is claustrophobic; the seats for the audience are positioned close to the side of the bed. The door is closed behind them and the smells of sickness and depression are firmly sealed in. The stickiness, the pervasiveness of smell is consciously employed here to create the sensation of inescapability. This is about illness and dying. The smells here are about our mortality. As the performer inhabiting this room for eight performances a day, the smells affected me. The sickening smell of Dettol that clung to my bed sheets, the airlessness of the room – this room of depression was a depressing one to be in. For Leslie, the toxic smell of the kitchen – the smoke and burning pork chop and smouldering hair – gave her a huge headache each day we performed the piece. For Lois, the overpowering perfumes, not to mention the overpowering perfumed chocolates, left her with a sickly sweet sugar buzz after the day's performances. This was a show about 'home sickness' that literally made us sick!

For all that the show literally gets up our noses when we are performing, the piece is none the less a compelling one to perform. As each group of audience members arrive and let themselves in, there is a renewed excitement about the encounter. There is a fearfulness and a delight in hearing four strangers making their way up the stairs, opening the door and entering the bedroom and suddenly being so close. So close that I can even smell on their clothes the scents from the living room and kitchen. Each performance feels like a very unique encounter with the audience. It is one of the things about the show that makes it so satisfying to perform eight times a day in a tour that must now have seen about 600 performances.

In the final stage of their journey, the audience members return to the living room where Lois is waiting for them. This time her camera is for their smell memories rather than her own:

> **Lois Weaver:** There you are. Come over here and sit down. Now you
> need to give me something before you go. A little something to keep me
> going. Something personal. I want you to think of a smell that makes
> you think about home or makes you feel homesick or maybe just sick.
> Tell me what it is, describe it and tell me what it reminds you of. I am
> going to capture it here, bottle it, keep it for later…

Audiences to *On the Scent* described this experience of telling their stories and hearing those of their fellow audience members as being very powerful. After experiencing the journey through the house, hearing the stories of home sickness shared by the performers they actively wanted to share their own memories triggered by the piece. Although sometimes unnerved by having to face the camera (and Lois!), they described a sense of relief at being able to respond to what they had just witnessed and experienced, and remembered. Through the interviews, an archive of smell memories and associations has formed as the work continues to tour, with each audience member contributing to the growing collection, imbuing it with something of their own essence.

On The Scent has been performed in 14 different countries and we have collected nearly 2,500 smell memories. The performance has taken up residence in many different homes, from its first performance in a small red-brick terrace house in West Bromwich as part of FIERCE festival in 2003 to a luxury Park

Avenue apartment in Manhattan, an historic building in Brazil, an ex-communist block in Shanghai, a council flat in East London, and a sun-filled house in Sydney – to mention just a few. The memories audience members share are poetic, funny, upsetting and endlessly surprising. There are cultural differences and collisions and it becomes clear that in working with smell we are also working with race, gender, difference and a fundamental element of what it is to be human.

Interview by Helen Paris with Lois Weaver and Leslie Hill from May 2009, during run of *On the Scent* in Cavendish Avenue, Cambridge, UK.

Helen Paris: What is the strongest experience of performing *On the Scent?*

Lois Weaver: One of the big things for me about the experience of *On the Scent* is the experience of performing for a few people. I love the intimacy of that. It was my first experience of it. It's so hard to get in a theatrical sense – I feel like I am in the room with the people rather than acting. I really feel like I am inviting them in to my room; inviting them into nostalgia for someone they know or associate with a particular perfume.

At the end of the piece, as soon as I say 'I want you to tell me something personal. Something that reminds you of home... or makes you feel homesick... or just makes you sick' and it's almost as if I see them leave the room for a moment. I know they are not listening anymore, they are tying to think of their smell, their memory. When I say 'something that makes you feel sick' that is the moment I get them back. In the performance we give them little pathways that trigger memories or that inspire them. I think that if we asked them for their smell memory immediately they came into the house we would get very different responses.

Helen Paris: Do you have a smell memory of the show?

Lois Weaver: Performing the show you lose contact with the experience of your own smell – every once in a while I get a scent of the lilies and if I smell the perfume *Eternity*, which is a smell I use only in the show, I get a sensation of the show, it's in the back of my head, it's a wide feeling – a creative place. It's the pace I go to be somebody else.

Leslie Hill: The strongest smell association for me with the show is the smell of pork chops cooking. That smell is very much a part of my past and makes me nostalgic for my grandmother cooking, frying meat on a high temperature with cigarette smoke in the air. That's very resonant for me in terms of my olfactory association with the show and also a smell that reminds me of childhood. When I throw the chop on the pan and blow cigarette smoke on the chop I see the audience look at me like I am mad, like 'what are you doing!' but then two or three seconds later they get the smell of the chop and the smoke and with anyone from thirty up there is a moment of recognition. It reminds them of the person in their family who smoked, or fried – a kind of 'ah yes, that smells like my grandmother' moment.

Editing the video clips is also a really important part of this project and the associations I have with it. It is so interesting to see the different territory and terrain that is covered in the audience members' stories. In terms of motifs that connect the different countries we've done the show in, there are a lot of stories about grandparents and childhood – maybe because it's hard for people to smell what their own homes smell like, so the memory of a grandparent's house has a vivid olfactory connection. In China, several members of the audience talked about the utter olfactory confusion in the wake of the explosion of products coming onto the market after communism eased up. During the communist period everybody smelt the same because everyone used the same one soap – so your mother smelt like your schoolteacher who smelt like you, and then suddenly there were 30 different types of shampoo.

Lois Weaver: In the show we did yesterday I saw someone really realise perhaps for the first time how powerful smell is. He remembered a smell and then his eyes lit up and he said 'when I think about that smell all these other images come up'. In that moment he was suddenly aware of the trigger that most of us know and don't necessarily give voice to it, but it was his pure discovery of that moment.

Leslie Hill: For me the most overpowering smell is the smell of the kitchen. The perfume smells when you spray it but then dissipates. But in the kitchen, even after only the first show, that smell is everywhere. It's a sticky smell and suddenly everything smells like that. When we were touring the show a lot for a few years I remember opening the camera bag and the camera smelling of those pork chops. And the camera is in Lois' room! It isn't even in the kitchen. And it's so strange that something that is so metallic can smell like this – like pork chops. The smell just sticks.

Helen Paris: Several of the responses to the show are that it's a very feminine piece and that the space we create is a very feminine one (even if the actual house owner is male!). I think as well as the relationship of smell and performance there is something about the relationship of smell and the female. I want to read you this quote:

> Smell, in turn, was now the sense of intuition and sentiment, of home-making and seduction, all of which were associated with women. It was maps, microscopes and money on the one hand, and pot-pourris, pabulum and perfume on the other. Significantly, however, smell was also the sense of 'savages' and animals, two categories of beings that, like women, were deprecated and exploited by contemporary Western culture.
>
> (Classen et al., 1995: 84)

Helen Paris: As creators and performers of this piece, how do you respond to the relationship of smell and femaleness?

Leslie Hill: The impulsive and associative are often denigrated in relation to the cognitive. The Cartesian split linked impulsive qualities to the feminine, rational qualities to the masculine but science has now blown this apart. The sense of smell is part of the instant impulsive rapid processing we do if based on our reaction to the environment we are in: what feels right or wrong or alluring or dangerous and so forth.

Lois Weaver: Nostalgia is associated with the feminine and is a way of marginalising us for being reflective.

Helen Paris: Has this experience of working with smell informed your other work?

Lois Weaver: When I think about making new work, most of my inspiration comes from a visual source. I now have a heightened awareness of the other senses as potential inspiration for writing. Also, working with people that way in the room has changed the way I feel about performance to a large audience. I think that now I am able to find more of the 'real' in a theatrical performance because of the reality of that intimate performance space.

We end here, a conversation unfinished as it is show time. We go back into the house into our separate rooms each with their own familiar scents. We await our next audience. To perform intimately and only for them and to capture and 'bottle' their memories like rare perfume.

SECTION 4

Certainties and Institutional Bias: Research for, into and through Practice; Research Criteria and Creative Intelligence

> Research is what I'm doing when I don't know what I'm doing.
> **Walter von Braun**

P ractice-as-research projects differ in substance and kind from conventional approaches, not least through their emphasis on the promotion of social and aesthetic change: as Laura A. McCammon sees it, this results in projects which are often participatory, with research as something done *with* participants rather than *on* or *for* them. (McCammon, 2005) Similarly, this book endorses, at least in part, the commonly held view that practice as research centres on practitioners researching in and through their own creative work. We can identify the types of researchers who put their faith in practice as those individuals who are generally disinclined to follow prescriptive patterns. What we see in place of prescription is a preference for the strength of practical knowledge, understandings and accumulated experience, and it is this which often leads these researchers into new fields of enquiry. Accordingly, practice as research can be seen to be a process through which performance makers are able to develop and deepen the abilities they already possess to make reasoned, autonomous and often professional judgements. Through research, practitioners can develop an increased critical awareness of the things they do in their own practice and of *why* they do these things in the ways that they do. Whether this in and of itself is enough to qualify as research, regardless of the rigours of contextualisation, is one of the questions this section and indeed this entire book will continue to wrestle with.

Performance practice as research fuses elements of aesthetic consideration with academic analysis. Etymologically, 'aesthetics' comes from the Greek term for perception. We know that perception is determined by one's belief system and we know that this in its own turn is created by the transformation of experiences into attitudes. Further, we can say that beyond the worlds of nature, classical art and arch commercialism there is rarely any unanimity in terms of what is or what is not aesthetically pleasing. We are able to say that the aesthetic exists and we can even make informed estimations as to in what form or to what measure any one thing can ever be aesthetically sound; but this is tempered by our knowledge that human judgement is innately interpretative and that interpretation is always in key ways personal. As notions of performance and aesthetics are as closely linked as they are, it is equally impossible to arrive at an unchallenged notion of what constitutes performance, or even what it is that distinguishes performance practice from the trial and error of non-performative research activity. We can make best guesses and not much more. Certainty exists only as an illusion.

And yet certainty is oftentimes the very thing we crave. We are most of us aware that one of the chief areas of difficulty for researchers is that we are working in an area that steadfastly refuses easy definition. The nature of research is that we are always likely to encounter that which falls beyond all but the loosest of categorising frames; just as we recognise the importance of theatrical performance without always being able to recognise performance when we see it, or even on those occasions when we do not. This is a difficult idea for some of us to come to terms with. If performance did not matter to us as much as it does then we would not be as obsessed as we are with ideas as to what performance is and what it is not. And this makes a complicated time for us all.

Research through practice suggests an element of artistry. We can identify certain aspects we might regard as useful, though not always crucial to the description of someone as an artist. Edging out on a limb we are able to say that artists are more adept, or aspire to be more adept, at encountering the complexities of life than non-artists. We can say this not least because artists are engaged in the day-to-day and project-to-project questioning of those issues that most affect us. Despite being at the centre of human existence these issues are rarely taken by most of us at anything more than face value. We can further say that (and more so than artists working in other fields) those artists whose medium is performance are charged with the immediate contemplation of these issues. Digital, retrievable technology aside, the moment of the work's completion is in one identifiable sense the moment of its exhibition. (For expert analysis of the shifting nature of multimedia performance see Skjulstad et al., 2002; Broadhurst and Machon, 2006; Kaye, 2006; and Dixon, 2007.) This is not to deny the importance of process, nor is it intended to suggest that the assessment of research should rest entirely on outcomes. The relationship of research product to research process is particularly vexed, no less than the relationship between content and form. As John Cage acknowledged:

> We know that unlike the discipline of philosophy, the role of the artist
> is to articulate her or his contemplation in a manner that marries form
> to idea and ideology to a sense of aesthetics... even when that sense
> may be no more than the artist's own. Form becomes an issue, even
> when the consideration of form leads to the deliberate abandonment of
> judicious choice.
>
> (Cage, 2005: 68)

Without asking questions that interrogate assumptions, practitioners become less than the term suggests... and less perhaps than it demands. They become no more or less than entertainers, copyists trotting out clichés in the manner of sentimentalists: and sentimentality, the repetitive act repeated because it provides familiar responses to familiar stimuli, is the death of both practice and research. This does not refer to repetition in pursuit of discovery, it relates to the repetitive act as a formula through which yesterday's idea is re-packaged as the art of today. Asking questions *through* practice, any more than asking questions *of* practice, does not mean that one should demand or even expect clear answers. The process has more to do with addressing issues. Any solutions sought and found are more likely to relate to the specific set of circumstances created by the work in question than to any globally significant responses. Accordingly, the default expectation of research as a process leading to factual certainty becomes the first casualty of practice... although as we shall see this can become an area of some difficulty when objective and verifiable clarification is replaced entirely by subjective belief.

This focus is concerned with two chief aspects, although the parameters of these will bleed and merge, weaving in and through the other's territory at will. One concern is to look at what might usefully define research practice; the other is to explore the area of practical performance and in so doing provide a contextualising frame for the discussions of work that have already begun to emerge through the book's case studies. In doing so the ground is prepared in a way that places my personal agenda upfront and clear. Clarity is not the same thing as ubiquity, and the views expressed in this book are knowingly open to and welcoming of challenge. Nevertheless, a central tenet of this publication is that there *are* commonalities in terms of what constitutes sound research practice and that without due adherence to these research is unlikely to exist as more than a value-less name. Needless to say, many of the case studies provide their own eloquent and experiential rebuttal to this claim.

Of the British university departments of Drama, Theatre and Performance that supervise postgraduate students, most have experience of students engaging in practice as research towards PhD, and the market is growing. The very ubiquity of the term 'Practice as Research' has allowed for a proliferation of conference papers, think tanks and publications, all looking, as we are here, for ways to create acceptable alternatives to the traditional thesis. A certain amount of confusion is inevitable and healthy. Written theses after all differ one from the other in substance and kind even before creative strategies and outcomes are brought in through practice; and progressive performance, like academic research, is recognisable by the creation of its own set of protocols. A fusing of the two forms leads if not quite to an Yves Kleinesque leap into the void then at least to a step into the unknown. Under caveats such as these this book threatens not so much to promise more than it delivers as to promise the delivery of not very much at all. Maybe all that we can hope to provide are minor responses to a major challenge. Certainly, no claims are being made here for 'Best Practice'. Whatever that often-dubious term might mean in certain locations, its utilisation here would be dogmatic in the extreme. There is no best practice for performance: only examples we can identify as effective under their own given circumstances of time, place and personnel. The same applies to research. The same applies to supervision.

Contemporary research in and through performance differs from normative patterns of academic enquiry, and the ways in which it differs continue to shift as we speak. In this context, the attempts at quantification being made here are added to the mix. The nature of research is quite naturally as fluid, fragmented and up-for-grabs as any other element of our relativist age; at a time when any two of us in a room are unlikely to agree on what constitutes performance, the chances of (inter)national concord over performance/research and its subsequent assessment are slim indeed. In its attempts at a twenty-first century re-evaluation of practice-based research in performance this book forms one part of the emerging corpus concerned with making some sense of this never-still challenge to mainstream research practices.

In many ways those of us who are engaged in this work as researchers, research assistants and supervisors have become increasingly adept at making things up as we go along, creating in situ the principles that locate what we do within some form of conceptual locus. In reading the present and writing the rules to accommodate it, the new is being endlessly crafted in the now. The paragraphs that follow in this section are not intended to close down the possibilities for research, for limiting in any way the creative and innately heuristic dimensions of learning through doing and of doing to learn. If this publication has the practical purpose it intends, it is in the making of certain suggestions that might help to take some (never all) of the guesswork out of what we do. For practitioners, not knowing what happens next is in the nature of the making and the ambiguity of chaos is something to be embraced rather than feared. For researchers a certain (though not complete) approach to prediction is demanded. It is in this overlap between freedom and focus that the creative practice-based PhD has begun to establish its academic claims.

With research as with performance, what takes place is determined in part by where it takes place. Because personal opinions so often relate to institutional aspirations these opinions always possess the potential to be compromised. Accordingly, and more than most of us care to admit, our personally held beliefs are often tempered, governed and even created by our professional aspirations. The locations in which research is carried out, alongside the names, expertise and affiliations of supervisors, place frames around practice which are every bit as telling as the ensuing practice itself. Research into classical content and contemporary performance techniques at the Shakespeare Institute is clearly different in kind from the same-named research at Warwick University, just a few miles distant; just as research into post-colonial narratology is different at New York University and Trinity College, Dublin. Less clear are the differences in kind, actual as well as assumed, that come with working with different tutors in the same university, even within the same department. Choice and allocation of supervisors is often a more haphazard activity than a good many of us might like it to appear to outside agencies and the pragmatic realities of internal and external workloads, alongside the myriad internecine battles that are the meat and drink of academic colleagues, mean that the most appropriate supervisory team is not always the one that the student gets.

Differences of policy and practice, taken with individually prejudicial approaches to ideas of and about performance (which are usually described as areas of particular interest), are not the only things that shape the student–supervisor relationship. Whilst the time-served principles of traditional robustness in postgraduate research are as valid today as ever before, there are, as our case studies have already started to reveal, legitimate practice-based research activities that make the identification of what is and what is not robust a difficult task. Ideas as to what constitutes the epistemic elements of research are often easier to locate and assess than the more slippery elements of idiosyncratic practice taking place under the auspice of practice-based reasoning. As well as being driven by the desire for change, universities are nothing if not bastions of tradition... exemplified externally by the arcane town-and-gown pomp of graduation days and internally by the wing-backed green leather seats of the hushed and tightly guarded Senior Common Rooms. As such, the tendency to cling to theoretical reasoning (knowing this and knowing that) is almost always seen as preferable to practical reasoning (knowing how and knowing why).

Carol Weiss has claimed that what happens most regularly with research is that, whilst it may well contribute to long-term 'enlightenment' in the field, a type of slow-drip 'knowledge creep' that occurs through the puncturing of old myths and the offering of new perspectives, it is less likely to have an immediate or even direct impact. (Weiss, 1972) Things are no different with performance, where changes are most clearly seen from the vantage point afforded by hindsight. Notwithstanding this, timeliness is an important factor in determining the appropriateness of practice-based research.

As long as we look for answers rather than questions, performance/research will always read as a contemporary exercise in comparative failure. It is only when we welcome the idea of address in lieu of solution that the debate opens up enough to make sense. Accordingly, the meandering contestations and questions that make up this book are not meant to lead to the finding of any absolute solutions. The offering up of conclusions has little or no currency in a book such as this that is unclear of the extent, at any rate, to which it stands as a research output or as an output on research. Absence of certainty is our only given and what we do not yet know is the thing that drives us on. We wonder when performance might stand as research, as we question the extent to which all performance work is intrinsically research-driven, and, come to that, whether all research is performative... inasmuch at least as it possesses the capacity to change, to make things happen.

The term 'performativity' is increasingly used to refer to almost every aspect of performance studies but in its most commonly shared sense it refers to J.L. Austin's argument that words are possessed of the power to make things happen, to create rather than merely describe, to create 'performance utterances' so that the words are also the deeds. (Austin, 1975) We ask if it is useful, feasible even, to distinguish between performance-as-research, performance-based research and research-through-performance. Despite the considerable efforts of, amongst others, ELIA (http://www.elia-artschools.org/), PARIP (http://www.bris.ac.uk/parip/) and PALATINE (http://www.palatine.ac.uk/), the only answers we seem to agree on amount to a maybe and a maybe not. We would probably agree that when practical performance, in its most inclusive sense, forms the core of the contribution to knowledge then that research can most logically be described as practice-based. Conversely, when the research undertaken is likely to lead primarily to new and/or advanced understandings about practice, we can say that this is practice-led. Beyond this point very little useful consensus exists. Hovering as we do between the rock of definition and the hard place of flexibility, we do not know whether to mark and measure everything we see or accept the fact that in doing so we lose as much as we can ever gain. Led by the nature of academia as the game of naming, the choice is always already predictive, but not quite yet prescribed.

Amidst this confusion there are some things we know, certain studies which help map out our route. Christopher Frayling's different readings of research *for* art, research *into* art and research *through* art, (Frayling, 1993) building as they do upon Herbert Read's writings of some fifty years previous, remain useful. As do Henk Borgdorff's study of arts research and development, (Borgdorff, 2006) Phillip Zarrilli's negotiations of performance epistemologies (Zarrilli, 2001) and Michael Biggs' study *The Role of 'The Work' in Art and Design Research*. (Biggs, 2003) Filtered through a growing recognition of the near-inevitability of autoethnography, these studies are informing the ways in which this book argues for effective working approaches to practical performance research.

We need, ultimately, to know three things first and foremost:

- What is meant by research in terms of performance?

- When does performance/practice assume the status of research?

- How do we differentiate between different modes of performance/ research?

Three more things follow:

- How is performance/research undertaken?

- How can it be supervised?

- How can it be assessed?

We begin to flesh this out by making a series of fairly blunt suggestions, which, building on Frayling and Briggs, distinguish between approaches to research. We can start with the notion that research into or on performance is investigation that takes performance as the object of study. There is no implication of any correlation between the nature of the study and its subject; indeed for many the assumption is one of dispassionate enquiry based on cool, analytical reflection. The impact of much contemporary thinking on the ways that one's subject positionality is never neutral goes some way towards mounting a challenge to the possibility of objectivity at source or summation.

Notwithstanding this, the myth of distance and distance as the myth of accuracy remain powerful and powerfully persuasive elements of university life. Because of this, research into performance, often historical and regularly undertaken at considerable emotional remove, is the type most often found in traditional humanities divisions.

Various theoretical frameworks wrought by semiotics, phenomenology, post-structuralism, deconstruction et al notwithstanding, research of this kind is still fundamentally about a process of investigation entered into from an external perspective. The study of performance as a live event brings its own peculiarities of observational analysis, subjectivity and application, but it is nevertheless the study *of* an event rather than study *through* an event. We can argue therefore that research into performance is the least complicated strand of our three, if for no more reason than that any distinctions between the studied and the student, and between the clearly differing natures of practice and print, legislate against the complex and complicating types of overlap we will encounter elsewhere in this book.

A second observation we can make is that research for performance is concerned with application: with the ways in which research can be used to develop performance. This is an approach to research that serves performance in much the same manner that performance has until relatively recently been held almost totally in the service of script. In this sense, performance is less inclined to be the object of investigation as its ultimate aim. This means that a type of binary can often be identified between the research that has been carried out and the practice that emerges as a result of research, and this is key in terms of what it is exactly that is being assessed. In fact, if we step away for a moment from our concentration on 'practice', we can see that performance which exists as a demonstration of research is often no more or less than a muddy mirror image of the types of illustrations, diagrams and graphs that might accompany and inform the standard written thesis. As the arts and humanities thesis is the articulation of research rather than *being* the research, so in this case is the written thesis that is in all but the rarest of cases submitted alongside the practice. The practice *informs* the thesis without ever (despite the best efforts of a fearless few) satisfactorily standing *as* the thesis. This is a hugely contested area, and the thoughts of practitioner–theorists such as many of our case study contributors provide valuable and well-reasoned arguments that stand in seasoned opposition to some of my own.

This research-for-performance approach might be favoured by students who are seeking to engage in artistic endeavour as modes of self-expressive activity, by practitioner–researchers who engage in processes that lead to the production of creative work for public consumption. When the aim is to create performances for public reception as much as to serve as vehicles for learning, the term 'research' can seem to sit somewhat uneasily. Unless this is addressed at an early stage by student and supervisor alike we can all too easily lose sight of what stands as practice as research and what stands as research for practice. In our collective rush to be part of the practice-as-research *movement*, where dissemination in print is increasingly seen as yesterday's news, we do well to remember that the most appropriate form for one's findings is usually going to be in and through words. For how else can thoughts, processes, methods and methodologies be better explained? It is hard to imagine someone successfully dancing the rationale for a research project or presenting a thesis on Beckett through three empty tin buckets lit on a stage. Some among us do not need to imagine this at all. We need only remember.

It is research in or through performance that is the most problematic of our three suggested approaches. It is so because it works in denial of any clean delineation between the practitioner and the researcher, between the researcher and the researched. The preferred aim here is to regard performance as an indivisible element of both research and result. This model of research-driven practice explores performance problems that are likely to be acknowledged and shared by the wider artistic and academic community. Because this work is undertaken in order to advance understanding, insight or knowledge in the areas of performance that it elects to address, the making processes turn rehearsal studios into something akin to laboratories… sites of formal experimentation. Unsurprisingly, given the reference to laboratory practice, we find that as well as being among the most complicated form of practical research to deliver, supervise and assess this is the area with the potential to yield the most provocative, stimulating and timely work. Because the student has little option but to proceed through a cycle of observing, analysing and intervening the work is inevitably fluid. It is the tension between the ephemeral qualities of performance and the permanence of a thesis that puts the search into research.

The work itself may tell us plenty, just as the processes undertaken might be innovative, even revolutionary, but these are often means towards a potentially different end. Research in cases like these can often read as an add-on, something applied retrospectively, with post-practice questions created to match the outcomes of the work: an *a posteriori* reasoning, from effect back to cause, from the particulars of performance as a blind to the generalisations of one's starting position. To reason *a priori* of course is precisely the opposite process, a way of reasoning from cause forward to effect, from abstractions to specificity, creating an intrinsically deductive and recognisable process. Seen in this way, *a priori* reasoning is theoretical, based on the logic of traditional research, whereas *a posteriori* reasoning is practical, based on experience, experimentation and practice. And it is this that needs if not quite defending then certainly explaining, for research questions as a starting point to formal enquiry are generally deemed necessary if the findings are to have any widely acceptable worth.

So, we run the risk with research through performance of ending up with that which can appear as assertions without investigation, results without enquiry and answers to questions never really asked: a difficult corner to defend, not least by a student in *viva voce*.

For practice to be acknowledged as research it needs first to satisfy a particular criterion. In this it differs in kind from other equally rigorous types of performance practice. Without denigrating the merits of other approaches, in order to be defined as research, practice-based investigation has no real option but to locate and address in advance a question or questions (problem or problems) before identifying appropriate practice-based means of addressing them. As noted at the outset, the issue is often one of address rather than answer, and the success or failure of research in the arts and humanities is rarely governed by the finding of permanent solutions. Scholarly activity reveals this to us in its concentration on method: we need to know the how no less than the why and the what.

Despite the vagaries of methods, what is common to all research through performance approaches is the understanding that there can be no easy separation between art theory and art practice and that each is as reflexive as the other. We can see this as an attempt to articulate some of this experiential knowledge throughout the creative process and in the art object. Creativity is a difficult phenomenon to measure and it is most often given value as a means towards a particular end. In a 2007 paper, PARIP researcher John C. Whelan began his introduction by asking the rhetorical question 'What does it mean to be creative?' Whelan developed his theme by stating that

> There is a difference between what I define as **"Practical** creativity" and "creativity" per se. When working on creating an original and experimental piece of live **performance** work "**practical** creativity" is the attempt to realise abstract conceptual ideas in **practical** three-dimensional reality, in the live space and time of "**performance**".
>
> (Whelan, 2007)

By the time students develop into researchers they are already in a state of relative creative stasis.

> Research shows that by age five, a child's potential for creativity is 98 per cent. By the age of ten, that potential has dropped to 30 per cent; at 15, it is just 12 per cent; and by the time we reach adulthood, our creativity potential is said to fall to a mere 2 per cent.
>
> (Robinson, 2000: 7)

Not all researchers, however, are equal in terms of their potential for creative thought and deed. In spite of the depressing figures given by Gerry Robinson, there is general agreement on what might be regarded as 'The Creative Personality' in adulthood. Whilst it is unlikely that every one of the following aspects will be found in any one individual, these features are common in creative people. (Freeman, 2006) It follows that they are equally common in students undertaking practice-based research in performance. Creative thinkers will usually possess:

- Conceptual flexibility

- Tenacity and perseverance

- Self-discipline and self-control

- The ability to integrate controversial content and controversial process

- A preference for the new and unconventional.

Despite the fact that many of these attributes would figure in common readings of intelligence, it is important to note that intelligence *per se* is not listed as one of the features of the creative personality. On the contrary, theorists have been at pains to separate out creativity from standard notions of academic intelligence. McGinnis, Roberts and Torrance suggest that intelligence tests have low correlation with tests for creative and inventive ability (McGinnis and Roberts, 1996) and that 'Measures of intelligence are either unrelated or related only marginally.' (Torrance, 1981: 55) As soon as we begin to scrutinise creative learning we see parallels between creativity and autonomy. Accordingly, it is autonomous researchers – recognised in these pages as those individuals who consciously control and take responsibility for their actions – who are the students who lead supervisors, examiners and subsequent readers into what is often an unfamiliar terrain.

Acknowledgment of the need for the articulation of what are the significant aspects of one's own creative practice does not make it the sole or even principle factor in terms of practice as research. Other elements are equally important, and even more necessary in terms of successful projects: a distillation of UK-university website criteria suggests that research usually needs to:

- Be specific, at the same time as it functions with demonstrable knowledge of a wider contextualising field

- Be accessible, at the same time as it reveals in-depth knowledge

- Develop extant knowledge in ways that make a contribution to thinking

- Be purposive

- Demonstrate originality.

In addition, practice-based research will usually:

- Involve a process of planning, doing, reflecting and refining

- Test a given hypothesis through action as well as analysis

- Be undertaken by a student with highly developed practitioner skills

- Be transparent in terms of process

- Seek the facilitation of change through the challenging of established assumptions

- Be creative and iterative.

In the context of this book, 'iterative' is used to describe a process of planning wherein key elements of practice are regularly reviewed by the student, often in moments of reflection in action. Any insights gained are subsequently used to shape the next step in the work. This involves systematic reflection as a means of developing practical investigations in situ, rather than merely reading the work in its entirety upon conclusion. An iterative working process, therefore, in which problems are identified and re-worked (if not always resolved) is almost always a central part of a practice-based researcher's methodology, insofar as it takes an intrinsically heuristic approach to the value of failures as well as successes. In this way all work becomes work in progress.

Progress and process are sometimes confused. Similarly the terms method and methodology are often spoken of as though they were synonyms. This is not the case and methodology is never just about method. It is in fact the philosophical basis and rationale for the particular method adopted. A researcher's methodology then comes from an informed study of methods, leading to considered choice and judicious application. The concern of methodology is with the philosophical assumptions that underpin one's research processes; conversely, a method is a specific means of collecting data, a means which functions as part of those selected philosophical assumptions. The key aspects here are of consideration, application and data collection, elements which need to be as transparent in practice-as-research theses as they are elsewhere.

If method and methodology are often incorrectly regarded as meaning the same thing, we can say the same about the relationship between qualitative and quantitative research. Distinctions between these approaches are rooted in philosophical ideas that see quantitative methods as associated with positivist, empirical research. Quantitative research is sometimes felt to be less than ideal in terms of its application to forms of social research, where qualitative research, with its innately anti-positivist leanings of exploration leading to subjective interpretation rather than objective fact, is usually (and increasingly) deemed more useful. In this way, quantitative research can be linked with pre-imposed structures and qualitative research with structures which are emergent, organic and fluid. A natural home for qualitative research then can be found in ethnographic, autoethnographic and practice-based structures, where questions are as likely to emerge from and through the research as to exist in full beforehand. To this end an imposed structure linked to a quantitative approach is likely to be appropriate when the broad research problem is well understood; an emergent structure linked to qualitative processes is more useful when the field of inquiry is less well known and when, as a consequence of this, an exploratory research approach is a natural part of the territory.

CASE STUDY 4

The Relationship between University Theatre and Professional Theatre: A Question of Method

Robert Germay

All directors are confronted from the start with a multitude of choices. The first concerns the repertoire, the choice of the work itself: will the play be scripted or scriptless, by one author or a collective collaboration? The first question then is '**What** shall we play?' These considerations normally precede the equally crucial question of the production itself, the '**how**' to play it.

Any theatrical production is faced with this dual problematic, but it is felt more acutely and exercises a particular constraint in non-professional theatre, whether it be purely amateur or taking place in a university setting.

I will not elaborate on the distinction between amateur and professional theatre: it is essentially statutory, i.e. monetary. (The reader is directed to *Du Théâtre amateur. Approche historique et anthropologique* by Marie-Madeleine Mervant-Roux, ed. CNRS-editions (Arts du Spectacle), Paris, 2004.)

There is also a real distinction between amateur and university theatre; though this does not imply a qualitative difference in aesthetic terms, for there is good and bad in both types of theatre – and in professional theatre as well. However, the nature (in terms of participants), the aim, and indeed the life of university theatre, i.e. theatre staged in a university context, are significantly different in most cases than that of non-university amateur theatre.

A first major distinction concerns the participants. Amateur theatre often attracts people of all ages from different social and/or professional spheres (e.g. hair stylists and bank tellers, butchers and the teacher down the street) while university theatre is mainly comprised of young people whose principal activity is studying, and studying is not a profession.

The second distinction is implicit in the first. The theatre these young people engage in is often related to what they are studying, whether it be literature, psychology, sociology, medicine, law, etc. Consequently, their commitment to the theatre often transcends that of a mere hobby and involves instead learning, discovery, and research, and not solely in the theatrical sense of these terms. The most obvious example is that of a play performed in a foreign language by students learning this particular language; but all subject matter taught at the university, even the most scientific, may find itself the focus of a theatre piece.

This is true of the three different categories of university theatre: spontaneous, assisted, and pre-professional (for further information on this subject please consult the AITU/IUTA website: Association Internationale du Théâtre à l'Université/International University Theatre Association, http://www.aitu-iuta. org/).

Let me now turn to my own experience as president/director of university theatre, in my case the TURLg – the Royal University Theatre of Liège (Belgium), www.turlg.ulg.ac.be. Our work by definition has been and continues to be confronted with the problems outlined above.

Let us examine first the question of **repertoire**, i.e. what plays to choose. We reject mere entertainments for works that lead the audience to reflect on man and the world he lives in (and has built), which is in essence the art of theatre itself. Our repertoire ranges from Aristophanes to Stoppard and Thomas Brasch, and has featured Shakespeare, Molière, Witkiewicz, Büchner, Pinter, Brecht, Fassbinder, Machiavelli, Mrozek among others.

Apart from the content, another important parameter is the **size of the cast**. At the TURLg, our system for recruiting actors is not based on auditions. Students from all disciplines – law, the human, natural or applied sciences, medicine etc. – are welcome to participate. Consequently, we usually start off with at least twenty volunteers, most of whom are complete beginners without much knowledge of acting or the history and/or theory of theatre. Thus we are restricted from the outset to choose plays with large casts where the major roles are not too demanding. This limitation is also an advantage: amateur university theatre can usually feature a greater number of performers than most professional companies can afford (in terms of payment).

In many cases things fall into place rather easily. Looking back over the repertoire of the TURLg over the last 30 years, we find a number of plays where this was the case: *Romulus der Grosse* by Friedrich Dürrenmatt; *Himmelwärts* by Ödön von Horvath; Durrenmatt's *Herkules und der Stall des Augias*; *Scherz, Satire, Ironie und tiefere Bedeutung* by Christian Dietrich Grabbe; *Die Versicherung* by Peter Weiss; *Velleytar* by Stanislaw Ignacy Witkiewicz; *Passion* by Edward Bond; *Rosencrantz and Guildenstern are Dead* by Tom Stoppard and Aristophanes' *The Birds*. These were all staged with twenty or so actors with few problems because they call for a crowd of peasants or city dwellers, a chorus, or random individuals. Sometimes we managed by adding characters not even present in the original (in *Mockinpott* by Peter Weiss, we had clowns act out transitions between scenes), and sometimes we double- and triple-cast certain parts (*Kennen Sie die Milchstrasse?* by Karl Wittlinger or *Lovely Rita* by Thomas Brasch).

We have also responded to this need for large casts by adapting stories or novels for the stage (*The Red Slippers* by Hans Christian Andersen, *The Pied Piper of Hamelin* by Robert Browning, *Encore heureux qu'on va vers l'été* by Christiane Rochefort, and *L'Homme qui rit* by Victor Hugo) and have even done adaptations of essays (*The Colloquia* by Erasmus) and films (*The Wizard of Oz*). The purpose has always been to let everybody have a turn at acting rather than simply appearing on stage. More interestingly, it has also happened that a strong desire to put on certain plays was long thwarted by the small number of roles in the original text, until this need to employ a larger cast led us to felicitous and considerable dramatic invention. Two examples of note are *Woyzeck* by Georg Büchner and the *Impromptu de Versailles* by Molière.

Let us first examine our **Woyzeck**, presented in 1983 to celebrate the twentieth anniversary of Liege's Germanic Language Theatre (Theater der Lütticher Germanisten). It was performed in German mostly by students of Germanic languages. This particular context was doubly daunting: on the one hand, we had to satisfy the expectations of aficionados of great German literature by adhering to a text they hold sacred; on the other hand, we also wished to realise our legitimate and natural desire to make a work dating from the early nineteenth century relevant to a 1983 audience.

The first problem was how to render this masterful text in two dimensions (ink lining a page) in three-dimensional flesh and blood on the stage. For a person steeped in the tradition of the theatre, this is like rediscovering America, but only at first glance, for we then had to consider the many concrete questions that are almost never asked when plays are analysed in literature courses (whatever the language). Questions as seemingly trivial as what do Marie, Franz and the Doctor look like? Does Marie love Franz? Did she make love to the drum major? What kind of knife? Of military post? And above all: what does this text still have to say to us? It is interesting to note that *Woyzeck*, written in 1836 but left unfinished, was not performed until 1913 in Munich. The same is true of the other two masterpieces by Büchner, *Danton's Death* – 1835/1910, Hamburg – and *Leonce and Lena* – 1836/1911, Vienna.

We thus had to choose a point of view: we decided to focus on the social aspect of the drama of soldier Woyzeck, all the while 'modernising' it. The work exposes the gap that opens up between men in a society that is founded on differences of class, of education, age, race, and gender. It also reveals the anguish of a creature exposed to a world which erects barriers that are antithetical to nature. Barriers that incite one to storm the barricades. That which was true in Büchner's time is true today, and this is what gives his *Woyzeck* its eternal worth. The paradox is that to perform the play today like some sort of holy writ would be platonic and ignore the work's militancy: this would in effect imply that the world represented in the play was itself holy, untouchable, an irremediable consequence of the human condition. Here, however, it is not human nature, but society and its rules that are implicated. This point of view, a product of our theatrical analysis, was the starting point for our direction of the play.

This implied a second consideration: the public, which can quite easily be led to weep over the sad fate of poor Franz Woyzeck, might not even recognize him if they met him in the street (the theatre of catharsis is alive and well, thank you). This dual reflection/conviction was crucial in terms of our attempt to modernise the play, and oriented our staging of the work as follows: Franz Woyzeck, a simple soldier living on a military post in 1830, could be a stagehand in a theatre today (the lowest rung of the hierarchical ladder) and his Captain (*der Hauptmann*) the director of the same theatre. The drum major, Franz's rival, would be the principal actor and star of the company (and play the role of the soldier Woyzeck) and in 'real life' would fall in love – that is, backstage – with Marie, the stagehand's girlfriend, etc. And the double of the doctor (who does experiments on Woyzeck) would appear as a guest of honour among the false public invited to attend the performance. The real public would thus experience a conventional performance of the classical *Woyzeck* (or at least a few chosen excerpts) with actors playing the main roles 'like in the theatre' at the same time as a parallel drama unfolded backstage involving the technicians and stagehands working behind the scenes on the actual play.

The large number of volunteers turning out for the play allowed us to double cast roles that were dramatically interesting, thereby killing two birds with one stone.

Although this necessitated altering the order of scenes and the original structure of the play – which in any event is a 'fragment' to begin with – we did present every word of Büchner's original text. This did not prevent certain professors of German literature from being surprised and baffled (at best) or offended and outraged (at worst) by our interpretation. But that was to some extent the object of the game. It should be mentioned that the public in general, which included many secondary-school students, appreciated our version of this great classic.

Heiner Müller wrote: 'To play Brecht today without transforming it would be to betray it.' Would this not apply to all the great classics? Our approach was similar with regard to another great figure in dramatic literature, a Frenchman this time: **Molière**.

It is also the mission of university theatre to put on plays that are seldom staged by professional theatres and thereby little known or unknown to the public; and this includes works by popular (not to say over-represented) playwrights. Such was the case with *L'Impromptu de Versailles*, whose very form as 'play within a play' dovetailed with our concerns during the 1980s, a time when the influence of postmodernism was rampant.

The plot is familiar: the King is coming ('in two hours', says the text) to witness a new play by Molière's troupe... and nothing is ready! Panic sets in! What to do? This theme and, as so often, the large number of willing actors we had no intention of turning away, were the inspiration for our dramaturgical reflection. Suppose the setting were no longer the court of Louis XIV, but a modern theatre? And what if the troupe of actors grappling with Molière's text while trying to 'modernise' it in the process (by employing modern costumes, diction and scenery) were harassed by their cast doubles, phantoms from Moliere's company in period costume, who were literally haunting the very space where the play would be performed? And what if it were not the King but the concierge of the theatre who was the ultimate artificer (or dreamer) of the whole affair, as the only 'real' character from the here and now on stage?

As we had the number of actors necessary, our *Impromptu* was thus able to feature two 'troupes' whose appearances on stage, sometimes alternating with each other and sometimes occurring simultaneously, required the audience to reflect on a relevant way to present Molière today. Our version was presented to acclaim in Belgium, France and Morocco, among francophone countries, but also encountered the same success in non-francophone countries (Germany, Lithuania and Bulgaria).

In the two examples just cited, the actors were young adults between the ages of 18 and 35.

Our final example concerns a group of adolescents (12–16 years of age) we directed in **Romeo and Juliet** by the great William S, the play being presented under the title *Roméo, Juliette, William, les autres... et moi*. (The TURLg organises weekly workshops for young people according to age group: 6–8, 8–12 and 12–16; sometimes these workshops lead to the creation of a 'real' production.)

Two major obstacles had to be overcome: on the one hand, the youth and inexperience of these teens confronted with His Majesty, Shakespeare; and on the other, the number of volunteers (about twenty) who we had no intention of using only in crowd scenes throughout the play. Once again these limitations obliged us to make crucial dramaturgical choices. Rather than presenting the play in its entirety, which would have been impossible given the time constraints we faced (a few months at the rate of one rehearsal a week) and the inexperience of the group, we decided to put modern teenagers on stage and have them question the meaning of this late-sixteenth-century masterpiece and how it might impact their lives today, in terms of their relationship with their parents and to power, the conflicts that beset our society, and the eternal themes of love, life, and death. We presented selected scenes from the play that lent themselves to 'staged' reflections of this kind, and this procedure in turn permitted multiple casting for many roles, especially the two main characters. We were also able to work in audio-visual devices, at times projecting video excerpts from some of the most illustrious adaptations of the play (Zeffirelli, Baz Luhrman, BBC) onto part of the stage decor, at others letting the young people film themselves choosing their period costumes from the wardrobes of the Royal Opera of Liège, and sometimes having them do filmed interviews of passers-by on the street who were asked point-blank questions about the play and its author. (We admit that the remarkable *Looking for Richard* by Al Pacino might have influenced our approach.)

Our decision to take on such a complex work by questioning it 'here and now', and by presenting only certain scenes rather than simply 'putting it on' in a conventional manner (which would have been impossible under the circumstances), turned out to be positive both in theatrical terms – e.g. the performance, in French, was greeted with enthusiastic applause from young German secondary-school students – but also in terms of the overall personal development of the participants. By discovering Shakespeare and reflecting upon the eternal themes that the great Will evokes in his play, they learned a great deal about themselves and their world.

Whereas professional theatres usually tailor the cast and the dramaturgy to the demands of the play in question, our approach has been to adapt the play and its representation to the constraints imposed by the use of volunteer actors – something that is mandated by the very nature of our work in the amateur university theatre *milieu*. Adapting to the real and particular needs of our actors, as well as their abilities, is an integral part of our method.

This is only a precondition, of course. This special cast must still give a performance that is worth seeing. As we said above, the doors of the TURLg are open every season to anyone (whether connected with the university or not) who wishes to participate in putting on a play. And lots of people do show up. The prospective actors can generally be divided into two categories: those who know nothing about the theatre, and those who have stereotyped ideas about it, which they want to replicate as quickly as possible. Those in the second category are usually the most difficult to (re)educate. Here too, a method is required: collective work, precluding any 'star' status for actors. This is a proven way of putting everyone's talent level, so varied at the outset, on a similar footing.

This is why we spend a great deal of time at each rehearsal (we usually meet three hours per week) on basic acting exercises – involving the body, the voice, space, concentration/relaxation techniques – before 'attacking' the play itself. Work on the play proceeds by means of numerous improvisations by different groups, each presenting its vision of such and such a character or scene. Those that work best are retained.

Collective work involves more than acting: it also entails a group reflection on dramaturgy, scenography, sound and lighting, right up to the actual staging. The final form the play takes is of course the prerogative of the director, the leader of the project. (We note in passing that we do not use professional directors but rather our own members who, after having appeared in several plays, express a desire to try their hand at directing.) This directed and selective pooling of participants' resources is a *sine qua non* for plays that are 'collective creations', i.e. not based on an existing play but on a subject or theme chosen by the group and/or the project leader. We have done several productions of this sort (*Quand je serai grand, L'Amour en noir et blanc...*).

Collective work as we practise it is an effective method to break beginners in quickly. The TURLg is not a school, but it does provide theatrical training. This is also a proven way to reconcile, as much as is possible, our status as an amateur theatre company and the demands of offering 'professional' quality entertainment.

It has often been said that there exists a particular TURLg **style**, and we concur, simply adding that 'if we have a style, it is the result of our **method**.'

But that is another story.

SECTION 5

Basic, Applied and Experimental Research; 10 Questions

> My joy is when you're possessed like a medium… lying around and this thing comes as a whole piece, you know, words and music, and I think well, you know, can I say I wrote it? I don't know who the hell wrote it.
>
> **John Lennon**

P ractice-based research is that which takes place along a complicated continuum: one which has the types of theoretical, book-based research activities commonly found in universities at one end and practice – which, whilst informed by research, is entered into with performance as its prime outcome – at the other. Every reader of this book, like its writer, is seeking some enhanced understanding of what it is that we increasingly do in practice-as-research terms. A simple sounding aspiration, but one made difficult by the breadth of innovative practice-based research being carried out in a range of countries and contexts. What it is that binds this work together is at times harder to discern than that which makes each project unique; and it is this striving for defining principles, amidst work that incorporates and indeed *creates* experimental modes, procedures and protocols, that is the challenge faced by all of us engaged in the serious study of performance.

At this point we can outline a series of ten questions. Taken together, these questions will form the usual core of a researching practitioner's early thinking.

1. What is practice as research in a performance context and how is practice as research positioned within performance studies?

2. What is the rationale for choosing appropriate methodologies for specific practical investigations?

3. At what point and to what degree is practice expected to 'speak for itself'?

4. What is the academic value of practice as research?

5. What are the most common and effective methods of documenting and disseminating practice as research?

6. What types of processes allow practice and research to inform each other?

7. What is the sequence through which levels of practice are changed by their own research imperatives?

8. What happens when practice as research becomes practice as thesis?

9. What will this practice reveal that other practices either omit or obscure?

10. What distinguishes experience from evidence?

Responding to these questions has, as we have seen, as much to do with addressing as answering, and this address might be seen to raise as many problems as it solves. Nevertheless, the questions cited here seem both reasonable and necessary ones to ask, particularly of PhD candidates who are considering adopting practice as an integral part of their research as well as constituting part of their overall submissions. Students following this research process need to be able to articulate ready and robust responses, and the demand for this needs to come from supervisors rather than being voiced for the first time by examiners in that which can feel like the do-or-die pressure of a *viva voce*.

Research can be broken down into three types. The first can be referred to as **Basic Research**. This is work undertaken in pursuit of new knowledge about observable facts. Basic Research approaches are not dependent upon any specificities of application: they serve rather as evidential means in their own right, as the gathering of information about existing phenomena. Because of its relative simplicity, this approach is not generally encountered in creative PhD work. The second type is **Applied Research**. As the name suggests, the new knowledge and information acquired through this approach tends to be directed towards a particular objective or application. Because this carries with it an amount of subject specificity in terms of development, it is an approach that is often exploited for the purpose of PhD. **Experimental Research** is the third type. Like other approaches it draws on extant knowledge; where it differs is in its drive towards the creation of new and often surprising innovations. The claim for originality implicit in PhD research makes this third approach one of the most useful as well as probably the most commonly encountered. And yet the three are rarely as discrete as this taxonomy suggests and neither is the need for originality in a PhD as great as the reading of university regulations would have most prospective students think.

Research can be concerned with a specific project or be almost entirely speculative in nature. It will usually have a fairly well-defined output, but the amount of any original contribution to thinking, knowledge and understanding that it brings to bear on its subject may well be relatively slight. It is, at any rate, almost certainly not going to comprise the most substantial element of one's thesis, even though it may well be the most significant.

It is axiomatic that this book would not have been written were it not for an essential conviction that there is a valid place in the broad area of research into performance for some of that research to be carried out by, in and through performative means. This conviction is tempered somewhat by a gnawing suspicion that some of what passes for practice as research in performance does so without having its claims for proof, truth and useful application sufficiently interrogated. Simon Jones makes a case for a reconsideration of the nature of evidence when he suggests that, in its fleeing of scriptural practices, practice as research in some ways stands outside notions of judgement, because 'if performance flees the known, no phrasing of judgement will recognise those aspects of the performance that make it worthwhile', (Jones, 2003) leading to a situation where practice as research stands ever more proudly as 'a matter of faith'. (Ibid.) In making a case for practice as research to be engaged with according to what it *does*, rather than through the dictates of regular academic discourse, Martin Welton similarly argues that 'performance allows the accessing of certain kinds of knowledge not privy to conventional academic practices of reading and writing which privilege "viewed" over "felt" experience.' (Welton, 2003)

As a former PhD student whose own research drew heavily on practical enquiry, any reluctant or even resistant tones that emerge in the writing here are informed by knowledge of some of the gaps my own work very nearly fell through, and very possibly should have done. Tones of self-critique aside, I am not alone I know in the wish for some, just some, of the nailed-down rigour we find in quantitative and science-based approaches to research; and whilst the near-exact repeatability of scientific data analysis is impossible to replicate in ephemeral performance activity the underlying argument of this book is that there is still a place in practice-based investigations for research which is systematic, informed and verifiable.

When Jane Bacon asks at a UK conference if practice as research needs to include some form of reflection that can be subsequently disseminated or whether practice in performance is sufficient in and of itself in research terms, we begin to see the power that has been accrued by the notion of practice-based work. (Bacon, 2003) It is only the insertion of the words 'practice as' that appears at first glance to lend this question validity. In fact, the question is extremely troubling... not in the sense of its provocative call to research arms so much as the fact that it can be asked at all. Wouldn't we all agree that critical reflection is a given of research, or, in the case of practice-based investigations, is the implication that totally different rules should apply? And if different rules do apply then how can we arrive at any equanimity in terms of measurement?

If this striving for new rules is the implication, and evidence suggests that it is, then the prospect of research through practice (an approach as old as research itself) being morphed into the new phenomenon of practice *as* research without due consideration to established research criteria is upon us as we speak. Whilst heeding Freud's notion that every denial is an at least partial affirmation, I should reiterate the fact that this concern is not based on a distrust of practice, neither is it about a desire to see ideas of research rooted fixedly into the past. Times change, circumstances shift, methodologies wear out and research moves into new methods and spheres of enquiry. As research has developed into the big business area it now is for universities, rather than being something carried out by a select few academics at particular institutions, there has been a concomitant need to increase the scope of what research might be and who might carry it out. Despite the reasons for much of this increase being concerned with financial rewards rather than epistemology, the increase is clearly a good thing.

And yet practice as research has provided routes into and through research for so many people that, like a cluster-funded avalanche, it has grown at breakneck speed into something seemingly unstoppable. Notwithstanding the claims its articulate champions make of researching in the face of institutional resistance, it is hard to see much evidence of resistance at all. Universities garner prestige through the health of their postgraduate provision, and we know that health equals wealth where funding is concerned. Accordingly, postgraduate students are measured at registration and completion: on a fiscal level continued registration and successful completion is what matters most to universities, with, in my experience, no particular concern for the research methodologies undertaken by particular students. A similar situation applies to members of academic staff: if one's practice can stand or be made to stand as a research outcome then everybody wins.

In this climate it is hard to maintain and voice an appropriately reserved view of some of the claims made for practice as research without being labelled a cynic... or worse, being seen as being somehow out of touch and resistant to righteous change: as the dread staid and conventional thinker. We know that with traditional research the end product is often very neatly tied up. A thesis with no loose ends is the aim, so that what we read is evidence that the research set out to explore *this* and it found *that*, and so the findings are *thus*. In this way research is almost always embedded in a problem-solving approach rather than the problem-creating that comes with practice.

Unlike this traditional research, performance practice is always messy and its manners are often bad. It neither does what it is told nor does it go meekly in the direction one would usually expect. It sits uneasily with many ideas of academic objectivity and verification. Its goals are often less well-defined and usually impossible to measure. It deals with jumps and starts, and sometimes complete revisions. It is unpredictable, maybe even at times uncontrollable. There is no blueprint for successful performance because creative practice thrives in no small part on the accidental. It is in many ways *governed* by the accidental. We are dealing with people and perspectives and events that shift over time and these can lead to different types of insights and frustrations to those encountered in library-based work. With practice the sense of purpose is likely to change in an instant, in a moment of despair or inspiration, as can what it is that is regarded as important or outcome-based. This creates something of a problem for PhD research. If we accept the idea (common with P-a-R) that a researcher doesn't know what it is that is being researched into until the work has been substantially carried out then this is a major departure from the norm. More than that, it suggests an emphasis on experimentation that is massively misleading. Research is always a step into the unknown, but we need to know a great deal more than the direction in which we are stepping if the journey is to have any research-worth. Unless experimentation is linked to an aim there can be no experiment. What we get in its place is play, and whilst it is hard to imagine any of us looking to argue play out of practice it is not the same thing as research.

Considered in this sense, this book might most accurately be referred to as a survey or report: a playing with ideas. Despite the fact that it will undoubtedly be framed within the context of my university contract as some form of research outcome – because as Peter Thomson sees it, one's written work 'qualifies as research by virtue, in large part, of its publication' (Thomson, 2000: 115) – I am not so sure that this will be an altogether accurate view. What this book patently is not is any kind of thesis. And the process of writing this book has not been unlike the process undertaken in practice. It started as an idea, as an itch to scratch, and it began with a rough sense of methodology; but as the introduction showed and every subsequent page has revealed, the ideas started with have been and continue to be unfixed by conversations, readings and performances encountered on the way. The case studies, so central to the book and yet almost completely unknown to me at the time of writing these words, will in their collective distinctions unravel any concluding words I offer long before we reach them.

It is to be hoped that this structure makes for a more interesting book than an entire body of my own words and thoughts would provide. And if this happens, again, everybody wins. But I can hardly claim as a legitimate research outcome a publication where so much that will be of value to readers has so little do with anything I think, and even less to do with anything I produce. Like performance practice, this book is more than a little messy and its manners are not always good.

CASE STUDY 5

That Spot in the 'Moving Picture' is You: Perception in Time-based Art[1]

Elena Cologni

In my video live installations I investigate the perception of time (psychological time), non-simultaneous artist and audience interchange in liveness, and the ontology/production of the video document. Particularly, how live recording, pre-recording and transmission can all be perceived as overlapping layers of representation of time, and unfold in duration.

> When we think of this present as what ought to be, it is no longer, and
> when we think of it as existing, it is already past... all perception is
> already memory.

> (Bergson, *Matièr et mémoire*, 166–167)

I refer mainly to time implied in audience fruition of works of art, where synchronicity of vision is not taken for granted. Where vision is considered only one of the instruments for knowing, as psychological studies have shown. I am thinking of appreciation of painting in gestalt terms for instance (example of use of perspective and distortions), Arnheim, the structuralist theory of perception of space. Aspects of these I have embraced in my art work in the adoption of gaps, the viewer's diachronic approach to human size objects (sculptures), the kinesthetics generated by ambients, and the relation between performer and spectator. In particular, the fruition stage I have described in relation to painting in my doctoral thesis, later illustrated, suggests a sort of audience involvement which is rooted in perceptual and psychological dynamics and is conceived as based on time. As my own media of artistic expression moved from 2D into performance and time based territory, the visual paradigm of composition within which I place a gap allowing for audience interaction overlaps with time. In this account I trace this journey of understanding (or research methods embedded) in my art practice. Moreover, I relate to the performance series *Mnemonic Present, Un-Folding,*[2] example of a continuous shifting of meaning in relation to the deferral of ontological value of performances' documents, and the current project *Experiential*, (www.elenacologni.com/experiential) to focus on the adoption of 'the gap' in the works. Also, in discussing the document's 'performativity' aspect, (Auslander, 2006) I look at continuous performance artist–audience exchange in the present. This present is expanded: from performance conception through to its reception, and documentation.

Positioning the Method of My Work

My research practice, mainly mediatised performances and installation, involves a specific interest in perceptual/psychological dynamics between artist (artwork/environment) and audience. In particular, Merleau-Ponty's concept of *chiasm/intertwining* is embedded by adopting various strategies to stimulate a continuous communication and position shift between artist and audience in the creative process, presentation and reception. Since my PhD, *The Artist's Performative Practice within the Anti-Ocularcentric Discourse* (1999–2003),[3] I placed my work within the critique of the ocularcentric Western philosophical tradition developed by twentieth-century French thought, as referred to by Martin Jay (1993) and Amelia Jones, adopting an evolutionary approach to test hypotheses through artistic experimentation. The thesis encompasses two main discussions in relation to my artistic practice to define: the emerging of the self and the concept of Chiasm/Intertwining in relation to inter-subjectivity in performance art. In creating my work, I challenged the static artist–audience relationship implicit in

Stretched Mirror, 300x300x500

the one-way perception of representations based on central-focus perspective and vision, by adopting strategies of two-way artist–audience interaction.[4]

This was also based on a long background study and studio work, since 1991, which included a strong interest in issues and methods of representation and perspective aimed at looking for 'the inaccuracy' within methods, pricking the eye of viewers. This is the first time I include some of that material from those sketchbooks, and bridge my previous work to the more recent and academic. It embraces aspects of psychology of perception, which, coming from my painting training and producing this body of work, I can relate to the 'design' of my performance pieces. Within these the perceptual element is mostly applied and affects the relationship between artist (artwork/environment) and audience. Some of my previous work (1994–1996) included, for example: reliefs and 3D pieces referring to areal perspective – the depth created by density of air in Leonardo's paintings, or curve perspective – based on the observation of the viewers' round eyes' surface and position in front of a building, to make them perceive straight lines as distorted and curved (these were compensated for in Greek architecture).[5] This body of work was mainly aimed at positioning the body in space. Even

Area, 1994 (glass, graphite, wood)

Area, 1994 (wax on perspex, pigment, wood, 40x200x15 cm)

Dentro e intorno 1 e2, 1995 (wood, glass, 100x100x40 + 100x100x40)

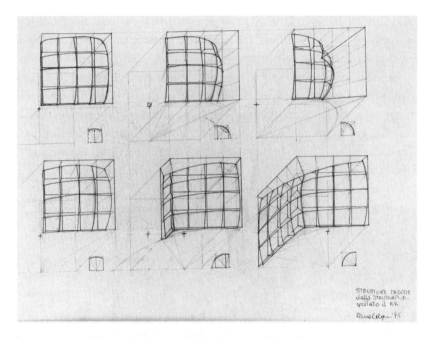

'strutture dedotte dalla struttura, b, spostato il pv' (structures deduced from structure b, moving viewpoint), sketchbook 1996

'Stuttura b, Visualizzazione di porzione della sfera percettiva in struttura modulare'
(structure b, visualisation of portion of perceptual sphere in modular structure), sketchbook 1996

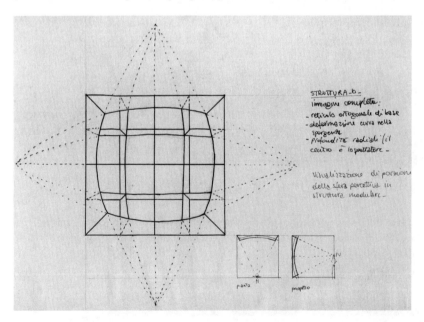

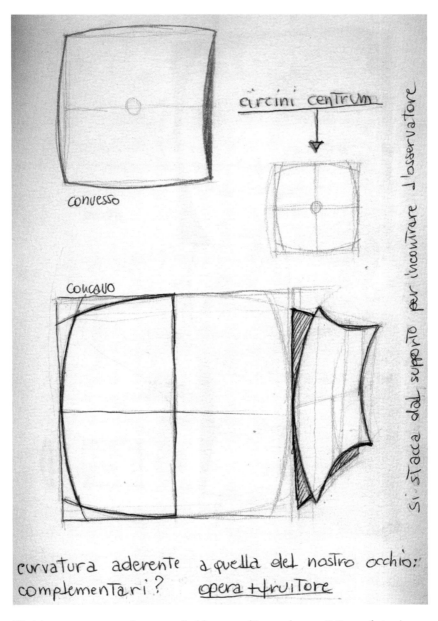

'Circini centrum, curvatura aderente a quella del nostro occhio: complementari? Opera+ fruitore'
(Circini Centrum, the curve adheres to that of our eye: complementary? Artwork + perceiver),
sketchbook 1996

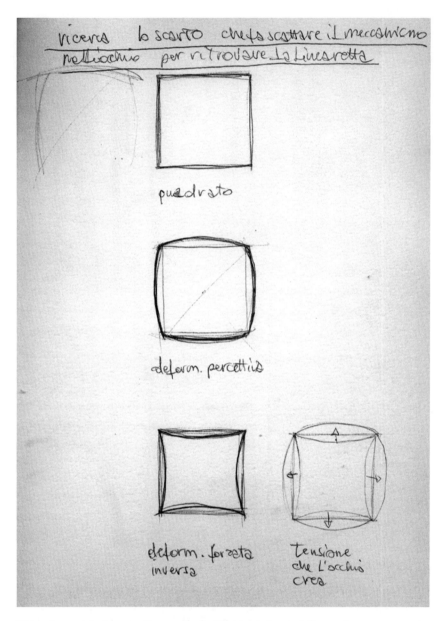

'Ricerca b, scarto che fa scattare il meccanismo nell'occhio per ritrovare la linea retta, per compensare' (research b, gap/scrap which allows for the eye to react by looking for straight line, to compensate), sketchbook

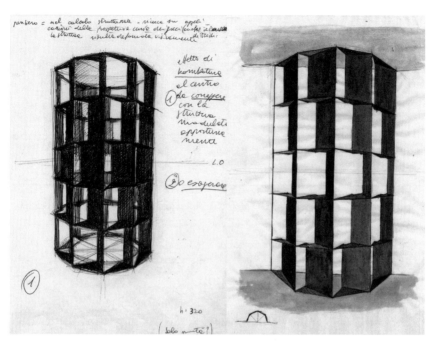

'pensiero: nel calcolo strutturale – ricerca sull'applicazione della prospettiva curva dei greci: la struttura risulta deformata verticalmente. Effetto di bombatura al centro da 1- <u>correggere</u> con la struttura modulate opportunamente, 2- o <u>esagerare</u>' (thought: in structural design – research on application of Greek curved perspective: the structure results vertically deformed. An effect of roundness in the central part is to be 1 – <u>corrected</u> with modular pattern, 2 – or <u>exaggerated</u>), sketchbook 1996

though there is an element of theatricality coming from minimalist sculpture, my references go back to ancient times. Since then I was looking at systems for including the spectator beyond the merely visual arena.

In this previous work, where I interweaved the conceptual and theoretical elements with my geometrical, abstract and diagrammatical compositions, I had instinctively addressed issues of perception in historical, philosophical and psychological directions, inscribing them into a fine art context. But as I worked on my formal research training I identified the process of *fruition* as crucial for the significance of my coming work in my PhD. The term 'fruition' is used to signify the verb of perceiving and becoming part of the work – labour finally coming to fruition; the condition of bearing fruit. The background to my use of the term 'fruition' to describe the process of delivery, reception and response to an artwork, is here traced as including issues of reflection and representation, in terms of optics and phenomenology.[6]

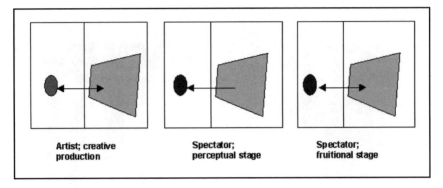

Stages of artist and spectator production of spatial context in relation to their activity (from my thesis)

Reflection and Self Representation

Rodolphe Gasché gives an explanation of the etymological roots of the verb 'to reflect', in the Latin verb *re-flectere*. In his view, this will suggest some of the more formal characteristics of the movements that compose reflection, as well as some of the fundamental imagery associated with this concept. *Reflectere* means 'to bend' or 'to turn back' as well as 'to bring back'. Gasché states that this turning back is significant for understanding reflection only if one recalls that in both Greek and Latin philosophy the term has optic connotations, in that it refers to the 'action' of mirroring surfaces in throwing back light, and in particular a mirror's exhibition or reproduction of objects in the form of images. Reflection signifies the process that takes place between a figure or object and its image on a polished surface. Gasché points out that from the beginning self-consciousness, as constituted by self-reflection, has been conceptualised in terms of this optical operation and perception, with the effect that self-consciousness has come to suggest a beam of light thrown back upon itself after impact with a reflecting surface. He concludes by writing that in this sense reflection is the structure and the process of an operation that implies that the mirror is mirroring itself, by which process the mirror is made to see itself. (Gasché, 1997: 16) The visual vocabulary of Western artists has been ordered and codified through a set of rules, amongst them that of visual representation. It offered the theoretical ground on which images could be built. Bernard Brunon writes that one of the aspects of representation relevant to self-portraiture is the characteristic straightforward gaze looking outward. This specific gaze is at the very centre of the major system of representation introduced in painting during the thirteenth and fourteenth centuries and carried through the Renaissance to the seventeenth and eighteenth centuries and beyond. This system, called 'one view point perspective' or 'single vanishing point perspective', for centuries fixed the painter's position in front of the model.[7] In my own artistic experiments the relationship with the spectator is investigated through considering his/her position of *fruition*. This was devised to clarify the process involved in my work, where I tend to incorporate the spectator's response mainly at the perceptual level – his/her presence is complementary to the meaning of the work. This also implied that this process is considered in stages and involves the passing of time, thus opening the discussion to the issue of non simultaneity between artist/artwork presentation and reception. The process of audience involvement is considered adopting a system including three stages: conceptualisation/production; perception; and fruition. In considering the fruition stage: the spectator here occupies a symmetrical position to that occupied by the artwork, it is a mirror composition. At this stage a meaning is produced, because there is a (conceptual) 'space' (later addressed as the gap) to be filled by the presence of audience. In this situation an

Las Meninas,
Diego
Velázquez
(1656)

exchange/interchange takes place as visualised in the diagram. Most of my work following on from this point has been based around this strategy, which I relate later to the concept of Roland Barthes' punctum and the Kanitza effect, and I have adopted practically through video manipulations, time gaps, and discrepancies in live pieces.

I now wish to establish a parallel allowing a better understanding of the function in the perceptual dynamics in art. I shall illustrate a fragment of the discussion regarding the painting *Las Meninas*, painted in Madrid in 1656 by Diego Velázquez, in which according to Martin Kemp, an introduced inaccuracy in the perspective construction allows for spectators' inclusion at a deeper psychological level than the more obvious surface effect of the mirror composition of the painting.

In *Las Meninas*, issues of representation and self-portraiture overlap to become one, and the interpretation of the composition and subject matter of this painting has been discussed.[8] I am interested in the non-scientific application of perspective by Diego Velázquez, as suggested by Martin Kemp, leaving 'space' for the spectator's subjective interpretation and input. The straightforward look in self-portraits does not necessarily coincide with the single-focus perspective for its spatial construction. This means that when, as it happens in *Las Meninas*, the perspective construction is not scientifically based on the position of the viewer and artist, then it no longer coincides with the painter's viewpoint either. Martin Kemp interpreted the construction of the space in *Las Meninas* aiming to find how scientifically Velázquez applied perspective rules that he might have been aware of because of his contacts with Italian painters. Kemp says: 'The setting of the "action" is quite specific – this is not the least original of its aspects – and can be identified as a long room in the Alcazar, adjacent to the painter's own suite of rooms'. (Kemp, 1990: 107) In his view, the perspectival clues are less obvious than they might be in Italian Renaissance painting, but they are definite enough. The vanishing point lies close to the central point of the door opening. The visual axis thus runs asymmetrically down the room along a line between two of the doors. The painter's own position in the picture can be determined as straddling the central axis of the room. Given the viewing axis, the centrally placed mirror cannot but reflect a relatively narrow vista which lies almost exclusively to the left of the central axis. The line of vision from the mirror would almost certainly have been intercepted by the large canvas. The painting would, therefore, represent a double portrait of the King and Queen. This interpretation corresponds to that of Palomino and is confirmed by the pictorial device of a red curtain visible in the mirror reflection. Velázquez would not have required advanced optical planning to achieve this effect, but simply his first-hand knowledge of what was visible in the room from a certain standpoint and what was (or would be) reflected in that mirror. (Ibid.: 108) Martin Kemp questions whether Velázquez did precisely recreate the view according to optical principles. In Kemp's view, it was directly recorded 'by eye' without a precise scaling of all the architectural forms, 'a conscious choice to openly challenge the perceptual limitations of the Italians' geometrical mechanics'. (Ibid.) In Kemp's view, one instance of Velázquez' s desire was to give a wider sense of the subtle processes of vision and how these can be magically evoked or paralleled in the medium of paint, thus achieving more than was possible with the drier mechanisms of linear perspective and geometrical shadow projection. 'No painting was ever more concerned with "looking" – on the part of the painter, the figures in the painting and the spectator.' (Ibid.) Kemp states that artists of high intelligence like Velázquez, concerned at this time with questions of visual representation, could set their understanding of perspective into a broader context of seeing and representation to fall into subjective interpretation based on their appearance to the viewer rather than theoretical constructs. The fascination of the painting rests in this non-scientific construction of

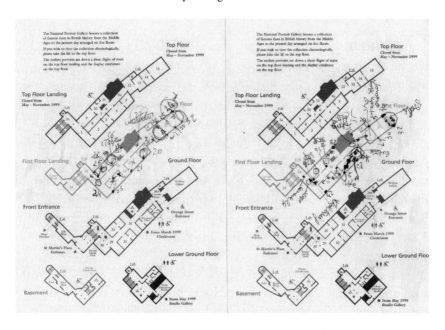

the space that, while giving the illusion of spatial engagement, also allows subjective interpretations where the fruition aspect of the work may be realised. Velázquez, by setting this composition in front of a mirror, realised a self-portrait: he looks straight ahead in the position that we occupy at the time of its fruition. Furthermore, Steinberg sees the main effect of *Las Meninas* as creating an encounter 'and as in any living encounter, any vital exchange, the work of art becomes the alternate pole in a situation of reciprocal self-recognition.... [Confronted with the mirror] we are, polarised selves, reflecting one another's consciousness without end, partaking of an infinity that is not spatial but psychological, an infinity not cast in the outer world, but in the mind that knows and that knows itself known'.[9]

The screen of the monitors is a meeting point for myself, as artist, and audiences in this following work, marked by a continuous change of position from in front and behind it. In the making of the piece *Ancora Cerca*, I was able to experiment with cctv systems, issues of documentation and time as well as self-representation. The work was performed at National Portrait Gallery, NPG, London 12–14 March 1999 and presented as an 8-monitor video installation at the Pinacoteca Tosio Martinengo in Brescia, Italy, between 6 and 24 April 2002. For this piece I worked with the existing video security system of the gallery. After having done some research on the ideal location for the performance within the space, I looked at the monitors to which the video-cameras would send the captured video information and made notes. '...room 17-cam 24 – coming from 18-sop between sculpture and entrance-watch camera; room 19-cam 25 – stop watch camera between glass case and sculpture; room 21-cam 26 – standing behind sculpture watching camera; room 22-cam 28 – walking from 21 in the middle and out; room 18 sitting on sofa...'. This enabled me to visualise the space from the viewpoint of the cameras – the space I would physically enter while performing. The performance took place on 12 March, the recording of it from the documentation on 14 March.

12 March – performance: I would stage an encounter with the warden watching the surveillance monitors in the NPG, by walking towards it and watching the video camera of each chosen room. As I address the camera in each room, I become a 'picture' in the gallery, yet the camera, fantasised as the *Gaze* of the Other is also, as it were, 'pictured' as the spectator sees me imaging what it is seeing and giving myself the things I lack and are looking for (meaning of ancora cerca).

14 March – video recording: I went back two days after (as required by the gallery for security reasons) and played back the tapes that were stored. I was surprised to find that the system reduced the footage by half, so that not all frames were kept. As a result the quality of the recording was poor. However, I placed the video camera in front of the screen to record the half an hour of the performance from each of the monitors: the recording of the action went through a number of filters. In the resulting video, the viewers see the evidence of the performance through the 'eye' of these surveillance cameras, that have videoed me walking from room to room barefoot, clad in a beige dress, and evoking a romantic spirit of the gallery by carrying a red rose. The spectators, at this stage positioned as the camera when watching the surveillance video or see stills from

Ancora Cerca, the video installation at Pinacoteca Tosio Martinengo and still from one of the 8 videoclips

Ancora Cerca, video installation and audience

it, are pictured by myself as I look at the camera. The spectators project what I might have seen from my vantage point in the gallery space. In this gallery dedicated to the construction of identity through picturing it, this performance makes the deep structures of that identity construction emerge, so we all become aware of how much both the artist and the spectator never fully or comfortably inhabit the illusory space of identification.

Even though this piece was inspired by my engagement at the time with the issue of the Lacanian Gaze, it was on its visual composition model, beyond the gaze, based on Merleau-Ponty chiasm that my practice found suitable ground. Furthermore, James Schmidt suggests[10] that for a description of the relation between self and other, Merleau-Ponty drew on Paul Valery's account of the 'exchange' of regards (before Lacan did). (Schmidt, 1985: 91) 'Once gazes interlock, there are no longer *quite* two persons and it's hard for either to remain alone. This exchange… effects… a transposition, a metathesis, a chiasm of two "destinies", two points of view. You take my appearance, my image, and I take yours. You are not I, since you see me and I don't see myself. What is missing for me is this "I" whom you can see. And what you miss is the "you" I see.' (Valery, 1970: 26) And you, spectators in front of the videos, while still looking (ancora cerca) for me disappearing from one screen and appearing on another, are reconstructing the spatial dimension with your imagination.

My particular interest in the psychological relationship between artist and audience, here seen as continually shifting in the creative process, as well as the construction of continually deferred meaning and ontology of the created document, has led me to develop a methodological frame also through my involvement in the Performance as Research in Practice[11] project and conferences. Since 2001 my investigation on the status of performance documentation, allowing for collection of research outcomes, was conducted by embedding the documents in the live events, overlapping research methodological tools with meta-linguistic art practice[12] as a result. My conference interventions have been mostly practical ever since, whereas the written material is usually published as contextualisation, documentation, or analysis of practice.

The intervention at PARIP was titled 'Tracing'. It was conceived to address the impossibility of fixing a moment in time (Derrida) and referred directly to the production of documents for research purposes. Amelia Jones states (in the live event) that the self is inexorably embodied, and yet she argues that the works suggest that this does not mean that the performed body/self is ever completely legible or fixed in its effects. 'Body art, through its very performativity and its unveiling of the body of the artist, surfaces the insufficiency and incoherence

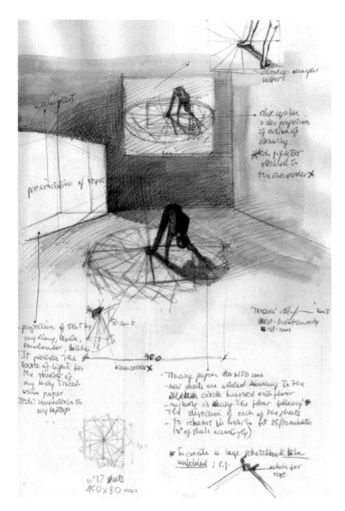

'Tracing', sketch for performance

of the body/self (or the body-as-subject) and its inability to deliver itself fully (whether to the subject-in-performance herself or himself or to the one who engages with this body).' (Alleque et al., 2009: 34)

A body is not self-contained in its meaningfulness; it is a body/self, relying on a receptive context in which the interpreter or viewer may interact with it where the body becomes a 'subject'.[13] Documents of the body-in-performance are just as easily contingent in that the meaning that accrues to the image of the body is open-ended and dependent on the ways in which the image is contextualised and interpreted. Seemingly, the video 'supplement' of the artist performing could expose the body itself as supplementary, as both the visible proof of the self and its endless deferral. Jones, by referring to Derrida, argues

97

that the sequence of supplements initiated by the Body Art project – the body 'itself', the spoken narrative, video – announces the necessity of 'an infinite chain, ineluctably multiplying the supplementary mediations that produce the sense of the very thing they defer: the mirage of the thing itself, of immediate presence, or originary perception.' Derrida notes that 'the indefinite process of supplementarity has always already infiltrated presence, always already inscribed there the space of repetition and the splitting of the self'. ('That Dangerous Supplement' in Derrida, 1978: 163) For the self is constituted above an 'abyss (the indefinite multiplication) of representation', a series of possible selves.

Derrida called the problematic of 'the trace' what splits seemingly identical reflections. He attributed the trace to the memory of an ever-receding origin that

'Tracing', University of Bristol 2003, stills from video documentation

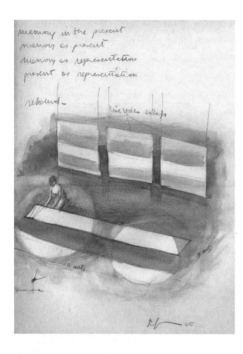

Mnemonic Present, Un-Folding, sketch and detail of action

always remains elusively outside of what it produces in the present. The temporal spacing of the trace never leads to spatial simultaneity and full visibility, but rather to interminable delay (diffèrance as deferral).

'Tracing' was performed as follows:

> *Action – I draw the shadow that my body casts onto tracing paper, on the floor, I position each sheet from the pile in a fan-shaped arrangement. 1st projection – live recording of a detail of the action: my hands drawing the shadow. 2nd projection – video with sound (also in Italian and overlapped). Extract: 'The supplement adds itself, it is a surplus, a plenitude enriching another plenitude, the fullest measure of presence. It cumulates and accumulates presence. It is thus that art, techné, image, representation, convention, etc., come as supplements to nature… Unlike the complement, dictionaries tell us, the supplement is an "exterior addition"'. (Derrida, 1978: 144–145) Supplement, added feature, addendum, addition, additive, appendix, bell, codicil, complement… tracing, copy, duplicate, archetype, carbon, carbon copy, cast, clone, counterfeit, counterpart, ditto, ectype, effigy, ersatz, facsimile, forgery…*

My hands were drawing the contour of the shadow my body was casting onto the paper. I was constantly re-inventing the line as the body moved following the

3, GAMeC Museum, Bergamo, Italy, 2005 (rolls of blank newspaper, three projections, two video delay systems)

7, in *Wonderful*, Trieste, Italy 2006 (rolls of blank newspaper, three projections, two video delay systems, cctv)

hands' movement. It is not possible to trace one's own shadow, and therefore it is not possible to document the movement of one's own body while doing it.

In more recent mediatised performances, such as the *Mnemonic Present, Un-Folding* series,[14] the use of the document as 'live-recording' and 'pre-recording' has opened up questions on the involvement of the audience and their perception of what is present, represented, how they memorise it; generating a form of 'present memory' of the event from which the notion of 'mnemonic present' takes shape. (Cologni, 2009) The latter underlines the significance of the act of recollecting memories in the present, a way of translating while representing reality, which affects the original trace of that memory. Our way of experiencing, conceptualising and translating reality makes sense in the present and through perception (issues of metamind in psychology[15]). It also relates to the way we experience it through video representation, no matter how delayed/deferred it may be, because even when we watch old footage we make sense of it in that very moment. Again, in the present.

From working material of *Geomemos*, Yorkshire Sculpture Park (April/September 2009), funded by Arts Council of England: *Conversation drawings 'Possibilities'* (Cologni's) and map of the lake area from Bretton Hall Archives, Leeds. The project collects memories from local residents, oral history as missing aspects from the documented history of how the private owned property was first acquired by the local authority and then became the YSP.

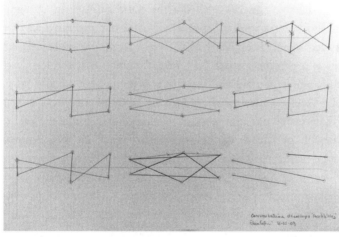

Through that 'making' of the series of nine performances based on two versions, I experienced the shifting in the creation of meaning in the re-staging of a performance. This concept deals with the impossibility of remaining coherent to a specific script or format, which is believed to be in the very nature of performance art (as opposed to theatre). A performance is not based on rehearsing a fixed script, but is fluid and depends on a number of factors including: the kind of context and audience; the artist's lived experience between restaging performances; the artist's acquired knowledge from previous performances; and the way the artist's body remembers the previous performance.

In this work as before, in terms of method, my re-occurring strategy is to locate/visualise a conceptual system with set parameters and work in a meta-linguistic fashion to overturn it: to create a paradox. In this sense, while focusing of the issue of the document, which should be evidence of performance for research purposes, I allow myself to prove that only by shifting the attention to accepting the failure of its purpose, and adopting the deferral of its meaning as point of reference, I essentially free myself/work from the static position an academic ground requires. This body of work is based on my belief that memory relates to the present of its becoming, in contrast with the early Bergsonian differentiation between memory and perception based on the assumption that the former is linked to the past (representation) and the latter to the present (action) (as in Deleuzean scholar Guerlac's latest book – Guerlac, 2006). Memory thus relates to perception dynamics and has an important role in processing information.

The conclusion of the *Mnemonic Present* project has led me to conceive a more complex set of issues around time perception which are being explored and developed in *Experiential*.[16] These are: time in fruition of mediatised performances for construction of performative self; distinction between reality and forms of its representation due to our perception of time (subjective time, simultaneity and continuity, retention and re-memorisation – Vicario, 2005); the reception of archival material in relation to live video; self-awareness generated by use of forms of dystonia (unbalance), i.e. between sound and vision.

The recent experimentation of gaps, scotoma (in the visual field), apnea (of breathing), amnesia (gap in memory), time-gap (transmission), is introduced to allow the audience to participate in the event because, just like a spot on a blank page, we/audience fill it in with our brain/life experience/imagination. Process which, if contextualised in relation to the Baudrillian concept of *punctum* and the perceptual Kaniza effect (a perceptual gap is where the eye goes to compensate for a loss): it enables me to define a strategy for the creative process in which the designed *perceptual lacuna* asks to be filled in by audiences. These are adopted,

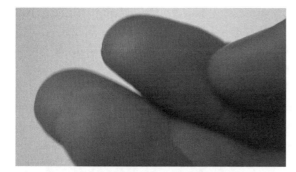

'Apnea' The Manchester Museum, (Human Remain Section) 2008

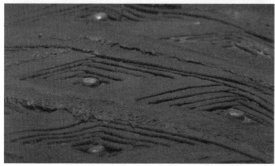

implied and experienced in my work in relation to the condition within which they happen: in liveness as site for continuous present, where performance art and live installation interchange take place. I specifically use various digital technologies postulating that continuous present can be constructed by perceiving reality as collapsed layers of its representations and time (i.e. memory, live documentation). In the *Mnemonic Present* series, *Apnea* and *Re-Moved* for example, making the audience aware of the passing of time as they are experiencing it (time gap in video), by being faced with an element of past experience in the present, allowed them to participate in its construction; this also mirrors the everyday life condition of relating to the world by referring to our memory archive in the perception of reality, and ourselves, in any given moment. The focus on time allows me to add to the broad notion of *liveness*. As illustrated, I argued that the audience's fruition of the event is due to the element of *gap*, more recently time-gap introduced to interfere with the experience of the passing of time, thus activating a psychological response and overlapping with the perception of the actual.

Re-Moved, 2008, Centre for Contemporary Art Glasgow, (installation view, stills from Scottish Screen Archive footage and video of participant)

With my investigation I contribute to the debate on the ontological value of performance documentation in parallel to Auslander's recent publication (Auslander, 2006: 1–10): embedding the document (e.g. video recording) in the event allows audience to witness its very production, thus emphasising the document's 'performativity' aspect. Philip Auslander discusses the status of documents in performance as performance concluding: 'It may well be that our sense of the presence, power, and authenticity of these pieces derives not from treating the document as an indexical access point to a past event but from perceiving the document itself as a performance that directly reflects an artist's aesthetic project or sensibility and for which we are the present audience.' The conceptual element highlighted by Auslander in defining intentionality behind the production of the document in an artwork, is relevant in the production of my work to claim that the audience is present in the artist's mind at the moment of its conception, and questions the parameters within which we assume that performative self is produced: by the artist–audience encounter in the presentness of the event. Embedding the document (e.g. video recording) in the live event allows audience to witness (participate in), and to influence the very production. In the context of my work, this is relevant to the claim that the audience is present in the artist's mind at the moment of its conception, where the process of fruition starts, and the interchange first takes place. All these elements contribute to question the notion of presen(t)ce in performance going beyond the sharing of a physical space and time. The creative process is essentially shared since very early on and the document is that of the-before-during-and-after. The research, or process, embracing such documents, is thus an activity which underlines a political position, unstable and not fixed, the position of the unfinished.

Links

www.cca-glasgow.com/events/creative_lab_3.html
www.elenacologni.com/experiential
www.elenacologni.com/memory
www.elenacologni.com/experiential/geomemos

Notes

1   This paper highlights some issues coming from my earlier artistic career, which are now linked to recent work. These were investigated and discussed at *Performing Presence: from the live to the simulated*, Centre for Intermedia, University of Exeter, UK, 28 March 2009; one day symposium for *Performed* at Wysing Arts Centre with Amelia Jones, Gavin Butt and Mel Brimfield, on 30 May 2009;

Creative Practice, Creative Research, Materiality Process Performativity, York St
John University, 15–17 April 2009; *Third International Conference, Consciousness,
Theatre, Literature and the Arts*, Lincoln University, 16–18 May 2009; also, part of
my fellowship at York St John University 2007–2009.

2   Part of the research project *Present Memory and Liveness in Delivery and Reception
of Video Documentation During Performance Art Events*, AHRC-funded project
conducted at Central St Martins College of Art and Design, London (2004–
2006). Cologni, E., *Mnemonic Present, Shifting Meaning*, Mercurio Edizioni,
Vercelli, Italy 2009.

3   Central St Martins College of Art and Design, University of the Arts London

4   *A Ritentiva*, solo show, Centre for Sculpture, Yorkshire Sculpture Park (catalogue)

5   Erwin Panofsky, Perspective as Symbolic Form

6   Not from a psychoanalytic view point, the Lacan's 'mirror stage' is discussed in my
PhD thesis, but is less relevant to the argument I am developing here.

7   Brunon, B., *Autoportraits, Here's Looking at Me*, catalogue of exhibition at Espace
Lyonnais d'Art Contemporain Ville de Lyon, 29 Jan – 30 Apr 1993

8   By various art historians and writers such as John R. Searle, George Kubler, Leo
Steinberg, Martin Kemp and Jonathan Brown. Some sources: Searle, J.R. 'Las
Meninas and Paradoxes of Pictorial Representation', in *Critical Inquiry*, University
of Chicago, Spring 1980; Kubler, G., 'Three Remarks on Las Meninas', in *The Art
Bulletin*, New York, June 1996; Steinberg, L., 'Velasques Las Meninas' in *October
19*, winter 1981.

9   Steinberg, L., 'Velasquez Las Meninas' in *October 19*, Winter 1981: 54

10 Schmidt addresses the definition of the Other through Merleau-Ponty's philosophy
and in relation to other philosophers and writers in Schmidt, 1985, pp.59–99.

11 PARIP 2000–2005, Bristol University

12 In the paper 'Documenting Performative Practice' (PARIP, 2003) presented as
video live installation, I illustrated how the documentation of performance art
pieces, in order to collect research outcomes, was subsequently incorporated into
the performance format itself. This process, supported by, while generating, its
theoretical critical contextualisation, thus became evidence of its status of research.
The 'video-live-installation' presentation was since adopted as a format of artistic
expression which incorporates research strategies of audience involvement in
the art-making process. My contribution to the 2005 conference is published in
Alleque et al., 2009.

13 Live performance, in fact, makes the intersubjectivity of the interpretative exchange
even more pronounced and obvious since the body's actions can be interfered with
and realigned according to other bodies/subjects.

14 Outcome of AHRC-funded *Present Memory* and *Liveness* in delivery and reception
of video documentation during performance art events, (2004–2006) details
also on www.elenacologni.com/memory. Other outcomes include: Mnemonic

Present, Un-Folding # 1, 'Performance Studies international # 11, Becoming Uncomfortable', Brown University, Providence, RI (USA), 2005. Mnemonic Present, Un-Folding # 2, 'International Conference Consciousness, Theatre, Literature and the Arts', Aberystwyth, Wales, UK, 2005. Mnemonic Present, Un-Folding # 3, Galleria d'Arte Moderna e Contemporanea (GAMeC), Bergamo Italy, 2005. Mnemonic Present, Un-Folding # 4, proposal per PARIP, Bretton Hall Leeds University. Mnemonic Present, Un-Folding # 5, 'Diverse Attitudini', a cura di BOArt, Villa delle Rose, Galleria d'Arte Moderna e Contemporanea Bologna, Italy, 2005. Mnemonic Present, Un-Folding # 6, 'Transversalities: crossing disciplines, cultures and identities', Departments of Film, Theatre & Television and Fine Art, University of Reading, 2005. Mnemonic Present, Un-Folding # 7, 'Warmhole Saloon', curator Joel Cahen, Whitechapel Art Gallery, London, 2006. Mnemonic Present, Un-Folding # 8, in 'Wonderful (Ibiscus section)', Trieste, Italy, curator Maria Campitelli, June 2006. Mnemonic Present, Un-Folding # 9, Tapra Conference, Central School of Speech and Drama, London, October 2006.

15   As discussed in Cologni, E., 'Present-Memory: *Liveness* Versus Documentation and the Audience's Memory Archive in Performance Art', in Meyer-Dinkgräfe, D., *International Conference Consciousness, Literature and the Arts*, Cambridge Scholars Press, January 2006.

16   www.elenacologni.com/experiential, funded by York St John University and Arts Council of England, outcomes include *Re-Moved*, Glasgow international '08, Centre for Contemporary Arts Glasgow; *Apnea*, Museum of Manchester, 2008, and *Geomemos*, Yorkshire Sculpture Park, April/September 2009.

SECTION 6

Feelings and Findings; Research Design, Research Prerequisites and Creative Processes

> All our knowledge brings us nearer to our ignorance.
> **T.S. Eliot**

B eing provided with access to a practitioner's research agenda, rehearsal notebook and critical bibliography does not necessarily furnish us with anything approximating to the type of reliability that the term 'research findings' still seems to imply. An approach to research that is based on a search for that which works is not the same thing as striving to understand how and why things work and where and under what particular set of circumstances they might work less well and why. It is at this point that theory starts to earn its corn, not as a series of sound bites so much as a way of identifying and making sense of principles and patterns, of allowing us to understand the extent to which our perceptions are innately provisional.

Theory allows us to look at practice in ways that recognise alternative possibilities and to proceed with investigative work in an appropriately considered way. It allows us to see that what might at first appear to be isolated idiosyncrasies in our own practice can have relatively widespread implications for practice *per se.* Inasmuch as research is inevitably concerned with the creation and dissemination of new understandings, an appropriately rounded engagement with theory is necessary. We use theory to develop unprocessed and/or instinctive practice into something meaningful and capable, perhaps, of making a genuine contribution to knowledge and understanding.

Barney Glaser and Judith Holton suggest that:

> A researcher requires two essential characteristics for the development
> of theoretical sensitivity. First, he or she must have the personal and
> temperamental bent to maintain analytic distance, tolerate confusion
> and regression while remaining open, trusting to preconscious

processing and to conceptual emergence. Second, he/she must have the ability to develop theoretical insight into the area of research combined with the ability to make something of these insights. He/she must have the ability to conceptualize and organize, make abstract connections, visualize and think multivariately. The first step in gaining theoretical sensitivity is to enter the research setting with as few predetermined ideas as possible – especially logically deducted a priori hypotheses.

(Glaser and Holton, 2004: 43)

Where practice as research is designed to contribute to the improvement of practice, those carrying out the research will first require some theoretical, and hopefully flexible, notions concerning what these ideas about 'better' practice might be. Without these ideas – which involve a public nailing of one's colours to a particular mast – there can be only a very limited framework for identifying either research intentions or outcomes. This is because research creates evidence relative to problems and questions. This evidence is presented in a manner that allows subsequent readers and viewers to determine the extent to which the researcher's findings can be deemed reasonable and considered: that they are reasonable in relation to the type of problems involved and to the types of questions being asked.

This demands an approach to research that is designed: the research demonstrates its intention to build upon a clearly identified problem or series of problems and promises to do so with an identifiable sense of purpose. This involves a research problem, a method of address, a rigorous regard for the application of evidence and a clear sense of what will be achieved through the research. In this way the initial problem is able to go a long way towards informing the type and nature of research questions asked, as well as shaping logical and coherent research aims and objectives. Analysing an aspect or aspects of one's own practice may well be an act of high-level reflection, with all of the analytical skills this implies; but in and of itself, that does not automatically amount to research activity.

As well as foregrounding problems, questions, aims and objectives, research includes identifiable strategies for making analytical sense of the information gathered. This allows for findings and conclusions; just as findings and conclusions create implications for future practice.

If one does not have a strategic understanding of research design – regardless of what terms are used to describe it as such – there is unlikely to be much research at all: at least not in the strictly academic sense. This is because whilst unexpected information may emerge and still be regarded as findings, an *a priori* research design needs to be in place in order for findings to justify the term within an academic context. Practice as research is particularly problematic here because it can lure researchers into the trap – and it often *is* a trap – of merging appropriate research problems and questions with a certain type of design for no more reason than that practice as research, for members of staff as well as students, as we have seen in our initial web search, has become the agenda of choice in so many university departments of performance.

The fact that a particular approach is fashionable at the moment does not mean that it is automatically the most effective of all available research methods. At varying points in our recent past, performance research based on semiotics has been in vogue, as has phenomenology. Bert O. States neatly described these two approaches as being premised on the oppositional views that in the former case 'everything is something else' whilst in the latter 'everything is nothing but itself'. (States, 1987: 8) For Patrice Pavis, research tendencies are considered main for ten years or so, which he breaks down as '1960–1975: dramaturgy; 1975–1985: semiology; 1985–1990: deconstruction; feminism 1990–1997: interculturalism, ethno-theatricality.' (Pavis, 2000: 70) Pavis argues that interculturalism led into 'the "science" of interculturalism [which] has become the leading discipline for numerous studies.... When it is mixed with biology and taken up by artists and brilliant "bricoleurs"... this produces a theatre anthropology which discovers universal principles and *ad hoc* sciences which mainly strive to justify and to extend the productions of their own theatrical or paratheatrical practices.' (Ibid.)

Clearly, no research approach can provide all of the answers. Just as clearly we can see that the particular foci of one's research approach can do much to create skewed findings. *Quod volimus credimus libenter*: we believe what we want to believe, and the temptation to find what we are looking for and disregard the rest is a powerful factor in all areas of research. In a field such as performance, where subjectivity is something of a given, its presence is almost inevitable.

It should go without saying that strong research projects stem most usually from good quality research questions and it is in the formulation of research questions that supervisory assistance tends often to be at its most attentive. Bella Merlin suggests that PhDs are 'primarily undertaken for pragmatic reasons: these days a doctorate is the basic requirement for any academic post'; (Merlin, 2004: 40) and the rush towards research, aligned to the need for PhD as a visa that is seen to expedite entry into a university lecturing career, has resulted in a number of people wanting the qualification without first having the questions to address. This comes with the attendant desire to be seen and classified as a researcher without having anything of value to research into.

Many of this book's readers will be familiar with students (if they are or were not those students themselves) who begin their process of solicitation and registration for PhD with no real sense of a problem that they wish to tackle, though most will have some sort of 'area' in mind. In order to have a question, one must first identify a problem; and in order to have a research design one must know what it is that one feels a pressing need to find out.

Unless a research design is in place at the start of one's studies, research is unlikely to proceed and develop effectively. To this end some of the mythologies of abstraction combined with the postmodernists' already historical malaise of their (our) anything-goes eclecticism have done research very few favours. The idea that, to paraphrase Lyotard, one can work without rules in order to establish the rule of that which has been made makes for a neat phrase in an undergraduate essay but it does little to prepare students for the rigorous demands that come (or *should* come) with the territory of postgraduate research. (Lyotard, 1984: 55) No matter how radical and subversive the aims of performance might be, it is a *practice*, a form, an approach that is always already built on the shoulders of earlier work. Even on those occasions when we publicly acclaim the new, we will often secretly desire the old and convention is almost always at the heart of performance... to the point where shifting one's paradigm from the well-made play to installation art might describe no more than a replacing of one set of borrowed rules with another.

Derrida reminded us that a performance would be unlikely to work if it did not 'repeat a "coded" or iterable utterance', (Derrida, 1988: 18) making the work identifiable in some way as a 'citation'. (Ibid.) In this way a practitioner who seeks to subvert the conventional expectations of performance does so in the service of recognisable principles, creating a 'reliance on the avant-garde's aesthetic strategies, which tend to preserve the very structures and principles they subvert'. (Callens, 2004: 47) As it is with performance, so it is with research. The idea that research can occur in a way that allows material to emerge organically without having strategies in place that are designed to make this happen is as naive as the belief that performers left alone in a space will create an extraordinary piece of work without some direction or plan. That this scenario is possible does little to offset the immense improbability of its occurrence. We always have some sort of map for making, even when this is a map of places we refuse to visit and of routes we are disinclined to follow. In these cases intentionality might emerge through a process of distillation and dismissal, but it still emerges and it still exists.

What is required for research is at the very least a sense of focus that can l accommodated in terms of objectives. That these are unlikely to be the same in 'research' and in 'practice' contexts is one of the things that makes practice as research such a difficult trick to pull off, despite its number of tricksters. This is not about making a case for formulaic approaches. It is often possible, even desirable, that an initial research problem is provisional, and that it is refined, adjusted and clarified as one's research processes develop. What matters is that the research has an initial direction and intention and that it addresses a problem that is capable of being resolved. The nature of resolve differs across disciplines and it is in the nature of performance, as it is with any art, that nothing is ever set in stone: quite the opposite in fact. Nevertheless, in all but the most exceptional circumstances, researchers are unable to address problems with any potential for verification unless the initial problem is developed into a question and from there into a strategy or design for implementation.

Every researcher, just like every practitioner, will develop their own particular ways of working. This is not in dispute and it is something to be remembered amidst the insidiously prescriptive language that is assuming dominance within this book's non-case-study pages. But the principles of research remain broadly the same. If they are to change because the research approach (e.g. research through practice) differs, then we are left with that which is likely to appear as a watered down version of something more arduous. Bleak words these may be, and they are words that will doubtless rattle the cages of some (I hope not quite all) of my colleagues in the arts; but the principle that the aim of research is to locate one's investigations as the relationship between a problem to be responded to and a question that facilitates this address remains.

Research is most often concerned with resolving a particular problem through the addressing of a question and of developing this into findings that add to subject-specific understanding in a communicable and retrievable form. This is as important as it is because as a permanent record of a university's academic standards a written thesis remains the document most suitable (and available) for continued (if infrequent) external scrutiny. That written theses are very rarely removed from their shelves is true to the extent that the well-known story of a newly qualified PhD student putting a $100 bill inside his library-held thesis and finding it untouched 20 years later seems as perfectly plausible as it does.

Undisturbed bills aside, arguments that form the core of research tend then to be based around a set of organisational and presentational premises, each of which draws the subsequent reader to a conclusion (*the* conclusion?) that the researcher intends to have accepted as logical, coherent and new. As readers or watchers, our roles are relatively simple. Our roles are to ascertain the extent to which the research and its findings are convincing and the extent to which this conviction has been arrived at via demonstrably rigorous concerns. It should be apparent then that a student stumbling upon a surprisingly new idea would not (safer perhaps to say *should* not) be rewarded with a PhD simply through finding the answer to a question that s/he had not known s/he was asking. This is so because research needs to develop from and through a sound argument: a process of enquiry, investigation, testing, validating, analysing, interpreting and concluding.

Research through practice is additionally complex inasmuch as it is usually grounded in vocabularies that originate in creative making rather than creative (post-performance) analysis. In its broadest sense the work acknowledges the ability of performance to embody thoughts and constitute theory. In order to secure the place and the status of practice-based research within PhD worthiness, a work's qualities need to be demonstrated as well as declared and described. Research through practice is intrinsically adaptable and it is able to assume a variety of modes; as such this approach draws upon, exploits and expands multiple representational forms. One of the strengths of research through practice therefore is its rejuvenating impact on our common perceptions of what research is comprised of. In this, the notion of making a contribution to knowledge is likely to exist as much in form, approach and type as in content, e.g. the 'thing' researched, discovered and tested. The contribution to knowledge is also and always personal inasmuch as the process affords opportunities for the fusing of roles that have most often been separated out at source.

According to Graeme Sullivan, practice as research is based on the premise that 'the imaginative and intellectual work undertaken by artists is a form of research'. (Sullivan, 2005: 223) The Sullivan view, which has harnessed considerable support in the arena of arts research, has it that intelligent practice results in works that are essentially theoretical statements, capable of taking and developing positions on issues of human significance. Traditional research in the arts and humanities sees identification as the prime goal, as an attempt, successful in part at least by definition, to apply prediction, causality and system to the seemingly chaotic. Research through practice on the other hand demonstrates more concern with the types of understanding that incorporate and work with the possibility of difference. Accordingly, results are often about seeing things differently and in different ways rather than arriving at explanation, with all of the attendant connotations of grouping paradigms together based on similarities. Indeed, we are able to go further than this and suggest that research through practice might demonstrate resistance at source to any and all attempts at hedging the complexities of creative endeavour into something manageable... preferring instead to leave the edges unsecured and open to endless interpretation.

There is something symptomatic of the creative process here. Creative makers are after all defined as much by their desire to seek problems out as their willingness to solve any extant problems that get in their way. Practitioners are thus quite logically drawn to the ambiguous, the marginal and the in-flux. Looked at in this way we are left with no option but to acknowledge some sense of shift in terms of the acceptability of findings; and as mentioned in this section's earlier musings, it is inevitable that this will lead to a change in the ways in which certain types of research activity are measured and assessed.

The prime aim of humanities research is the understanding of concerns that are regarded as significant within the field. We know by now that these concerns can be approached and indeed articulated in different ways. When the researcher is also perhaps that which is being made subject to research the drift takes us away from humanities and forward into the arts. It is no accident therefore that the theorisation of visual arts practice has shown the way to those who are committed to the developing understanding of performance practice.

Susan Melrose acknowledges the origins of practice-based research when she reminds us that 'organised discussion of these issues was led by Art and Design and not by Theatre or Performing Arts'. (Melrose, 2002) Notwithstanding this formal impetus, theatre practitioners have their own tradition of conducting research that has informed and developed our contemporary understanding. Certainly the history of the twentieth century from the early Futurist manifestos of Marinetti through to the writings of Sarah Kane and the biotechnological performance practices of Stelarc is a history of change, innovation and progression. These developments, however, are the result of primarily individual not to say idiosyncratic and disjointed energies. As such, ideas are built upon in what are often repetitious ways. The result of this is development which does not always demonstrate the type of purposive interrogation one expects and perhaps demands from research.

CASE STUDY 6

Bleeding Narratives

Yoni Prior

> During the exorcism scene in *The Dybbuk*, in which I was mostly on all fours, and carrying another actor, I would sometimes either graze my knees, or find that some of the red pigment from the floor had stained them, making it appear that I had sustained injury. Mid-season, I noted that the applause seemed louder on the nights I appeared to bleed.
>
> (Yoni Prior, journal entry)

> We have tried to say, silenced sometimes by repression, and sometimes by the knots in our own tongues, not that the play speaks thought, but that it is thought.
>
> (Hollis Huston, 1992: 128)

What follows is a necessarily and, I hope, usefully subjective testament to the creation of *Levad*, a solo theatre work devised with theatre director Barrie Kosky in 1993, in which I functioned as co-creator and performer. I draw upon part of the 'conception to performance' account of the collaboration I wrote as a Masters thesis, in which I responded to a call from Patrice Pavis for researchers into performance to return to the studio and interrogate the 'actuality' of our processes as performance-makers. As such, it constituted an attempt to describe what Pavis has called 'the dramaturgy of the actress' (Pavis, 2000) – the mapping of a journey through the process of creation and performance, and an identification of co-ordinates and points of reference, both practical and theoretical within that terrain.

In her paper *Performance as Research/Performance as Publication*, (Richards, 1992) Alison Richards distinguishes between 'research *about* theatre/drama practice' and 'research done through, or... *by means of* performance'. *Levad* was made in a 'professional', rather than an 'academic', context, and the thesis formed a post-mortem reflection upon its making,[1] placing my research in an odd space between these two poles. In the mid-1990s there were few, if any, established research models which allowed an artist to theorise their own practice, or which honoured the complexity of the process of making a work of theatre. I chose to 'testify' through the 'thick description' defined by Clifford Geertz, (1973) a methodology which presumes that the theory is embedded in the practice. The treatment of the process, not as theoretical construct but as narrative, allowed me to map the multitude of intersections between multiple discourses which provided both content and context for the creative process. In particular, because *Levad* was theatre *about* theatre, much of this discourse was literally being negotiated on the rehearsal or stage floor as we translated it into performance.

This study draws upon that research, with a focus on the shift from the phase of creation and rehearsal into that of performance, and on a set of unforeseen occurrences which both proved Spalding Gray's theory of the 'unifying accident, in which something so strange happens… that it suddenly unites the audience in the realization that we are all here together at this one moment in time'[2] and sparked a multiplication and merging of narratives within and around the performance event. These events revealed a crucial nexus between the 'actual' and the 'acted' in the experience of performance, and sparked a peculiarly reflexive process of manipulating meaning in the creation and editing of *Levad* for, and in, performance. My hope is that there is value to be found in the particularity of the instance, and the way in which it points to interconnections between 'fragments of lived experience, texts, images, spaces, bodies, theatrical styles and historical documents'.[3]

The Exile Trilogy

Levad (the Hebrew word for 'alone') formed the third part of *The Exile Trilogy*,[4] works which were loosely based on key texts and songs from the canon of Yiddish theatre, incorporating aspects of Jewish history, ritual and culture. The works of the trilogy were linked by a thematic of possession, in which fictionalised characters, based on actors from the Vilna Troupe, famous in the heyday of the Yiddish theatre in pre-World War II Europe, found themselves trapped in a space between life and death, attempting to traverse the worlds created by 'their fractured and displaced recollections'.[5] The lone protagonist in *Levad*, Eva Askenfeld, who appeared in the first two parts of the trilogy, was a composite of a number of famous actresses in the history of the Yiddish and Israeli theatres.[6] Our intention in making this performance was to extend metaphors established in the first two parts of *The Exile Trilogy* – those of the wandering spirit of the performer, the struggle to reconstruct fragments of memory, and the linking of the idea of the Jew and the actor as proxies of public suffering – by placing the character alone in a 'memory mill', visited by fragments of her eventful life, and of performances she had given.

> Levad is the self-induced exorcism and trial of a performer, a mother
> and a voyager. She is alone. In her solitude, nourished by desert air,

she constructs a theatrical memory necropolis populated by silent characters, invisible streets and ruptured dreams. She is pursued by nameless voices, voiceless names and voided cities.[7]

The set, designed by long-time collaborator Peter Corrigan, featured a massive corrugated iron wall, out of which protruded a number of metal channels. At the rear of the space was a tall wooden mill, in which were lodged signs indicating streets in Warsaw, Melbourne and Tel Aviv. In a front corner of the stage, unconcealed but not on the set, was the piano at which the director–accompanist sat. The entire stage space was covered in a thick layer of rock salt. Unlike the setting in earlier works, which, in the main, effectively utilised the features of the dilapidated mechanics workshop in which the shows were built, the set for *Levad* was built during the rehearsal process and was not installed in the relatively featureless theatre until the production week.

The phase of the process I want to focus upon here sees us reach the point at which all the strands in the elaborate weave of the work, and in the working process, coalesce – sometimes in ways which were unexpected and salutary.

Running Through, or Just Running?

As we moved toward production week, and the shift from the rehearsal room into the theatre and onto the set, we began to run the piece in its entirety. The performance was constructed around a series of scenic fragments which repeated with variations, and which saw the character shift, often abruptly, between rehearsals, performances, queues, attempts to exit, attempts to remember lines and names, attempts to inter objects in the salt, attempts to disinter things from the salt, and songs in Yiddish and Hebrew. By the time we moved into the theatre, we had a work in five movements, composed of 78 scenes, and running approximately 75 minutes.

This was also the moment in which we began to feel the imminent gaze of an audience. Inside the text, notions of gaze – looking at, being looked at, demanding attention, diverting attention, avoiding the gaze – proliferated. Both the fictional actress (Eva) and the actual actress (Yoni) were negotiating the business of being scrutinised. The phrases 'Look at me!' and 'Don't look at me!' recur. In the opening scene, she complains to the invisible director that a fellow actor is not looking at her: 'I must have a pair of eyes to work to.'[8] Another rehearsal scene sees her demanding of the (invisible) cast that they should all be 'looking in' and 'looking worried'. The process of acting was being defined by qualities of 'looking', and of 'directing' trajectories of gaze.

In contrast, there were moments of pain and weakness in which she did not want to be witnessed and retreated, crying 'Don't look at me!' This repeating motif of retreat recalled Benjamin's 'Angel of History', an early inspiration. (Benjamin, 1973: 259–260) Her face was 'turned toward the past'. 'The chain of events' which is her history was compressed into a 'single catastrophe', in which she was 'irresistibly propelled into a future to which [her] back is turned'.

Repetition

As the sections we ran became incrementally longer, the moments of respite in the rehearsal room were fewer, and I began to develop some notion of the actual effort the performance was likely to cost me. Work sessions became rehearsals – less inventing, more repetition. I was working with one eye constantly on the white board in the corner, where the scene sequence was written up in detail. This 'running order' (a term which comes to have an ironically literal meaning later) was nearly fixed. We were engaged in making small adjustments and edits, a process of excising smaller fragments, or tucking them in between episodes, and layering references to other moments into individual scenes. We were enchanted by the structure and its endless possibilities. The structural conceit of 'theme and variations', and the narrative conceit of the rhizome of memory, made almost infinite intertextual reference theatrically plausible. Only the looming opening night curbed the impulse to elaborate.

It is also likely that the highly schematic structure of the piece was, at least in part, a response to the limitations of the rehearsal and production schedule. By accident or design, we made a work about time; about trying to push the narrative of a lifetime into the frame of the time it takes to execute 'a series of compacted challenges'. We made a story about trying to compress time, and about an actress who was pushed through her paces at a rate faster than she wanted to run.

Barrie and I were also moving from a co-devisor relationship to one of actor and director. If I was to be ready for opening night, I had to learn and refine the performance by means of the repetition (or rehearsal) which had become such a significant motif in the piece. I became impatient with Barrie's interventions. My hold on the piece still felt very tenuous and so suggested changes, or interruptions to the 'running' of sections, evoked both anxiety and exasperation. The demands on memory were substantial, and I was fearful of forgetting what happens next, or of launching into the wrong variation of the many repeated scenes. I needed to commit these actions to 'body memory' – to absorb them to a level where they were near-reflex. The character, too, fears forgetting, and we linked some scene fragments through the incorporation of strange journeyings up and down the channels muttering lines and names. Constant repetition also allowed me to develop an internal 'graph' of the flow of physical energy and effort through the piece, and judge how to husband that energy economically.

We left the creation of the final scene until the eleventh hour. This is partly because we were waiting for the street sign to arrive to explore the possibilities of that machine. We knew that the mill needed to be denuded of street names by this point, symbolically removing all signs of the possibility of escape, and that we would use the song *Farges Mikh Nit* (Forget Me Not) as a final plea that there might have been some enduring meaning to the ordeal she had just endured, and the ordeal that had been her life. We knew that she would climb the edifice and disappear within it, and we agreed that there should be no release, no blinding insight – only the entombment, and the disappearance. In the final instance, the fear of forgetting was replaced by the fear of being forgotten.

> Peter Corrigan: 'It could have been self-immolation… it could have been all sorts of things. I happen to think that, after the appalling battering this individual had taken she's found some peace.'

> Y.P.: 'I suppose I always felt that it was a parallel of what was actually happening to me myself in that moment. Just let it go, just stop.'9

Working the Set

A week before the opening night, we moved into the theatre. A rapid process of reorientation took place to adapt to the actual dimensions of the set. My gaze, the trajectory of my voice and my physical orientation needed to re-site all my invisible co-actors in the new space, and the empty seats in the auditorium indicated how far my voice must travel to reach the audience. The tonnes of salt on the floor absorbed any moisture in the atmosphere. This meant that much of the time my mouth was dry, making a double demand on vocal production. We concealed water bottles in the set, and choreographed several moments into the performance where I could steal a mouthful of water.

There was also a significant gap between the audience and me in terms of 'worlds'. In the mechanics' workshop where we performed *The Dybbuk* and *Es Brent*, audience and performers sat, metaphorically and materially, in the same dark and disintegrating space. In the Beckett Theatre the audience sat in upholstered seats surrounded by warm polished wood and looked down upon an island of salt and distressed metal. They seemed, metaphorically and materially, a long way away.

Tom Wright: '[The dimensions of the Beckett Theatre] reduced it down to being like a mouse in a shoe box, you know, scientists just watching a mouse negotiate a series of compacted challenges.'[10]

Peter Corrigan: 'I certainly think that there is a metaphor of – some idea of endurance and survival. It struck me as having a sort of Blakean connotation... it took on the appearance of something like some rather excruciating nineteenth-century mill... to put you up and down the channels, around and around like mice running around the sort of wire trays. The mechanised nature of what you had gone through. I thought that there would be times when you would be fighting the set a bit, which is... not necessarily a bad thing... It struck me as rather moving in the way the actress had been put through this work experience. That you had to *work* all the time... It's also extremely interesting to see actresses work. Most of them just loll around the stage.'[11]

YP: '...because of the set, I didn't have to feign certain things. I can't run. I can't do anything else but shuffle on this surface. Getting on to that salt made a whole shift in what my body was doing. And I was starting to work with the sound of my feet shuffling on that metal channel, or the sound of my feet crunching through that salt becoming a whole other text.'[12]

The movement onto the set also wrought a series of significant changes in the physical execution of the performance, rendering some things harder to perform, and others easier. I could begin to distinguish between those actions or inflections of action which I must 'feign' or 'act', and those which merely require execution. I had developed a shuffling gait for the character in her repeated journeys along the metal channels. Once I attempted to travel the slippery surface of the metal, I found I could do so *only* by shuffling if I were to remain vertical. Traversing the deep salt forced a new gait, making the effort involved unconcealable. Once the signpost was installed in the space, the 'character' of the effort of climbing it and removing the remaining street signs was also dictated by the difficulty of manipulating the object, and of maintaining my grip as I tugged the heavy signs out of their slots and dropped them to the floor. Perhaps the most obvious example of these 'accidental dramaturgies' was the 'shower of blood' in the final scene. The dramatic collapse, mid-song, which we had choreographed in the rehearsal room lost its melodramatic elegance as I gasped and shuddered uncontrollably under the sudden downpour of cold water on my overheated body.

In short, the concrete, material aspects of the set made their manipulation into 'real work', adding another layer to the already multi-layered text of 'work' through the tension between the actual and the fictional 'work' being executed on stage. Coincidentally, it also added another layer to the musical orchestration of the text as the sounds of the body interacting with the actual environment were integrated into the 'score' of the work.

Director/Sadist/Author?

Levad opened in the Beckett Theatre on 23 March 1993. At the end of the first week of a four week season, I became ill and the company was obliged to cancel scheduled performances for a week. The speculations surrounding my illness, and the way in which it affected both the audience reading of the work, and my own re-reading of the work, proved extremely significant.

In the week I was away from the show, rumours abounded regarding the nature and severity of my illness. The virtuosic nature of the previous work of the company, and the physical and emotional demands it made on the performers, had been frequently commented on. Helen Thomson, reviewing the performance in the *Australian* commented that, 'What makes the entire trilogy so memorable is its ambitiousness… combined with a willingness on the part of actors and director to push themselves to new limits. The demands made on the actors are punishing and sometimes physically dangerous.'[13]

> Levad is written for and performed by Yoni Prior. Kosky has now
> created three compelling, unique works….[14]

Since authorship of the work of the company was, more often than not, attributed to Barrie, and since he had been so frequently and publicly critical of a lack of courage and rigour in contemporary Australian performance, the public perception which characterised him as a martinet director mercilessly driving performers to, and beyond, their physical and emotional limits was both reinforced and amplified by my illness. This perception, however, reveals a naive view of the relationship between the Actor and the Director in the process of making any work for the stage, most particularly when that work is not the realisation of a prewritten text, but is being created in the rehearsal room.

Despite frequent public assertions from Barrie that the work of Gilgul was a collaboration between peers – 'You've got to remember that in that company of six actors, there are three directors, that there are writers… and that's what makes it all exciting…'[15] and, in the case of *Levad*, despite being advertised as 'devised by Barrie Kosky and Yoni Prior', authorship of the work of the company continued to be attributed to Barrie – acknowledging no distinction between the function of the 'devisor' and the 'director'. Following this logic, then, the rigours of executing the work were interpreted as having been visited by the director upon compliant actors, making him responsible for their consequent 'suffering'.

The attribution of authorship (or 'auteurship'[16]) in a collaborative performance-making process is a problematic issue. A singular, signature, or successfully integrated performance style or aesthetic is, more often than not, assumed to be the product of a single and singular vision – that of the director. The fact that the contribution of the performer/author in the creation of any performance work is so often rendered invisible by the needful invisibility of the work in the rehearsal room has led to a mythology which characterises the actor as the passive, compliant instrument of the director. This assumption is even more flawed when we come to examine performance work which is particularly body-based; where the idea is transmitted through the 'character' of the lived, trained body of the performer, and therefore dependent on its residing in the particularity of that body for its meaning. The fact that I could not be replaced in *Levad* when ill is a case in point, not because there were no actresses of sufficient ability to perform the piece, but because so much of the piece depended for its meaning on its transmission through my body, and because so much of the performance text had no actual existence outside my body and my memory.

Here, again, was a bleeding of one narrative into another. In the narrative we invented for *Levad*, the actress, Eva, has claimed 'authorship' of the role of *Mireleh Efros*[17] – or, rather, of her version of the role she has 'made her own'. We imagined Eva as part of the tradition of 'grand dames', such as Sarah Bernhardt and Hana Rovina, who made their reputation by singular, 'definitive' interpretations of a particular role or roles, and who might therefore be seen as 'authors' of the character, if not the text. Part of Eva's resistance to the director's interpretation of the text, therefore, derived from a reluctance to relinquish 'creative control' of the rights of an embodied 'authorship' to a disembodied other.

Life Imitates Art

Upon my return to the show I began, however, to realise that the progress of the narrative is less dependent on 'my' character than I had supposed, and that the orchestration of the performance was less dependent on the actor than I had previously presumed. Barrie was a visible presence in the performance – not inside the world of the play, not in 'costume', not 'in character', but identified in the public imagination as The Director. There were, therefore, two directors present inside the event; the fictional director in the auditorium in the rehearsal scenes, and the 'actual' director sitting at the side of the stage. Barrie's double role as co-performer and director rendered our relationship, and readings of the performance from within and without, fairly complex.

In post-show note sessions, I developed some resistance to his judgements, partly because I felt that his function as a performer was restricting his view of the overall shape and sweep of the piece. We could not reach an agreement regarding the pace of the performance. I felt that he was pushing the show too fast, and another strand to the double narrative of resistance was being played out in a battle between us for control over the performance. As in the scenes between actor and director in the play, the understanding was that I would 'try it and see' with regard to director's notes. Nonetheless, when it suited me, I 'forgot' or 'misinterpreted' his instructions. Barrie, however, coerced compliance with some of these instructions by driving the rhythm of the performance from behind the piano.

> YP: 'I had far less control over this piece in terms of the narrative actually emanating from the character, than I thought…. In fact, a lot of those points where the narrative jumps forward… actually came from beyond me… [in] a narrative where so many of the moves forward were actually spurred by a lighting cue, a music cue or a movement in the set… [as if there were] this whole other power outside… another character, or a great big god figure, pushing the lights and turning the music on and pushing me around the traps!'[18]

Back to the Salt Mines

My return to the show after a week of cancelled performances was riven with anxiety. Many of the critical responses to this particular work, published during my absence, had pointed to the difficulty of its execution, and I was concerned that these stories would bleed into, perhaps obscure, the story of the piece. Would the audience reading of the piece be coloured by the rumours of my collapse? Would they be looking for signs of illness, waiting to see whether I could make it to the end of the show without collapsing? Initially, I felt a substantial pressure to appear well and in control in order to redirect the gaze from me to the work.

> 'Yoni Prior's performance is confident… and vulnerable'.[19]

> '…Prior's obviously driven performance…'[20]

I was hardly in the right show or character, however, to deliver a performance of 'fitness', and here a capacity to analyse and theorise the performance event became a protective mechanism. I found myself sifting through those aspects of the performance which I must 'act', and those which I need not. As with the 'work' involved in manipulating the set, the performance of this piece cost me considerable effort which I was, at first, at pains to conceal. I felt I was revealing a visible, palpable lack of competence. In self-defence, I concluded that I must make this incompetence a sign – to 'claim it', integrate it, make it appear deliberate. Compelled to confront the limitations of my material body, I needed to make a series of crucial distinctions about what was 'actual' in the moment, what of the actuality to reveal, and what to conceal – to determine which aspects of the present experience were material to the fictional moment.

In response, I selectively ceased to conceal the effort. What I could not conceal or control must be incorporated. If I could not conceal it, I could inflect it. I allowed the breathlessness. I allowed myself to lick my lips when my mouth was dry. I could not 'finish' gestures, so I allowed them a rough, unfinished quality. In Sydney, later that year, I performed *Levad* at the end of a three-month season in which we presented all three parts of *The Exile Trilogy*. My voice was raw and cracked from overuse. No matter how I economised its use, and no matter how much salt (!) or aspirin I gargled, this could not be remedied. I could only try to 'claim' it as intentional, which worked – sort of.

> 'Her singing is often so bad one must assume this is deliberate – the old performer has lost her art?'[21]

At both a deeper and more general level, this process of mining the 'actual' and claiming selected pieces of it for inclusion in the fictional/'acted' begs the question: 'What am I doing when I "claim"?'. What is it about what I am doing, or *not* doing, or, more particularly, *how* I am doing or not doing it, which signals that 'I *know* what I am doing'? Perhaps, to borrow a maxim from Grotowski, it is a 'not doing' – a way of operating '*via negativa*'? (Grotowski, 1968: 18) Is the signalling of intention as simple as a failure to falter – to leave no pause, to refuse to allow any interruption to the rhythm, or to allow my gaze to waver from its proper object? The whole mechanism of my body/mind must respond to the idea/moment which is comprised of layers of actual and fictional material.

This activity relies upon the translation of a rationalised **self-consciousness** into a near-objectified **technique**. I became the 'Spect-actor', watching myself and sorting through not only past experience (personal history/experience, the inscription of the performance text on the body/mind in rehearsal) but through present experience and the making of moment-to-moment decisions regarding the revelation, concealment, adaptation or description of what is present **in the moment** to, or for, the witness/audience. In this sense the experience was both raw and constructed, actual and fictional.

Making another Text

So how did these reflexive narrative strands coalesce? If we accept that my task as actor became the acknowledgement and identification of the multiplicity of texts present in the performance arena, and the bending of these strands to my purpose, what metanarrative was created by the collusions between the actual and the fictional? If we substitute the discourse of history for the discourse of the theatre, and the role of the Jew for the role of the actor in this performance, an analogous narrative is constructed.

In this memory mill, history moves through her body. Its rigours are imposed upon her body, and its effects inscribed upon it. Attempts to locate a place of physical safety or comfort are constantly subverted as she is driven or pursued by forces she has no control over. A certain safety lies in the enactment of the ritual which defines her 'role', but the dynamic of the history of the Jew is characterised by constant destabilisation which pushes the subject at a pace which defies dignity and endurance. Actions are broken and unfinished – scenes cannot resolve because she is constantly shifted forward by 'cues' imposed from without, and the abrupt movement of objects in the environment. Despite her resistance, she is 'processed' through this ordeal by mechanical elements at the command of a Director (History). Without any direct reference to that monumental event, the Holocaust is always in the peripheral vision.

In *Levad*, the narrative of history, both internal and external, was expressed as action on and through the body. Experience was made incarnate. A second text emerged as the effort of executing that action told on the body of the actor in signs of exertion – weariness, breathlessness, sweat, strain in the voice. Images of 'stoic endurance' in the frame of the piece knit the impact of the fictional history on the fictional body/character into the impact of the real history/time on the real body/actor.

In the ambiguous time/space occupied by Yoni/Eva/actor/Jew, my material 'living' body underwent a present ordeal, representing a body undergoing a present ordeal, which was a compression/collage – a reliving – of the life of her body. My 'actual' discomfort was not commensurate with the pain history had inflicted upon this Jew/woman/actress. My hope was that, by claiming the intersections, I could claim some control over the text made by 'actual' circumstances – and push it into a 'double space', destabilising the 'actuality' of my discomfort and moving it towards a potential metaphoricity. By this blurring or bleeding of the lines between the actual and the fictional, might the audience be brought to read the impact of the actual (historical)/fictional forces represented on the fictional character by responding to the impact of the actual/material forces on the present actor? (Auslander, 1997: 99)

Notes

1   In fact, issues of research methodology and intellectual property which arose
    in negotiating my candidature later informed the frameworks we developed for
    practice-as-research post-graduate awards in my own department at Deakin
    University. Despite more than a decade of lobbying, the persistent reluctance of
    the Federal Department of Education, Science and Training in Australia, and of
    the Australian Research Council, to acknowledge artistic practice as legitimate
    research continues to marginalise practitioner–researchers in the university sector.

2   S. Gray, *Spalding Gray's Monster in a Box*, videorecording, directed by Nick
    Broomfield, produced by John Blair (Chatsworth, CA: Image Entertainment
    (Distributor), 2006)

3   Richards, A. and Prior, Y., 'Theatre of Exile: the possible and the improbable in the
    work of Gilgul Theatre, 1991–1997' in Belkin, 2008

4   The first two parts of the trilogy were *The Dybbuk* (1991), based on S. Anski's
    iconic text of the same name, and *Es Brent* (*It Burns*) (1992), based upon Elie
    Wiesel's play *The Trial of God*. In each of the performances the director, Barrie
    Kosky, accompanied the songs, and provided a partially improvised soundtrack
    from a battered piano in the space. Sources:

    Anski., S., *The Dybbuk* in Landis, Joseph C., (editor and translator), *The
    Dybbuk and other Great Yiddish Plays* (New York: Bantam Books, 1996)
    Wiesel, E., *The Trial of God (as it was held on February 25, 1649, in Shamgorod)*,
    trans. Wiesel, M. (New York: Random House, 1979)

5   Kosky, B., Director's Note, the *Dybbuk* program (Gilgul Theatre, 1991)

6   The creation of the character was strongly informed by the life history of Hana
    Rovina, an actress who began her career with the Habimah Theatre in Moscow,
    and moved with the company to create what is now the National Theatre of Israel.

7   Kosky, B., program note, *Levad* (Playbox Theatre, March 1993)

8   Prior, Y. and Kosky, B., performance text of *Levad*, Gilgul Theatre and Playbox
    Theatre (1993, unpublished)

9   Recorded conversation between Peter Corrigan and Yoni Prior (22 April 1996,
    unpublished)

10 Recorded conversation between Tom Wright and Yoni Prior (20 May 1996,
    unpublished)

11 Recorded conversation between Peter Corrigan and Yoni Prior (22 April 1996,
    unpublished)

12 Recorded conversation between Peter Corrigan and Yoni Prior (22 April 1996,
    unpublished)

13 Thomson, H., review of *Levad*, *Australian* (newspaper), Australia, 26 March 1993

14 Scott-Norman, F., review of *Levad*, *Bulletin* (magazine), Australia, 6 April 1993

15 Recorded conversation between Barrie Kosky and Alison Richards (14 June 1995,
    unpublished)

16   The term 'auteur', as related to the role of the film director, is summarised by Eric Rhode as 'the ultimate authority and the sole arbiter of a film's meaning... they required one consistency only: that the director should have a strong personality and that he should be able to project his convictions'. (Rhode, 1976: 530)

17   The play which the actress in *Levad* continually returns to is *Mireleh Efros*, frequently called 'The Female King Lear'. Gordin, J., *Mireleh Efros* (Hebrew version translated and adapted by Miriam Keyney) (Tel Aviv: Or-Am publications, 1987).

18   Recorded conversation between Peter Corrigan and Yoni Prior (22 April 1996, unpublished)

19   Caleo, M., review of *Levad*, *Melbourne Times*, Melbourne, Australia, 31 March 1993

20   Boyd, C., review of *Levad*, *Financial Review*, Australia, 2 April 1993

21   Morrison, P., review of *Levad*, *Australian Jewish News*, Sydney Edition, 17 December 1993

SECTION 7

Methodologies; Thesis Statements; Fallibilism; PhD Outcomes; Performance Studies

> It has not been definitively proved that the
> language of words is the best possible language.
> **Antonin Artaud**

O nce we begin to ask ourselves research questions such as 'What will
be discovered, decided or understood as a result of our enquiry?'
'To which organisations or individuals will the results of our search
be of benefit?' and 'How will our results be collected, tested and refined?' we
are obliged in these pursuits to seek out the most appropriate methodologies
to follow. And how are these decided? Researchers will usually look for
a methodology that allows for active dynamism throughout the period of
investigation, for such is implied if not quite demanded by a timescale that is
at once intensive and extensive. Because a practice-as-research methodology
that is dynamic is one that finds ways in which the constituent elements of
performance can be usefully deployed beyond the known, it is likely that
the process of discovery will evidence flexibility, awareness, responsibility,
ethical consideration, creativity and experimentation: these are staples rather
than deviations in performance practice as research. All of these may well be
demonstrated in the substance of practice – in the process – but what of the
dissemination of one's findings? The investigation of original performance
processes necessarily has a practical imperative and for some the practice *is* the
thesis.

This leads us to question the extent to which a thesis should have to be
submitted in written form. Since we know that information can be communicated
in a variety of ways it is hard, tradition aside, to create a cogent argument that
legislates against purely practical dissemination. We have already seen an
emerging history of practice-based documentation that challenges conventional

systems of notation. In cases like these the 'thesis' is still assumed to exist in terms of its key and essential elements, so that the generative methodological and informing elements are still operative, albeit in often unexpected ways.

If we are to accept the equivalence of practice to a written thesis, or to argue that the creative work presented *is* the thesis, we need to have some clear idea of what a thesis is usually taken to mean.

We can start by saying that the term 'thesis' comes from the Greek *tithenai*, meaning 'to put': accordingly a thesis is an as-yet-unproven statement put forward as a premise in an argument. It is a means of advancing an original point of view that has arisen from one's research. A thesis is therefore most commonly regarded as a document that articulates both research and findings and that is subsequently submitted in support of candidature for a higher degree or professional qualification. The thesis is maintained by argument and through this it is able to develop, contextualise and defend its findings. A thesis can be implied rather than stated directly, but it will always be capable of distillation into some form of statement that provides a condensing of the argument or analysis that the thesis will go on to provide. This act of condensation is most often referred to as a thesis statement. Thesis statements are useful to both researcher and reader. For each, the statement will offer a guide to the argument, with the distilling of ideas into one clear reminder of what it is that the research is intending to accomplish.

Regardless of their levels of complexity, almost all theses are capable of being reduced to a single question. This necessitates developing an area of address into a specific question; and the answer to this question can stand as the thesis statement for the work. A thesis statement needs to answer a question about the issues the work will explore. In this situation the researcher's task is to decide what main question is being addressed.

A strong thesis statement will usually include the following attributes: it will engage with a subject upon which reasonable people could be said to disagree; it will articulate one chief idea; it will focus on a subject that is appropriate in research terms; and it will briefly assert the researcher's conclusions. A good thesis statement therefore is charged with taking some sort of stand, of indicating the point of the work, expressing the main idea and demonstrating that the thesis will be dealing with a manageable topic. Intrinsically, a thesis statement is not a statement of fact: its function is to articulate a debatable point of view which the thesis will substantiate and defend. Thesis statements are then demanding of the very proof that further reading makes a promise to provide. They make claims that require some proof, some supporting evidence or explanation, and it is this that makes thesis statements deal in debatable points. A thesis that is not an *ipso facto* invitation for some form of argument and debate is not in fact a thesis; more likely it is a report: a valid form of documentation, but not what we would regard as a thesis.

A PhD thesis will usually involve starting with a hypothesis and then collecting evidence to support it. In almost all cases before one can write a thesis one first needs to collect evidence that will be offered in its support. The essence of a thesis then is critical thinking rather than the laying out of experimental data. Analysis forms the heart of the work and it is likely to demonstrate a concentration on principles, inasmuch as it will state the things learned through the period of research and not merely the facts behind them. The facts that result from and through research are data, whereas the concept of knowledge demands that data has been made subject to analysis as a means of producing new and useful information. Because a given of a successful PhD thesis is that it makes a contribution to knowledge it stands to reason that the submission of data alone is never going to be enough. Data alone, or a document in which the data far outweighs analysis, is indicative of a research report rather than a thesis.

Another identifiable feature of a successful thesis is that it will probably draw only those conclusions that are warranted by the research. This demands that researchers are careful only to draw conclusions that their evidence supports. This is not to deny the idea of speculative research, as distinctions need to be drawn between research based on informed speculation and findings based on proof. The ideas of Charles Sanders Pierce provide a useful echo here. For Pierce feelings were often legitimised into proof as a consequence of the skill of the experienced guesser. Nevertheless, Pierce was consistent in his belief that the idea of feelings functioning as findings was an exercise in fallibilism. In this sense Pierce is a touchstone for those critical writers and thinkers who claim the authority of certainty when their/our ideas are, like everybody else's, premised on the fallible and unsure.

In normal circumstances (i.e. with an entirely written thesis based on externally verifiable data) researchers will usually refrain from stating particular judgements unless or until they are in possession of the results from reasonably controlled and repeatable experiments. Even on those occasions when the cause of specific phenomena appears to be obvious, experienced researchers will rightly hesitate before asserting conclusions without the support of solid, substantiating evidence. We can say that a thesis is an intellectual proposition that serves to present the key findings from an individual's research. (See the case study from Whalley and Miller for an example of when this sense of individuality is constructively subverted.) It is the main idea of one's research and is usually the end product of a substantial period of academically verifiable investigation. Because a thesis is normally the culmination of a research project, the writing will most often start when all investigation has been completed. There are alternatives to this model of course and practice as research, where work that forms the thesis is often also that which stands as process, is a clear example of this.

International and institutional nuances apart, and following *viva voce*, academic decisions for written PhD submissions will normally fall somewhere on this list:

1. The work is accepted as a pass with no corrections.

2. The thesis needs minor revision. The nature of these revisions commonly includes the rectification of errors of spelling or grammar or additional clarification in terms of methodology. If these revisions are relatively modest the examiners may decide that student should be awarded a PhD on the understanding that the candidate will re-submit the revised document within an agreed period of time.

3. The thesis requires extensive revision. When this happens the thesis will need to be revised substantially before being resubmitted. Typical problems here include theoretical or methodological issues. Again, depending upon the severity of the revisions candidates may or may not be required to re-submit the thesis with a second *viva voce*. The period of revision is likely to be significantly greater than that demanded for minor revisions.

4. The thesis is regarded as unacceptable for PhD, but the award of M.Phil is offered.

5. The thesis is totally unacceptable. This verdict is given on those occasions when the thesis requires major revisions, bordering on a re-write, and when the *viva voce* defence has made it clear that the candidate is incapable of making such major improvements. On very rare occasions a thesis can be failed without the candidate being offered the opportunity of attending a *viva voce*.

Of these possible outcomes, numbers 1, 4 and 5 are fairly easily adaptable to submissions that are made up in part by practical elements. The second and third options are potentially problematic, not least because the ephemerality of much practical work, alongside the once-only aspects that are frequently part of its nature tends to legislate against post-submission amendments. It becomes clear at this point that practice as research is one thing, whereas practice as thesis is something else entirely.

The standard requirements of a thesis are that it will demonstrate ability to pursue original research in a particular field of study and that this will be based on an appropriately comprehensive understanding of the varying research techniques and concepts appropriate to the discipline. Practice as research is obviously one such technique within the performing arts. Equally obviously, it is never going to be the only one. A thesis is expected to articulate the results of a programme of research which may reasonably be expected of a student after completing an agreed period of supervised registration, and this will comprise the student's account of relevant investigations undertaken. Furthermore, it will represent a distinct and significant contribution to the subject. This will be through the discovery of new knowledge which reveals and is premised on the implementation of critical judgement. A thesis will also be expected to pay due attention to previously published work on the subject. With practice-based work it is reasonable to assume that this will be extended to include work that has been performed or otherwise made public in a variety of non-literary forms. The submission needs to make clear the variety of sources from which information has been derived, alongside the extent to which the work of other scholars in the field has been used. Above all, a thesis needs to demonstrate a student's ability to design and carry out an independent research project.

All of these can be achieved through a submission that is practical in part. A potential difficulty arises when the written element is strong and the practical work is relatively weak. If practice underpins the research, as well as forming the critical foundation of the thesis, then the risk of everything collapsing as a result of practical inadequacy is high... and this is a more difficult failing to remedy than in the written elements of theses, where clarity of rationale tends to be favoured over creative expression.

We can move on from our remarks regarding research theses towards an articulation of the type of practice being focused on in this and other sections. Whilst most readers will be already familiar with current issues surrounding practice and performance it is worth spending some time on a defining of the field as it applies to this book. The area of academic theatre study has witnessed many changes in recent years. Of these, one of the most significant has been an almost annual reconsideration of nomenclature, with institutions changing the names of programmes as much to appeal to a shifting undergraduate market as to reflect the particular nature of study. As we have seen, 'Theatre' and 'Theatre Studies' remain popular, as do 'Drama' and the increasingly adopted 'Performance Studies'. Performance Studies suggests an inclusive approach, one that is not only able to accommodate liminal forms, but which actively and progressively welcomes the problematic into its fold. That which sits (or sat) in the margins of theatre and/or drama is able to assume a centre-stage position in performance in ways that, in Richard Schechner's terms, have initiated a 'wholesale reconstruction of curricula'. (Bial, 2004: 8) Schechner observes that most theatre departments do not train professional artists, that those who *are* trained are unable to find jobs and that 'elite live performance such as the so-called "legitimate theatre" is shrinking'. (Schechner, 1992: 8) In a climate such as this Schechner suggests that most theatre departments should get out of the study of theatre and move towards the more conceptually and practically legitimate field of performance. (Ibid.)

Ritualised and shamanic activities, anthropological approaches, inter-cultural procedures, theatre-of-barter, dance-theatre, rule-based work, installation and gallery practices, media interventions and body art have all found their natural home in the contingent, enabling and endlessly eclectic area of performance, rather than the more (seemingly) restricted fields of theatre or drama. The name of a subject, however, is distinct from attitude and approach, and one reader's performance is another's theatre and yet another's drama. The word 'performance' as it is adopted in the pages of this book is most often taken to stand for contemporary work that challenges, develops and sometimes subverts the key conventional codes of theatre; for work that is concerned with interruptions, uncertainty and doubt. Accordingly, the research practices explored in our case studies have this in common: that they operate not so much beyond the normative values of theatre and drama (although some clearly do) as that they comprise a challenge to conventionalised notions of cultural authority and closure.

As Brooks McNamara claims:

> Performance is no longer easy to define or locate: the concept
> and structure has spread all over the place. It is ethnic and inter
> cultural, historical and ahistorical, aesthetic and ritual, sociological
> and political. Performance is a mode of behaviour, an approach
> to experience; it is play, sports, aesthetics, popular entertainment,
> experimental theatre and more.
>
> (McNamara, 1996: 17)

Whilst Schechner tells us that we should:

> situate theatre where it belongs: among performance genres, not
> literature. The text, where it exists, is understood as a key to action,
> not its replacement. Where there is no text, action is treated directly.
>
> (Schechner, 1988: 28)

Performance Studies is inextricably concerned with forms and areas of performance not typically accommodated within the field of Theatre Studies; in this context we can say that Theatre Studies tends to be theoretically informed and analytical, concerned with throwing light on certain ideological processes inherent in theatrical practices and productions, whereas Performance Studies is more inclined towards the utilisation of performance as a means of viewing events that are not easily accepted within the usual theatrical terms. Performance Studies in this way can be regarded as an approach to knowing that is theoretically informed by theatre but which will often step outside of normative theatre-orientation in its endeavours.

For the purposes of our understanding here, performance then can be reasonably defined as practice in which the actions of an individual or a group at a particular place and in a particular time are seen to constitute the work. A broad enough definition for most. But this idea of constitution is made subject to challenge by practice that sees itself as one small cog in a large wheel of receptivity, reciprocity and intervention. What we find in these tentative stages of description is that the very uncertainty and doubt that we promote and defend problematises all but the most guarded of attempts at neat articulation. We can try again and say that unlike the connotative understandings most of us will probably share of theatre and drama, performance is able to occur at any time and anywhere and that whilst this 'anywhere' can certainly include theatre buildings it is in no way limited to or by them. This is a useful distinction, albeit in no way authoritative or binding.

As we have already started to see from the case studies, space in contemporary performance research is rarely regarded with anything close to the parsing emptiness of Peter Brook's to-be-performed-in, even in the non-space utilisation of the British motorway network as envisaged by Miller and Whalley's innovative fusing of text and objects, location and action, travel and time. Time, in fact, is one of our very few relatively safely defining features, as what distinguishes performance from the field of fine art, where much performance might on the face of things be equally well-housed, is its relationship with time. Fine art plays often with time, without time being one of its intrinsic elements. Fine art then is always concerned with objects and space, even when these objects are readymade or absent; whereas performance is driven by action and time, even when those actions are inane or unseen. A series of concise and articulate interrogations of contemporary performance practices (not least those offered by Franc Chamberlain and David E.R. George) can be found in Murray and Keefe's *Physical Theatres: A Critical Introduction* (2007).

An often-used and only slightly out of favour term for performance is time-based art, and this may well be the most honest description we could use. Honest, perhaps, but also more than a little cumbersome. We do better at this stage to say that performance can be any situation that involves elements of time and space, intention and action, performer and spectator, without being necessarily reliant on all of these being present or being present at the same time. Some sort of testing of the relationship between performers and spectators (between the doing-to and the done-with) is an indication, if not quite a given, of the type of progressive performance work being undertaken at this point in the twenty-first century, and it is one of the strongest links between the otherwise quite diverse case studies drawn upon in this book.

The lines between art-forms, as we well know, are seldom cleanly drawn. The medico-operational work carried out on Orlan is critically regarded as performance at the same time as the deposits of her fat that are removed via these performances are subsequently sold on as art objects. The performance status of her surgical procedures undeniably lends art value to the galleried objects that remain. Conversely, Jackson Pollock's splattering actions gave added credibility to the canvasses he was able to sell and yet Pollock's processes, performative though they doubtless were, never threatened to be taken seriously *as* performance. A certain acceptance of the difficulty of naming is apparent. By the same token, a willingness to allow one's personal agendas and levels of comfort to be challenged by approaches to practice that are deliberately contradictory and radically difficult to read is necessary if one is to engage constructively with research that makes practical exploration both its content and its form.

Performance is further complicated as a term because in various other contexts the same word might refer to the execution of a particular experiment in science; or in linguistic terminology as the producing of an utterance. Elsewhere, performance relates to the activity of a unit or the measurement of some output or behaviour, as in the performance of an engine under stress. In the context of this book performance is regarded as that which explores theatre-based and/or drama-based activity without the relatively restrictive frames that using the terms theatre or drama in its title would impose. The case studies that form the experiential spine of this book range from the casting of plays for international audiences, the choreography of space and an olfactory series of performance events, through to explorations of narrative and pedagogy and each in one way or another stretches the idea of what constitutes progressive performance-related research.

Stretched to near breaking point it may be, but theatre remains the predominant referential term, rather than music or even dance; though each of these comes close enough to touch, and case studies from these disciplines, from contributors such as Yves Knockaert and Leena Rouhiainen, are comfortably accommodated in this study of research located in and through practice.

It is this stretching of theatrical convention and expectation that puts the search into research and in this it serves as a reiterative statement of the book's intent and, hopefully, of its usefulness. As with all acts of research, this book is only ever one aspect among many. The various references, taken with the bibliography, function as signposts towards other acts, events and writings; and this larger world of publication serves less as the marginalia to this book so much as a vast resource within which this work takes up its own small space.

CASE STUDY 7

A Mono-trilogy on a Collaborative Process in the Performing Arts

Leena Rouhiainen

> *Previously visited by our faces, hands and bodies, a table corner at a dimly lit cafeteria is alive again. It is endless; words keep pouring out of our mouths in turns as excitement moves in ebbs and flows from person to person. Our limbs hardly keeping still, we drop names, concepts, images and experiences on the table. A cluttered array of ideas, books, laptops, hands, lattes and ashtrays piles between us. And anticipation keeps figuring who you are, who I am with you and what we are doing together... Perhaps I'll know more next time.*

The Frame

In this case study, written with the support of the Academy of Finland, I will discuss a collaborative artistic process that I undertook together with the musician–sound designer Antti Nykyri and the architect–scenographer Toni Kauppila. I myself am a dancer–choreographer, and our explorative project that produced an installation–performance entitled *Passage* (Väylä) took place between the years 2007 and 2008 in Helsinki. Initially, we set out to explore our shared interest in *space*. It involved observing urban sites and their social choreography as well as our personal experience of commuting between our workplaces and homes as well as rest or stillness. The following pages contain my reflections on the initial stage and workshop of our collaboration with some literary or theoretical quotations that stimulated our work.

In describing our process I will implicitly deal with the emergence of that sensual, perceptive, imaginary, intellectual, bodily, material, practical and technological space we enacted and worked in. Maurice Merleau-Ponty points out that our existence is primordially spatial because it is oriented and mobile. We are directed towards different modes of consciousness and different kinds of relations to others and the world through our habits and actions. In its lived nature, space carries the meanings of the manner in which we inhabit the world. According to him, lived space is a situation, the spatiality of a lived event. In this sense he considers the experience of space to be 'interwoven with all the other modes of experience and all the other psychic data'. (Merleau-Ponty, 1962:

286–287) He also claims that 'there are as many spaces as there are distinct spatial experiences' and that 'the description of human space could be developed indefinitely'. (Merleau-Ponty, 1962: 286–287, 291) De Certeau (1988: 117–118) takes Merleau-Ponty to discuss a space that is not a theoretical construction, but a space of practice, operations, mobility and a poetic space of mythical experience.

As I address features of the above-described kind of space, I will look into those experiences, actions and thoughts of mine that were instigated by our collaboration. I will also deal with the realms of research and writing. They began to trouble me as I constructed a view on the in-between space the three of us enacted. These realms, for me, became part of our space. Research also informs the manner in which this paper addresses our process. I found support for my reflections from conceptions of artistic research and narrative methodology as well as phenomenological notions on space.

On Writing as a Part of Artistic Research

As the subsequent sections contain ruminations on an artistic process as well as some notions of the embodied and practical knowledge it relied upon, this paper could be understood to belong to the field of artistic research. Henk Borgdorff (2004) suggests that research *in* the arts in contrast to *on* the arts is a form of practice-based, processual and performative research with a contextualising point of view. While aiming at expanding our knowledge and understanding of artworks and the at least partially tacit artistic processes, such research allows experimentation in practice and interpretation of this practice to be its component parts. (Borgdorff, 2004: 12; 2004: 6) As rehearsals with Antti and Toni began, we needed to explore the practical grounds of our collaboration. How we work together, what we actually do, what we think of what we did and how we continue further, became important concerns. This need to construct a means to share our practice and interact with each other by doing and talking initially swallowed our interest in space. But it was a necessary process to allow for a communal space of interaction as well as a practical approach to emerge between us. This demonstrates the process-orientedness of our approach.

What is more is that written articulation is often considered a part of artistic research. It supports both reflection and dissemination of the diverse knowledges involved in artistic undertakings. Laurel Richardson suggests that writing is a method of inquiry: a way to discover and learn to understand an issue of interest. She claims: 'I write because I want to find something out, I write in order to learn something that I didn't know before I wrote it'. (Richardson, 1994: 517) This is how I felt about my writing. She further argues that writing does not reflect social reality. As it produces meaning, it simultaneously constructs social reality. (Richardson, 1994: 516, 518) While Antti, Toni and I were working together, and as I made notes during and after each day with them, I noticed that my writing and additional reading became part of our artistic process. I made comments on what I had written and between us they opened conversations about our collaboration. For some reason, different texts attracted my attention during the days we worked, too. They formed a reflective mirror against which I contemplated our process and gave me insights into what we were dealing with and how to continue working. In fact, Hannula, Suoranta and Vaden (2003: 32) argue that artistic research becomes part of what is researched, the object of investigation, and changes the latter.

On the other hand, being aware of the fact that I was planning to write about our collaboration made working on my diary somewhat special. I wrote some anecdotes about my experiences or simply jotted down words, which a few hours or days later I filled out in order to present more complete descriptions and thoughts. I noticed that it was impossible to document much of anything of the freely flowing and lively conversations we had or much of the actual dancing. I was so engaged with them both. They seemed to need my full attention to be enlivened. I was faced with the challenge of being an artist–researcher doing two things simultaneously: exploring our artistic practice in and through art-making itself as well as reflecting upon this creative activity not for the ends of art-making itself but for telling about it to others in writing. I actually dealt with a double construction of reality in my writing: my notes on our daily work and the text produced by my ruminations on writing about our process and the notes. And I noticed that my writing was somehow troubled, which I believed had something to tell me about the nature of artistic practice and reflection upon it.

In general, in the human sciences it is understood that the researcher is part of the research with her interests, background and the skills, traditions, conventions, instruments as well as languages she operates with. (Hannula et al., 2003: 35) In the process related to this paper, I keenly felt that as an artist-researcher I could not clearly distinguish between when I was dealing with art and when with research. They interweaved and informed each other. Co-relatively, Hannula, Suoranta and Vaden write: 'artistic practice and scientific practice occur in one world, in one person, in one being'. (2003: 34) Juha Varto (2000), in turn, argues that being part of, or in the middle of, what one is researching makes knowing challenging. Because the object of knowledge is not distinguishable from the knower, one cannot see clearly. Knowing turns out to be fragmentary, and a unified understanding or coherent conception of the object is not achievable. (Varto, 2000: 38–39)

Being immersed in the process I was investigating is one aspect of what made writing and reporting about the process challenging. But also, the fact that I was dealing with a new way of collaboration with two people I had not worked with before had a lot to do with it. In writing my notes, there were many moments in which I felt mute, unable to grasp or articulate what had gone on between us – even if at the moment I was quite enthusiastic and felt productively engrossed in whatever we were working on. Some of my notes felt redundant. Those that felt interesting were revelations about new themes that I could work upon or a few crystallised articulations about what we thought we were dealing with and why we felt some things worked and some did not. Also, more poetic descriptions of shared moments evoke something of what I had experienced.

As I struggled with my approach to writing I recalled the dance historian Susan Foster's words on improvisation:

> The improvised is that which eludes history.... History, however, keeps track almost exclusively of the known. It focuses on those human actions reiterated frequently enough to become patterns of behaviour.... Historical inquiry has neglected to question how certain actions slide easily across representational fields into the historical record and others are persistently unnoticed. It has tried to ignore actions resistant to written description.
>
> (Foster, 2003: 4)

When one is retrieving understanding of lived processes and improvisation, it is imperative to allow oneself to be immersed in them and to take sufficient time to gain a sense of their nature. This notion describes an aspect of the phenomenological method in the sense that Merleau-Ponty writes of it. For a philosopher to gain access to the lived character of the world requires an opening towards the world through a state of wonder. The philosopher should leave her preconceptions and personal motives behind and allow the world to speak through her. Gaining sense of the lived nature of what is observed is not attained through conscious effort. Rather, it entails that the philosopher has perceptual faith, can endure the unclear and allows enough time for her or his wondering to bear fruit. (Rouhiainen, 2003: 95; Heinämaa, 2000: 104–105; Merleau-Ponty, 1962: xiii)

The novelty of our practical collaboration challenged my orientation. Probing the ways we worked together, what my dance was about in relation to Antti's and Toni's work, thinking of making notes alongside of all the other practical issues we were solving, as well as considering how to manage to write on the process, placed me in a deep sea of questioning. I needed time to allow impetus to grow and to gain perspective on what we were dealing with.

A Story in the Making

> Every story is a travel story – a spatial practice.
>
> (De Certeau, 1988: 115)

As I wrestled with writing about our collaboration, I noticed that my thinking was influenced by our earlier encounters. Our meetings and the days we worked together began to determine the structure of my writing. I was trying to tell a story about the time we spent together. The subsequent text follows a sequence of beginning, middle and end and could be understood to follow a narrative logic. Therefore, the account that I constructed on our collaboration could be considered a story, an artistic–scholarly tale. And I found some grounds for constructing it from notions related to narrative research.

Narratives interpret the temporality or processes of life in human terms. The way in which narrative reasoning constructs reality is by being contextually embedded and looking for particular connections between events in a causal manner. (Richardson, 1990) Therefore, the ability to tie different *spatial* and *temporal* elements together through a causal plot is characteristic of narrative research. It does not attempt to determine an event by situating it in only one defining category; rather, it attempts to delineate the manner in which it is related to other spatially and geographically situated happenings. (Saastamoinen, 2005) Stories or tales are usually differentiated from narratives as a subcategory. Stories are more straightforward accounts of actual events and experiences concerning human life.

In following the aim of creating a good story from chosen episodes that enable a logical plot to emerge, narrative research makes it possible for a piece of research to interlink a variety of textual or symbolic material related to a socio-cultural practice. Even different research methods and writing styles can be combined to produce grounds for new and shared understanding of an issue. (Heikkinen, 2001; Richardson, 1994) I am following this advice in combining my notes, some poetic images on our process, with a few more theoretical conceptions. Moreover, in this kind of an approach to research, the origins of the source materials or orthodox methodology are considered less important than the experimental process of creating new understanding. (Heikkinen, 2001; Lincoln and Denzin, 1994)

Stories can also be considered to be spatial practices. They position, mark boundaries, map structures, open vistas, move ideas, interconnect agents etc. De Certeau writes: 'Every day [stories] traverse and organize places; they select and link them together; they make sentences and itineraries out of them. They are spatial trajectories'. (De Certeau, 1988: 115) So as I am constructing this somewhat scholarly tale on our artistic process, I am actually constructing a space. After all, 'the story does not express a practice. It does not limit itself to telling about a movement. It *makes* it.' (Ibid.: 81) In some respects, my tale might turn a dynamic, interactive, mobile and ambiguous space into a more organised, stable place, as it offers a view from my perspective only. Nonetheless, since 'space is a practiced place' and 'stories… carry out a labour that constantly transforms places into spaces or spaces into places', I hope that this paper involves at least an intermittent dynamism. (Ibid.: 117, 118)

The First Task

> Sit, stand, walk but do not talk.
>
> Muffled noises with glassy paths of electronic and human motion.
>
> Step after step a mixture of limbs in locomotion, upright directed elevators, diagonal escalators, TV screens with their mind-protruding commercial clips and a spherically ticking clock.
>
> Here I am sunken into the heaviness of my joints, muscles and other organs – an onlooker on an ergonomically designed seat. I mere meat.
>
> The passivity of observation: a peaceful distance in the proximity of goal and effort consuming busy bodies.

I wrote this poem about the site I took Toni and Antti to see. It was my urban site of rest in between commuting from my workplace to my home – waiting for the bus at the central bus station in Helsinki. For me the poem functioned as an emblem of a lived experience. I take it to preserve the felt-sense I had of this urban space. In fact, it became a map of my emplacement at the bus station. According to Gaston Bachelard, a poetic image offers the opportunity to experience linguistic spaces. Language as this sort of an image is not a means of expression but the surging forth of a living reality. (Bachelard, 2003/1957: 42, 50, 51) Merleau-Ponty argues that, in poetic expression, the object of expression and the expression itself are inseparable. A poem is a string of living meanings that illuminate a situated attitude or approach towards the world. (Merleau-Ponty, 1962: 151; Heinämaa, 1996: 97) I used my poetic emblem to extract movement themes for our workshop, such as walking and sitting or moving backwards and down as you do when you take a seat.

As our first workshop period approached, we presented our first ideas and drafts on materials to each other. I showed my poem and physically demonstrated the related movement themes. Toni presented his idea of a spatial construction, a site for our performance. In his drawings, he had visualised a patch of rouged floor on which I would dance and onto which he could project video material. He also presented two video clips he was working on. They were based on material he filmed at the bus station in which people walked as well as a moving map of a route from Helsinki to my home he had retrieved from *Google Earth*.

Antti had created an instrument that could produce static sounds. He made a wooden box and glued three pieces of sandpaper of different roughness on top of it. Under the sandpaper he placed contact microphones. He also built reconstructed loudspeakers in which he separated the middle- and high-frequency elements from each other, placing the first close to the ground and the latter some two metres higher. The sounds that Antti played with this instrument were mixed through a computer program.

I was impressed by the visualisations Toni had made of his ideas. Antti's musical instrument, in turn, affected me even in my dreams. I dreamt that he had constructed a wall-size-poster-kind-of-sandpaper-construction anybody could touch and create music with. However, I was a bit perplexed about the ways in which the three of us worked. Antti and Toni seemed to be able to present quite exact and concrete material already. For a moment I felt inadequate and considered the bodily medium excruciatingly vague and contingent.

Even if I acknowledged that we all began our work from ideas that we found interesting and allowed them to push us into the concrete act of producing something tangible, visible and audible, I began thinking about our mediums and their technological nature. Don Ihde's line of reasoning helped me to gain some insight into my experience and even a slight envy of the tools Antti and Toni worked with. He suggests that:

> we can 'read' or 'see' ourselves by means of, or through, or with our
> artifacts. We can – in technological culture – fantasize ways in which
> we get beyond our physical limitations... In this mode of technofantasy,
> our technologies become our idols and overcome our finitude.
>
> (Ihde, 2002: xiii)

I guess I would have enjoyed getting out of my body and being able to construct something altogether new. Now I had to rely on what, through my life, my body and dancing had become, which at moments feels all too familiar. However, what Ihde further argues is that technical devices extend the polymorphism of bodily possibilities and that the ultimate goal of virtual embodiment is to become a multisensory bodily action. So far, monosensory, either visual or audio, media have dominated the scene. (Ihde, 2002: 7–8, 9) Antti's and Toni's expressive mediums could be viewed as being monosensory ones. Their devices and medium offer restrictions to what they can present, just as my body with its habits restricts my performance. Obviously they do this while they also allow for performative possibilities. Slight deviations from the familiar can offer paths for change and discovery.

In fact, in its habits the human body incorporates different kinds of techniques through which it operates in its daily activities. It likewise contains a virtual dimension. Ihde opines that the image-body is a virtual body through a non-technological projection. In his view, these projections can radically change our situation and our sense of our own bodies. (Ibid.: 5, 7) With a similar line of thinking, Foster argues that dance-related practices utilise two dimensions of the body: dancers perceive their bodies and do this through certain perspectives. The former is about understanding the lived and motional nature of bodily actions, while the latter relates to an imagined ideal. (Foster, 1997: 237–238) Dancers imagine possible movement sequences, and focus upon their body to perceive how their bodies accomplish them, and while the body does so they identify their projections in their bodily performance. However, a bodily act never fully achieves a body ideal, which is affiliated with completeness and leaves nothing to be desired. The body responds in its own way by producing unimagined, even unwanted, results, and the imagined projection remains incompletely realised. (Weiss, 1999a: 1, 21; 1999b: 131; Merleau-Ponty, 1962: 100) Perhaps this relates to the sense of vagueness I felt in front of Antti's and Toni's more technological approach. I imagined that they could achieve something more determinate through their work than I could – an illusion.

Nonetheless, I still felt I could not proceed any further with my work, unless I concretely improvised together with Antti and Toni. I had no preset ideas as to where I would like my dancing to end up. I was eager to explore with the few movement themes I had chosen and to allow more to emerge as I entered into a bodily dialogue with their work.

Let's See What Comes Out of This

I started our first workshop by working with Antti. Toni could join us only later in the week. What we did first was to clean the studio space that had been given for our use at the Theatre Academy. It was a recording studio approximately 50 square metres in size. Then Antti began setting up his sound equipment and I marked a space, which I imagined resembled the size of the platform Toni had planned, on the floor with white tape. Antti placed his equipment on the floor next to the 'dance space' I had outlined. He played some music for me to gain a picture of how he modified the sounds he produced with his instrument through the computer. Then we improvised together for the first time.

> I walked on the border of the dance space. I mimicked walking with different parts of my body, fingers on the floor, lying on my side and moving forward like an undulating amoeba. Antti's music made me move in a rather minimalist and fine-tuned manner, emphasizing each new movement by stopping in between, utilizing secluded body parts in movement. Afterwards, Antti pointed out how the newly fashioned loudspeakers together with the sounds he played created an atmosphere of a large space. I began to think about my rather inward focus. Should I perhaps try to use a mode of projecting, directing my motion more into outer space than I had?

During the week we continued our collaboration in the studio in a somewhat similar fashion: exploring our own practice, improvising together and talking about what we did and experienced. The second day, Antti fine-tuned his instrument and I explored movement material on my own. It felt good to work on our own tasks together in the same studio.

> *Moving body shapes, statues – stillness in shape, position. Remaining in one place in one stance.*

> *I dance with my arms a lot – there is a lot of movement in my arms, fingers... Could I dance with my legs in a similar way, too?*

At the end of the day we wondered about how to make our very concentrated effort accessible to the audience. We questioned whether beginning the performance by arranging things and warming up in an everyday manner would help the audience to settle into a comfortable interaction with us. We also wondered whether talking would offer a relaxed or open atmosphere. But we also acknowledged the difficulty of talking spontaneously while dancing or playing music. So for the next day I took with me George Perec's book *Species of Spaces and Other Pieces* in Finnish. While I danced, Antti both played his music and read a section of Perec's text aloud.

> *Text by George Perec, words by Antti, muffled human sounds including echoed walking and talk emanate from the loudspeakers. Me walking around... more and more awkwardly... jerky movement – means stillness in between, a chance to listen, become aware, searching, uncertain movement, carefulness, bound flow, demonstrating spatial distances and spatial relations – pointing outwards, projection, space between body parts... erasing, pointing, measuring, showing... Perec's words on parking*

a car have an effect on my doing, uncannily I demonstrate actions, shutting
a door, walking away from the car... Then the words stop leaving a silent
mumble intact... intensity amplifies... I find myself on my knees fiercely
paddling my arms backwards...

In discussing our experience we both noticed how a new space of perception
had opened as one of the performative elements was left behind. When Antti
stopped reading Perec's text and only his music and my dance remained, it felt
as if a reorientation had occurred, a curious but intriguing questioning. We
both noticed this shift. In fact, we wondered if we had hit upon some dramatic
principle or convention of the performing arts more generally. For me something
else happened, too.

I was interested by a new theme of movement that came about in the
improvisation: measuring space with my movements and body parts...

'It is very difficult to conceive of time and space as distinct elements,
because measuring space always involves measuring time and vice versa.
Time is measured through movement that occurs in space. The ancient
Persians measured distance by using the concept of *parsang*, by which
was meant the journey a man travelled on foot within an hour'.
(Van Kerkhoven, 1993: 25 – trans. L.R.)

Measuring and walking do connect!

In addition to measuring space, I kept to my basic movement theme, walking,
throughout our workshop.

Stopping into stillness, commencing again, how the sole of the foot touches
the floor, in what possible ways and angles can it do so? What happens
to my spine, rotating shoulders swinging or stiff arms? How do my fingers
walk? What other area can I rotate other than my spine and shoulders and
to what extent? What catches my eyes when I walk? Where is my focus
and head directed to... inward, outward, up down, sideways, forward? Is
my gaze open, receiving and communicative, or closed, thoughtful?

'To walk is to lack a place. It is the indefinite process of being absent
and in search of a proper'.
(De Certeau, 1988: 103)

And we were undertaking our quest with some origins in urban space.

'The ordinary practitioners of the city live "down below", below the
thresholds at which visibility begins. They walk – an elementary form

of this experience of the city; they are walkers. *Wandersmänner*, whose bodies follow the thicks and thins of urban "text" they write without being able to read it. These practitioners make use of spaces that cannot be seen; their knowledge of them is as blind as that of lovers in each other's arms. The paths that correspond in this intertwining, unrecognized poems in which each body is an element signed by many others, elude legibility'.

(De Certeau, 1988: 93)

On the third day, Toni began collaborating with us. He set up his computer and video equipment and built a high tower from unused loudspeaker stands so that the video could be projected from above onto the floor. When he was done, Antti and I improvised with a structure that emanated from utilising Perec's text. Afterwards we had an intense discussion about the manner in which we ought to be working. Antti and I were already trying out some structural ideas. Toni wanted a more experimental and open collaboration. We had originally opted to allow the unfolding process itself to determine the end result. But our eventual performances formed an ever-present background that influenced our exploration. Still, it was important to be reminded of an openness and simultaneously to acknowledge the shared goal we were working for – some kind of performances.

With Toni we covered the floor with white paper for the video images to be visible. In my dancing I became very concerned about how to relate to the projected video images. I had trouble seeing them in our improvisations. After all, they were projected onto me or onto the floor, and I could not continuously look at myself or the floor. I lost a sense of integrity in my dancing, as I tried to dance in dialogue with the images and the music. After talking with Antti and Toni, I decided to quit trying to relate consciously to what they were doing. I began searching for a more somatic orientation to my dancing again. A more spontaneous relation to Antti's and Toni's work seemed to emerge.

> *I lie on the floor on my back. My left arm hovers towards the ceiling. Fingers palpating the air. Then my fingers gather together and bend to form a loose fist. My wrist bends and my hand starts falling towards the ground as my elbow follows. My forearm drops heavily on the floor. Immediately my arm shoots back into the air again. An intense diagonal reach and tension in my arm pulls me into sitting. My body folds, my knees bend and I find myself sitting on the side of my right leg... How determined my arm was to pull my torso off the ground...*

I am on my side and lift my head to look at the rest of my body; a shadow moves across it over my legs, there is a streak of white light on my waist. I turn to look backwards to see if my body makes a shadow on the floor. It does, and pushing with my arms I allow my head to draw me into a back extension...

I walk in a circle sideways, crossing and opening my legs alternately... Invited by the music my arms open to the side... The sounds call me further and I notice that I walk outside the actual performing space and after a few paces I sit down and start watching Antti play.

During the second week Toni decided to add in another video projector and to use two computers. He had filmed and edited a bit more material. Now the white ceiling above the paper floor had moving images running over it, too. Dancing with the ceiling projections made my sense of space fuller, truly three-dimensional or actually multidimensional. There were intensities to react to all around me, the video projections above, below and on me, sound throughout the room, Toni in the front of the room, Antti on the side. I realised that the projections on the white floor and the ceiling created a highlighted performance arena as well as a kind of extended *kinesphere* for me. In our previous improvisations, on occasion, I had roamed all around the studio. Now it felt imperative to do so. I had to surpass the arena, why I am not quite sure.

In his dance or movement theory, Rudolf Laban introduced the term *kinesphere* to denote that human motional space that transcends the surface of the body and is delimited by the extensions of the limbs. The kinesphere – or as it is also called, personal space – is defined by the areas we can reach without locomoting in space. (Laban, 1966: 17; Moore and Yamamoto, 2000: 193) For us personally, it could therefore be viewed as having something to do with some kind of familiarity or at least accessibility. (Casey, 1998: 224) In sticking to the projected spatial areas in my dancing, was I sticking to a comfort zone or working with a necessary minimalism? After all, I did explore walking through different body parts, starting from different positions, working on the floor and in upright position, moving in one place and moving all around the studio. Following some of Edmund Husserl's thoughts on kinesthesia, Casey suggests that:

> What walking introduces is the fact that I must first of all unify myself before I unify my environs. I cannot walk at all if I am utterly disjointed; to walk is to draw my body together, at least provisionally; and to do so is to constitute myself as one coherent organism.
>
> (Ibid.)

Observations and questions continued, but for now this partial and fragmentary story is ending. Carrying Antti and Toni with me, in it I have tried to convey what our early collaboration generated in me. Much was incubating and not quite relatable. Nonetheless, I think we learned to endure the incompleteness of our process as well as to offer room for, and to listen to, each other. Simultaneously, we continued questioning and re-interpreting what emerged in and between us through our collaboration. This thrust us forward.

> I have stopped my motion in order to rest, and I sit on a white paper patched on the floor for projecting video material onto. I make my observations. Toni has climbed to the top of a ladder and is fixing the video apparatus – redirecting its focus. Antti kneels to my right and peers into a computer screen while testing his equipment and playing some soft echoey sounds every now and then. Quiet concentration. Our tiny and soundproof studio is a secluded world all of its own. Satisfied, I turn back to my motional rumination and continue exploring how differently I can walk with my fingers, arms, shoulders, hips, legs and feet and while standing, sitting, lying on my back, on my side…

SECTION 8

Practice as Research as the Dominant Orthodoxy; the Nature of Evidence

> Creativity is first of all an act of destruction.
>
> **Pablo Picasso**

As the objects of performance study have diversified, close examination of the processes and event of performance has emerged as something of an industry in itself. As a late response to the blind-date marriage of phenomenology and postmodernism, scholars and practitioners alike have created a drift towards a state wherein performances can no longer be seen to exist without reference to the spectatorial debates that frame them. This in its own turn has given rise to the establishment of certain types of practical work assuming, and being granted, status as university-sanctioned research activities.

This is not to suggest that the linking of research with performance is anything new. The twentieth century saw numerous practitioners whose work was highly practical in outcome at the same time as the investigative and research qualities were clear to see... and not just in hindsight. These researching practitioners – and we can think immediately of luminaries such as Stanislavski, Meyerhold, Brecht, Grotowski, Barba and Brook – created a legacy of intelligent and often intellectually vital work that did much to shape their own time and ours. What differs now is the sheer scale of practice-based research. That which was once in the sole domain of some of the world's greatest thinkers and makers in their chosen theatrical forms now peppers the pages of countless curriculum vitae; and regarding oneself (or at least *describing* oneself) as a practising researcher is an increasingly commonplace type of catch-all activity.

A consequence of this is a feeling of saturation, with a great many university department staff pages proclaiming the view that any and all practice is practice as research and that every member of staff is a researching practitioner. It is not easy to locate the point at which so many of us began to reinvent previous practical work as research activity, but it is hard to avoid the sense that this is so from the claims being made. Now, some of this work is and was undoubtedly research-driven; but I suspect that just as undoubtedly much of it is and was not. If evidence is required in support of this I can put forward much of my own back catalogue of early practice, none of which was in any significant way research-driven at source and almost all of which I have subsequently found myself describing in relatively straight-faced research terms that have been steeped deep in interview-speak exaggeration.

If we have reached the point where any practical endeavour, from directing an end of year production to dimming the lights and altering one's voice in order to give a conference paper, is being regarded (and submitted) as practice-based research activity then the small world in which we function would appear to have gone a little mad and those of us who function as the by-proxy gatekeepers have conspired fully in the madness. No surprise to Alvis Hermanis, who concludes after a 25-year period of fully participatory observation that theatre attracts 'people with mental problems'. (Hermanis, 2008: 9) Appropriateness notwithstanding, the extent to which Hermanis has his tongue in his cheek (or not) is not for us to know, but his words, provocatively indelicate in intent, strike something of a chord. Should each and every performance from the past be reinvented as a research project? Should we be blithely re-defining every playwright, director, designer and actor that's ever been as a researching practitioner?

Bizarre as this sounds (although I am aware that to some it does not sound bizarre at all) this is already happening. It happens every time we tidy up a curriculum vitae and decide that the performance we happened to devise ten years ago was more than that; it happens every time we talk up or invent the research importance of a twentieth-century theatre project we might well have embarrassed ourselves in, or a television camera we perhaps ambled awkwardly in front of; it happens every time we project the myth (and project it so ardently that we begin to believe it ourselves) that we were engaged in high-quality research endeavours even without knowing that such was the case, as though the retrospective application of a label somehow makes it so. It is an act of self-delusional profile-raising that would be laughable if it were not so prevalent. And how many among us can enter a genuine plea of Not Guilty to these charges? As the previous paragraph shows, certainly I cannot. And there is a very good reason why hordes of us buy into and propagate the illusion. We do so because it has become rare to find an advertisement for a full-time UK lecturing post in Theatre, Drama or Performance that does not make such great play of practice as research that to locate ourselves as other than accomplished in this is seen at best to denigrate the quality of our work and at worst to appear naïve and out of touch with contemporary developments. And those brave, confident and honest enough to risk these calumnies are seriously under-represented on the job-interview circuit, as they are when they apply for promotion or tenure, research leave, sabbatical or publishing contract. Not every lecturer is as honest as Franc Chamberlain, who states that whilst he is committed to the making of performances, 'Sometimes these performances have a research imperative, sometimes not.' (Thomson, 2003: 162)

Chamberlain's words are in accord with those issued by SCUDD (albeit as far back as 1998) where a proposal was made that 'while it should be acknowledged that high quality creative work (including professional practice) is undertaken that might qualify as research, there is other work, however "well researched", that might not'. (Piccini, 2004: 192)

As Simon Jones sees it, the symbiotic relationship between an engagement with practice as research and the enhancing of one's subsequent employability is a positive move, signalling as it does an end to those mutually exclusive boundaries that saw practice as always somehow subservient to published critique:

> The candidates most sought after for posts in performance studies in the rather buoyant jobs market fall into two clear categories. Those young academics emerging from practice-based doctoral work, whose experience has been within the logic of performance studies; whose natural and reasonable ambition is to research and teach through practice. Or artists who are entirely at home with submitting their practice to the reflective and critical discourses at work in the academy.

> (Jones, 2003: 5–6)

Jones' words are in no way incorrect, but they do perhaps reveal a little more than they intend. If we look at the statement from an outsider's perspective (i.e. outside of the practice-as-research orthodoxy) the opportunities for Jones' 'young academics' who do *not* emerge from practice-based work start to look bleak indeed, with intimations of a barely concealed closed-shop recruitment. More than this, if the ambition to teach and research through practice is normal and reasonable, then the implication follows that teaching and researching in other ways is at once abnormal and unreasonable. As we will see with the section on autoethnography that follows our next case study, the urge to state one's case with conviction can lead to a sweeping dismissal that sits awkwardly within the humanist liberal arts ideology of respectful tolerance for alternative views. That there has been a shift in the axis of power at universities is clear to see; but this power could be usefully tempered with understanding that there are more ways than one to pursue knowledge of one's subject, and that practice as research does not hold a monopoly on scholarship. It is worth remembering as well that for most of us, in the UK certainly, our embrace of Performance Studies had at least as much to do with the books and articles we had read as with the practical work we saw: a state that leads some of us to wonder at what point words on the page become a burden to understanding.

In terms of performance study, we can trace ruptures between words about and words for, and between articulation and experience, to the point where academic scholarship in the subject began to throw off its status as literary add-on. We have become increasingly and justifiably confident in our collective assertions that a history of making work impacts on seeing and of understanding performance as an event in itself. In the same way we have rehearsed our somewhat less justifiable arguments that appreciation of performance is something denied to those approaching drama first and foremost as an object written rather than as an event done. Our new(er) argument, and it is one with even less justification, is that performance studies sees systems of writing as inadequate... and that only through performance itself can we begin to 'exceed the fixity and encapsulation that characterize categorical language.' (Greiner and Assumpção, 2009)

Jones' statement about prioritising practice-based research is given credence by recent advertisements such as this from Royal Holloway, University of London (February 2009). In a call for applications for the position of Associate Professor in Drama, the copy reads:

> This post offers an outstanding opportunity for a senior academic with
> an international profile in practice-based research to take a leadership
> role in a department of dynamic scholars. The department is entering
> an exciting new phase in its development in which practice as research
> will take a central role.

In the contexts of phraseology such as this it is easy to forget that practice as research is one approach among many. And it is this: an *approach*... a way of dealing with a particular research problem at a particular time in a particular way. It is a mind-set switched on for a specific activity or series of activities. In this way, P-a-R is a selective and hopefully appropriate methodology, not a life choice.

Whilst shifts in research focus such as those articulated by Greiner and Assumpção have called attention to practice, which seems both logical and right for our subject, this can be problematic when the results we are offered are akin to athletes basing books around the feelings they experience when participating in sports. Interesting as reports like these may be, it is not easy to see what turns, indeed what *can* turn a description of experience into a thesis with anything approaching verifiable findings. In fact, research undertaken by and on athletes is almost invariably scientific in terms of data collection and measurement. What it is that is argued through the findings may be contentious (one could almost say that it needs to be contentious) but the processes undertaken *en route* to conclusions need to be rigorous and transparent. The idea that a thesis investigating athletic performance might involve a boxing match or round of golf in lieu of 40,000 words of written analysis is hard to imagine, and yet this is precisely what we get when the focus is on theatre performance. This is, of course, an arguable point, and nobody working through theatre practice as a research process would accept the idea that the suggestion is anything other than crudely reductive. And yet, potentially limiting though it may be, the parallels are there for all to see.

Gabriel Egan is aware of this when he notes that in Sports Science 'it's not enough (nor, indeed, even necessary) to do the running, jumping, swinging etc., but rather one has to be able to collect and impart knowledge about these activities. A really good high jump would not, I think, meet most people's criteria for "research", whereas a thesis/book about the diet and training regime that made it possible probably would.' (Thomson, 2003: 173) Indeed, as Neil Beasley, writing from experience gained as Senior Performance and Improvement Manager at Sport England confirms, 'sports scientists spend many hours in front of computer screens digitising athletes' joint centres in order to run biomechanical analysis.' (Beasley, 2009) This is done, logically enough, in order to provide both athletes and coaches with significant data on the internal and external forces that act upon the human body. Beasley continues: 'Exercise physiologists go to great lengths to determine which variables differ between mediocre and great performers; these measurements are subsequently investigated in order to adjust training techniques, manipulate the movement execution and improve performance.' (Ibid.) Despite differences of physiology and aesthetics, these levels of applicatory investigation set high aspirational standards for practice-based theatre performance.

If submitting practice is a choice, reflecting on practice is a given: every performative decision is in some ways always already an act of reflection even when that reflection is subconscious or seemingly intuitive. Reflective practice is also problematic, not least when the practice in question is one's own. Reading the self is an elusive exercise, precisely because there is no one self to read and because the selves of the maker, the reader and the writer will not drop easily and uncomplainingly into compartments labelled *id, ego* and *super-ego*. Long experience has shown us that the employment of the personal, evidenced in reflective writing, need not function at the expense of a wider and more generic publication of knowledge. The relationship is one of collusion rather than collision, with the necessary critical discourse being at once contained *within* and exercised *through* the product itself. Research which leads in intended ways towards advanced understandings is given credibility by its inclusion into new or newly articulated ways of working: the process is then intrinsically developmental and progressive. As art influences art, rather then being hermetically sealed and untouchable, so research influences research. Reflective research is determined by readings, writings, thoughts and actions, which are determined by their own creators' histories and influences.

Performance consists of a series of broadly recognisable conventions, and conventions are the stuff of tradition. Inasmuch as we can say that progressive practitioners (in whichever field they operate) seek to free themselves and their work from the shackles of tradition, they will often do so by locating their own processes within the work of other, similarly minded makers. Thus one set of traditions is exchanged for another. What this means is that radical developments, truly original examples of practice, are rare indeed. The progressive practitioner is engaged in a dialogue not with the past so much as with her or his own interpretations of the past, alongside those of a host of other practitioners. In this way the fixed sequence of the past is challenged. It is challenged inasmuch as one of the unspoken tenets of progressive performance practice is an attack on the very idea that the glories of the past can be preserved in new work by the inculcation in any one spectator of theatre memory as reverence.

If the maker's self is more than a filter through which influence and invention coalesce into practice, what then might it mean to show oneself through practice, to make oneself both performatively and analytically visible, to offer oneself up in order to be read as 'subject'? Michel de Montaigne's *To the Reader* reveals an introduction to a number of key issues here, issues for which his text also provides explicit illustration. (Frame, 2003)

Montaigne's writings of 1580–1581 include an extensive justification for devoting a book to the 'trivial topic' of himself. Whilst admitting that his topic was relatively unimportant, he argued that this was offset by the fact that he knew his subject so much better any other author could hope to know his. Montaigne's implication was that knowledge of one's self was the most complete and perfect form of understanding. Because that which Montaigne describes is more than (just) an introduction to the idea of the self-reflexivity of his and our time; it also speaks to us of the ego of the artist. The signature of the artist, we might say, is not placed as is usual in visual art practices at the bottom right-hand corner of the work, at the last point at which the Western eye, conditioned to the reading of a page from top to bottom and from left to right, will ever reach: the last word in every sense. Neither is the author's name on the front cover, spine and title page of the work, clearly visible yet always part of the frame rather than the work. With Montaigne's statement that he was the subject of his own work the signature, the author's name, is at once enunciator and enunciated: the subject of the maker takes for itself the position of subject-proper, both part of the frame and also that which is being framed.

The comments here are quite overtly presupposing application to a particular type of work, the type of work indeed where one's self, or one of one's selves, is made into the work's theme, and the autobiographical and/or autoethnographical aspects of these approaches will be discussed as we move through the next section's pages. To a large extent, however, the complexities of reading one's own practice are there for any of us who make study of our own working processes, whether these are primarily interpretative or compositional, whether they serve the creation of the self-as-text, deal with extant published material or are concerned with development through collective application. The key question then is not what type of work is one reflecting upon so much as how accurate can one's act of self-reflection ever be?

CASE STUDY 8

Performing with Trees: Landscape and Artistic Research[1]

Annette Arlander

Performing landscape is the overall theme of my ongoing research project in which I try to explore how to perform landscape today. Through performing landscape I have for instance tried to show time take place. While performing a still-act[2] in front of a video camera, the events taking place in the background, in the landscape, can come to the fore. When repeating this with regular intervals during long periods of time and by condensing the material by editing, the slow happenings (or abrupt changes) not discernible in real time can be seen and shown.

Generally I use a three-stage working method for performing landscape on video. Firstly I repeat a still-act or a simple action in the same place in front of a video camera with the same camera positioning, with regular intervals during long periods of time. Secondly I condense the material by editing, preserving the chronological order, but choosing only a fragment of the action and using various durations. Thirdly I combine several video works to form an installation or exhibition in a specific space. For the fourth stage (the research part), I describe the work and reflect upon some aspect of the material (the videos, the working notes and the documentation from the exhibition) in relation to some question or some concept from another field and write about it for a research context. The still-act, for instance, borrowed from anthropology and dance studies.[3]

The above working method is in itself quasi-systematic. The data gathered by video documentation could be used as research for a study in weather and climate changes, for instance. But they do not really tell about performing landscape, except as a form of demonstration, an example: 'You could do it in this way'. However, I prefer to use my art work as research data, rather than as a demonstration of research outcomes, perhaps because I want to be free in creating the work, and to choose what aspect to reflect upon afterwards. 'In the artistic research experience studies experience, producing new experiences.' (Hannula et al., 2005: 59)

In the following I am discussing performing landscapes with trees, based on a presentation written in response to the question 'what strategies and forms of performance do working with landscape as a medium inspire or necessitate?'[4] I propose that the action or position of the performer easily turns the focus away from the environment. Or alternatively, makes the performer completely indistinguishable. However, a blurring of the boundary between subject and environment can be created, from the point of view of the spectator, I have to add.

The trees I have performed with in recent years are five all in all: one birch tree, three pine trees and a spruce. Three of them are situated on the island of Harakka in Helsinki, two are growing on Koivumäki (Birch hill) in Kalvola, 120 km northwest from Helsinki. The works created with them and used as examples are: *Sitting on a Birch* (2006), *Year of the Dog in Kalvola – Calendar* (2007), *Year of the Dog – Sitting in a Tree* (2007), *Day and Night of the Dog* (2007), *Shadow of a Pine I–IV* (2007) and *Under the Spruce I–III* (2008). I will try to look at how the relationship between the tree and the human performer shifts in these projects, from being a background or support for the human protagonist, like the birch, to being the leading character with the human figure invisible, as in the case of the spruce.

Background

Performing with trees has not been a central occupation of mine. I was prompted to look at the trees I have engaged with while trying out various ways of performing landscape, thanks to a presentation at the PSi conference in Copenhagen 2008.[5] Dee Heddon showed a documentation of a performance where she was standing with a tree leaning against her shoulder, or that is how I remember it. My exercises with trees have been more conventional. There is a tradition of protecting trees through various activist actions in Finland, a country dependent on its forest industry. The Koijärvi movement of the '70s – where young people, some of whom later formed the green party in Finland, protested against the destruction of a forest by chaining themselves to trees – had recently been discussed in the main Finnish newspaper.[6] An event which I did not take part in: I was a good family girl studying theatre at the time.

My own history with trees starts with fiction. A radio play in three parts, *Keijut (Fairies) I–IV*, from 1999, based on Irish fairytales and visits to Annaghmakerrig, Donegal and the Aran islands, had the protagonists named after trees. They were, according to the druidic tree horoscope, based on the birth dates of William Butler Yeats (William White Poplar), Samuel Beckett (Samuel Sycamore) and Seamus Heaney (Seamus Rowan) as well as myself (Ann Fir), translated into Finnish, as Ville Valkopyökki, Samuli Vaahtera, Janne Pihlaja and Anne Pihtakuusi.[7]

A more recent (still ongoing) project where individual trees have been involved, 'in person' as it were, is called *Puut Puhuvat (Trees Talk)*, and consists of small monologues. The first trees talking on Harakka island – a birch, a rowan, an ash, an alder and a sycamore – were speaking Finnish for more than two months during the summer 2003.[8] At the ANTI Contemporary Art Festival in Kuopio in 2004,[9] some trees in Minnan Puisto Park – an oak, a sycamore (again) a linden tree, a pine tree, and a black fir – were not talking many hours before the headphones were stolen. At an outdoor exhibition in Helsinki created with MA students of performance art and theory, a willow tree had a chance to speak a little longer in April 2006. And during the summer 2008 in an environmental art exhibition *Taiteen Tiet – Hiidentie* (*The Ways of Art – Old Gnome's Way*), along an ancient country road in the Salo region, with the next group of students, two apple trees (one by the road side, the other near an old mill) had longer speeches of approximately half an hour. This rather theatrical or fictional way of performing landscape, using trees to hang stories on, I nevertheless still hope to continue with, and find talkative examples of all of the trees or bushes in the tree alphabet (beth-luis-nion).[10] In the following I will shortly describe the first version of the project, which set the tone for the rest of the series.

Performing as Trees

The first *Puut puhuvat* (*Trees Talk*) consisted of five monologues, presented in the outdoor exhibition called *Reviiri – taidepolku* (*Territory – Art Path*) arranged by the artists' association on Harakka island in July–September 2003. The five stories could be listened to with headphones in five different places, from five different trees, along the path. After compiling and writing the texts, I read, recorded and edited them and arranged the presentation. The technique was simple and the production costs minimal. The stories were played non-stop on small CD-players and audible through headphones. They were presented in a contemporary art context, though outside in the summer time, but they were not visual art, not really audio art (since mainly text), not really performance art (since recorded). Perhaps you could call them site-specific audio plays.

The 'art path' of the summer exhibition arranged by the artists on Harakka followed the existing nature path, which was created in order to protect the fragile areas. *Trees Talk* was one of the works placed along the path. On the poster it was presented as follows: 'Today we say ABC, once the alphabet was birch, rowan, ash, (beth, luis, nion) and alder... The talk of trees and talk about trees.' The trees could be heard talking from headphones hanging from the branches. The CD-players were hidden at the roots or in the foliage and they played five monologues non-stop for two and a half months. I chose the trees so I could get electricity by cable. Information was provided on small cards hanging next to the headphones, and the main sources listed: Robert Graves, *The White Goddess* (Noonday Press,

1990, orig. 1948); Roisin Carroll, *The Crane Bag* (Irish Ogham Publications, 1997); Reija-Tuulia Heinonen-Rivasto, *Druidien puuhoroskooppi* [the Druids' tree horoscope] (Ateena-kustannus, 1997). The text fragments were translated into Finnish and transformed into first-person narration. In addition to some botanical facts they consisted of historical and cultural information (Graves), advice on the spiritual path addressed to the listener (Carroll) and psychological characterisations (Heinonen-Rivasto).

According to Graves, the fourth letter of the beth-luis-nion (birch-rowan-ash) alphabet was alder and the fifth was oak. I included the sycamore, though it does not belong to the beth-luis-nion, because there is only one growing on the island and it is beautifully situated, whereas the two oaks are tiny and insignificantly placed. Rowans and birches abound; the only ashes grow at the corner of the so-called nature house; and all the alders – exceptionally old and beautiful, the pride of the island – are concentrated in the southern part, far from potential sources of electricity. In the end the talking trees were (following the path and not the alphabet): the Ash by the nature house, the Alder on the eastern shore, the Rowan in the north west, the Birch in the north and the Sycamore on the hill in the centre between the houses.

The monologues were short (5 x 4–6 minutes). The structure of all of them was roughly the same: first a short presentation – 'My name is Betula, though around here they call me Birch'; then some advice addressed to the listener – 'I will help you when you are about to start something new'; then some history – 'in ancient times evil spirits were expelled by beating with birch twigs'; and in the end some personal psychological talk – 'according to my friends I am graceful, sophisticated and reserved...'. The texts were compiled in a hurry and I was not really happy with them. However, more important than *what* the trees were saying was the fact *that* they spoke. Although the work was shallow, it was surprisingly well received as information and as a gesture.

In this work the starting point was not my own experience, but playing and fantasy: what would a birch (or a rowan, ash, alder or sycamore) say if it could speak? What would it sound like? My own experiences were completely downplayed. Actors could have read the monologues, without significantly changing the meaning of the work; it was not important who the interpreter was. The fact that the trees were talking, had a personality, feelings, character traits, cultural history etc. in short, extending human needs, values and qualities to concern trees, was regarded as a statement, anthropocentric or not. Because of the fictional dimension, the work was rather theatrical, and could be regarded as an entertainment–statement. The trees did not speak environmental politics, did not demand the right to vote etc. *Trees Talk* was a fiction, almost a fairy tale. Compared with, for instance, recording their sound or registering their movement in the wind, the trees functioned more like puppets. The monologues were based on facts and conveyed cultural information, but described neither my experience of the trees nor the trees' experiences of me or of their environment. They were stories and addressed to the listener, explicitly 'as if' trees would talk.

To illustrate the paradoxical in the situation, my interaction with the landscape could be compared to a similar attitude towards people. What if instead of trees, I'd gathered people from five different ethnic groups, collected some legends once attached to them by others, transformed those into monologues and demanded the people to present those texts in my own language, or asked them to sway gently in the background while I performed the texts myself? Regardless of this paradox, I was trying to take up the challenge presented by Italo Calvino at the end of *Six Memos for the Next Millennium*, and interpreting the challenge literally, naively, if you wish:

> Think what it would be to have a work conceived from outside the self,
> a work that would let us escape the limited perspective of the individual
> ego, not only to enter into selves like our own but to give speech to that
> which has no language, to the bird perching on the edge of the gutter,
> to the tree in spring and the tree in fall, to stone, to cement, to plastic...
> (Calvino, 1993: 124)

Performer and Environment

In some of my recent attempts at performing landscape by means of video, trees played a prominent part in a different way. They will be used as examples in order to discuss the problem of the performer–landscape or performer–environment relationship.

As a reference point and framework for my reflections, I present some formulations by Baz Kershaw in his *Theatre Ecology* (2007), though these works were created for a visual-art context. One of the key aspects of his study is the realisation that humanity must sense itself as part of a 'performance commons' that it shares with all organisms, as well as the 'environmental commons' such as air, water and soil. (Kershaw, 2007: 14) The relationship between artist and landscape or performer and environment, even the use of those notions in opposition, is part of the legacy of modernism and the 'enlightenment' which placed nature and culture, 'man' and 'environment' against each other in a potentially disastrous opposition. (Ibid.: 15)

Kershaw starts with the common understanding of ecology as 'the interrelationships of all the organic and non-organic factors of ecosystems' and 'the interrelationship between organisms and their environments, especially when that is understood to imply interdependence between organism and environments.' (Ibid.: 15) He maintains that performances in all their manifestations involve the interrelational interdependence of 'organisms-in-environments', or, following deep ecologist Arne Naess, constitute 'a relational total field' in which everything is interdependent and cannot easily be assigned to clear distinctions. He uses the obvious example of eating, through which we become part of our environment, or, the environment becomes part of us. (Ibid.: 16)

There are complicated interdependencies between every element of a performance event and its environment and, as he notes based on his own practical experiences, the smallest change to one factor of a performance will effect change in all the rest. And more importantly, a 'theatrical performance is not a system that is different *in kind* from other ecological systems, though of course like them has its own peculiar characteristics.' (Ibid.: 24) This is obviously the case also with less-complicated performance systems, like actions built around a camera, a human being and a tree.

According to Kershaw, the 'foundational contradictions of theatrical performance' – such as 'that it is both real and not real, i.e. it exists always in an ontologically subjunctive mode' or 'that it is both ephemeral and durable, i.e. it exists always in a transitive mode where one state implies another to come' – make performance 'in many if not in all of its manifestations a paradoxical affair'. (Ibid.: 25) However, in terms of performing, whether in daily life, in front of an audience or for a witnessing camera, the distinction between what is the performer and what is the environment is mostly quite clear, at least for the performer herself. I am aware of what is a part of me and what is not me while embedded in the landscape, aware of my dependency or even emotionally merging with it. From a spectator's point of view, however, the situation can be different.

Kershaw discusses Gregory Bateson's famous idea of a change from the individual, family line, subspecies, or species as units of survival into a different hierarchy of units, like gene-in-organism, organism-in-environment, ecosystems and so on. 'Ecology in the widest sense turns out to be the study of the interaction and survival of ideas and programs (i.e. differences, complexes of differences, etc.) in circuits.' (Bateson, 1972: 49, quoted in Kershaw, 2007: 24–25) In his version of ecosophy further developed in *The Three Ecologies*, Félix Guattari maintained that the ecology of the mental, the ecology of the social and the ecology of the environment must be thought of as interrelated and inseparable.

(Guattari, 2000: 53) According to Kershaw this implies a paradox as a fount of knowledge for ecology itself. (Kershaw, 2007: 25) He quotes Bateson's example from 'Pathologies of Epistemology':

> You decide that you want to get rid of the products by human life and that Lake Erie will be a good place to put them. You forget that the eco-mental system called Lake Erie is part of *your* wider eco-mental system – and that if Lake Erie is driven insane, its insanity is incorporated in the larger system of *your* thought and experience.
>
> (Bateson, 2000: 492, quoted in Kershaw, 2007: 247)

Understanding thinking as a process that takes place in the natural world as well, he explains that an idea is a 'difference' operating as part of a structure of circuits. 'The difference – let's say between "hot" and "cold" – enables these circuits to work as a system in which "self-correctiveness" or trial and error becomes possible.' (Kershaw, 2007: 247–248) The feedback produced by trial and error in these systems will push them either towards a state of equilibrium, or to 'runaway', a state of self-harm. There is no point in separating organism and environment since according to systemic thinking they are aspects of the same system. In the words of Bateson: 'What thinks is the total system which engages in trial and error... The unit of survival is *organism* plus *environment*.' (Bateson, 1972: 16–17, quoted in Kershaw, 2007: 248)

Along the same lines, Félix Guattari claimed (in 1989) that nature cannot be separated from culture: in order to comprehend the interactions between ecosystems, we must learn to think transversally. (Guattari, 2000: 54 quoted in Kershaw, 2007: 249) He criticised Bateson's theory, however, for its conception of context as encompassing action, like in organism + environment (action + context), whereas, according to him, an active 'rupture', can transform the contextual system 'as it takes it on'. And this seems meant to merge rational thought and imaginative intervention, Kershaw explains. (Kershaw, 2007: 249) For him transversal thinking is paradoxical, and as Guattari exclaimed, 'no one is exempt from playing the game of the ecology of the imaginary!' (Guattari, 2000: 57, quoted in Kershaw, 2007: 249) So he responds by offering his thought experiments as a kind of ecology of the imaginary.

In some sense you could say most art is providing exactly that, imaginary options, possible models. So what should we imagine today? How could we perform landscape in a way that does not strengthen the dangerous fantasy of a self-sufficient subject being fully independent and ontologically severed from the world?[11] How could we express or make explicit, explicitate (to use the term of Peter Sloterdjik, adopted by Bruno Latour)[12] the interrelationship and interdependence between human beings and the environment, performer and landscape, me and a tree?

As humans we are totally imbued with earth's biosphere, and cannot survive without it. So how could we possibly access a critical perspective that would be beyond it? How can we solve a problem whose solution is another version of itself? After presenting this recursive dilemma or vicious circle, Kershaw brings in Po-chang's ox and paradox. 'Asked about seeking the Buddha–nature Po-chang says. "It's much like riding an ox in search of the ox!" The quest is a search for itself.' (Kershaw, 2007: 52) This is the dilemma not only of the artist–researcher who is mixing the object, method and outcome of research, but for all who study landscapes in the midst of them.

Performing with Trees

By performing landscape with trees I have tried to move beyond my previous way of performing landscape by being *in* an environment – which I of course also am doing – and to understand landscape in a more material way. While sitting on a birch I was sitting on a birch, but now, looking at the work in retrospect, I can try to understand what kind of approach to the performer–environment relationship (or action plus context-problem) or the nature–culture split that work implies and perhaps unknowingly propagates... This kind of self-imaging (to use the term of Amelia Jones)[13] is a kind of ecology of the imaginary as well, or at least a thought experiment or 'model' of that relationship, regardless of intention.

In performing landscape the human figure easily becomes the main thing and the landscape recedes into the background to serve as scenery, as a backdrop. Performing landscape comes to mean performing in the landscape. In order to search for alternatives to this predicament, I want to look at some attempts where I chose a specific element in the landscape to work with, to perform with, in a more co-existing sense; that is, a tree. Instead of performer and environment we could then look at performer and co-performer, in this case a tree, where the tree comes to stand as a representative of the environment, as an entity on a more 'equal footing' with a human being.

On the basis of my examples, which I will shortly describe in the following, we could preliminarily distinguish three modes of use:

- A tree as support (to sit on, to hang from, to lean on) as in *Sitting on a Birch* or *Year of the Dog in Kalvola – Calendar* (see Images 1 and 2).

- A tree as co-performer or 'neighbour' to share with (to lie next to, to sit with, be a shadow of) as in *Shadow of a Pine I–IV* (see Images 3 and 4).

- A tree as shelter (to sit in, to hide under) as in *Year of the Dog – Sitting in a tree* and *Day and Night of the Dog* as well as *Under the Spruce I–III* (see Images 5, 6 and 7).

If we speak of blurring of the boundary between performer and environment, that means blurring the boundary between performer and support, performer and co-performer or performer and shelter. This is relevant mainly from the point of view of the spectator. As a performer I can experience some kind of interconnectedness with my environment and imagine a kind of shared existence with a tree, but I certainly do know the boundary between me and the tree, there is no real dissolving taking place from my point of view. That merging is a semi-fictional construction produced on video.

To develop the three alternatives – support, sharing, shelter – we could perhaps distinguish three different approaches to the relationship between performer and environment more generally:

- Contrast or contradiction where the human figure stands out from the environment through movement, by performing an action or by providing an opposing colour in the landscape.

- Confluence or sharing, where the human figure seems to dissolve into the environment to some extent, by participating in the relative immobility of the elements in a landscape, sharing the changes of the seasons and the weather with them.

- Camouflage or chameleon-like disappearance, where the human figure is hidden and can no longer be distinguished in the landscape.

Playing with words, we could call these strategies contrast, confluence and camouflage or why not differing from, dialoguing with, and dissolving into the landscape. And of course all these terms open up a whole set of new questions. Nevertheless, in all of my examples the performer is clearly distinguished from the environment. There is no real blurring of the boundary, no merging with the landscape, except in a visual sense, and no 'explicitation' of interdependence, as far as I can see.[14]

An example of contrast, of performing with a tree as support is *Sitting on a Birch*. There is no doubt the human figure is the main character. The role of the tree is to provide a fixed point to return to, a support that stays the same regardless of changes in the seasons or the weather. The birch serves as support literally, like a chair or bench to rest on. Only a small part of the tree trunk is visible. The image is framed to fit the human scale. The red scarf creates a strong contrast to the greenery or to the snow in the landscape. Emotionally, I might have experienced that I performed together with the tree, or even performed the tree in some way, but in the images the tree serves as a backdrop or scenery, almost like a prop (see Image 1).

Image 1. Still from *Sitting on a Birch*

Year of the Dog in Kalvola – Calendar belongs to the same category, though with less contrast between performer and environment. An old pine tree serves as support by providing a branch to hang from and a trunk to lean on. Turning her back to the camera makes the human figure less prominent and creates more balance, a possibility of dialogue between the human and the tree. Both are standing next to each other though only the human figure can be seen in full. The colour of the scarf creates less of a contrast to the bark of the pine, and the action is performed once a month rather than once a week (see Image 2).

A kind of coexisting or even confluence, sharing or performing together with a tree, is accentuated in *Shadow of a Pine*, where their distance from the camera makes the human figure and the small pine tree more equal; both are rather isolated on the seashore. The title accentuates the attempt to let the pine tree

Image 2. Still from *Year of the Dog in Kalvola – Calendar*

become the protagonist, with the human being as a momentary shadow. In a still image this impression is possible, but on video, when movement is involved, the action of the human figure catches the attention. The pine tree and the human figure are video filmed from two opposing viewpoints, first with the city in the background and then facing the open sea. The same action is thus repeated twice. In a one-channel version of the video the human figure is sitting next to the tree first with the city, then with the sea, as backdrop. In the installation version four different positions are separated into independent but synchronised sequences. Lying on the cliff upwards or downwards is repeated from both angles. In one of them the cliff covers the human figure completely, except when she is turning from lying on her stomach to lying on her back. In this case the human figure is really disappearing out of sight, though accidentally. The work is based on the idea of some kind of co-existence, however (see Images 3 and 4).

Another kind of disappearing takes place in *Year of a Dog – Sitting in a Tree*. The tree is used as shelter, but the tree and the human are shown only partially. The image is framed so that only part of the trunk and one branch is seen. And only half of the back and shoulder of the human figure sitting in the tree are visible. The framing of the image does not reveal the size of the tree or the height

Images 3 and 4. Stills from *Shadow of a Pine I* and *Shadow of a Pine II*

of the branch. In some images the figure seems to merge with the tree. The editing creates an illusion of continuity. The human figure seems to be sitting in the tree for a year or to have grown to become part of the tree. *Sitting in a tree* could be understood on one hand as confluence or sharing and on the other hand as chameleon-like disguise. Perhaps the human figure is seeking shelter in the tree in order to look at the surrounding landscape from a safe hiding place (see Image 5).

Image 5. Still from *Year of the Dog – Sitting in a Tree*

In *Day and Night of the Dog*, the same image is video filmed during Halloween with the camera somewhat closer and with two-hour intervals, thus with most of the sessions in complete darkness. The human figure is sharing the existential conditions of the tree, as it were. The confluence or partial merging of the human and the tree, the performer and environment, is produced by the editing. Due to the close up, the human presence is stronger than in *Year of the Dog*. The experience of the performer was mostly relaxing and meditative during the weekly visits, whereas performing the day-and-night sessions left the overriding impression of dampness (see Image 6).

Image 6. Still from *Day and Night of the Dog*

A chameleon-like disappearing into the landscape – partly due to a miscalculation – is most evident in *Under the Spruce I–III*. The spruce is the only tree of its kind on the island and situated quite centrally, next to the remains of an old garden grown wild. As a sequel to the pine tree on the shore, video filmed from two opposite directions the previous year, I wanted to examine three different perspectives: a wide view showing the spruce in full, a view from the path showing the surrounding vegetation, and a subjective view from under the spruce, from the point of view of the spruce, as it were. I imagined the human figure would be visible sitting under the spruce, though this is not the case in most of the images. Thus the final triptych with three parallel and synchronised videos is really a portrait of the spruce. The hints at a human presence, in the beginning and at the end when the human figure is going to sit under the spruce and returns from there, do not have much impact on the whole. In most images there are no indicators that a human being is sitting under the tree. In terms of the relationship between performer and tree we could say this is a case of camouflage, of chameleon-like hiding, a complete disappearing of the performer in, behind or under the tree, dissolving into the landscape (see Images 7a, b and c).

Images 7 a, b, and c. Stills from *Under the Spruce I–III*

Imaginary Models

If we think of these relationships as imaginary models for the relationship of human beings and the environment, none of them provide a good image of our real position of interrelatedness and dependency. The woman sitting on a birch is the human being opposed to nature, trying to experience a contact and even confluence but performing a contrast and remaining fundamentally separated from the landscape. The woman hanging from the pine tree and leaning on it is engaging with the environment in a more dialogical manner, seeking support and comfort from nature through an anthropomorphic relationship, as it were, and leaning on the tree trunk as on the shoulder of some wise wizard of the forest. However, the relationship is basically one of separation, though with romantic overtones. The woman lying on the cliff below the pine has a different relationship to the environment, since she assumes a position in the landscape which is unlike her expected behaviour. She is creating an aesthetical relationship to the environment, in a double sense. Firstly for herself by focusing on the sensual experience of lying on the cliff in different positions; and secondly, by creating an aesthetical image for the spectator, by positioning herself in relationship to

173

the tree in the image. The relationship to the landscape is more playful and could perhaps be called dialogical. There is a connection between the human and the environment at least visually, in display. For the woman sitting in a tree the relationship is altered on a visual level, since the image of a fragment of the tree and a fragment of the human creates an impression of merging, or some sort of confluence, perhaps. Although the woman is surrounded by the tree, hiding within it, she might seem visually to have become one with the tree, at least to some extent. For the woman sitting under the spruce the performer-environment relationship is different again, since now the performer seems to have disappeared altogether, or has positioned herself behind the camera, in the subjective close up from under the spruce. But these images – though downplaying the role of the human figure – do not provide a sustainable or recommendable imaginary model for the relationship between human beings and environment either; they do not indicate interdependence in any obvious or easily understandable way.

I have tried to look at these works of performing with trees as examples of performing landscape, in order to see whether some useful strategies could be extracted from them. And I have come to formulate these three strategies – contrast, confluence and camouflage – which are options of the visual relationship between performer and landscape, but none of which are really suitable or sustainable models for our relationship to the environment in general. So the question remains open for more trials and errors...

Notes

1   This text is based mainly on a paper 'Performing landscape with trees' presented
    at the conference Living landscapes in Aberystwyth in June 2009, but contains
    material from several other presentations. For a recent publication describing parts
    of my research in English, see Arlander, 2008.

2   André Lepecki uses the notion in his book *Exhausting Dance – performance and the
    politics of movement* (New York and London: Routledge, 2006).

3   'The "still-act" is a concept proposed by anthropologist Nadia Seremitakis to
    describe moments when a subject interrupts historical flow and *practices* historical
    interrogation.' (Lepecki, 2006: 5) See also Seremitakis, C. Nadia, 'The Memory of
    the Senses, Part I: Marks of the Transitory' and 'The Memory of the Senses, Part
    II: Still Acts' in *The Senses Still – Perception and Memory as Material Culture in
    Modernity* (pp.1–18 and 23–43) ed. C. Nadia Seremitakis (Chicago: University of
    Chicago Press, 1994).

4   See the call for papers for Living Landscapes, http://www.landscape.ac.uk/
    2009conference.html (2 July 2009).

5   For information on the conference PSi 14 see http://www.interregnum.dk/ (2 July
    2009).

6   *Helsingin Sanomat*, the monthly appendix, June 2009

7   *Keijut (Fairies) I–IV* – bedtime stories from Ireland. Anne Pihtakuusi (Ann Fir)
    goes to Ireland to find out about fairies and she writes letters to her beloved from
    there. She tells about the landscapes she encounters and about three men, which
    she imagined into those landscapes, and especially those strange fairy stories that
    they tell her. The radio play in four parts was compiled, written and retold in
    Finnish for the Radio Theatre by Annette Arlander. The main parts are played by
    Katja Kiuru as Anne Pihtakuusi (Ann Fir), Taisto Oksanen as Samuli Vaahtera
    (Samuel Sycamore), Jarmo Mäkinen as Janne Pihlaja (Seamus Rowan) and Jari
    Hietanen as Ville B. Valkopyökki (William B. White Poplar). Pirjo Jyrälä was
    responsible for the technical realisation, with Mauri Päivistö as assistant. The
    producer was Mauri Ahola. *Fairies I–IV* was broadcasted in the series *Radio theatre
    after ten o'clock* on Tuesdays 4, 11, 18 and 25 July 2000 at ten past ten p.m. See
    www.harakka.fi./arlander, the section titled 'old works'.

8   For information about the exhibition, see http://www.harakka.fi/2003/reviiri/
    index01.shtml (2 July 2009).

9   A description of the work and some images can be found in Annette Arlander
    'How to Turn Landscape into a Performance, How to Carry Out a Place?' in
    Mirka Niskala (ed.) *ANTI – Contemporary Art Festival 2002–2006 Time-Based
    and Site-Specific Contemporary Art in Kuopio*, Savonia University of Applied
    Siences, Series D 2/ 2007, pp.49–61. The current website of the festival goes back
    to 2007 only, http://www.antifestival.com/.

10 For a popular overview of the tree alphabet, see for instance http://www.angelfire.com/journal/cathbodua/Ogham.html.

11 According to Lepecki, Brennan is particularly insistent on the centrality of the subject experiencing his or her being as fully independent and ontologically severed from the world as constitutive of the modern process of subjectification. She identifies in the self-sufficient monadic subject the psychic work of a particularly alienating 'foundational fantasy'. (Lepecki, 2006: 11) See also Brennan, 2000: 36.

12 In 'A Plea for Earthly Sciences', his keynote lecture for the annual meeting of the British Sociological Association in April 2007, Bruno Latour referred to the ecological crisis and to the notion of 'explicitation' coined by Peter Sloterdjik: 'Everything that earlier was merely "given" becomes "explicit". Air, water, land, all of those were present before in the background: now they are explicitated because we slowly come to realize that *they* might disappear – and *we* with them.' (Latour, 2007: 2)

13 Images and projects which are not self-portraits in the traditional sense, but which enact the self (often of the artist her- or himself) in the context of the visual and performing arts (including film, video, and digital media) participate in what Jones calls 'self-imaging – the rendering of the self in and through technologies of representation.' (Jones, 2006: xvii)

14 'All the tree cares for or wants from you is that you breathe and piss', as a participant at the conference presentation of the first version of this text remarked.

Heuristic Research; Autoethnography; Immediacy and Self-Reflexivity

> The average PhD thesis is nothing but a transference of bones from
> one graveyard to another.
>
> **James Frank Dobie**

John Cage asserted that the self should only rarely be the subject of art, (Cage, 1995: 70) and yet we can recognise self-portraiture as a form with strong historical precedents. Further, we can see, and no less in performance terms than in visual art, that it is generally reliant on four elements for its existence. These elements are the artist as subject (as model, as theme); the event or object that accommodates the expression; the image of the self, the 'myself' within the artist's own notions; and finally the reading of that work undertaken by spectators and/or viewers. All performances are self-portraits to an extent: the selves of the director, designer, writer, performer et al. Of these it is the performer, usually but not always, who is the most highly visible and yet the least powerful. In the traditional theatre sense, performers usually tell other people's stories and the name above the title is rarely the name of the artist (of the subject) who is seen.

This is subverted by the possibilities for direct encounters offered through performance. Catherine Elwes describes performance as 'the real life presence of the artist [who] takes no role but her own. She is author, subject, activator, director and designer... within the performance tradition, she's understood to be conveying her own perceptions, her own fantasies, her own analyses.' (Elwes and Garrard, 1980: 42) By putting one's own body and experience forward within a live (arts) space the artist becomes both object and subject within the frame of the work and, as a consequence, this situation allows the artist to interrogate and articulate that relationship. We can say therefore that the performing of oneself is a feature of performance, even something central to it, whereas the submergence of self into character is a defining trait of acting. Potentially problematic binary this might be, yet it chimes with Philip

Auslander's view that constructing aspects of oneself rather than acting the part of a constructed other occurs through 'The blending of real and fabricated personae and situations that occur when performance personae assume the same functions as "real"'. (Auslander, 1994: 78)

Reflective practice embraces notions of heuristic research methodologies. Heuristics has its etymological roots in *heuriskein*, a word meaning 'to find'. It is more broadly associated with the idea of a search for information and knowledge which is as closely linked to internal and personal development as it is to the key principles of fact-finding most commonly associated with research. In this sense heuristic research is not necessarily concerned with whether or not a thesis can be shown to contain something that is innately correct so much as the extent to which it produces a *potential* solution: this creates an embrace of trial-and-error procedures that sees error as being no less valuable than success. Clark Moustakis explains this by arguing that heuristic approaches allow for and indeed demand that the opinions, feelings, moods and intuitions of the researcher are present throughout the period of research and that, in addition to an increased understanding of the area being studied, the researcher will also chronicle the specific phenomena of increased self-knowledge and awareness. (Moustakis, 1972: 37)

Heuristic processes offer an embrace of notions of self-discovery. As such, these processes are aligned to the kinds of creative research most likely to be employed in the type of work under discussion in this book, in that the very act of discovery leads the discovering researcher to new points of knowledge and new directions to take. In this we see evidence of an immersion process with heuristics which necessitates an openness and receptivity to the fluctuating and often frustrating rhythms of research and rehearsal. In many ways heuristic processes do not merely share a number of common features with the putting together of creative projects; they are creative projects in their own right. This means that heuristics function as much more than a peg to hang one's work on, as in effect a neat legitimising agent... heuristic research articulates a way of thinking and a way of thinking *about* thinking. For Paul Rae this understanding of 'artistic and research practices as mutually implicated in a process of invention [allows us to be] simultaneously invested in and led by the work as it unfolds'. (Rae, 2003)

Because the primary concern of heuristics is with the nature of knowing, whatever thoughts and attitudes exist in the mind of the researcher/maker, however temporary and disconnected they may appear to be, are imbued with the capacity to shift the process of investigation on into new fields of thought... a situation which Rae sees as an accommodation of anxiety. (Ibid.) Accordingly, research into the ways in which a practical performance project is being made is one thing at the same time as it is also another. The process provides space for the extension and development of a knowledge which is subject-specific at the same time as the self of the researcher is enhanced.

Yasuo Yuasa makes distinctions between knowledge gained *through* the body and the knowledge one might have *of* the body. (Zarrilli, 2007; Yuasa et al., 1993) According to Shigenori Nagatomo, body knowledge of this first kind can be contrasted with 'intellectual' knowledge inasmuch as 'Intellectual knowledge is a particular mode of cognition which results from objectifying a given object, which propositionally takes a subject-predicate form, and which divorces the somaticity of the knower from "the mind" of the knower'. (Zarrilli, 2007: 59) A consequence of this is that Nagatomo's notion of intellectual knowledge is always innately secondary, lacking the immediacy and oneness of judgement that is felt, experienced and ultimately inarticulate. Like Artaud's essays on theatre that needed to be lived through rather than written, this describes a proposition that sees the body as something that creates its own object of knowledge, as something that unashamedly elevates body-feeling over mind-knowing: the root and branch of practice as research.

This links with the concept of tacit knowing, which comes from Michael Polanyi and which is often cited as a legitimising agent in the field of practice-based research. (Polanyi, 1983) Polanyi's notion has been misrepresented over time until it has started to read as shorthand for a form of knowledge that is wholly or partly inexplicable, and by default as a rationalisation of inarticulation. It is worth remembering, however, that Polanyi was writing about a process – tacit knowing – and not a form of knowledge in and of itself. The premise underpinning Polanyi's idea of tacit knowledge is that we are not always aware of the knowledge we possess, or of the ways in which this knowledge might be valuable to others. Polanyi's argument is that the effective transfer of tacit knowledge is not something that can be easily achieved, requiring as it does a high level of personal contact and trust. (Brohm, 1999) Polanyi's most famous statement is that we know more than we can tell, and it is hard to disagree with this. Nevertheless, agreement with this, as well as agreement with the idea that tacit knowledge is hard to describe, falls some way short of buying into the idea that tacit or embedded knowledge functions as a means of bypassing those very processes of transforming tacit knowledge into explicit knowledge through codified articulation that lead to the transference of knowledge. And it is this transference of knowledge that is the key principle of research.

Polanyi suggests that there is a type of knowledge that is not explicit and articulated, but unspecifiable, implicit, and tacit; he develops this into the subsequent suggestion that in any activity there are two different levels of acquiring or using knowledge. These are 'focal knowledge' and 'tacit knowledge', where the former is about an object or phenomenon in focus while the latter functions as a background to what is in focus, assisting 'in accomplishing a task that is in focus'. (Parviainen, 2007: 17) Again, it is hard to disagree with this. It is equally hard to see Polanyi's views as antithetical to the view that practical investigations, insofar as they are broadly tacit, serve usefully as a means of framing and contextualising the focal knowledge of a research submission.

Acknowledging that experience is often of and through the body is not quite yet the same thing as buying into the idea, put forward by no less than Marcel Duchamp, that any and all decisions made in the construction and execution of art stem from intuition and can not therefore be translated into any form of spoken, written or even imagined self-analysis. Duchamp had it that:

> In the creative act, the artist goes from intention to realization
> through a chain of totally subjective reactions. His struggle toward the
> realization is a series of efforts, pains, satisfaction, refusals, decisions,
> which also cannot and must not be fully self-conscious.... The result of
> this struggle is a difference between the intention and its realization, a
> difference which the artist is not aware of. Consequently, in the chain
> of reactions accompanying the creative act, a link is missing. This gap,
> representing the inability of the artist to express fully his intention, this
> difference between what he intended to realize and did realize, is the
> personal 'art coefficient' contained in the work... the relation between
> the unexpressed but intended and the unintentionally expressed.
>
> (Duchamp, 1957)

Continuing this theme, Barry Edwards suggests that:

> Practice does not come from thought. It is a physical encounter with the
> world. This is the key characteristic of practice – it is not reflective, it is
> active. Attempts to modify the primitive and intuitive nature of practice
> (by attributing it with reasoning or rational thought, for example) will
> always fail, because whatever it is that arises from such changes may
> well be of interest, but it will not be practice.... The creative process is
> a matter of being lost one minute and suddenly finding yourself 'in the
> clearing' the next: and that's about it.
>
> (Edwards, 2008)

Clearly the thoughts of Duchamp and Edwards, separated as they are by half a century and notable differences of field, pose something of a challenge to the drive of this book. If practice is indeed something mediumistic and inexplicable then by definition all attempts at linguistic rationalisation are doomed to failure, no matter how cognisant of and sympathetic to the nuances of performance they might be: a fact that would render all written analyses of practice redundant. This is distinct from the historical mistrust of the self as a topic of research, a mistrust that sees scholarship as an activity that reports from the sidelines of activity and which keeps researchers' voices neutral, to the extent that the proper voice for research is held to be no voice at all.

A challenge to this assumed homogenisation comes from autoethnography. Autoethnography is a way of researching and writing that seeks to connect the personal to the cultural, placing the self at all times within a social context. In this we can see a link to Kenneth Pike's 1954 idea of the emic as an account of behaviour in terms which are meaningful to the world of the researcher, inasmuch as an emic reading is innately culture-specific. An etic account, conversely, is a reading in terms that are culture-neutral, in that one's findings can be applicable to a range of cultures. On a High Street level, we see, in either the faux Italiana or the re-packaged Seattle of every chain store coffee shop, the supposedly geo-culturally specific when in fact the only sense of place that matters is between which shoe store and pharmacy these slices of caffeinated stage sets are housed. To relate to this in more overt performance terms, a Broadway/West End production of *The Lion King* is etical in its rigid adherence to a prescribed and English-speaking mise-en-scène, even though its content makes a claim to be emical in its *Hamlet*-derived and Disneyfied depiction of African wildlife. Autoethnography is intrinsically emic in that texts are regularly written in the first person and contain self-consciously relational, reflexive and highly personalised material.

Autoethnography is seen to differ from autobiography (albeit with some obvious overlap) in the etymological claims for research-validity of 'ethnography', as opposed to the storytelling of 'biography'; nevertheless, autoethnographical reports are often presented as stories of experience: a fact that can render them diary-like and even self-indulgent in tone. One could say that autobiography starts to morph into ethnography at the point where researcher/writers understand their personal histories to be implicated in larger socio-cultural frameworks and take steps to make their own experiences a lens through which other experiences can be pulled into focus.

According to Marjorie DeVault, 'personal writing is useful for exploring the unexpected and thus for bringing to light aspects of "ordinary" experience that are typically obscured'. (DeVault, 1997: 226) Whereas in the past, cultures and subcultures were regarded as relatively discrete and clearly delineated, in today's globalised world national and cultural identities have become somewhat unfixed. Accordingly, the drive to re-establish and re-state individual and social identities is possibly stronger than ever, in that the investigation of personal narratives can yield insight into our constantly changing and differently complicated lives. Ann Oakley suggests that:

> the act of knowing is an extremely complex endeavour: not only do
> different human beings know different things, bringing different values,
> beliefs and perceptions to what they know and how they know it, but
> the act of knowing and what is known are often irredeemably fused...
>
> (Oakley, 2000: 291)

In a research context, autoethnography implies experiential knowledge, containing not only the period of the study in question but also the interweaving of past and present knowledge. In other words, autoethnographical research investigates knowledge regarding the feeling of what happens, rather than having a focus on what happened. The standard methodological frameworks we are increasingly seeing are linked by the belief that there can be no such thing as value-free research and that any research undertaking has to be viewed in the context of its particular approach to the idea of objective truth. Mark Evans believes that 'If there is a weakness [and a strength?] to... self-reflexivity, it is that it betrays the writer's allegiances; nonetheless, it is a betrayal that suggests the power of the radical to seep through, inform, and even transform our intentions and experiences.' (Evans, 2000: 122) Evans' words, written in response to Kershaw's deployment of memory as document, create an insightful resonance in their acknowledgement of the power relations and prejudices that inform all research approaches. Approaches such as these lead to analysis that is intersectional, deconstructive and laden with awareness of doubt, corresponding in turn to an innately postmodern way of thinking: a type of thinking that in its embrace of multivalence refuses fixed form. We know well that a feature of postmodernism is the absence of faith in any theory or approach having a universal claim to being seen as privileged... except, perhaps, the privileging of subjective self-experience. This leads to approaches to knowledge and understanding where epistemology, ontology and axiology jostle for space in a research world where all enquiries reflect the standpoint of the enquirers, and where no practice is ever neutral.

Practice through research in performance is often distinguished then by its embrace of subjectivity, not least because individual researchers' practical engagements tend towards findings that are difficult and even impossible to test. As a consequence, practice-based research methodologies will often focus on specific processes undertaken rather than on that which might or might not be contained in the 'finished' work produced. We can identify this as a concentration on forms of procedural explication. The difficulty facing researchers is of finding ways of articulating key aspects of their creative processes in a manner that resists accusations of self-justification and navel-gazing. It is in this climate that autoethnography has emerged as a near-compulsory word in the practice-based researcher's vocabulary. Despite the primary subject of autoethnography being the writer's self, the form has (in theory, at least) a wider relevance insofar as the self is constructed by the social *milieu* and bound up with its surrounding culture. Norman Denzin describes autoethnography as 'a turning of the ethnographic gaze inward on the self (auto), while maintaining the outward gaze of ethnography, looking at the larger context wherein self experiences occur'. (Denzin, 2003: 258) Denzin's words echo Luce Irigaray's belief that 'We have to discover... words which don't bar the corporeal' (Irigaray, 1985: 43) and Howard Barker's faith in the narratives of performing bodies to be expressed through the beauty of language. (Barker, 1997: 114)

The logic of autoethnography is that the act of writing about the self will always contain more than self, it is 'a form of self-narrative that places the self within a social context'. (Etherington, 2004: 139–140) More than this, we learn that at best autoethnographic texts are able to reveal the 'fractures, sutures, and seams of self interacting with others in the context of researching lived experience'. (Spry, 2001: 720) That which the researcher lives through is then about more than the narrative of one experience because it involves interaction and is inherently social and cultural. Rather than speaking only of itself, writing the autoethnographical self can, according to Amanda Coffey, 'be viewed as part of a greater trend toward authenticity, and as part of a biographical project. It can be seen as part of a movement towards the representation of voices in social research.' (Coffey, 1999: 118) Authenticity, however, is a relentlessly problematic notion, in writing no less than in life. There is no such thing as an objective, innocent, primary document. No such thing as a piece of writing that tells an untrammelled truth. A methodology based on autoethnography is ultimately no greater a guarantee of the truth of experience than any other:

> The document... is the result, above all, of an assemblage, whether
> conscious or unconscious, of the history, the time and the society
> which have produced it, and also of the ensuing periods through which
> it has continued to be used, even if perhaps in silence... in the end,
> there is no documentary truth. Every document is a lie.
>
> (De Marinis, 1985: 383)

Autoethnographical writing differs further from autobiography in that whilst it is able to present an individual perspective it is one that also makes connection to a more collective understanding. In this way it is an approach that recognises and moves within communities rather than focusing on purely individualised experience, hence autoethnography's switching of bios (a life) for ethnos (a people). It is in this understanding of self as something innately relational that autoethnography becomes more than just a word. And it *is* often used as just as a word; a word that lends the type of research credibility that autobiography is inclined to lack.

Within performance studies, the term autoethnography remains contested, even maligned. As a reflexive account of one's own experiences situated within the culture of performance research, as well as within the specific cultural *milieu* it functions as a part of, autoethnography is always as much about cultural accounting as critical reasoning, as much about a foregrounding of experience and of narrative as an academic enterprise as it is a straightforward research report. Whilst some members of both the academic community and the publishing industry argue forcefully for giving autoethnography critical credence, the absence of an objective voice is used as criticism, even when we know that writing 'one is left to question' rather than 'I questioned' will often amount to no more than a stylistic sanctioning of the idea of distance.

There is of course more to the wish for objectivity than some people's reluctance to read the continued use of the personal pronoun in a PhD thesis; and whilst writing oneself out of the frame can be something of a sham exercise when one's research is thoroughly focused on personal experience, the request for those experiences to be made subject to contextualisation, analysis and interpretation and to be written up in such a way that an informed reader can make sense of the researcher's findings seems reasonable enough. It is this giving shape to narrative investigation that moves autoethnography from the private, raw data of the diary into the public domain of research. The better, more balanced endorsements of autoethnography, such as Nicholas L. Holt's call for the development of appropriate evaluative criteria for such work, acknowledge that 'those who produce autoethnography are at risk of being overly narcissistic and self-indulgent'. (Holt, 2003) There is much to be said of the dangers of composing a thesis which reads as an exercise in the researcher researched, where the bulk of evidence presented offers little proof other than its own autoethnographical verisimilitude.

CASE STUDY 9

Un-telling Myself: Performance (Preparation) as Research

Felix Nobis

Since the storytelling revival of the 1960s and '70s, the art of the storyteller has been viewed with increasing interest from a range of academic disciplines. The early investigations of folklorists, anthropologists, and narratologists have been advanced, in recent decades, by researchers whose concerns are pedagogical, motivational, and therapeutic. Interestingly, the fields of theatre studies and performance studies have been slower to engage with the intrinsic performativity of contemporary professional storytelling practices. Until Michael Wilson's *Storytelling and Theatre* (2006), platform storytelling made only an occasional contribution to studies of contemporary theatre practice, while in the field of performance studies, discussion of storytelling in tribal rituality has only recently been complemented with discussion of storytelling in the radically performative practices of monologists such as Spalding Gray, Ron Vawter, and Heather Woodbury. (Schechner, 2002; Etchells, 1999; Farquhar, 2000)[1] In recent years, performance theories have not only acknowledged storytelling models, but, increasingly, interrogation of storytelling practice has contributed to a better understanding of established theories of performance.[2] It is fertile terrain and it is far from exhausted.

A significant body of primary material has emerged to inform this discussion. Detailed interviews with storytellers (Wilson, 2006: 148–200), with audiences (Sturm, 2000), and active participation in storytelling projects (Ryan, 2008) have invigorated theoretical discussions of storytelling, while also focusing scholarly attention on such practical aspects as were long the domain of classroom how-to manuals.[3] It is to this body of knowledge, dynamic and evolving, that I have turned to inform my PhD thesis, a theoretical study of theatrical storytelling practice(s). Almost inevitably, I have found myself dealing with an incomplete body of knowledge, and one to which I am able to contribute.

Having trained and worked as a professional actor, I have increasingly focused on performing spoken narratives in a range of settings from classrooms to arena-size stadiums.[4] From 1998 to 2004 I worked as a professional storyteller, touring two performances internationally. In this case study I focus specifically on the performance of my own translation of the epic *Beowulf*, which I presented, sometimes three times a day,[5] in theatres, churches, universities, halls, school classrooms and school basketball courts throughout Ireland, the UK, the USA and Australia. The conditions of such touring are not conducive to evolving or maintaining performance routines; yet, during this period, I devised a procedure of physical and vocal warm-ups which provided a consistency to a performance that was otherwise responding to a broad range of performative conditions. In this case study I do not interrogate my public performances, but consider instead the private performance of preparation, a performance dictated by personal requirements, experience, training, and informed intuition.

This performance lasts approximately an hour, and follows a performative pattern of stretching, enacting, amplifying and retracting. It begins with a physical stretching of muscles, incorporating a cardiovascular circulation of blood. I then focus on specific physical movements of the story, repeating, stretching, and exaggerating the actions to extremes of physical magnitude. From this, I retract, performing the same actions by focusing energy inward into various parts of my body, enacting them silently within my entire being, reducing movement until I merely sense the performance, allowing it to play out in the stillness of my body. My vocal performance follows a similar pattern. I begin by gently stretching muscle groups: diaphragm, jaw, tongue and soft palate. I then exercise my vocal range by reciting passages faster, louder, lower, slower, exaggerating vocal features until I release vocal pressure and return to performance levels, intimate levels, and silence, articulating the words in a voice-less, mouth-less, motion-less performance. It is a performance of contrasting physical energies, of processes and recesses and enacting extremes. It is a performance of in-forming my body, but it is also a performance of un-telling myself. Roland Barthes observes that 'narrative is… simply there, like life itself'. (1977: 79) I see my role as storyteller as one of privileging a particular narrative amidst a complex web of others. In preparation, I not only tune voice and body to speak a story, but seek to un-tell other, distracting, stories that clutter a storytelling event. Through this enactment of preparation, I seek to 'perform myself' into a storyteller.

To clarify this notion, I make the distinction between 'I practice' and 'my practice'. With 'I practice' I refer to a process of rehearsal and recitation, measurable in hours or months spent exercising and improving, polishing and preparing, pacing and placing and performing dry runs. Publicly, 'I practice' is expressed through 'my practice' and might be gauged by the standard of a public performance or the ease with which I execute my role. 'My practice' refers to the individual relationship I have with a broader, timeless, borderless, practice of storytelling. Fused in the term 'practice' I identify not only my performative preparation, but my praxis, and the professional tradition of which my praxis is part. I propose this intersection as a site of investigation. In the process of 'I practice' I in-form my body and by interrogating this practice I seek to inform my research of professional storytelling practice(s). Davies warns of a 'reflexivity that continually spirals inward, a process that is ultimately destructive of one of the two pillars of social research, a belief that we are able through these activities to learn about things outside ourselves, not knowable through introspection'. (2008: 18) My research, however, spirals outward, from the known body to the unknown body, and, in the over-arching framework of my thesis, to distant and unknowable bodies, seeking to understand storytelling practices that extend beyond my own.

Body

Physical preparation can be a private process, often self-taught, intimate and difficult to articulate. Where volumes are devoted to preparation of the actor, storytelling manuals seldom include more than a comment on voice or a note on stance, and generally overlook physical preparation altogether.[6] In order to 'embody a self on stage', Ronald J. Pelias proposes that 'the performer must develop a flexible and responsive body' which may also be able to 'function as a methodological tool'. (2008: 186) I develop flexibility and responsiveness through a series of physical exercises, yet in enacting a corporeal performance of physical warm-up, I become aware of a conflicting, counter-performance that arises within me and seeks to erase the traces of the first. Over time I sense my performing body competing, in corporeal demands, with my storytelling body. On one hand, I prepare – through breathing, stretching, and focusing – for particular performative needs 'which do not respect the habitual conditionings of the use of the body'. (Barba, 1995: 15) On the other hand, the state of energy dilated through such extra-daily body technique feels at odds with a preparation that allows me to disappear behind the story, or, as practitioner Daniel Morden puts it, 'become invisible in order to allow the story to work its magic'. (Quoted in Wilson, 2006: 84)

The balance between a 'hot body' of 'performer's power presence' (Barba and Savarese, 1991: 54) and a 'modest' body that 'just disappears' (Pullman in Ryan, 2008: 85), is fraught with implication for the contemporary storyteller. I share Patrick Ryan's concern that 'We put too much effort into the story*teller* performance and not enough in the story*telling* performance', agreeing that 'the genuine teller must be part of the norm, not distinct from it'; (Ryan, 2008: 68) however, in 'I practice', I negotiate such agreement with a deep-felt personal need to prepare, practise, and physically transform my body into that of a storyteller. This conflict of intuition cannot be negotiated theoretically, and calls instead for physical engagement and corporeal mediation.

In 'I practice' my body prepares to be seen, and not be seen, and it tests and flexes its presence and absence. Barba provides the example of the nō theatre's *kokken*, who, in assisting the main actor, are required to 'perform absence'. (Barba, 1995: 17) In such absence, Barba observes, the *kokken's* extra-daily energy is present, just as it is present in stillness and immobility. (Barba and Savarese, 1991: 94) In my storytelling warm-up I seek to achieve a performance of absence through an expression of presence. I perform to the point of losing myself, exaggerating and exerting, before enforcing stillness and stifling impulses. I emerge and recede, as if flexing and releasing a muscle. Langellier and Peterson observe that the 'storyteller does not change bodies to become a narrator or a character or a listener... Both narrator and character are sensible to the extent that they are dimensions of the storyteller's bodily conduct'. (2004: 9) In 'I practice' I prepare my body to be present in order to be a teller, while also preparing myself to be invisible in order to become the story. The working and the weighting of this balance is reflected in the efficacy of 'my practice'. Nuala Hayes warns that 'the flashy, showy stuff puts the focus on the performer rather than the story', (Wilson, 2006: 84) and audiences interviewed by Sturm generally support these views. (2000: 295) Liz Weir cautions, 'I've been in situations where the audience are embarrassed, either because the performer is so hyper, or superior, or whatever. I'd rather be more natural, except it's natural with a layer, a varnish on it.' (Wilson, 2006: 200)

In my physical warm-up, I enact a performance of varnishing/vanishing, through stretching, flexing, and testing extremities before retracting and returning to a former shape. I seek a balance between energy and neutrality approaching the contained *enérgheia*, articulated by Barba, which is 'ready for action, on the verge of producing words'. (1995: 55) Yet this is not enough. The action prepared for and words produced are not constant. They do not pre-exist, but rather demand to be created in collaboration with an audience. Storytelling is a collaborative act and in contemporary practice, causality is seen as a hallmark of 'genuine' storytelling. (Ryan, 2008: 69) Causality, however, need not preclude a purposeful process of preparation, and the shaping of a story*teller* who is able to adapt to and inspire a story-listening audience. I prepare what Dundjerović calls a 'peripheral consciousness', to 'use all external elements from outside reality (most importantly audience presence) as personal resources (stimuli) to play with'. (2009: 12) I prepare for my storytelling to be collaborative, but I also prepare a platform from which to collaborate. Privileging egalitarianism in my performance risks underestimating the messiness of actual storytelling transactions: disruptive individuals, recalcitrant school-classes, age-inappropriate bookings, cultural restrictions, contractual obligations, inaccurate information, bad acoustics, laziness of facilitators, each of which may make radical demands on me as story*teller*, and call upon performative skills, that I either will, or will not, be able to meet. In my process of 'I practice', I prefigure performances of exaggeration and extremes of physical magnitude, not because I am likely to perform this way for an audience, but so that these performances exist within me, silently contributing to my story*teller* performance, even if not present in the exigencies of any individual story*telling* performance.

Wilson writes that 'storytellers in performance are not less physical than actors, but differently physical', (2006: 80) and in the enactment of 'I practice', I identify procedures which reflect the different physical demands of my storytelling. I do not prepare my body for a pre-set performative presence, but strive for a malleability of presence, open and equipped for different inputs, and able to respond with different tellings. In stretching I prepare for the unknown and unexpected, while in retracting I seek neutrality and a return to a storytelling self, varnished but not necessarily burdened by an inflexible storytelling persona. In the final stages of preparation I find myself actively shaking off the warm-up process. I chat with a stage-manager, investigate the performance place, and seek to reconnect with the real and actual. In such activity, I sense my knowing-body enacting a performance of return from which I can build, again, in collaboration with my audience.

Throughout periods of preparation, my body has learnt its own processes which it begins to enact largely without cognitive assistance or interference. In so doing it reflects theories that occasionally seem in conflict, but which exist within me as a practitioner. My body has developed layers of knowing, trained responses and informed judgements, which I can only begin to approximate with theoretical understanding. Yet by interrogating 'I practice' I inform my understanding of a relationship between 'my practice' and existing theories of performance. By interrogating my preparatory performance as research, I gain a foundation from which to incorporate ontological aspects of being into an epistemological study of knowing.

Voice

A distinction between physical and vocal preparation is predominantly one of classification. The body, and the voice that emanates from that body, prepare themselves concurrently regardless of warm-up structures I impose. For Cicely Berry, preparation of voice and body are linked at a level of musculature:

> Speaking and using the voice is partly a physical action involving the use of certain muscles, and, just as an athlete goes into training to get his muscles to the required efficiency, or a pianist practices to make his

fingers more agile, so if you exercise the muscles involved in using the
voice, you can increase its efficiency in sound.

(1982/1973: 9)

Paul Zumthor invites vocal performance to be read as corporeal performance
by asking 'does not every song contain, at least by way of the mouth, its own
articulatory dance?' (1990: 156) By interrogating my vocal 'I practice', I discover
that the relationship between vocality and corporeality – as distinct from the
relationship between vocality and intentionality – can further contribute to an
understanding of 'my practice'. Having discovered that knowledge may be inherent
in some routines of practice, I consider the value in disrupting such routines.

From a process of translating the Anglo-Saxon text, to the discipline of
daily tellings, my familiarity with the structure and articulatory patterns of my
performance of *Beowulf* is intimate. I have never forgotten lines nor lost myself
in the design of the story's telling. When making adjustments in the moment of
performance – by shortening or lengthening sections, or including or excising
passages – I am able, with little effort, to take up the story's strand, and continue
with its unravelling. On tour, however, I return to Cicely Berry's *Voice and the
Actor* to incorporate new exercises into my vocal warm-up. One such exercise
involves use of a bone-prop, 'a small prop about the thickness of a pencil, of
varying lengths, which you put between the teeth to keep the jaw open and steady.
It has a groove each end into which your teeth can fit to prevent it from jumping
out under pressure from the jaw'. (1982: 49) The purpose of the bone-prop is to
heighten awareness of vowel and consonant construction and to 'place in your
mind the exact movement of the muscles'. (Ibid.: 50) Upon placing the bone-prop
between my teeth and speaking passages of the performance text, I find that I
stumble in the 'articulatory dance' with which I am so familiar. My concern is
not with the bone-prop, but that my *Beowulf* story has become partially recorded
in the muscular memory of its own performance. Upon investigation, I find
that even though this articulatory record departs, sometimes dramatically, from
prompt copy or written text, it serves as a truer record of my current telling than
anything that is published or printed.

Stanislavsky warns against reeling off lines:

> It's one thing to go out in front of a respectful audience and reel off
> 'tum-ti-tum', 'tum-ti-tum' and exit. It's quite another to get down to
> business and be active! The first way of speaking is 'theatrical', the
> second, human. We not only feel these parts of our lives but see them
> with our mind's eye.

(Stanislavsky and Benedetti, 2008: 409)

As an actor I immediately become concerned that the engine of my storytelling practice is not legitimate 'business', but 'tum-ti-tum', 'tum-ti-tum' and that my performance has become more 'theatrical' than 'human'. As a storyteller, however, I suspect that more is occurring than a reeling off of lines, and that my mind's eye is focused and actively engaged in performance. Stanislavsky writes, 'the whole script is accompanied by mental images in our mind's eye just in the way the actor pictured them... Look at them closely and describe what you see and hear as fully, deeply and clearly as possible'. (Ibid.: 410) In my transition from actor to storyteller, the mechanical order of my performance has altered. Rather than seeing images in my mind's eye and describing them, it seems I am leading with the words, allowing them to function as the bow of the performance, cutting into the story and moving it forward while the images, and responses, trail. My concerns as an actor are different to my concerns as a storyteller. For Stanislavsky, the 'main concern in performance is that our mind's eye should always reflect mental images which relate to the character'. (Ibid.: 409) I question whether the mental images that I see belong to me as storyteller, or to a storytelling 'character' that Ryan and Wilson identify as the storyteller's 'mega-identity'. (Wilson, 2006: 70–73)

I return to the rehearsal room, prepare for performance, and bring my inquiry before an audience. The images that appear to me unbidden are influenced by an informed understanding of the period and the structure of the poem, but also by my personal relationship with the work as a whole. In its telling I might glimpse textbook diagrams or undergraduate Sutton Hoo reproductions, yet I might as readily glimpse certain locations where I immersed myself in the process of translation. I picture movement: a trail of figures approaching the sea or the balance of a boat's hull upon the water, but I also become aware of my sensual response to the poem's imagery: I recall familiar landscapes or a personal moment's looking out to a stormy ocean.

The images are told to me by my personal relationship with the story, but they no more drive the telling than I control the events that take place. It is not my responsibility to describe my images 'as fully, deeply and clearly as possible', as they are no more real or authoritative than the images that the audience creates in response to the words. Rather than describing images for the audience, I *join* with the audience in *discovering* images, allowing them to emerge from the words as I speak them. The events performed by the Stanislavskian actor are experienced in an immediate present, while the events told by me as a storyteller occur at a more Brechtian distance. I am observer in these events, and even my role in them is observed from a temporal and/or geographic remove. I am able to invest the events with immediacy, re-discover them with my audience, animate them, feel them, explore and engage with them, but I find that I am unable to live them their first life without a falsity that detracts me from my storytelling. I may tell of my current relationship with the story, but I always *relate*, a verb that finds its stem in *referre*: 'to bear or carry back'. (OED) I suspect that the motor of my storytelling is not found in my storyteller's mega-identity or inner life but is predominantly located within my physical, corporeal self, and my relationship with the story as it exists beyond me. The life of the storytelling lies in the muscularity and the machinery of vowels and consonants, linking 'vocal energy with the energy of the word'. (Berry, 1982: 43)

Interrogating my performance of vocal and corporeal preparation, I discover an intuitive balance between storytelling functions. On one hand, I prepare a vocal engine that unravels the story through articulation, and on the other hand I prepare an actor who responds to the story in its telling. By interrogating 'I practice' I discover a process radically different to my practices as an actor. The division is not definitive. Emotion colours the voice as it is lived through the body, and can exist in the words as they are spoken. They may catch up with each other, but when emotion overtakes voice I fall into the flashy, showy stuff that Hayes claims puts the focus on the performer rather than the story. Such findings are preliminary. I do not propose a new performance paradigm to embrace every performative function, but I do acknowledge a muscular vocal performance as a vehicle that propels my story, and a flexible, responsive body that allows me, in collaboration with the audience, to respond to it.

Not every aspect of 'I practice' is readily translated into research data. I am aware of important outcomes which I am unable to articulate fully but which transform my everyday consciousness into that of a storyteller. Such a transformation acknowledges the ritualistic element of enactment, taking into account the relationship between corporeality and consciousness. In 1975, Evan M. Zuesse proposed that 'Ritual is difficult to interpret precisely because it is so *present*, so fulfilled in itself, that it can dispense with further interpretation or native exegesis (and often does)'. (1975: 517) In the intervening decades, performance theory has contributed to a vocabulary which allows such interpretation to begin. However, the deep knowing of when a particular enactment is complete, or if a ritual has been committed to, or a warm-up successfully enacted, represents a body-knowledge that I am still seeking to decipher. An unsatisfying 'I practice' does not necessarily translate into a poor public performance; however, without sensing the completion of a preparation I feel cluttered and distracted. Routine and repetition of 'I practice' assist in a process of un-cluttering the dull and the daily, and can clear the way for a focused telling.

Zuesse proposes that 'Ritual gestures forth the world as meaningful and ordered. It establishes a deep primary order which precedes the world that can be spoken, and out of which the word proceeds, to which it returns.' (1975: 518) In the repetition of movements and sounds of 'I practice', I distance myself from the internal and external distractions that Marie Maclean identifies broadly as 'noise', (Maclean, 1988: 3–4) and approach an order from which I am able to focus on the important, relevant, narratives. In this way, 'I practice' serves not only to inform my corporeal self, but to un-tell my cluttered and everyday self, although I acknowledge that such a distinction only begins to address the deep sense of knowing when a performance is ready, and when a balance is found between storyteller, story, and self.

Through 'I practice' I gain access to a source of knowledge which contributes to my theoretical understanding of other professional storytelling practices. It offers a foothold in a practical known, from which my research advances to a theoretical unknown. As it currently stands, 'I practice' is a private performance, enacted by me as practitioner, and examined alone by me as researcher. Evaluating such practice presents a range of methodological challenges, but the value of the model cannot be measured against its ability to produce conclusions of scientific certainty. It calls upon a different range of measures, such as those advanced by narrative inquiry, of honesty, authenticity, transferability and economy. (Webster and Mertova, 2007: 21) Ultimately, however, the reliability or validity of 'I practice' must be measured, not by how well it serves as a methodological tool, but by how well it serves 'my practice'. The investigation must not detract from the performance and specific challenges must be acknowledged. (Pelias, 2008: 190–192) Increasingly, I view 'my practice' not as an extension, but as a defining aspect of my role as a researcher. As my theoretical research progresses I find I have a dual obligation, performative and investigative, to further develop 'my practice', and to maintain 'I practice', not only in order to advance a practical knowing, but to inform a theoretical understanding.

Notes

1   Although studies such as Richard Bauman's landmark *Verbal Art as Performance* (1977) scrutinised oral narrative in performance, the predominant concerns remained folkloric, anthropological and linguistic. (Bauman, 1977: 3) Distinctions, however, are not always clear. Dell Hymes suggests that 'the roots of "performance theory" and "ethnography of speaking", and also "ethnopoetics", are intertwined'. (Foley, 1995: 8*fn*) For discussion on the history of theatre and storytelling, see Wilson, 2006: 11–33.

2   See Langellier and Peterson, 2004: 1–31; 2006; and Cohen-Cruz and Schutzman, 2006.

3   There are some excellent volumes on the practical aspects of storytelling. See McKay and Dudley, *About Storytelling: A Practical Guide* (1996).

4   From Dec. 2007 – March 2008, and May 2008 – Sept. 2008, I narrated the arena spectacular *Walking with Dinosaurs: The Live Experience* on its Australian and American tours. See Felix Nobis, 'Working with Dinosaurs: Narrative Techniques in the Arena Spectacular', Monash University, 14 April 2008, *Drama and Theatre Studies Feeds* <http://arts.monash.edu.au/drama-theatre/feeds/2008/nobis-working-with-dinosaurs.php> (accessed 9 June 2009).

5   I refer here to a season of high-school and college performances in Pittsburgh, PA, 25 Oct. – 8 Nov. 2002, produced by Unseam'd Shakespeare Co., partly funded by the Grable Foundation. <http://www.grablefdn.org/old%20ref%20files/2002grants.pdf> (accessed 5 Feb. 2009).

6   McKay and Dudley offer comments on the voice and the importance of hydration in their practical volume *About Storytelling: A Practical Guide* (1996: 49–50).

SECTION 10

Truth and Doubt; Epistemology and Ontology; Thesis Demands

> I know it was wonderful, but I don't know how I did it.
> **Laurence Olivier**

The drift towards autoethnography has gone hand in hand with the postmodernists' raising of doubts over the privileging of any one method for obtaining authoritative knowledge about experience. Taken alongside an increasing distrust of truth, to the extent that any assessment of the quality of analysis and desire for evidence of findings and trustworthiness in data is seen as increasingly irrelevant, we can see some of the reasons that practice-based investigations and practice as thesis have taken root as they have. In autoethnographical terms, the subjectivity of the researcher is seen as a resource for understanding the deeply problematic and deeply contentious world under investigation. The experiencing self becomes then something to be capitalised on rather than kept in the wings, and the ability and willingness to write one's individual experience up into something possessed of academic and cultural currency is, as Simon Jones has pointed out, both logical and desirable.

As a consequence of the resolutely personal nature of practice-based data, data which is drawn from and for the most part *comprised of* performance-making experience, research is often methodologically idiosyncratic. This amounts at times to models of deliberate approximation rather than assumed exactitude. Practice-based research is concerned with the advocating of approaches that seek the indeterminate, the unfixed, the radical and the ambiguous; it is an approach that regards attempts to settle issues conclusively as indicative of bad practice as well as false order. If practice-based research is a useful umbrella term, the projects that function beneath its brim display their own unique set of concerns, each of which Patti Lather identifies as being simpatico to the new research gods of multivalence and fluidity. (Lather, 1996: 533) This absence of fixity – that same absence that can be so problematic in terms of pre-determined research questions – can lead to forms of data re-presentation which are, in Elliot Eisner's terms, productively ambiguous. (Eisner, 1997: 8) More significantly than this, they are leading research away from its historical focus on the nature of knowledge, the epistemic, and towards the nature of being, the ontological. In this regard, practice-based research makes a good case for *deserving* to be the default approach that it has so clearly become for PhD students of performance… which casts a different, and differently sympathetic, light on Jones' claims.

Conventional research methodologies contrive to create evidence in support of the particular argument being made: data is collected strategically and employed for the purposes of elucidation, clarification and confirmation, and the thesis-intention is, as we have seen, primarily concerned with the pursuit of reliability, replicability and validity. In their subversive challenge to these conventions, practice-based and autoethnographical research methodologies have resulted in their own metanarratives of idiosyncrasy harnessed to institutionally sanctioned conformity. As the agenda of progressive practice is always in some ways to disrupt, challenge and decentre the status quo, so the agenda of practice-based research is to replace the desire for objective rationalisation with a claim for more subjective research outcomes, which demand and are often based upon first-person descriptions of performance processes. To see this as a logical approach to investigations of the logic-defying personal art coefficient that Duchamp wrote about is to acknowledge the potential of practice-based research to approach the complexities of creative making on an equal (and equally informed) footing. The widespread adoption of practice-based study has done much to develop a new way of viewing the in-the-moment ontology of performance rather than the epistemology of post-performance (post-practice) reflection, and it is easy to lose sight of this in the dust raised by struggles between one set of research conventions and another.

Whilst with epistemology we can say that knowing demands understanding, with ontology the act of doing defines being. In this sense performance is innately ontological, hence Richard Foreman's adoption of the term in the creation of his Ontological-Hysteric Theater. The knowing–being interface is at the heart of performance research. Roberta Mock and Ruth Way articulate this in their rationalisation of the distinctions and overlap between programmes that are described as Performance or Theatre Studies (where study suggests epistemology) and Theatre Arts (where art implies ontology). (Mock and Way, 2005)

It is worth reiterating some of the connections between practice-based research, autoethnographical writing and the lingering tenets of postmodernism. Many more battles have been fought over the excesses and absences of postmodern performance than any of us could ever recall, let alone recount, yet what matters here is not a concern for the knowing nature of much recent performance so much as a familiarity with the idea that objectively obtained and linguistically neutral certainties are no more than politically assumed illusions. The adoption of this idea leaves little room for research strategies based on working hypotheses that are comprehensively testable and less still for the reproduction of normative research values.

In an academic world where all views are increasingly seen as valid and where the need for proof is exiled alongside truth, the researcher's personal relationship to the topic has assumed a new primacy. Personalised, subjective, idiosyncratic and autoethnographical methodologies do not easily accommodate concerns for communicable validity and reliability, and the very situatedness of most practice-based studies legislates against the collection of data in ways that are either prescriptive or traditionally empirical. On the contrary, the individual, not to say *unique* manner of the research will often lead to the creation and utilisation of methodologies that are hybrid in the extreme. From a postmodern perspective, researchers pursuing normative patterns could be said to be exercising concern with the preservation of academic privilege, whereas those opting for the disruptive patterns of practice-based work are mounting a loose collective of resistance to the (old) ideas of distinctions between the researcher and the researched.

Stanley Aronowitz's smart description of these nascent practices as approaches in pursuit of the 'ineluctability of difference' (Seidman and Wagner, 1992: 296) locates these differences between the belief that research utilises theory to locate new ideas safely within established thinking and the belief that research is concerned with the creation of departures that are so divorced from the depersonalised, distanced and objective realms of orthodoxy as to be out on the very edges of acceptability. Not all notions of acceptability share the same criteria, however, and as Bruno Latour has argued, a collapse to the type of objective order demanded by conventional research is a given of 'the modern constitution' in that it 'renders the work of mediation that assembles hybrids invisible, unthinkable, unrepresentable'; (Latour, 1993: 34) the differing foci of modernism and postmodernism are acknowledged in Latour's claim that modernism 'allows the expanded proliferation of the hybrids whose existence, whose very possibility, it denies.' (Ibid.)

Henk Borgdorff notes that 'Gradual but noticeable liberalisation has occurred in recent decades in terms of what is understood by "research" in the academic world', (Borgdorff, 2008: 91) whilst Foucault tells us in *The Archaeology of Knowledge* that discursive understanding is not:

> an ideal, continuous, smooth text that runs beneath the multiplicity
> of contradictions, and resolves them in the calm unity of coherent

thought; nor is it the surface in which, in a thousand different aspects, a contradiction is reflected that is always in retreat, but everywhere dominant. It is rather a space of multiple dissensions; a set of different oppositions whose levels and roles must be described.

(Foucault, 1972: 155)

Seen in this light, one could take the view that coherence to established practice is no more than a tugging of one's forelock to tradition; a tradition that roots knowledge alongside respectful obedience rather than dissent. Developing Foucault's ideas we can read the demand for truth in thesis terms as synonymous with the type of power relations that see the hard sciences as always already superior to the soft science approaches that have come to epitomise the liberal arts.

Inasmuch as Foucault sees truth, or more accurately 'games of truth', as something impossible to separate from structures of power, the successful completion of a PhD thesis allows entry into the power/knowledge world of academic acceptability: an exercise akin in key ways to the entry-by-invitation world of freemasonry.

Foucault uses the term power/knowledge as a means of exposing the idea that truth:

is produced only by virtue of multiple forms of constraint. And it induces regular effects of power. Each society has its regime of truth, its 'general politics' of truth: that is, the types of discourse that it accepts and makes function as true; the mechanisms and instances which enable one to distinguish true and false statements, the means by which each is sanctioned; the techniques and procedures accorded value in the acquisition of truth; the status of those who are charged with saying what counts as true.

(Foucault, 1988b: 131)

A thesis demands that readers understand clearly the ways in which data was collected, generated and analysed. In this way the reader is shown how results were obtained. This is significant because the ways in which data is gathered can have a massive bearing on how findings are arrived at, and how trustworthy these findings appear. It is becoming commonplace to encounter practice-based research theses where neither data nor findings are regarded as central, or even particularly important; but the regularity with which these absences appear says more, perhaps, about the drive to recruit and accommodate PhD candidates than it does about our collective desire to hold onto rigour and reason in the face of post-Foucauldian doubt.

Foucault rarely wrote an ordinary sentence, and yet we have seen his intellectual legacy of subversive resistance to the powers of orthodoxy translated into a series of evasions and false arguments that, despite appearing to be concerned with expansion, are in fact incredibly reductive. The 2001 PARIP Symposium, held at the University of Bristol, brought together a number of highly regarded academics. The bulk of these made cases in one way or another for practice to be legitimised as *ipso facto* research. Many of these amounted to reasonable and well-reasoned claims; others were more directly provocative, such as Toby Yarwood's contention that if only we learned to re-position 'the paradigm of practice and research, emphasizing their similarity and co-dependency' we would realise that 'practice IS research (and research IS practice) and the use of simile (AS) only weakens the issue.' (Yarwood, 2001) Yarwood continues in this vein with his statement that 'Practice-based research degrees should be accepted as normality, not anomaly.' (Ibid.) In the context of Yarwood's status at the symposium as a postgraduate practice-based research student it is impossible to distance his notion that practice IS research from claims that practice IS thesis, an idea which is given a further twist by Angela Piccini, who asks whether 'engagement between audience and performance [might] be enough to testify to the research and to the dissemination of knowledges to the community'. (Piccini, 2004: 198)

The notion that practice *is* research is a meaningless and ultimately empty conceit, for what does it actually mean? It is worth pausing for a moment at the enormity of the idea that any and all practice is research: not research-driven or research-informed; not *sometimes* imbued with research-worthiness; not that research and practice might *sometimes* overlap. These possibilities (each of which demand a particular kind of attentiveness) are sacrificed to the false certainty that practice is always already research, and it is in this way that both practice and research are reduced to facile terms.

Inasmuch as both autoethnography and practice-based research can be read as attempts to subvert those conventions of academic behaviour that render the living, moving, breathing selves of researchers invisible, they are processes that worry away at many of the in-print certainties this book's pages contain. And long may that be the case. Just as practice-based research might not make a watertight seal with traditionally accepted research activities into performance (and that term is certainly not being used here pejoratively), so the criteria for library-based research may need to shift in order to accommodate the emotions, memories, inventions and interruptions of autoethnographical theses that document practical outcomes.

CASE STUDY 10

In Tränen unendlicher Lust:
An Artistic Inquiry into an Innovating Audiovisual Lied Project

Yves Knockaert

The romantic Lied: a stiff-suited vocalist or a singer in a dazzling dress stands rigidly next to a piano; at the piano a pianist, also in a suit, or a lady pianist in an equally striking dress. At best, the colours and style of their attire are somewhat harmonious, although this is not necessarily a requirement. The singer (male or female) keeps his or her hands immobile, places them on his or her thighs, or leaves them hanging along the body, or folds them together. A sober gesture or facial expression is sometimes used to emphasise the content of the performed song lyrics, although this is not really necessary: only the music matters. Whereas the song as such has evolved in the musical field outside of classical music circles into a comprehensive whole containing song, dance, video, fashion, and social behaviour, and has, as a popular art form, become a public favourite, the romantic Lied has remained a professionally well-conserved museum piece. There are after all excellent interpreters, vocalists who are Lied experts and pianists specialised in Lied accompaniment, but they are comfortable with merely performing the music itself and the position of the genre within the classical music circuit and its traditional conventional setting.

Research Question

Lieve Jansen, singing teacher at the Lemmensinstituut Leuven (Lemmens Institute, Louvain), had been pondering for quite some time what she could do to confront her students, young people of today with an eclectic interest in many musical genres, with the romantic Lied in a contemporary, interesting way. This was not a question in itself, but a consideration made for the listener as well. She did not just question herself, but also her colleagues, and in this way found much support in the search for possible answers. Is it possible to present the Lied in a contemporary manner, able to captivate an audience? Is it possible to formulate answers beyond the obvious usage of visual effects such as lighting, accessorised costumes, and staging? Or find a solution that doesn't necessarily imply dance? The research question was sharply focused on the visual presentation of the Lied based on its own specificity, its intrinsic qualities, in full contrast with the artificial addition of external effects. From the outset, Lieve Jansen considered collaborating with the fine arts field for the visualisation of those intrinsic qualities, ranging from the content of the lyrics to the social context of the nineteenth-century Lied.

She found her ideal research partner in video artist Wim Lambrecht, teacher at Sint-Lucas Beeldende Kunst Gent (the Visual Arts department of Sint-Lucas Ghent). During the selection of the Lieder she came across two exceptional artist couples, both of whom have made a unique contribution to the romantic Lied: Robert Schumann and Clara Wieck; and Gustav Mahler and Alma Schindler. This unique finding led to the inclusion of gender questioning into the project. Obviously, it was always the researchers' main concern to develop the singing voice itself in the most ideal way and to investigate whether the altered circumstances of the vocal performance, as investigated in the project, would also affect the development of the voices of the participating singers. This led to the involvement of Wivine Decoster, researcher at the voice lab of the medical faculty of the Catholic University of Leuven (Department of Neurosciences, Experimental Laboratory, Departement Neurowetenschappen, Labo Experimentele ORL, K.U. Leuven).

This formed the base for the In Tränen unendlicher Lust project. The name of the project refers to the last verse of the poem Ich kann's nicht fassen, nicht glauben by Adalbert von Chamisso, included in Schumann's volume Frauen – Liebe und Leben (this is the original notation of the title, often listed as Frauenliebe und –leben).

The Gender Research

First, the most important aspects of the gender and voice research are briefly considered, followed by an extensive investigation of the fundamental research question. The romantic Lied gender question was originally not solved by the composers, but by the publishers, who developed a simple commercial response to the question: a Lied is written for a high or a low voice, the high voice being a soprano or tenor and the low voice an alto or bass. This allows the singer's gender to, as it were, be changed in the function of the Lied, and even more so in the function of the poem upon which the Lied is based. The poet may have written from an unmistakably male or female point of view, but this is utterly ignored by the publisher, with or without the consent of the composer. There is even more to consider, making the gender issue all the more complex: how is the gender (M/F) of the I-subject in the poem handled by a poet (M/F), and a composer (M/F)?

This threefold M/F relation leads to a myriad of combinations all of which will throw a different light on the Lied's gender issues. However, this leads to considerations of a more theoretical nature, while in fact this project is mainly concerned with the (visual presentation and) performance of the Lied. This brings up the question of the gender (M/F) of the performer, coupled with all previous M/F considerations. This means that, in fact, the project is based on experimentation with the exchange of and between M/F. What happens when a man sings a Lied based on an original poem written around a female I-protagonist? The example par excellence is of course Frauenliebe und –leben. What happens when a woman sings a Lied with a male I-protagonist, which is the case – again considering Schumann – in Dichterliebe? The adoption of a trans-gender position has caused the singers participating in this research project to reflect upon their interpretation and has severely influenced the way in which the Lied is brought. The interpretation becomes much more refined and more conscious of gender positioning when the singer actually 'returns' to his or her own position (man singing as a male I-protagonist, woman as a female). This will not escape the attention of an attentive audience either, even if it hasn't been specifically pointed out or explained.

Anke Gilleir (literary theory and gender researcher, department German Literature, University of Leuven) confronted the singers (M/F) with various elements relating to the research project's gender issues.

The Voice Research

The question whether or not acoustic voice research has a place in the whole of this artistic project is indeed a valid one. In the first place, a number of reasons can be listed which not only concern this very project but also apply to virtually every research project that focuses on voices. At the same time it needs mentioning that it is highly advisable to combine laboratory research with artistic research. Voice research can have a preventive function in that it can avert fatigue or injury. It can act in a therapeutic way through the spectrographic visualisation of voice behaviour, indicating singers' correct and incorrect voice use. This visualising enables a very precise handling of barely audible matters. Voice research can show a singer why a certain passage in a Lied causes difficulty: research can indicate a problem with articulation, tone formation, correct pitch, vocal impulse, etc. In this research project concerning the romantic Lied voice research can contribute to the development of the interpretation specifically.

In her evaluation of the entire project, Wivine Decoster wrote that she considers the image of the singer as entirely unique because of the physical approach regarding body language, facial expressions and gaze, movement and space, direction and mise-en-scène; because of the combination between this physical approach and the link both between the lyrics and the musical score on the one hand, and the singer and the pianist on the other hand; and also aspects such as control, intention, distance, contact, and communication. Behind this complex whole lies a universe of experience, emotion, control, musicality, understanding, knowledge, willpower, technique, conviction, readiness, skill, ambition, enthusiasm, (self-) confidence, alertness…

At first sight, acoustic voice research seems quite alien to the artistic content of the research project, which made it quite difficult for the researchers to convince the commission who control the allocation of the research grant at the start of the project about the importance of this research element. After all, the commission failed to see how what they considered as a purely medical matter could have an impact on an artistic research project, let alone affect the interpretation in a stimulating way through visualisation and comparison. This research does not end with making obvious conclusions: it goes much farther than merely making comparisons between voice conditions at different time intervals. This kind of measuring allows the mapping of physical differences between different singing voices according to a variety of parameters: loudness and pitch range (intensity and frequency range), vocal force in the high, middle and low tessitura, flexibility of the voice, stamina, breathing technique, etc. The physical voice research also allows investigation into an individual singer's interpretation. Not just the physical progress, but the entire evolution of an interpretation can be mapped through the voice research, making it possible to determine the most appropriate interpretation. The spectrographic visualisation focuses intensely on the fine tuning of the singing, making it a veritable piece of interpretative research.

This facilitates the formulation of comparative answers (approximating objective scientific answers) to the specific questions concerning the success of an interpretation; the subtle differences that seem inaudible but are, however, of great importance. A few examples: starting one moment too soon or too late; not immediately reaching a specific pitch – but reaching for it from a lower or higher level (with a minimal, almost inaudible glissando); delayed or premature vibrato on a vowel; vibrating in a direct, intense way or increasing and decreasing the vibrato; stressing consonants or stretching them somewhat longer than normal; singing (thinking) the first consonant of a word at the pitch level of the next vowel; retaining energy until the utmost last moment of a phrase, especially in a descending melody line, which ensures that the rich overtone spectrum remains maintained; etc.

The effect of the body movements of the singer can also be measured exactly by the spectrogram. In conclusion Wivine Decoster writes:

A spectrogram is like a mirror. Without any form of concealment it translates the bare facts of the sound as a product of a complex and fully mental, emotional, and physical activity. As an objective source of information it plays an important part in the development and/or analysis of the actual singing voice. It helps vocalists to gain insight in their own performances and stimulates their development. Using the spectrogram in the singing practice enables the singer to see relations that were previously unclear or perform at an entirely unexpected level. [...] Once the spectrogram is understood as a mirror of the singing voice, the singer will be able to read it just like a score. As with musical notation, the spectrogram will incite an auditive representation, readiness, intention, and physical realisation. The expressed sound becomes an aural image, which, like sheet music, can be varied upon in terms of vocalisation.

Of course, it is impossible to confront the audience with the spectrogram; but working with visualised sound became an interpretative exercise for the researchers and singers. This makes it artistically interesting and innovating at the same time to have either one singer sing the same Lied in a recital various consecutive times, with subtle interpretative nuances, or have the same Lied successively sung by different singers. It seems even appropriate to leave the correct execution according to the score behind and have various vocalists sing the same Lied together. These interpreters can stand at large distances from each other, hereby introducing the visual image into the Lied interpretation, obviously leaving the 'singer standing stiffly next to piano'-style behind.

The Space

Throughout their research, Lieve Jansen and Wim Lambrecht have experimented with different aspects of space and image, as well as the positioning of singers and pianists. If the singer is relatively easily positioned away from the piano, this is obviously not the case for the pianist. Considering the size and bulk of the piano as an object, this has direct and important spatial implications. An upright piano, however, is quite different from a grand piano: it evokes a cosy domestic atmosphere. The upright piano is placed in the living room; this was also the case in the romantic nineteenth century. The presence of a grand piano transforms any given space into a concert hall; the upright piano turns it into a salon.

Also, the sound quality of a standing piano is quite different from that of a grand piano, recreating a typical – perhaps even Biedermeieresque – domestic atmosphere reminiscent of the nineteenth century. The researchers have organised numerous presentations in early-twentieth-century townhouses with art nouveau influences, houses with a particular history, such as for instance the L'Ecume des Jours house and the Ligy house, both situated in Ghent, and a villa by Horta in Renaix. The Ligy house has been uninhabited for quite some time and is in urgent need of repair. The stuccoed ceiling has come down in various places, the wall covering is ruined, the floors unstable. The selected houses served as living heritage piece, memento, and reference object at the same time. They recalled the nineteenth century, the salons where the romantic Lieder must have originally sounded. This is not a stage, but an atmosphere, impossible to recreate in a concert hall.

This space allows the audience to be mobile: it moves from the one salon to the other to listen to the next Lied. It moves to the stairway hall where a Lied with a dramatic turn can be presented as if it were a short play. The audience is free to choose its place: closer to or farther from the piano, on or under the staircase. The varying spatial positions allow the audience to adopt various approaches and enjoy one Lied various times, each time from a different perspective. The salons are furnished with antique furniture; décor attributes in a concert hall, but in this setting authentic reminders of romantic life, the backdrop to a literal 'Frauenleben', as in the title Frauenliebe und –leben. The attributes, the dramatic usage of a stairwell, the mobility of the audience: all these elements are absent in a classical concert hall, or are introduced as 'exotic' décor pieces. The presentation in early twentieth-century houses makes the audience's experience of the Lied more authentic; at the same time it is also experimental, in that the audience is 'active', not to say 'interactive' with the music and the environment.

Wim Lambrecht intentionally wanted to stage a few presentations in a 'Lied-unfamiliar' setting, such as a theatre for instance, quite different from a concert hall. This was the cause of 'Verfremdung' for the singers: performing in an inappropriate space produces a strange acoustic experience; to be invited to sing standing still in an environment geared towards action equally so. How is the interpretation of the Lied affected if the vocalist stands askew, on the verge of falling over? How is the audience's experience of the Lied different when this physical act of 'almost falling over' is incorporated into the performance? Even stranger: a blindfolded singer tries to find his/her way on the stage. He/she is unable to communicate with his/her eyes, his/her facial expressions hidden by the blindfold. The hands are used to find the way gropingly, trying to avoid bumping into something, carefully. The hands are no longer used to express the content of the Lied.

Another oddity: a wide white millstone collar choking the throat, preventing comfortable singing: a rigid image coupled to a 'rigid' voice. The 'voce' doesn't sound as pleasing as it could, aesthetically beautiful; it is suffocated in a way.

Is it permissible to constrict a voice, use it as an element in an artistic research that almost smothers it? Once more it is clear that ultimately the goal is reached: the audience experiences the Lied in a different way, this time not in a different situation, since the audience is seated facing the stage in the theatre just as it would in the concert hall, where the action unfolds. The confrontation occurs through the inability of perceiving what is being sung since the singer has been blindfolded, forcing the listener to just listen, to become a mere 'listener', invited to elaborate his or her own visual imagery, if this were at all necessary. With the wide collars the spectator can literally witness the singer being restricted. He literally hears what he sees; the voice is bound by the wide collar. It is impossible to hear anything other than what is visually presented: what is heard is the reflection of the frustration of being bound, the inability to free oneself. The singer is led to an unprecedented experimental interpretation of the Lied, precisely because of the theatrical intervention; this approach yielded unexpected results for the research project also.

These 'new' interpretations proved unacceptable for those music lovers who approach the Lied and the singing voice through the traditional aesthetic of beauty: the voice of the singer should not be constricted, beauty should not be spoiled. They brought these elements into the discussion and indicated having been shocked at first, explaining that this was in fact the result of the unfamiliar experience the Lied had provoked: non-beauty as Lied aesthetic. Wim Lambrecht explained his position as follows:

> This is the very first time I present the Lied in a theatrical context. This time, the visitor will look the Lied straight in the eye(s). More thought is going into how the Lied will leave the body. Since the theatre setting was chosen, we will be confronted with the absence of 'resonance'. This space is conceived for the speaking voice. The singing voice will be subjected to exhausting and physical circumstances.

> Paradoxically this will bring a different kind of drama to the foreground. Drama of an utmost intimate character. This artificiality is furthermore enhanced through the usage of scenery, lights, costumes, and attributes. All the quintessential elements of 'stage play'. Will the lighting sing to the Lied? Will the voice become a chiaroscuro? Will the singer draw traces of light next to traces of shadow? Will there be space cleared within the darkest corners of this performance where memory can touch upon the body of the Lied? How much time does one need to look through the darkness, make the gaze waver and stray off into what was and what can be expected?

After these experiences, theatrical elements and situations obviously also appeared in the salon settings of the townhouses. A singer goes to stand in front of a large mirror and sings a Lied. He/she is permanently confronted with him/herself and with the audience in the mirror. This is yet another setting in which the audience can experience a Lied. The audience sees the singer only from the 'expressive' back; depending on his position the spectator either sees the expressions of face and hands, or not. The audience sees itself in the mirror: the listener is watching himself as he/she hears the Lied. He/she is forced to confront him/herself with the Lied.

The Image

As a video, artist Wim Lambrecht has explored his own medium to find solutions concerning the presentation of the Lied. The unconventional visual presentation of the Lied through the utilisation of video equipment in the early-twentieth-century houses has brought the audience into new situations in which the Lieder can be experienced. By means of camera usage and live on-screen projection of recorded images in one room, and microphone recording and 'projection' of recorded sound in another, it is possible to separate the singer and the piano from one another. The spectator has to make choices: the live experience of the piano implies seeing the singer on a screen and hearing the singing through loudspeakers, or perhaps faintly live from a distance, from another floor or room in the house. He can now try and find the source of the singing, following the trail of the voice until he ultimately comes to the singer, accompanied by the sound of the piano through the speakers. The exploring listener listens in a different manner; he/she combines voice and piano in an explorative way into a new interpretation of the Lied. It goes without saying that the singer and pianist's interpretation of the Lied in this unfamiliar setting requires absolute concentration: there is no eye contact between the two musicians, it is impossible for them to be close together in the same room and sense each other or breathe together. This situation creates an extra dimension for the video artist: the combination of images and live music can be incorporated into a video artwork. Wim Lambrecht has presented the idea of the singer as 'femme fatale' through the character of Salome (not unimportant in nineteenth-century music, especially opera). The head of St. John was brought to Salome on a platter: at last she was able to kiss him, beheaded. This was not about love, but about power: a gender theme par excellence? Are love and power not secretly interwoven in countless nineteenth-century romantic poems and consequently in many Lieder also? Was this not the real question regarding the two artist couples this research project focused on? Who held power: the composer Robert Schumann, unable to perform as a pianist after a self-inflicted injury paralysed his hand; or his wife, piano virtuoso, celebrity, enormously popular with the public, especially when she performed pieces other than Schumann's?

Who held power in the Gustav Mahler and Alma Schindler couple? Why did he forbid her to compose music after their marriage? Why was she only allowed merely to copy his music? Is this how he tried to tie her to him? It was she who held power over the world, through her wide and open outlook on culture, her passion for art, which she combined with flirting and passionate affairs with lovers, all of them artists. The head of St. John the Baptist becomes the head of the singer, presented on a television screen on the platter of the piano. This is just one example of the many ways in which the utilisation of video can bring a new dimension to the Lied, not only where use of space and spatial separation is concerned, but definitely by inviting, more even, forcing the audience to listen to the Lied in an entirely different way.

The Challenge

In the whole of the research project, the challenge was the greatest for the singers, especially Lieve Jansen who had taken on the responsibility for the research. The above report clearly indicates that the singers were challenged in many ways to interpret the Lied differently than before. Ask ten singers to sing a serious Lied with a small self-made newspaper hat on their heads, and chances are nine of them will run off immediately. For the one who didn't run, this project turned out to be both a blessing and a burden. Unusual, strange to borderline extreme circumstances put greater strain on rehearsals, concentration, communication, mutual respect and understanding, and open collaboration. First, the unfamiliarity of the (classical) musical field with the video medium, and vice versa, has to be overcome and transformed into an exploration of each other's discipline and an investigation into the possibilities and opportunities both artistic disciplines have to offer. It is a fact that this kind of project requires a greater effort from the singer than a mere familiarising with sheet music and performing after studying and rehearsing with the piano.

How can a singer be convinced to perform in situations going from strange to including voice-blocking activities by means of attributes? This is only possible because the whole group of researchers and singers have understood that the research was significant for them and created a surplus value, that it was a challenge which at the same time presented many playful elements, that the confrontation with a video artist in a multidisciplinary collaboration opened new perspectives regarding the interpretation of the Lied. All of these elements can feed a singer's interpretation, bring out new possibilities, and make clear that the future of the Lied lies with interdisciplinarity. Surely, the musicians must have felt that the Lied's audience is old and grey but that precisely through these experimental settings they can reach out and appeal to a new, young(er) audience. After all, the Lied itself is not old and grey, but was reborn in this research project as a contemporary, up-to-date genre.

The Framework

This research project occurred within the frame of projects subsidised by the Instituut voor Onderzoek in de Kunsten (Institute for Practice-based Research in the Arts (IvOK)). IvOK is responsible for the policy regarding practice-based research in the arts as part of the Associatie Katholieke Universiteit Leuven (Catholic University of Louvain Association). This association contains three departments of audiovisual and fine arts, an architecture department, and a music department. The subsidising of the research projects is competition based. The granting of subsidies requires the presentation of a well-founded research problem together with a listing of research methods and a time plan. Ideally, the research group consists of experts both from within and outside of the association, with the additional condition that an art department collaborate with at least one other K.U. Leuven department (be it art-related or not).

Facts

The project started December 2005 and ended June 2009. The principal researchers were mezzo-soprano Lieve Jansen and video artist Wim Lambrecht. Anke Gilleir conducted the gender study and Wivine Decoster was responsible for the voice research. The poems were translated into Dutch by Geert Kestens, assisted by Anke Gilleir.

A total of twenty presentations were organised in locations such as the Royal Opera De Munt/La Monnaie in Brussels, the Lemmensinstituut in Louvain, and private houses in Ghent and Renaix, amongst others. Wim Lambrecht gave a number of lectures presenting video material. He presented the project together with Lieve Jansen at the Dag van het Artistiek Onderzoek (Artistic Research Day) in Ghent in May 2008, and in March 2009 at a session of the artistic research programme 'Into Research', also in Ghent. Both these organisations are part of the Instituut voor Onderzoek in de Kunsten

(Institute for Practice-based Research in the Arts, IvOK). Lieve Jansen and Wivine Decoster gave a number of lectures – together and individually – about the project, and specifically about the voice issues. In this way, the project was presented at the international Pevoc 7 conference in Groningen (NL) (2007), at the Voice Symposium held on the occasion of the opening of the Centre of Excellence for Voice (Expertisecentrum Stem) of the Medical Faculty of K.U. Leuven (2008), and at a workshop held during the international Pevoc 8 conference in Dresden (D) in 2009.

The following people participated in the recitals and performances: the sopranos Greetje Anthoni, Hratsuhi Aramian, Annemie Cobbaert, Gunta Davidcuka, Wannah Organe, Charlotte Panouclias, Marina Smolders, the mezzo-sopranos Ana Naqe and Lieve Jansen, the countertenor Bart Uvyn, the tenors Jan Caals, Govaart Haché, Steven Marien, Laurens-Alexander Wyns, the baritone Peter Maus; the pianists Stefaan Celen, Maaike De Zitter, Michel Stas; the actor Bram De Jonghe; Guy Cuypers, Henri Eliat, Ian Gyselinck, and Jan Pauwels of the Aorta group took care of the set construction; Jos Verlinden, lighting; Pauwel De Buck, Johan Vandermaelen, and Jeroen Vandesande, sound; Bas Rogiers, graphic design.

Lectures and workshops were organised in the frame of this research project. Authentic locations were visited, such as the Mahler–Freud walking-tour in Leiden, as well as locations where Mahler conducted, such as Amsterdam and The Hague, guided by Eveline Nikkels, president of the Gustav Mahler Foundation in The Netherlands.

There were programme brochures with explanatory texts concerning the research project at all presentations. Wim Lambrecht held various lectures and participated in exhibitions with videos which were made during the project. The project was discussed in various publications. The project was included in one of the Cahiers (no. 12) in the series of Cahiers van het Instituut voor Onderzoek in de Kunsten (Cahiers of the Institute for Practice-based Research in the Arts) which presents the results of the artistic research projects. This cahier contains texts by the various researchers: *In Tränen unendlicher Lust. Een artistiek onderzoek naar een vernieuwend audiovisueel liedproject,* Leuven, Acco, 2009, ISBN 9789033473630 (Dutch).

The Researchers

Mezzo-soprano Lieve Jansen has established an extensive repertoire of baroque to contemporary work ranging from Lieder and opera to oratorio on the international scene. Since 1985 she has taught singing and given master classes at the Lemmensinstituut, department of the Hogeschool voor Wetenschap & Kunst (Lemmens Institute, University College for Sciences and Arts). She is project leader of the In Tränen unendlicher Lust research project and has participated in various research projects concerning voice-related issues.

Wim Lambrecht is a visual artist. He teaches at the Experimenteel Atelier van Sint-Lucas Beeldende Kunst Gent, also a department of the Hogeschool voor Wetenschap & Kunst (Experimental Workshop of Sint-Lucas Visual Arts Ghent, University College for Sciences and Arts). He teaches image research at this academy and organises the Filmavonden (Film Evenings). He is also project leader of the In Tränen unendlicher Lust project, operating in the beloved field between image and sound, and specifically focuses on the human voice.

Wivine Decoster is doctor in Speech Language Pathology and Audiology. She is senior professor in Logopedische en Audiologische Wetenschappen (Speech, Language and Hearing Sciences) at the medical faculty of the K.U. Leuven. In her teaching and research she focuses on all the aspects of the human voice: prevention, optimisation, pathology of the speaking and singing voice in various age, professional, and patient groups. She coordinates these voice-related activities at the Centre of Excellence for Voice (Expertisecentrum Stem).

Anke Gilleir teaches German literature at K.U. Leuven. Her research themes are German literature by female authors (eighteenth to twenty-first centuries), literary theory and gender, historiography of literature, literature as cultural heritage, and literature and politics.

At the Crossroads of Research Cultures; Type A, B and C Research

> Research is to see what everybody else has seen, and to think what nobody else has thought.
>
> **Albert Szent-Gyorgyi**

B ack in the early days of post-1960s physical theatre there was a feeling that words were dishonest evasions whereas the body was about truthful communication... or even communion. Four legs were good, two legs were bad and for every effective application elsewhere there were hundreds of students dressed in black and barefoot, scuttling aimlessly around on all fours or prancing like wild horses making faux-Artaudian cries of anguish. Physical performance became the default form for innovative work. And we believed it, and we believed in it. That time passed and for better or worse we moved from animalistic physicality through irony to post-irony; through neo-realism to post-dramatic presentations; through site-specific performance to site-sympathetic work and on to in-yer-face theatre, thinking all the time that things were getting better, believing all the time that we were somehow getting closer to the truth – even when that meant denying all notional possibilities of truth itself.

As practice is as strong or weak as those who work through it, so research methodologies are limited in their effectiveness by those researchers who employ them. The idea that practice-based research is the flame-carrying future of performance or that its disciples should be somehow fast-tracked into positions of influence is a worrying trend and one that does little, ultimately, to further the cause it intends to support.

It all boils down to our lingering postmodern love affair with relativity; and where all truth is relative so validity becomes something of an irrelevance. If truth, and therefore evidence, is all relative the principle of research as something bound to objective verification seems to collapse in on itself. Yet it remains the case that evidence, in whatever form it is offered, is a prerequisite of research outcomes; and whilst one's evidential findings are almost inevitably subject to challenge, it is the way in which that evidence is reached that says much about its voracity.

Practice as research is not ultimately helped by those advocates who look constantly for evidence that supports their claims for its values. This is so because the evidence that matters most is evidence that survives in the face of all efforts to disprove it. Like all irrational beliefs, that which can be asserted without recourse to evidence can be dismissed without recourse to evidence. Something is challenged only when it is tested. Without that challenge we are left with tenuous findings based, seemingly, on the type of confirmation bias that always finds what it is looking for, because it refuses to acknowledge anything else.

There is a sense in which we can identify some of the generic concerns of practice-based research in a more historically conventional British educational context. In a lecture given to the Teacher Training Agency in 1996, David Hargreaves called for educationalists at all levels to be able to pose answerable questions and to know how to find supporting evidence systematically and comprehensively. Hargreaves argued persuasively that this needed to exist alongside the ability to read such evidence competently and to undertake critical appraisal and analysis according to agreed professional standards, ascertaining and organising the importance of this evidence with a view to determining its relevance to one's particular needs and environments. (Davies, 2008: 109) For Hargreaves this is evidence-based research: making one's practice less susceptible to political ideology, conventional wisdom and wishful thinking.

But what is it that constitutes evidence? We can perhaps agree that evidence is only that which works, inasmuch as everything affirmed needs to have first been tried and tested out. Because evidence is something that furnishes proof, we know that before we can claim and use this as a status label we need to be able to measure the outcome of the activity in question. Furthermore, we have to be able to develop a procedure of relating the measured outcomes to the activity in order to transform that relativity into evidence. Hargreaves does not see much of a problem with how outcomes are constructed and yet he is adamant in his zeal for structures which allow for enquiries that can accommodate the meanings different people attach to different activities and which allow for the broader long-term consequences of them. Hargreaves' commitment is to the experiment as the only means for settling disputes relating to educational practice and as the only way of verifying educational improvements; and it is in this way that his thoughts and writings remind us that practice-based research has its roots in evidence-based analysis.

Once an idea for a question has been determined, it is an historical given of research that this will be framed in a way that is likely to yield the most effective and accurate results. Developing our overtly educational theme for a moment we can cite the pedagogical theorists Hubbard and Power who list three important suggestions when framing their approach to teachers' research questions. The first is that the question needs to be 'open-ended enough to allow possibilities to emerge'. (Hubbard and Power, 1993: 23) They also suggest choosing research by considering what is thought interesting or intriguing in one's own situations and contexts. Thirdly, Hubbard and Power advise teachers to 'investigate broader teaching dilemmas that have arisen'. (Ibid.) The ways in which this evidence-based and education-based pattern can inform our understanding of what is at the heart of research through practice in performance are immediately apparent. Indeed, simply replacing Hubbard and Power's words 'teaching' and 'teacher' with our own 'performance' and 'performer' allows for a relatively seamless adoption.

It is self-evidently the case that investigative activity has to be possessed of certain aspects in order for it (for *practice*) to qualify as research. Research is, after all, no more or less than a way of questioning. Essentially, this refers in the arts to our desire to ask and attempt to answer questions we want to learn about rather than, given the choice, those that others assign or give to us. It is these 'real questions' (Brady and Jacobs, 1994) which are often the most rewarding for researchers to ask, develop and learn about. There are a number of important factors that propel researchers forward through practice. One is an examination of those parts of one's own practice that have worked well, aligned to a willingness to share those experiences with other practitioners. By conducting research that tries to understand why certain techniques, approaches, or strategies have been successful, researching practitioners can learn more and tell us more about their own processes. A second force that drives researchers on is that they are able to address their own most telling concerns. In this we see that it is just as important to attempt an understanding of what is unsuccessful as to focus on what it is that works. By conducting research through practice we can better examine our own practical and performance-making strategies and make the adjustments necessary to improve what it is that we do.

Practice-based research in performance exists, to paraphrase Patrice Pavis, at the crossroads of a great many cultures, each with distinctive approaches to qualitative interpretation, each with different points of focus, each with value systems that are as likely to exclude as to overlap. The terminology used to describe activities is likewise difficult to pin down. 'Evidence-Based

Learning', 'Reflective Practice' and 'Action Research' are no less useful terms than 'Practice-Based Research' and its derivatives, although each description carries its own barely hidden agenda. The ebb and flow of boundaries reveals at core a radical disagreement as to the ways in which practice-based research in performance can be defined, measured and judged. And this is made even more problematic by the recent introduction of metric analyses of research outcomes, where the cool measurement of publication, citation, importance and application becomes the key determinant in one's academic research profile. At such a time and in the face of such difference of opinion we do well to adopt a line in which practice and research seek recognition as integrated activities, one borrowing freely from the other in a mutually supportive and developmental fashion.

For many practice-based researchers any approach that attempts to create a binary between practice and research amounts to an invidious demand. For some of these researchers the practical and written submissions are regarded as equal in weight and significance, with each element speaking in its own language to examiners and subsequent readers; for others the importance of practice is such that a written thesis at once reduces the visceral intelligence of the created work and forces the student into the submission of a doubly demanding doctorate: effectively two theses for the price of one. For Katy Macleod, a long-time champion of the idea that art is always already an intrinsically theorising activity, practice is well able to produce and stand for the research aspects of a thesis. Indeed, practice, when it is submitted alongside a written thesis is forced by academic historicity to serve as little more than an illustration of theory, rather than as the form that drives and contains it. (Macleod, 2000)

From the Macleod corner we are introduced to the argument that the conventional PhD use of extant theories to shore up new propositions needs to be reconsidered in the case of practice-based research. Whilst the evidence of collective investigations such as those carried out by PARIP in some ways supports this view, the fact that a number of universities are changing the ways in which practice-based research is supervised, supported and assessed does not necessarily amount to a constructive departure from tradition... only a departure. We know that institutions are becoming more and more amenable to the idea of flexible ratios of practical work and written texts, with universities increasingly determining their own understandings of the ways in which written texts relate to practice, including the amount of words required. Despite these institutional freedoms, it is rare at the moment to find a UK university that is happy in the general scheme of things to accept a written thesis of fewer than 40,000 words, regardless of the depth and scale of practical submissions.

In her incisive 2000 study, Macleod offers a reading of three distinct types of written theses in support of or combined with practical submissions. For Macleod the first approach, which she refers to as Type A, involves renewing and/or positioning the practice so that the written text provides a specific reading of the artwork. Type B aims to put a theoretical context around the methods involved in making the artwork: in this approach the written text is regarded by the researcher as integral in terms of framing the work. Type C strives to reveal the practice: here the written text is integral and complementary to the artwork submission... notwithstanding this, the artwork here *is* the thesis inasmuch as it is seen to offer a theoretical proposition. (Macleod, 2000) Macleod cites the 1974 insistence of the CNAA (Council for National Academic Awards) that the thesis (i.e. the aspect of argument and *value*) is contained primarily in written form and that this must be laid out in an appropriate theoretical document: what practical work exists as part of the submission must be presented in clear and subservient relation to the written work. This is clearly a Type A thesis in Macleod's terms.

The quality of Macleod's contribution to thinking in the field of arts research is justifiably assured; and yet her insinuation that art is enough – that it has the capacity to be both research (with all its contingent accountability) and art (affording space for endless interpretation) – amounts to a position which, for this writer at least, is easier to applaud instinctively than to defend systematically. In fact, Macleod's proposition that art practice is indicative of advanced intellectual thinking is itself something of an exercise in faith over reason, a type of hyperbole where the first line of defence is also often one of attack. As with a great many arguments, the drive to convert can override the need to convince and factions are formed where none need exist.

CASE STUDY 11

Partly Cloudy, Chance of Rain

Lee Miller and Joanne 'Bob' Whalley

What follows is an account of the collaboratively undertaken practice-as-research PhD Whalley and Miller completed in 2003 out of the Department of Contemporary Arts, MMU, Cheshire.

It is difficult to know how best to begin writing an account of our PhD, not because writing about our research is an alien experience (after all, we submitted over 95,000 words upon completion), but precisely because of the weight of words already attached to our thinking about it. As one might expect, our post-doctoral research has grown out of and been informed by the formative experience of our PhD, and much of our subsequent work has borrowed from, developed out of, or strip-mined ideas that belong to our PhD. How might we begin to offer a perspective in this context, in a context where what we think now is so heavily informed by what was written then?

It is not just what we have already written that haunts us; there is also the spectre of things not said. Of the pony that only does the one trick and the fear that we will forever be **that** couple. You know, the ones who pick up bottles of piss, the ones who got married in the service station, the ones who cannot seem to do anything by themselves.

Since the completion of our PhD, all our subsequent practice as research has inhabited spaces that tend to be transactional in some way – that is to say, they are rarely spaces of dwelling, never *home* in the most traditional sense. We could start this account with a discussion of the research imperatives of each piece that has grown out of our doctoral research, but that might not be the most helpful place to begin. Instead, we will slide back into the confessional. Perhaps we are obsessed with journeys, with the things in between A and B simply because we are not well travelled. 'Well travelled' suggests a certain glamour, a movement, a freedom where the world is something with which you are intimately familiar. To us, it speaks of a sophistication that does not sit well in our bodies. We don't do sophisticated, we don't do at ease. We do gauche, we do awkward and we do them very well. No, we are not well travelled. But there are 104,000 miles on the clock of our current car, and we hit 24,000 miles on our last one, 24,000 miles for the second time. No, we aren't *well* travelled, but we are *much* travelled.

As always, we have moved too far forward, and we articulate our concerns before we have offered any context, and we seem to be running the risk of writing something that has nothing to do with our PhD, or our subsequent post-doctoral research or perhaps even with practice as research more generally.

Except that it does.

The narrative of our practice as research does not start cleanly, and upon reflection, perhaps we were a little confused by the terminology. Whenever we thought about the word 'practice', we thought about giving things another go, about getting things wrong, no judgement, no strings attached. It is fair to say that we have never really been the 'measure twice, cut once' type. It is no surprise that we were initially drawn to the sound of practice as research, trying it once, making a 'balls-up' and having another bash. Imagine our surprise when we joined the fray, entered the debate where practice might not mean doing something until you get better at it. It might be about having a practice, a body of practical skills that might be utilised and worked through. A practice was something that we definitely did not have. We were not following a route out of training and into a deeper thinking about that training, nor were we developing ideas formulated from our Masters degree. And we were always, decidedly **we**.

Our context does begin with us, from us. It begins a long way from the academic context one might imagine. It begins on the fifth of December 1995, the date we moved to Penrith. To be accurate, we moved to a house about half a mile outside a small village called Yanwath, about three miles outside of Penrith. A series of mundane life choices, following careers we thought we wanted, led us there. But those careers turned out to be something of a mis-step, so we got married, bought a dog and decided to enrol for a Masters at the (relatively) nearby Lancaster University. Because of the costs involved, we both worked for a year to build up our funds, Bob at a local pottery, Lee at a call centre in Carlisle. By early 1997 we had saved enough for one of us to begin the Masters. A coin was tossed and in September Lee began studying full-time for his Masters in Contemporary Theatre Practice. Soon Bob changed jobs and was working split shifts at a local hotel as a chambermaid. As Bob could not drive a car, it was necessary for Lee to drive her to work before seven in the morning and then begin his commute to Lancaster. Bob would get a lift home at three, and Lee would try to be back from Lancaster in order to take her to the hotel for the beginning of her second shift at seven in the evening. In January 1998, Bob began working for an independent art gallery in Kendal. This meant that Lee could drop her off and pick her up on his way to and from Lancaster.

Without realising it, the road or perhaps more specifically the motorway was becoming a silent partner in our relationship, with the M6 between junctions 40 and 32 becoming an increasingly familiar stretch of road. Following the completion of Lee's MA, Bob began her Masters programme, but because she still could not drive, she took a room on campus and we lived apart from September 1998 to June 1999. The stretch of M6, already familiar, became increasingly significant. It was the road that separated us, and the road that allowed us to meet again. Throughout this entire period (1997–1999), the M6 was undergoing a series of road works. It began in 1997 with resurfacing between Penrith and Shap, and slowly the various plant and people operating it moved down towards Lancaster, as if undertaking the same journey that we so regularly made.

It was during the time that the road works had made it down as far as Kendal that our practice-as-research PhD took its first faltering steps. In early 1999, the motorway just after junction 31 was reduced to two lanes. Drivers were required to travel along the hard shoulder, and because of the volume of traffic moving through a reduced space, the speeds were often well below the posted 50 mph limit. It was on this south-bound stretch of motorway that our PhD really began. Travelling at approximately 10 mph, Lee noticed a bottle resting on the edge of the hard shoulder. It was a two-litre, blue plastic mineral-water bottle. It had no label, and was half-full with what appeared to be urine.

The next time this journey was made, both of us were in the car, and as we approached the bottle, Lee recounted his observation to Bob. As luck would have it, the traffic came to a standstill just as we drew alongside the bottle. Bob decided that there was only one way to discover if Lee's suspicions were correct, so she swiftly opened her door and picked it up. It was this one action that began the research project that this account discusses, and it was in that one moment that the shape of our research project was decided. Without Lee, Bob would have been unaware of the presence of the bottle; without Bob, Lee would never have thought to pick the bottle up to see if his suspicions were correct. It was in the space between us, sitting in a stationary vehicle on the M6 that it began.

Having seen one bottle, we began to see them at regular intervals along the hard shoulder, and we began to collect them. Knowing that these were the product of people, Bob felt uncomfortable about simply taking them, and so it was decided that we would make an exchange. At first we left behind whatever we had in our pockets (coins, tissues, paid utility bills). This soon developed into keeping a selection of treasured items in the car; items that had been given to us as gifts, things with some provenance, things we could exchange for the bottles of urine we found on our travels. A ritualised behaviour developed around stopping on the hard shoulder, which performed the outward signifiers of mechanical failure. Because of the illegality of stopping unnecessarily on the hard-shoulder, Lee would activate the hazard warning lights, open the bonnet, stand in front of the car and scratch his head. Throughout this, Bob would be executing the exchange, collecting the bottle and leaving the treasured item behind.

As we began to talk to people about our growing collection of bottles of urine, we became aware that there was something developing, something that was at that point instinctive, but something that was seeking articulation, looking for a frame that would allow it to develop beyond these small exchanges and become more visible to the general users of the motorway. Our interest in the motorway and the position it occupied within society, and the collaborative manner in which the research project developed was established at the moment we picked up the first bottle of urine. Our resultant practice as research grew out of a more formalised articulation of the instincts that fuelled that first exchange, one that would lead to an explicit consideration of the implications of space, place and collaborative practice.

Joanne/Bob Whalley and Lee Miller
Request the pleasure of the company of
....

to celebrate the renewal of their Wedding Vows
at Roadchef Sandbach Services
M6 Motorway between junctions 16 and 17
on Friday 20 September 2002 at 12.30pm
Formal Dress
RSVP at your earliest convenience

Entitled *Partly Cloudy, Chance of Rain*, the practical element of our research
was publicly conducted on Friday 20 September 2002 at the Roadchef Sandbach
Services between junctions 16 and 17 of the M6 motorway. A site-specific,
durational performance piece, it included the renewal of our wedding vows, the
location of which was intended to problematise Marc Augé's conceptualisation of
the motorway as a 'non-place'. Augé states that:

> [i]f a place can be defined as relational, historical and concerned
> with identity, then a space which cannot be defined as relational, or
> historical, or concerned with identity will be a non-place.
>
> (Augé, 1995: 78)

We felt that this was only a partial account of the motorway, one that ignored
the subversions of its 'normative' usage, and our PhD sought (amongst other
things) to challenge the conceptualisation provided by Augé. Thus the project
had its inception in an inclination to provide a qualification of the account of
the motorway as a 'non-place' and, in its development, contest the notion of
postmodern, or to more accurately invoke the language of Augé, supermodern
spaces lacking co-ordinates or histories. As the project developed, it expanded to
include a consideration of the nature of collaboration through an exploration of
Gilles Deleuze and Félix Guattari, a concomitant challenge to the individualist
location of knowledge creation, and a consideration of poststructuralist theories
through an examination of dialogism, heteroglossia and the multi-accentuality of
the sign, paying particular attention to the theories of Mikhail Bakhtin.

As one might imagine, given our inclusion within this book, our eventual PhD
was what Susan Melrose terms 'mixed mode'[1] in form, consisting of practice,
documentation and a written element. The term 'thesis' was used to describe
the relationship between each of these outcomes, a simple strategy employed to
resist the reification of the written element. The writing was always seen as one of
multiple sites of articulation of the knowledge we generated, and as such, it could

only ever be a partial attempt to articulate the knowledge generated throughout three years of our PhD.

This idea of partiality and the development of knowledge in the spaces between elements, led us to a consideration of Deleuze and Guattari. The construction of *Partly Cloudy, Chance of Rain* echoes the construction of *A Thousand Plateaus* in that it encouraged a resistance to the pull of the metanarrative. *A Thousand Plateaus* presents the reader with multiple, seemingly disparate concepts. This multiplicity encourages the text to be read as open, and thus resist closure. By following a similar structure in the construction of *Partly Cloudy, Chance of Rain*, we encouraged the audience member to resist the closure of an 'either/or' position, and invite her instead to embrace a 'both-and' reading of the performance–wedding event.

Just as the knowledge generated by the practical element was partial, the written element did not claim to offer a totalising account of accrued and reverberating knowledges. Much has been written about the embodiment of knowledge, and of the tensions between cognitive and haptic processes in the generation of knowledge. These debates were never central to our PhD, and so we will resist rehearsing a debate already skilfully explored by theorists such as Merleau-Ponty (1962), Bourdieu (1990), Foucault (1969; 1980), Lakoff and Johnson (1999), and developed by a range of performance practitioner–researchers.

It was enough for us that the written and practical elements both had differing but interconnected jobs in the overall development of our thesis. Reading the written element of our submission would never replace standing in the service station as we renewed our wedding vows; likewise the renewal of said vows did not seek to provide the wealth of contextual and theoretical material expounded within the writing. Both sites were in dialogue with one another, with knowledge being developed in the interstices. Indeed, the knowledge generated between these two sites was similar to the manner in which knowledge is generated between the two of us, in the manifold conversations, discussions and arguments that constitute both our research and our life partnerships.

Given that ours was the first practice-led PhD research project within the arts to be conducted in an entirely collaborative fashion, the joint nature of our approach was necessarily reflected upon throughout the written element. For the most part, the written submission employed the traditional voice of academic discourse. However, in an attempt to account for the multiplicity involved in its construction, there were occasional ruptures in the discourse, allowing space for a more reflective, playful voice. Perhaps interestingly, we made the decision that within the writing there would be no attempt to indicate if it was 'Whalley' or

'Miller' responsible for the construction of particular sections of text. As with the practice, our writing was collaboratively constructed, with both of us having worked on all sections of the text, ensuring that the knowledge produced within the writing was generated between us in a field of influences. This writing strategy remains, with all of our post-doctoral research having been jointly authored, utilising the strategies developed throughout our PhD. Letters are written, notes are passed. One will speak while the other types, and occasionally we will sit at the same keyboard, our fingers falling over one another in an attempt to get our thoughts out while still responding to the other's ideas.

Since the installation of *Partly Cloudy, Chance of Rain* we have written and spoken about this event in five different countries, spanning two continents. We have presented the work at conferences, workshops and sessions discussing alternative models of postgraduate research. We have spent more time revisiting this six-hour portion of our life than is healthy, and now we find ourselves returning to it again. But perhaps for the first time, we are encouraged to ask ourselves 'why?' Not why did we stop to collect that first bottle, not why did it develop into a six-hour durational performance that included the presence of a choir, a band, a pianist, twenty performers dressed as brides and grooms, two photographers in our employ, plus another four or five from various media outlets, a TV crew, an Anglican priest, fifty family and friends and the two of us. Rather, the 'why' we are encouraged to address is concerned with the choice to explore any of this through practice.

Following our initial discovery of the abandoned bottle of urine, and the subsequent musings that resulted, we could have offered a perfectly coherent qualification of Augé's thesis, locating it within an appropriate field of enquiry, and leading to a traditionally constructed written thesis. Of course, the conjoined nature of our venture might have been problematic in such a context, but let us park this concern, and focus instead on our pull towards practice. The performance installation referred to above was our attempt to provide the users of the service station with a practical, rather than cognitive, challenge to Augé's conceptualisation of the non-place. Although recognising the operational validity of Augé's thesis, the performance of *Partly Cloudy, Chance of Rain* was our attempt to provide a counter to the behaviours of the non-place (those of transit and transaction) by disrupting the experiencing of the space.

As previously stated, the research project began with an observation, a chance encountering of a discarded bottle of urine on the hard shoulder. What followed was not a simple musing, the response did not stop at the conceptual; the project developed out of a physical response to the initial observation, it took the form of a subsequent collection of the bottle, and this in turn developed into a series of performative exchanges. From the outset, thought and action were wedded; we could not conceive of a response to the encounter that did not include stopping and collecting the bottle. And as we have already stated, without Lee, Bob would never have seen the bottle; without Bob, Lee would never have stopped to collect it. In that moment, the subsequent nature of our PhD was defined. A thinking found articulation in a doing, a thinking that was shared between two, perhaps akin to what Charles Stivale means when he adopted the term *'pensée à deux'* (1998: xi) to write about Deleuze and Guattari. Seeing a bottle of urine, discussing its provenance, picking it up and eventually developing recurrences of the phenomenon into a number of exchanges, was the result of a series of observations and concomitant actions, all of which led us to use practice as a research methodology. Even though it began without an explicit contextual framing, it began as the result of a question, a question that eventually necessitated the inclusion of further 'traditional' research methodologies. Both the actions executed on the motorway, and the research undertaken within the academy, were vital to the development of our PhD.

It became clear that two very distinct discourses would need to be employed to the same end: the traditional academic discourse as evident in this piece of writing, and the less overtly academic inscription of the site-specific performance. It is possible to make a case that performance work, created and presented within an academic context, might assume a certain amount of prior knowledge from its audience. While it differs formally from the written articulation, performance work presented as part of a practice-led PhD is likely to share something of the established academic context. It could further be argued that practical work presented within an academic context can expect its audience to have experience of, or interest in, the type of performance with which it is engaged. Being located in the public space of the service station, *Partly Cloudy, Chance of Rain* could assume no such thing. Despite having invited 50 guests to the venue in advance (including various representatives of the academy), we were aware that the majority of our audience would encounter the work as part of their daily use of the service station, and thus without any predefined conceptual framework.

This realisation led to an engagement with the writings of Mikhail Bakhtin, and particularly the concepts of 'dialogism' and 'heteroglossia'. Bakhtin suggests that there are a multiplicity of 'speech genres' at play at any given time, each recognisable to, and appropriate for, different encounters (1994). We were keen that *Partly Cloudy, Chance of Rain* accounted for the differences within our audience, and it was through a consideration of Bakhtin that this became possible. Thus, an exoteric–esoteric aesthetic was developed in the project. The exoteric refers to that to which the majority can relate, or understand. It references a populist tradition, as opposed to the esoteric, which suggests understanding from a limited, particular group. Broadly put, the exoteric is the majority of the users of the service station, whereas the esoteric would be the few, probably those invited guests who were operating in their capacity as representatives of the academy. The majority of PhD research might assume a certain 'expertness' from its reader, indeed its purpose is often to add to the accumulated levels of expertise. The inclusion of practice within our project meant that we could assume no such expertise, and as a result we needed to develop strategies to account for the various types of audience.

It was this recognition that led to the development of an exoteric–esoteric aesthetic. At the beginning of the project, we had discussed the development of a piece of devised performance that could be installed in a service station. However, it became clear that any piece located in a service station would have to take the general users of the site into account, and therefore needed to be constructed with them in mind. Thus, Bakhtin's concept of heteroglossia (literally many-voiced) encouraged the construction of a piece that would employ exoteric and esoteric aesthetics, in order that it could be read by as wide an audience as possible.

Of course, by deliberately positioning our research outside the academy, coupled with the bottle that began the whole process, it was (and still is) possible to read our project as entirely parodic. While there was always a ludic element to the project, it is vital to state that the research was never simply a 'piss take', a pun all-too-readily available to the casual observer. While there was a deliberately playful element running throughout the project, there was also a sincere attempt to engage in a series of theoretical debates, and in our own way to add to the 'expertness' of the field. It is this balance between the parodic and the sincere that is most evident in the vow renewal, but something that also ran throughout the entire project.

In the case of the vow-renewal ceremony, its role was to oscillate, to occupy a both-and position in terms of potential readings. When recounting her experience of the day, Lee's mother still talks about her experience of the vow renewal as a 'fluttering' in her perception; one in which she was aware of the event as a performance, but equally aware of its position as a socio-cultural ritual. Her 'fluttering' resisted settling on one position even as the vow renewal was enacted. In contrast, a colleague referred to the event as a 'wacky arts project' prior to the event, and likewise after the event used the same description to articulate the piece. However, in the moment of the vow renewal, she was seen wiping tears from her eyes. These tears suggest that, for the duration of the renewal at least, the event ceased to function as a 'wacky arts project' and began to operate more as a sincere act of the affirmation of our love.

Which brings us briefly to Ludwig Wittgenstein, specifically his discussion of the duck–rabbit. (1968/1953: 194) We came across this simple line drawing in the final throes of writing up our PhD. It slotted into what we had been thinking with an elegance quite unlike anything else we had encountered. As we wrote about it, we became enthralled by the idea that once the rabbit had been seen, the duck is always infected by its presence, and (of course) vice versa. Once seen, it cannot be unseen. The response offered by Lee's mother, and the reading we make of our colleague's tears equate to our 'seeing' of the duck–rabbit.

These two responses, offered as anecdotes rather than 'proof', serve to point to the way in which the vow renewal functioned as both a parodic and a sincere act, providing the audience with a dialogic experience that could not simply be reduced to the position of either/or, accounting for both the exoteric–esoteric aesthetic. As both a sincere event and a parody of itself, it conformed to Linda Hutcheon's definition of the postmodern in which she states:

> [p]ostmodernism offers precisely that 'certain use of irony and parody'…
> As a form of ironic representation, parody is doubly coded in political
> terms: it both legitimizes and subverts that which it parodies.
>
> (1988: 101)

In order that our qualification of Augé's non-place might be successful, it was necessary that space was provided for the wedding ceremony to function as a sincere event. However, at the same time we needed to provide space for the event to read as parodic, to ensure that we were not simply replacing one monologic conception of space with another. In this way the employing of parody can be articulated as a postmodern strategy of resistance, subverting and affirming that which is represented. By employing parody and sincerity within the same moment, we were ensuring that both the exoteric and esoteric aesthetics were accounted for.

In many ways, it is this fluttering, or at least the potential for fluttering, that practice-led research can offer in a way that more traditional modes and methodologies might struggle with. Of course, the location of our research within what can broadly be termed poststructuralist discourse afforded us a certain licence. By locating our research within a poststructuralist context we allowed ourselves the opportunity to resist certain fixity of meaning, and also the space to embrace a challenge to individuated notions of knowledge creation. This resistance is further illustrated by our embracing of a both-and approach to the exoteric–esoteric aesthetic and place/non-place.

The consideration of the types of knowledge generated by *Partly Cloudy, Chance of Rain* discussed above perhaps requires us to offer a further consideration of the location of this research project, and more broadly practice as research, within the domain of theories of knowledge. Our PhD attempted to resist the closure presented in the acceptance of an either/or response, suggesting that we were developing a thesis[2] that opened up space for a multiplicity of responses, rather than closing down the text to a singular response. This both-and approach is perhaps most explicitly evidenced in the collaborative nature of the research project. By working collaboratively on both the practical and written dimensions of the research project, we sought to resist the singular position of originary generator of knowledge. In so doing, we further resisted indicating to the reader which of us 'owns' the knowledge generated – in fact our account of the collaboration suggests that neither of us owns the knowledge, noting instead that it is located in the space between us.

By resisting an either/or response to knowledge, by working in an explicitly collaborative manner and locating our research within a poststructuralist frame, we provided little room for the concept of falsifiability as famously outlined by Karl Popper. Popper states that:

> [w]e can say of a theory, provided it is falsifiable, that it rules out, or prohibits, not merely one occurrence, but always *at least one event*.
>
> (2002: 70)

Popper's theory of falsifiability determines what statement/theory can be classified as science, and what can be classified as what he describes as 'non-science'. The deliberate slippage we employed, firmly locates their work under the heading of non-science, with more in common with the 'language analysis' (Popper, 2002: xix) of which Popper makes a critique in his preface to the English edition of *The Logic of Scientific Discovery*. In it he states that falsifiability is required for a system to achieve the status of empirical:

> [b]esides being consistent, an empirical system should satisfy a further condition: it must be *falsifiable*. The two conditions are to a large extent analogous. Statements which do not satisfy the condition of consistency fail to differentiate between any two statements within the totality of all possible statements. Statements which do not satisfy the condition of falsifiability fail to differentiate between any two statements within the totality of all possible empirical basic statements.
>
> (Popper, 2002: 72–3)

From this point of view, it is clear that our practice-as-research PhD cannot possibly be defined as empirical. It is not concerned with falsifiability, and deliberately resists this kind of closure. If Popper's model is accepted as a definition of scientific knowledge, then this questions further the type of knowledge generated by our research project.

Of course, in the early-twenty-first century, it is possible to draw a distinction between the empirical/verifiable knowledge created by the hard sciences and the knowledge paradigm in which we located our practice-led PhD. Much of our research concerned itself with what could be described as experiential knowledge, knowledge that develops as a result of observations made in the field. Unlike Popper's knowledge based on falsifiability, these observations cannot be proved or disproved, merely reflected upon. It is for this reason that we did not seek to overwrite Augé's concept of the non-place, but instead augment it with a reminder of place, in an attempt to keep both concepts in the continual play of both-and. Evidently our practice-led research was exploring 'soft' knowledges, rather than the 'hard' knowledge propounded by Popper. This consideration of 'softness', which should not be confused with a lack of rigour, reinforces further the need for us to have undertaken our PhD utilising practice as research as a methodology, allowing as it does the use of practical explorations of theoretical models. Thus, 'soft' knowledges, which valorise the experiential, supported our strategies of dissemination, which sought to generate knowledge in the location in which it was developed. *Partly Cloudy, Chance of Rain* functioned in such a way, allowing the service station to be both a site of contestation and of generation.

As a result of that first bottle of piss, and all that followed it, we have spent most of the past 12 years looking out of various windows, at varying landscapes as they blur by. We are much travelled, and we suspect that the much-travelled couple probably does not engage in the voyage of discovery. Their travels are unlikely to be the kinds that lead to some sort of edification. They are much more likely to engage in the kind of journey that ends on a stranger's doorstep with a Kirby™ vacuum cleaner or something in tow, and a hopeful smile on their face.

The much travelled probably clock up the miles out of necessity. Maybe they have a partner who lands a job in a far off place, a partner who ups sticks and moves to the land of milk and honey, leaving their other half behind, and so they are forced to travel 500 miles a week just to try and keep the old familiar routine in place, even if it does creak, groan and threaten to buckle under the weight of expectation. But that is another part of our shared history, part of the research and life partnership that is so messily entangled, and we are in danger of moving away from the PhD, and down the subsequent roads we have taken.

But these are roads that we must resist, as that is not where we want to take you this time.

The blurring of landscapes, the buckling of expectation and the strained smile of the much travelled. Where the miles speak of promises, not discovery. The space between *A* and *B*, occupied out of necessity; so we find ourselves sitting here, stationary but thinking about movement. Thinking again about how the research began, and where it could take us, has taken us. Away from where we were, from the fixed point of one there, imagining the shift to another. Except of course that oversimplifies. We are never moving away from one fixed point, and we are always moving towards a multiple. The 'there' we have left has always been plastic, a shifting point we imagine to be fixed, even as it is in flux. And so we are brought to the beginning that we imagine we start with and from, even though we know it oscillates; the beginning that is **home**.

Notes

1   In her essay 'Entertaining Other Options…' (2002), Susan Melrose writes about the status of the practical element in relation to the written thesis, in what she terms 'mixed-mode' submissions.

2   It is important to remember that we offer this term as a definition of the combined outcomes of the project.

SECTION 12

Mode 1 and Mode 2 Research; Dissemination; Professional Doctorates; Qualitative Issues

> If we knew what it was we were doing, it would not be called research.
>
> **Albert Einstein**

Michael Gibbons argued in 1994 that from the mid-twentieth century on a new context-driven, interdisciplinary and problem-focused form of knowledge production emerged. This approach to learning, which Gibbons opted to call Mode 2 Knowledge Production, often involves multidisciplinary teams of practitioners, working with randomly emerging stimuli, in contradistinction to the discipline-specific investigations, predictive and more obviously goal-oriented research of Mode 1 thinkers. It is clearly the case that the type of thinking, research and practice explored in this book generally adheres to this Mode 2 ideal.

We have reached a point in our academic development where industry-driven concerns are shaping investigations to the extent that knowledge is increasingly regarded as being at its most effective when it impacts most overtly on socio-economic factors. (Malfroy and Yates, 2003) It follows that the relationship between academic and professional practice is more blurred now than at any time in the recent past. It follows further that the very idiosyncrasy of PhD research makes it eminently capable of accommodating these changes in foci, and it is able to do so, some would argue, through a shift from Mode 1 to Mode 2 thinking. We can observe that Mode 2 thinking functions most effectively within varying contexts of application and that, as Gibbons reflects, this makes knowledge applied through Mode 2 approaches 'inevitably performative'. (Edwards and Usher, 2002: 147)

Notwithstanding the necessity to result in work that makes a contribution to knowledge, Mode 1 research, the type most often encountered in conventional PhD routes, is predicated upon learning for its own sake: learning that, if it leaves the university at all does so either reluctantly or late. In this sense Mode 1 knowledge tends to stem from traditional academic subjects and disciplines. As our $100 story has illustrated, most written theses know no shelf lives other than those provided by university libraries and most are referred to, if they are referred to at all, by subsequent researchers through inter-library loans. Mode 1 knowledge demonstrates concern with the pursuit of universal truths and objective findings articulated in identifiably codified structures: the stuff of university tradition. In comparison, Mode 2 knowledge tends towards immediacy, relevancy and application: the very heart and soul of performance practice. Mode 2 knowledge is also transdisciplinary, in that it is likely to involve the 'close interaction of many actors throughout the process of knowledge production' (Gibbons, 1994: vii) and it is inextricably linked to the finding of solutions to problems as they emerge, rather than pre-determining each and every response. Mode 2 approaches then are characterised as the production of knowledge from and through application. Its practitioners often have disciplinary training from Mode 1 institutions and education but their work tends to be transdisciplinary. Whereas Mode 1 is hierarchical, Mode 2 is heterarchical in that it is group based, rather than remaining focused on the work of individuals. Whilst Mode 1 researchers are concerned about certification, verification and approval from the academy, Mode 2 researchers seek validation through application.

The changes wrought by Mode 2 knowledge production have started to subvert many of the conventional ideas of thinking about the ways in which research is organised. This is so as a result of the strong focus on application and interdisciplinary that underpins Mode 2 thinking. It is this blend of methodological hybridity and 'real-world' usefulness that upsets the traditions of discipline-specificity and peer assessment. Whereas Mode 1 research is investigator initiated and discipline based, Mode 2 tends towards problem-focused and interdisciplinary research: research entered into within a context of use. We should bear in mind amidst these qualities that whilst the notion of Mode 2 research has attracted a number of followers, it is some way short of being universally accepted.

One perceived problem with Mode 2 work is that it blends descriptive and normative elements, creating more of a learning ideology than a research theory. There is also something self fulfilling within Mode 2 approaches inasmuch as these are in essence about types of learning that cannot be authoritatively encoded in traditional forms of scholarly publication. Mode 2 research is based around a highly reflexive dialogic process, an egalitarian exchange between researchers and research subjects; and these egalitarian aspects are often utilised to such a profound degree that the basic vocabulary of research becomes almost redundant. A consequence of this is that our usual notions of accountability have to be massively revised.

Broadly speaking, we can characterise Mode 1 research as being:

- Entered into by individual academics;
- Produced in universities;
- Mono-methodological;
- Subjected to qualitative assessment through peer review;
- Subject or discipline-based.

Mode 2 research is, equally broadly, the pursuit of knowledge that is:

- Often produced by and in teams;
- Produced in non-university locations
- Transdisciplinary;
- Subject to application-based accountability.

Mode 1 research is based on the objectivity of knowledge and is dependent upon the notion that validated understanding needs to be rooted in some type of objective reality. This is the historical foundation that has given legitimacy to knowledge: testing findings against previously established ideas of objective truth and/or correspondence with an objectively real world. It doesn't take much familiarity with a postmodern vocabulary that worships doubt to see how dated these ideas can be made to appear. Indeed, postmodernism's challenge to traditional forms of knowledge has brought us to the point where researchers across a number of disciplines have abandoned all claims to objectivity, relying instead on a faith in the virtue of interlinking relativities. Our innately postmodern understanding arrived at through Mode 2 approaches is then characterised by a problem-solving approach to specific issues, as opposed to a context governed largely by the interests of an academic community. As such, my own slightly cautious approach reveals a more deeply embedded faith in this traditional idea of the academic community (and in knowledge-transfer rather than knowledge-production) than I would usually care to admit, and my partial reservations should be viewed in the light of this shamefully confessed conservatism. Caution aside, we can applaud the Mode 2 idea that research should be useful to someone other than the researcher.

The usefulness of practical arts research is diffuse and inferential, and consequently difficult to measure and circumscribe. Practice as research has always possessed more than its share of Mode 2 characteristics, long before the term was coined. We can see that a Mode 1 approach is entered into within a context of new theoretical knowledge discovery whilst Mode 2 approaches are more logically concerned with practical explorations which, whilst sanctioned by universities have their truest application in the professional workplace. Indeed, for Robin Usher the researcher's workplace 'becomes the site of research'. (Edwards and Usher, 2002: 15) Under circumstances such as these we can begin to see potential distinctions between the practice-as-research PhD and the PhD by more conventional routes, not simply because of the ways in which research might be carried out and submissions might be framed but by the differing types of knowledge provided. In terms of fitness for purpose, this leads us to question the extent to which the PhD by thesis alone is most obviously a doctorate for professional academics and (with apologies for the crudeness of the binary) the PhD through practice is a more suitable doctorate for artists. We consider this because the differing provisions of knowledge might lend themselves to differing post-PhD environments. The phenomenon of artists in residence does much to make light of this, but the number of professional practitioners lending their experience to institutions on a short-term basis is relatively low.

In lay terms, we can describe the conventional PhD as being concerned with academic investigation by (usually) inexperienced researchers and the PhD by practice as concerned with action research engaged in by (usually) experienced practitioners. We can also see issues in terms of the ways in which work is retrievable and capable of dissemination. Whereas the conventionally written thesis is easily capable of being disseminated, it rarely is; by contrast the performative elements of a practice-as-research thesis are likely to be disseminated more widely, even though they are almost impossible to retrieve with any accuracy.

Practice-as-research Mode 2 PhDs are usually expected to conform to similar regulatory aspects as conventional PhDs, which are assessed by thesis alone. Because the standard university practice is to accept practical work as part of an overall submission – so that, together with a 40,000–50,000-word written thesis, it makes up an equivalent to the 'gold standard' of 80,000 words – we often find regulations that are re-written to accommodate this distinction; but this rarely results in anything other than a fifty–fifty split based on notions of the practical work's 'equivalence' and not much more. The processes one goes through in terms of research are only really significant inasmuch as they are seen to be appropriate to the subject in question and to be rigorous in the ways they are applied. Whilst one's research approach is massively important to the researcher, it is what emerges from this (in this case the thesis) that matters to examiners and subsequent readers. This is an important point for us to note because any practical work offered as part of the overall submission is seen as an integral part of the thesis rather than something that is largely seen as being of illustrative worth.

The term 'practice as research' is then often misleading. Grotowski's *Towards a Poor Theatre* and Brook's *The Empty Space* are examples of entirely written outcomes that stem to a large extent from practical research activities: these are examples of practice as research, which are very different things to productions of *The Constant Prince* and *A Midsummer Night's Dream*, which we might more usefully, or honestly, refer to as examples of research as practice. There is more to this than mere word play. Mode 2 knowledge notwithstanding, our understanding that research processes inform research findings does not negate our knowledge that this is not always or automatically the same thing as offering research processes *as* findings. The information gleaned from and through practical investigations is not worth more than information gathered through any other research form and we need to be careful to guard against thinking it so.

Perhaps it was inevitable that the recent proliferation in publishing within our subject area (see Thomson, 2000) would lead to some sort of backlash, so that practice, seen as actively *doing*, would start to nudge aside writing, seen as passively *talking about*; but this is not reason enough to conflate process and outcome into a generic embrace of practice as either innately research driven or satisfactory within the strictures imposed by PhD.

A PhD is not the only terminal academic qualification available to researching practitioners. Research programmes leading towards a professional doctorate qualification are widely known and used across a range of applications, and yet the professional doctorate (ProfDoc) is largely unknown within the subject area(s) covered in this book. ProfDocs differ from PhDs in approach and assessment rather than quality. What we often find with ProfDocs are two-stage processes, with the first stage concentrating on research training and the second moving forward into specific research projects, 'where the university, the candidate's profession and the particular work-site of the research meet and intersect in specific and local ways'. (Garrick and Rhodes, 2000: 127)

On the face of it this is what we find in conventional PhD-by-practice registrations; the difference here is that ProfDoc students are by definition engaged in ongoing professional work. This distinction is central inasmuch as one of the tensions of the practice-as-research PhD involves the qualitative assessment of any non-written work submitted as part of the overall thesis. While the status of professional practice is no automatic guarantee of quality it remains a fairly reasonable indicator. We can say this even though we know that professionalism is something of a moveable feast when it comes to performance. Earnings from professional practice can be so small and/or sporadic that it is quite common for one's supplementary income to outstrip vastly any payment received for professional performance work. The opposite also applies (although with reduced regularity) whereby brief periods of highly paid employment can lead to a 'professional salary' that has little or nothing to do with any engagement, immersion or even interest in performance.

ProfDocs originated in the USA, where they were initially developed in the field of education. More recently the qualifications appeared in Australia and the UK in areas including particularly Education, Business and Law. We can connect the emergence of the ProfDoc to the widening role and remit of universities in the production and transference of knowledge, linked to growing acceptance of evidence-based research and reflective practice and the development of work-based learning, the need for more professional/industrial relevant programmes and the proliferation of access into Higher Education. The increase in structured PhD programmes, demands from the workplace and various funding council recommendations to develop transferable skills have lead to the integration of some ProfDoc elements into traditional PhDs... not least into arts-based PhDs by practice. Stan Lester makes this link explicit when he describes the emergence of 'practitioner doctorates' as heralding a new type of ProfDoc that focuses on practical activity which also embodies a high level of professional scholarship. (Lester, 2004) For Lester this creates a PhD with an emphasis on creative practice rather than on the rigid adherence to codified research methodology.

A 2004 report from the UK Council for Graduate Education suggested that Professional Doctorates are a development of taught doctorates, distinguished by the fact that the field of study is a professional discipline, rather than an exercise in primarily academic enquiry and scholarship. Because the research aspects of ProfDocs are inevitably focused on professional practice, 'it is possible for the work to make an original contribution to the way in which theory is applied, or to the nature of practice within a profession'. (UKCGE,

2004: 7) Stuart Powell and Elizabeth Long concur, describing the Professional Doctorate as an award where the field of study is 'a professional discipline and which is distinguished from the PhD by a title that refers to that profession.' (Powell and Long, 2005: 8)

Key features of Professional Doctorates are:

- A concentration on professional practice;

- Focus on the researcher's professional development;

- A shorter thesis-length than for conventional PhDs, but with an equal requirement for originality;

- A greater concentration on taught elements and the specification of learning outcomes.

A number of practice-as-research PhD routes share these features, with the taught element being the only aspect that one rarely sees. That aside, the similarities and overlaps are patently clear. The PhD demands that students make substantial and original contributions to knowledge and demonstrate the ability to make a continuing high-level contribution to their subjects whilst the ProfDoc makes equal demands in relation to research, but links these more openly to the concerns of professional practice. A PhD is usually awarded solely on the basis of a substantial written thesis, whereas a ProfDoc is usually earned on the basis of a portfolio of practice and written accompaniment. In this way we can see that the distinctiveness between the ProfDoc and the PhD are being challenged by recent changes in PhD programmes. Indeed, practice-as-research PhDs have more in common with Professional Doctorates than they have with conventional PhDs and the reasons why Professional Doctorates have not been embraced by universities as tailor made for practice-based investigations into theatre, drama and performance remain something of a mystery.

CASE STUDY 12

Corpo, Carne e Espírito: Musical Visuality of the Body

Johannes Birringer

1. Audio-Visions

If one were to look for critical studies of visual composition in contemporary multi-media performance, one would probably be disappointed: the available literature on mise-en-scène and intrinsic relations between performance (acting, dancing, performing audio-visual interactive enactments) and acoustic/visual/ kinetic projection in the technologically driven media performances of the last two decades is sparse. Although practitioners in theatre, dance and performance art at times delve into their processes of composition to discuss collaborations with designers, interactional composers, and programmers, it is rare that we learn about the specific challenges encountered in the aesthetic creation of 'performance systems' that integrate performer and audio-visual/responsive environments, especially the various architectures of projective environments.

We also don't hear enough about the specific challenges of delimitation in performer techniques applied to interactive mise-en-scène – a sensitive subject perhaps that is understandably undertheorised since the integration of digital technologies in live performance often requires extensive technical problem solving, delaying the compositional process or determining modifications of the performer techniques, for example asking dancers or actors to adapt their movement to help the computational system (and its movement-tracking or sensing instruments) to 'recognise' the performers' gestures properly. Technologically driven performances almost always limit or modify performer virtuosity, and thus the software to some extent qualitatively constrains what bodies can do and what they like to do with the 'machining architecture', a term used by architect Lars Spuybroek to define the virtual organisation, not the actual structure, of a machine or a system and its component audio-visual, tactile, procedural or dynamic properties.[1]

Critical studies are only now beginning to catch up slowly with the evolution of hybrid arts and digital performance, and consequently, with the assimilation of independent new media arts and collaborative networks into the spectre of research methodologies – conceptualised in academic institutions, arts organisations, specialised labs or cross-disciplinary research centres – that underpin the development (R&D) of new work.[2] Rather than addressing the outer frameworks that may (or may not) support experimentation and artistic production within (presumed) interdisciplinary university research contexts, I shall examine the intrinsic aesthetic and technical demands for systems integration in a particular compositional process which conjoined my London-based laboratory with Brazilian composer Paulo Chagas and an ensemble of Brazilian musicians and vocalists. The practice-based research process for the digital oratorio *Corpo, Carne e Espírito* culminated in three public concerts commissioned by the FIT Theatre Festival in Belo Horizonte (June 2008). It was encouraged by prior artistic projects on interactive audio-visual performance carried out since 2002.[3]

When I refer to 'performance systems', I specifically address stage works or open installations that are built with a combination of physical performance and computational feedback systems which allow the real-time manipulation of the digital stage and its various data flows. Such manipulation, in my experience, involves programming and design of the interactive architectures, and thus shifts the (older) roles of the scenographer or the artists who contribute design (stage scenery, costumes, lighting, video/film projections, and sound) into a kind of instrumemtal live performance context, namely real-time interactive audio-visual spaces where software computing or live coding has added a rich dimension of 'cross-patching'.[4] Such cross-patching and connecting processes generally link aesthetic aims with technological innovation and issues (e.g. technical problems) of extending functionality introduced by electronic and engineering instruments. On the theatrical level, choreographing physical performance is also a digital process patching the coded 'bodies' (the imaged figures or resultant abstractions) into the temporal medium of projective space. My role as a choreographer/ stage director therefore is not easily distinguishable from that of a designer or programmer. The artistic research, which I present as a case study in the following pages, is predicated on complex collaborative strategies of composition and temporal mediation/interactional performance.

Primarily, I want to examine the role of music/sound in relationship to physical imaging, and the role of visual real-time image manipulation in relationship to music, positing the conceptual and perceptual resonances between performance, image and sound as one of the key areas of research in contemporary audio-visual art. The proximity or distance, the complementarity or dissonance, between the 'images' of a performance and the accompanying sound, or between music performance and accompanying images, is a complex, continuously fluid and changing phenomenon. In interactive performances we also cannot speak of visual and audio 'tracks' since the tracks are not edited beforehand but generated in the performance. What is at stake are the connections and discrepancies that are being built and designed for the reception of a live concert or installation, for *audio-vision* and the multi-dimensionalities of hybrid acoustic–digital works which stretch from the physical action or gestures to the manifold projections of the virtual.

Visual sound, visual music, sound images: how to address this complex combinatory phenomenon and compare how sound and image behave? How to imagine composing and performing images to music, and to examine how each element in musical performance and visual composition plays its part in figuration, narration, temporal rhythm or temporalisation/vectorisation (of static or dynamic scenes) to generate complementary effects, duplication, repetition, counterpoint and contradiction? Furthermore, rather than adopting interpretative models from studies of sound art or film sound (for example the intricate critical analyses in Michel Chion's *L'Audio-Vision*), I suggest here that we look at the performance-making practices and constitutive stages of production, articulating the methods through which relationships between physical imaging (mediated through camera, editing and real-time manipulation) and musical performance, between mapping of images to sound or mapping of sound to bodily movements, are created.[5]

Our pre-production for *Corpo, Carne e Espírito* begins with the paintings of Francis Bacon – those famously irritating portrayals of distorted flesh and writhing anatomies which inspired the composer to create a series of short compositions later combined into a full-length oratorio for chamber orchestra and vocalists (eighteen sections). The leap from painting to music is a stretch, but one of course recalls Bacon's amazing studies of Velázquez's portrait of Pope Innocent X, with the distorted screaming mouth wide open, amongst so many other denuded bodies he painted in seemingly arrested figural contortion, with silent openings or sockets from which the organisms might escape. Paulo Chagas approached me with the proposition of creating visual images for his oratorio, the particular sequencing of which was open and not determined when I begin to work on the visual script. I had collaborated with Chagas before, on several dance/music productions, so there was a strong basis of trust between us allowing for continuous experimentation. After many months of online exchanges, and in-depth scrutiny of Bacon's painting technique, I start shooting film in the studio, envisioning the visual material of the physical performance to be pre-edited for an open, live improvisation with interactive software patches programmed as a kind of choreographic scenario for triptych projection of digital images. I want to mix the projective image live in real-time during the music performance.

Figure 1

Paulo Chagas conducting *Corpo, Carne e Espírito* at Klauss Vianna Theatre, Oi Futuro, Belo
Horizonte, Brasil, 2008. Yiorgos Bakalos on triptych screen, live processing by Johannes Birringer.
Music ensemble: left to right standing: Eládio Pérez González, Sérgio Anders, Mônica Pedrosa;
percussion (right): Sergio Aluotto; string quartet (front): Frank Hammer, Eri Lou Nogueira, Cleusa
Sana, Pedro Bielschowsky. Photo courtesy of Luca Forcucci.

This approach harbours many intricate problems. Firstly, I will examine
the resonating capacity of the digital, asking whether the animated gestures
of projected bodies can in fact complement or connect at all with the acoustic
sensorium and the emotional intensities of 'pure' listening. Secondly, I offer
some production notes from working with kinaesonic gestures or real-time
interaction with 'image groups' or 'libraries' inside the software patches used for
the performance with the musicians. My observations derive from working with
a form of live coding (real-time composition or improvisation) that layers and
manipulates the shot material into time images and 'synchronous objects' that are
projected alongside the music performance.

The first problem of course arises when translating painting into digital
film, creating photographic studies of the actors' bodies. The translation is

also inspired by the music composed by Chagas for the various sequences of the oratorio, but the photographed bodies remain silent and do not respond to the music. The projected bodies' sensation-levels or thresholds do not possess visualised sound; the projections do not materialise in sound and its source (of sound). My images are in fact soundless, while the performance of the oratorio creates a full musical world separate from the (visual) action on screen. The spectator/listener can watch the instrumentalists and the vocalists, but cannot locate the point of audition as that of the visual figures in the film scenes. The whole notion of a place of audition in our work is complicated, as visual bodies and music are disjunctive/autonomous even as they appear together (united); the visual gesturality of the musicians might even be heightened by silence of the projected figures. Yet the oratorio is also distinct from opera (and its often-stylised, exaggerated gestural and scenic vocabularies), from silent cinema which borrowed opera's punctuative musical effects, and from film scores using orchestral music and leitmotif techniques for narrative synchronisation or the expressive symbolisation of action scenes. Chion rightly points out that 'in opera the frequent synchronising of music and action poses no problem, since it is an integral part of an overall gestural and decorative stylisation. In the cinema such synchronisation must be handled more discreetly, so as not to be taken as exclusively imitative or slip over into the mode of cartoon gags.'[6]

Opting for non-synchronised, discreet visual sequences, I largely focus on the internal rhythms and cadences of the visual space and its sensorial impressions. A careful interpretation of Bacon's melting flesh-bodies suggested the use of the specific kinetics of digital visuality, preparing short tracks for microtonal image manipulations and frame-by-frame corruptions, as a kind of counterpoint to the sustained integrity of the oratorio's musical form, its precise score, internal structure, and virtuosic performance conducted by Chagas himself in the concert. How could I 'conduct' the bodies-to-be-projected? The conducting happens on two levels, first in the shot selections, then in the real-time programming. In our laboratory, we have come to believe there is something in the connection between the gesture and the interference with the 'image group' by the performer or programmer that might re-emerge as a signature with a distinct, poetic video quality. For the production process it is crucial to plan the filming for the signature of image manipulation. We don't create a movie clip or static images (stills), but asynchronous objects *designed to be interacted with*. The digital objects are incomplete without the interaction.

Much of the initial shot selection is done with actors performing in the nude. If music is, or has been considered, the most abstract art form of all the arts, its relationship to the erotic or pornographic imaginary is necessarily convoluted, since the nude body evokes a certain naturalistic or explicit dimension, a loaded dimension that can also be dangerously close to slapstick. Surely, serious classical composition and rigid experimentations of the twentieth-century avant-garde (after Mahler, Berg, Webern, and the younger generations of composers influenced by Stockhausen, Boulez, Berio and Ligeti) abstain from the burlesque and chaotic proliferation of subcultural genres exploiting the base slapstick materiality of sexual imagery or the corrupted low-fi trash aspects of video, especially hand-held video (in advertising, reality TV, celebrity and internet porn, S/M video, manga, gun erotica and other comedies of tremor). Avant-garde music is not without its own slapstick potentials, however, if you recall Kurt Schwitters' *Ursonate* and the notorious beginning of this sound poem ('Fümms bö wö tää zää Uu, pögiff, kwii Ee, Oooooooooooooooooooooooo...'). The pornographic counterpoint to avant-garde music interests me precisely because of its faltering, indeterminate nature, the uncertain anticipations that might be aroused by the digital 'deformation' of the body and its diffusion beyond the single frame (single screen). The multiscreen configuration I designed creates a kind of orchestral spatialisation of the images; and, secondly, the 'unnatural' movement of the projected bodies also disrupts the rules of representation or diegetic logic. The emotional affect of the music cannot easily supply any logic to the multiple frames; it cannot explain the images.

Filmmaker Andrew Repasky McElhinney, admired for his provocative *George Bataille's Story of the Eye*, chose to shoot his underground porn film as a silent movie, letting the camera just capture ambient location sound and then editing the sound and mixing it with additional audio fragments. The fragmentation, McElhinney believes, is an advantage of what he prefers to call 'filmed radio', leaving the visual text open enough to allow the spectator to process it *after* seeing it.[7] There is a very strong dynamic of anticipation and thwarted gratification in *Story of the Eye*. Other filmmakers, such as Martin Arnold, use found footage from B-movies to de-animate and re-animate particular frame sequences – again as silent film – in order to 'scratch' the filmic image and even delete figures within an image sequence, throwing narrative continuity out of kilter and generating a nervous fluttering, a hysterical twitching of image-as-motion. Most interestingly, in a collaboration with choreographer Willi Dorner, for a dance–film piece titled [...], Arnold decomposed graphic sexual scenes from found pornographic footage, using extensive computer technology to actually erase the filmed figures from the existing film material and leaving only the holes, their absent presence, in the projected digital performance space.

A certain dismantling of the visual, or the destruction of figuration, also lies at the bottom of my approach to *Corpo, Carne e Espírito*. It requires creating a space for the hearing of forms of not clearly discernible bodies, flesh or meat, following Bacon's images/colours of meat that flow and seep, almost as if their visual direction could be felt as a touch of sound. Bacon's pink and orange flesh often causes pain in the viewer, as we stare disbelievingly at swollen, elongated, hysterically deformed flesh and carcass, something human becoming something animal or abject in 'diagrams of sensation', as Deleuze called them.[8] These diagrams, like the open mouths of Bacon's 'Heads', scream at us, since they are highly graphic, sensational, and at the same time blurred, wiped and scrubbed. Their blurrings are (like) the scream of voice confounding the meaning of sound that escapes from a mouth, throat, diaphragm, lung or deeper inner cavity. This blur is the pornographic dimension which cannot be clearly described because we cannot see what escapes, what breaks down kinetically in the organisation of the bodily organism. The visual blur also does not have any clear points of convergence in the music, or the musical instruments (cello, violin, percussion, etc.), unless one interprets dissonances as anxiety producing or ominous, and most of such semantics of listening cannot but be highly subjective. Nevertheless, I now want to explore how music, in this sense of the gestural, kinaesonic blur, might complicate the partition of the perceptible and build/sustain the non-linear, non-dramatic procession of visual decompositions of the body.

2. Phantasmic Silent Dance

The *Corpo, Carne e Espírito* oratorio has five parts, with the first two parts comprising three sections each, and the last three parts comprising four sections each; the parts are interlinked by four silent entr'actes. During the short entr'actes, each of the vocalists steps forward to the edge of the stage and sings silently into a microphone. The image of mouth and face is captured by a camera and transmitted to the triptych screens. What the audience sees are the heads of the baritone, the counter-tenor, and the soprano, and finally the coupled heads of the two male vocalists, engaged in a teasing duet, a lovers' discourse that is silent but doubled (on screen) in real time, distanced from the front to the back, enlarged. Mouths wide open, eyes wide shut – what the live camera feed captures are slightly blurred (the feed is processed in the interactive software patch) orifices, muscle tissues, skin, jawbones, the large cavities at the back of throats where voice would break through if we could hear it. Yet the microphone here amplifies only silence. For these scenes I decide to use a live feed; all other pre-recorded scenes are mixed and layered through computer programming.

Figure 2

Entr'acte 4, with Eládio Pérez González, Sérgio Anders, *Corpo, Carne e Espírito*. Video still: Johannes Birringer.

'In the sensory zone of audibility which the microphone transmits to us', Rudolf Arnheim suggests, 'there is probably no direction at all but only distance.'[9] Silence, with voice only implicitly present, creates a particularly intimate distance or proximity, a circular contrapuntal scenario in which unrequited love and desire overlap as if in a fade-out. But a silent scream resonates in our imagination, and is not Arnheim's Gestalt psychology examining why we see or hear things as we do, and whether there is a partition between what can and cannot be seen or heard, a partition between what can and cannot be coupled together? In the visual design I develop for *Corpo, Carne e Espírito*, I seek for such partitions rather than attempting to illustrate the music composed for the five parts of the oratorio, allowing the sound and the instruments to stretch their full expressive potential, according to Chagas' structure:

1. Directionality from slow to fast – electronic sounds; opening of space

2. Opposition between live-performance/electronic and large ensemble/ solo; alternation of spaces

3. Alternation between solo/ensemble; different characters and atmospheres

4. Alternation between solo/ensemble and consonance/dissonance; dissonant mood

5. Directionality from voice to ensemble; sense of development; consonant mood.[10]

Silence creates much more expectation than music, Chagas agreed, and in the oratorio's main musical sections he initially used very reduced harmonic material – based on a system of intervals (a lot of major 7ths) and a repertoire of extended techniques for string instruments – for example, the technique of pressing the bow against the string for producing scratching sounds. In the music for voices, he used a contrast between modal melodies and harmonies that recalls medieval and early renaissance polyphony, and unusual sounds produced through or in combination with breath, whispering, speaking. There are directionality as well as recursive and fractal structures developing contrasts inside contrasts, and musical gestures that pulsate simultaneously with symmetry and regularity, asymmetry and irregularity.[11] Such compositional elements might also be used for the digital images and animations, but I try to create a separate dynamic in the visual projection of colours and bodily forms, aiming at quietly fragmenting spaces of something quiveringly present, breathing, unstable, contracting and expanding. These spaces do not visualise sound, nor are they diegetic, nor adherent to any linear or chronological notion of time. Rather, they affect optical consciousness through an indirect, underhanded mode of visual volubility which I call *granular digitality*, in analogy to granular synthesis (e.g. varying the waveform, envelope, duration, spatial position or density of the sound grains, amplitude modulation, random reordering, scattering and morphing). On three screens, the projected images undergo various glitch infestations and granular depressions which continuously both articulate and dearticulate the frames of the body.

In a sense, this technique of digital granularity means translating Bacon's paintings into luminescent and ghostly video surfaces/skins created through the projection, a graphing of motion that often appears as if still, animated yet deanimated, nervously hovering over an unconscious sensation of the videographic objects (male bodies, female bodies, heads, part objects, contours, armatures, pools of colour, pellicles, silk cloth, striations, shutterings). Just as Chagas' music attempts to capture the poetic of Bacon's universe and invisible forces behind the surface of bodies, not necessarily related to anything realistic, concrete and objective, the video and the digital software transpose 'obscene' images into

Figure 3

Part 5, Scene 17 (Handicapped), *Corpo, Carne e Espírito*. Photo courtesy of Luca Forcucci.

virtual abstractions. None of them speaks 'to' the music or expresses anything that one might think one is hearing. Contrary to Chion's notion of the audiovisual scene, the music does not anchor the images. The graphics, then, cannot function as visual track or diegesis, and the music does not constitute a film sound track or underscore driving the action image or setting/propelling atmospheres. Independent from one another yet intertwined, the quasi-cinema of a visual dance of objects and the music imprint different sense experiences on the listener, sensations wrestling with sensations.

While preparing *Corpo, Carne e Espírito* for the premiere, I was reminded of Hélio Oiticica's ideas for the 'suprasensorial' aspects of colour extending into space and creating sensory stimuli in the environment through enactment, through the wearing of the Parangolés as habitable colour or garment that incites the wearer to move/play with its luminous qualities, rhythms, and intensities. In his late work of the 'Quasi-Cinema' installations, Oiticica arranged whole rooms as inhabitable tactile–corporeal spaces provoking a delirious sense of materiality (colours, fabrics, projections) as *penetrable*, an experience he called *vivência* and considered an intermixture, a concretion, of the real and the virtual.[12]

While it is true that the listener can find a way to allocate time–space or emotional or narrative meaning even if heterogeneous acoustic spaces are immersed into each other, complex musical compositions stretch beyond the probable to peculiar, invisible spaces and conflicting dimensions that intermingle without ever unifying within a larger whole. Regarding the acoustic realm of the radio as a new technological artform, Arnheim proposed that the constant permutations and migrations of polyphonic sound create an ambivalence ('appropriate for the future') and virtuality of unresolvable probabilities and inexplicable differences. You will 'make countries tumble over each other by a twist of your hand, and listen to events that sound as earthly as if you had them in your own room, and yet as impossible and far-away as if they had never been.'[13] The layerings of electronic, instrumental and vocal music in *Corpo, Carne e Espírito* generate this sense of delirious ambivalence, stretching out, and as in the case of most operatic arias, we cannot quite understand the words sung by the vocalists. They remain blurred. But at the same time, Chagas' music contains a very high degree of 'graphic' resonance, of a gestural physicality that is of course 'performed' live, visible right there to the audience. At times I reduce this visibility by having very low light on the musicians, while the triptych screens (hung upstage above the musical instruments that fill the stage) glow with the colour fields of projection, a deep crimson red, followed by turquoise, cold white, soft orange, wrinkled and folded textures of fabrics, pleats of skin.

It is the uncanny contradiction within the projected images themselves which complicates the sensuous and erotic temptation, the desire to reach by the twist of your hand as if you could touch the far-away object. You sense the fabric but your tactile sensation is deceived, the cloth does not hide or adorn the unusual body shape, two twisted arms grow from a yellow torso, reaching up, elongated, as if a butoh dancer's hands were now plucking an imaginary feather from the glittering plumage of a rare bird. The disjunction between the musical and the visual can impact our senses in powerful ways, illuminating the deficits of visual hard-core graphics and allowing for a larger elasticity of the mental spatialisation.

Invoking the material aspects of sound, Arnheim emphasises its multifaceted and abundant nature, as this is how he understands *materiality*, 'the affective capacity of sound: sound as movement, as metamorphosis, as a material repetition of ephemeral differences that generates intricate lapses – convoluted lapses with many velocities, all viscous, elastic, capable of sequences, but certainly also capable of simultaneity, of retention, of anticipation, of slowing down and speeding up, of multiple intervals, a thousand times folded and refolded – that, finally, breach all confines and burst forth into boundless musicality.' The manner in which Arnheim describes sound is thoroughly sexual and erotic; Serge Cardinal is more modest and comments that musicality here is not a 'plain and comfortable metaphor: it proclaims a liberation provoked by manifold affinities, through forces that appropriate perception.'[14] This musicality, I suggest, runs through Chagas' music for the oratorio; it is gripping and sometimes teeming with dissonant intensities that transport the listener to a state where perceptions are conveyed into the darker, phantasmatic realms of fetishised glamour or pain.

3. Filters of Decomposition

Most of the video footage for *Corpo, Carne e Espírito* was shot in the studio, with five actors and dancers; some of it was shot outdoors. Then hundreds of small QT movies and animations were created to be manipulated in real-time interactive processing. The projected images circulated on the curved triptych, displayed in various configurations: all three images are the same (but not played at same tempo); all are different; or combinations of one different plus two the same, with side by side or left/right/centre juxtapositions, one image alone or two images alone, etc. Slowed down to crawl almost indiscernibly, most of the time images are non-linear and looped, evoking an intensified sense of movement in place. Others are manipulated frame by frame, the microfilms becoming inconclusive image-spasms.

In the concluding pages, I shall discuss the visuality of some of these mircofilms, without claiming that I could define how you might perceive, interpret and remember body shapes or parts of a body or spatial forms or colours in the particular context of a music concert. Rather, I am claiming a

Figure 4

Part 2, Scene 4 (Knife/Violation), *Corpo, Carne e Espírito*. Photo courtesy of Luca Forcucci.

certain power of exhilarating affective sensation which arises from *Corpo, Carne e Espírito's* projection of unusually warped or dissolving figures/figural objects. Chagas wanted me to envision a connective tissue between flesh and the spirit; it is hard for me to fathom where the latter comes into play, its possibility must rest with the audiences.

The disjunction between the musical and the visual, I argued, impacts our senses in unexpected ways, illuminating the dearth of visual pornography associated with abject or hard-core transgressive sexual images. The naked flesh, the knife gently cutting through meat, the running dog, the fetishistic costume of power (in the Pope scenes), the vegetal green and the orange colour fields – none of these microfilms presumes a sense of transgression, titillation, excessive splendor (Lingis) or the Bataillean erotics of profanation and defilement.[15] But they evoke possibilities of seeing how we would not have imagined seeing a body (human, animal, male, female) or an eroticised curve, a tremor, a spasm, the difference between taut muscles and sagging flesh, a young female body balancing on a chair, an older man lying exhausted on the floor, an eye stroked by a violin bow, a mouth wide open, incongruously distorted.

Part 1, Scene 1 (*Birth*) opens with three fields of red coloured cloth which reveal subtle creases but nothing else on all three screens of the triptych. In the centre screen, very slowly, a bent over naked body becomes visible underneath the red, with hands and fists opening and closing in slow motion, extending the uncomfortable posture for the duration of the scene without relief.

In Part 1, Scene 2 (*Prison*), the colour changes to a clinical white. Abstract 'shuttering' becomes visible in the centre. On the left, a person is becoming slowly visible under the white. An interrogation scene: the prisoner–body squirms on a chair. On the right side, slowly a cage appears, a still figure stands inside the prison. This is a 'real' documentary photo, taken in Guantánamo. The figure is barely visible, but the sensation of cold, whitewashed walls prevails and provokes a colder air.

Bacon was drawn to pathological, forensic as well as X-ray images and incorporated them in early paintings; he had collected scientific photographs showing how the skin was folded back to reveal raw flesh, and curiously, he was also attracted to 'spiritist' manifestations. He seemed particularly fascinated by the traces of light on photographs exposed for a long time, and manifestations of ectoplasm for him were consonant with the chronophotographs of Etienne-Jules Marey. The striations he painted over his figures have been associated with the 'shuttering' technique in photography; the curtains, veils, cubes and cages that 'hold' the figures (e.g. the Pope portraits) also served simply as a device for 'seeing the image more clearly.'[16] At the same time, these stripes generate a kinetic effect; they are lines that appear to move as in a flickering 16mm film projection. I tried to create this shuttering effect in the interactive video animations for this scene, using special filters that provoke the still images to flicker.

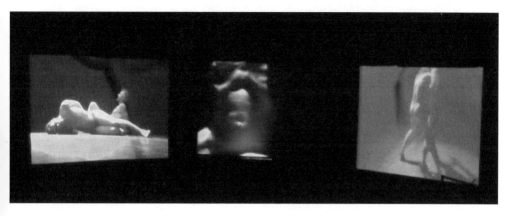

Figure 5

Part 1, Scene 3 (Men's Love)), *Corpo, Carne e Espírito.* Video still: Johannes Birringer.

In Part 1, Scene 3 (*Men's Love*), the colour changes to dark white and grey, with a blue tint. Two male figures are seen left and right, and later also in middle, intimating a scene of two men after coitus; they are exhausted, they lie separate, then squat together. The quiet scenes are interrupted by a more convulsive, harsh erotic sense of love making between men, wrestling with each other. They are full of anticipation for the sport of love.

Later, in Part 3, Scene 8 (*Shaving*), a voluptuous female body is seen pressing her flesh against a milky glass pane; we see her turn her back against the glass and press against it, her spine distorted in many wrinkles of white flesh, then her arms move her body around and we see her full breasts in a slow motion, with hands held forward as if to show us the lines on the palms, skin meshing with plexiglass to immerse us into a sexual (mirror) space. The televisual screen becomes the very skin of touch, the woman's hand fondling our eyes looking at her naked body which cannot be fully seen.

After the third silent entr'acte, featuring soprano Mônica Pedrosa, Part 4, Scene 11 (*Love*) reverts to the thematic evocation of love in the aria sung by Pedrosa downstage right, a haunting melancholic threnody hovering in empty space, only a faint image appears on the left screen, slowly growing more distinct,

Figure 6

Part 3, Scene 8 (Shaving), *Corpo, Carne e Espírito*. Video still: Johannes Birringer.

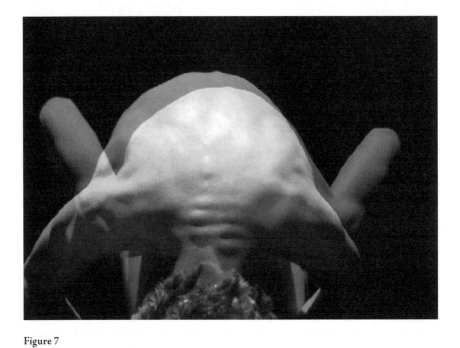

Figure 7

Part 4, Scene 11 (Love), *Corpo, Carne e Espírito*. Video still: Johannes Birringer.

as if emerging from the singer's open mouth. The doubled image of a man's torso turned upside down, slowly moving (together as if one), a man auto-erotically entwined with himself, becoming animal-like.

In Part 4, Scene 13 (*George Dyer*), during an exquisite violin solo performed by Frank Hammer, we see another 'portrait' this time of a formally dressed man in profile, looking to his left, then looking to his right (on left and right screens), while in the centre there is a full facial close-up of a young woman. 'Dyer' looks at the face in the centre which is stroked by the bow arm of the violinist, the strings cutting across the face causing the woman a kind of ecstatic pain. She responds as if in the throes of *jouissance*, her face, eyes, mouth, teeth and cheeks twisting in arabesques filtered with changing tones of colour.

Figure 8

Part 4, Scene 12 (George Dyer), *Corpo, Carne e Espírito*. Photo courtesy of Luca Forcucci.

Earlier, in Part 4, Scene 12 (*Pope*), the voices of soprano, countertenor, and baritone, along with the string quartet and percussion, intone a rapturous, powerful cacophony of sounds, while the microfilms project a seated authority figure (a woman dressed in majestic purple and golden silk coat) who gestures with her outstretched arms as if ordering us, commanding our attention. All three popes on the screen are depicted with a slow zoom into their faces and their wide open mouths, and the sequence-images then freeze in the final instance, holding the scream. The hands are now invisible, but they are remembered as claws, birdlike extremities that clutched at something invisible.

Figure 9

Part 4, Scene 12 (Pope), *Corpo, Carne e Espírito*. Photo courtesy of Luca Forcucci.

Part 5, Scene 18 (*Handicapped*) features a short text (sung) from Francis Bacon – 'I think about death every day' – accompanied by shifting musical sonorities that are by turns strikingly beautiful and abrasive, and conjoined with abstract and figural images that are heavily filtered in the interactive software processing. On one side we see a woman's face covered with soft honey; the contours of the face gradually melt away. On the opposite side, another fleshly body is digitally anamorphosed, slowly decomposing into fragmented trunk, limbs, belly, thighs, filtered out into yellow, ochre, and orange colour scratches and stains. In the middle, a sequence of still animations is seen of a couple appearing to make love on a bed. The colour red returns, as abstract moving squares begins to flicker, suggesting boxes or framings that enclose the disappearing bodies.

Figure 10

Part 5, Scene 17 (Handicapped), *Corpo, Carne e Espírito*. Video still: Johannes Birringer.

The graphic momentum of the visual scenes is achieved through heavy filtering in the software. The Isadora software refers to these filter objects in the patch as 'actors', and I act with these actors in real time to affect the colour tones and saturations, the contours, the figure, and the vibrations of pixelation in the field. I rarely use the real speed of the filmed images or their unfiltered RGB colour values; rather, I continuously vary the frame-by-frame motion, and the light intensity and transparency values. The broken tones of the figure make the bodies appear layered, shadowed, and emergent, just like the 'accidents' Bacon mentioned as mounting on top of each other. The particular aesthetics of real-time video synthesis, with its permutations of resolution, zooming and graphic morphing effects, can thus intimate the quasi-cubist technique in Bacon's painting, when he combines various limb positions (in his 1967 *Study for a Portrait* based on photographs of Henrietta Moraes or his mysterious 1953 *Sphinx I*) or depicts anxious, disjointed bodies in flux (*Study for a Pope*, 1955; the crucifixions, George Dyer portraits, or the late *Triptych* of 1991) and places their curvilinear, mutating forms against greenish grounds or black voids. The graphic image choreography implies a kind of kinaesonic metabolism: motion and decontouring shadows glide slowly as if animated by the ripples of sound (waves) created by the orchestra, and yet the music – and the musicians' gestural performance – remains mostly outside the visual space. At the same time, the music cannot but infuse (project) perceptual mechanisms and emotional tones onto the images. The quivering voice of the baritone creates a 'personality' for the image of falling or enmeshed bodies: it inevitably manipulates sensory perceptions of the morphology of the image.

Yet unlike some of my previous interactive performance works, in which dancers control the image manipulation through their kinetic behaviour and technique (movement/gesture), in *Corpo, Carne e Espírito* I use the computer keyboard and touchpad to 'conduct' the real-time processing of media parameters directly and intuitively, auto-scopically: as I hear the music performed live, I enact the image transformations in the software. This is not an external, merely operational (functional) action, but needs to be considered expressive, since I make instinctive, immediate decisions which have no safety net; I can certainly hit the wrong note and get the 'pitch' or 'glissando' of the frame manipulation wrong, and this will instantly show up on the screens, even if the audience may not recognise a visual mistake. Interacting with a software technology, while my sensations and perceptions of the live music are in a heightened state of anticipation for the live coding, thus requires rehearsal and a technique which becomes embodied and articulate over time. This software performance technique, driving image processing algorithms that are mathematical but result in visual output, involves making split-second judgements similar to the rapid thinking of musical performance improvisation. Real-time control of an interactive computer system, therefore, demands a particular sensitivity for the tempo and granularity of visual time. Musicalising the images, the projective visual world, is a technique of unfolding the frames, bit by bit in time, just as music is an unwinding of experience of time.

The music for *Corpo, Carne e Espírito* is essentially dialectical, with unresolved tensions of complementary worlds of modal melody in conflict with the 'noise' of strange phonemes (consonants), extended techniques on the stringed instruments, effects on the strings and percussion. 'Everything is fragmented', the composer suggests, 'and pushed to the limit of the possible. Nothing stays; there is a constant transformation of the material trying to develop something but it doesn't go anywhere.' This suspension crystallises, in my mind, the indeterminability of the graphic organisms in the visuals. Attracting darker and more warped recesses of the mind/imagination, some of the images might compel different chambers of the erotic imagination, produce haptic sensations that are as coagulated as the dissolving, superimposed figurations. We can create various scenarios to explain a body's mannered postures, twisted shapes and isolated, disintegrating wholeness, or we can accept them as real. The intensities here are evolving, incomplete, there is no brutality of fact and no allegory of futile erotic vandalism. The dilation of the clothed or nude form quietly intimates a surreal flow, a leakage that makes it hard for the eye to discern a consistent presence. The effects of this flow, however, can be felt on a deeper affective level where the listener might realise, after processing the experience, that no identification (with flesh or spirit) was readily available to the sensual imagination. Rather, the 'visual' counterpart to the music suggests a particular fluidity between (perceiving) body and projected informational objects (images, colours, space, events) which imbricates a range of different sensations and tactile responses to the digital devolution of the body.

Acknowledgements

Special thanks to Paulo Chagas, the musicians, and to all my collaborators of the DAP-Lab, especially Paul Verity Smith whose photographic work and conceptual explorations of the interactive image were instrumental for our practice.

Notes

1   Cf. Lars Spuybroek, NOX: *Machining Architecture*, London: Thames and Hudson, 2004: 6–13

2   Steve Dixon's *Digital Performance: A History of New Media in Theater, Dance, Performance Art and Installation* (Cambridge, MA: MIT Press, 2007) is perhaps the most comprehensive study to date of the use of new technologies in the performing arts. It is part of the MIT Press 'Leonardo' series of books, edited by Roger Malina, focusing on new media arts, and the series includes important studies by Susan Kozel (*Closer: Performance, Technologies, Phenomenology*, 2007), Frank Popper (*From Technological to Virtual Art*, 2007), Oliver Grau (*Virtual Art: From Illusion to Immersion*, 2003), Lev Manovich (*The Language of New Media*, 2001), all the way back to Mary Ann Moser and Douglas McLeod's *Immersed in Technology: Art and Virtual Environments* (1996), which offered case studies of several large-scale research projects conducted at the BANFF Center in Canada. Gabriela Giannachi's *Virtual Theatres: an Introduction* (London: Routledge, 2004) is a theoretical account of hypertextuality and the theatricality of interactive technologies but rarely engages with performance practices. Christiane Paul's *Digital Art* (London: Thames and Hudson, 2003) is an illustrated guide of artists and artworks since the 1980s, distinguishing between work that uses digital technology as a tool to produce traditional forms and work that uses it as a medium to create new types of art (net art, software art, digital installation, virtual reality,

etc.). I present a critical and aesthetic engagement with these practices in my book *Performance, Technology, and Science* (New York: PAJ Publications, 2008), and make reference to a few other studies that resulted from workshops, e.g. Martina Leeker (ed.), *Maschinen, Medien, Performances: Theater an der Schnittstelle zu digitalen Medien* (Berlin: Alexander Verlag, 2001) and Söke Dinkla and Martina Leeker (eds), *Dance and Technology/Tanz und Technologie: Moving towards Media Productions – Auf dem Weg zu medialen Inszenierungen* (Berlin: Alexander Verlag, 2002), or from theoretical approaches to new media-performance, such as Susan Broadhurst and Josephine Machon (eds), *Performance and Technology: Practices of Virtual Embodiment and Interactivity* (Houndmills, Basingstoke: Palgrave Macmillan, 2006), and Freda Chapple and Chiel Kattenbelt (eds), *Intermediality in Theatre and Performance* (Amsterdam: Rodopi, 2006). In *New Visions in Performance: The Impact of Digital Technologies* (Lisse: Svets & Zeitlinger, 2004), Gavin Carver and Colin Beardon collect essays from both critics and practitioners, and their focus on design stands out amongst most of the other books. An overview of new media art movements and their gradual institutionalisations can be found in Mark Tribe and Reena Jana, *New Media Art* (Cologne: Taschen, 2007). One of the most provocative books of case studies, investigating interdisciplinary arts and science research, is Joke Brouwer, Arjen Mulder, Anne Nigten, Laura Martz (eds), *aRt&D: Artistic Research and Development* (Rotterdam: V2_Publishing/NAi Publishers, 2005).

3   My interest in interactive performance evolved gradually from numerous multi-media dance and theatre productions I choreographed in the 1990s, and from my involvement in dance and technology workshops (introducing software use and development) I attended or conducted since 1994. I began to work with interactive installations since participating in 'Real-Time and Presence: Composing Virtual Environments', a 2002 workshop organised by Trans-Media-Akademie Hellerau e.V. and CYNETart Dresden. In the following year, 2003, I founded an independent media lab in Germany (http://interaktionslabor.de) which is open-source collaborative and driven by the changing participant communities that meet there every summer. At Brunel University (where I teach and direct the DAP-Lab), sustained research has been enacted since 2006 (http://www.brunel.ac.uk/dap).

4   Cf. Anne Nigten, *Processpatching: Defining New Methods in aRt&D*, PhD Thesis, Central St Martins College of Art & Design, University of the Arts, London, 2006

5   Michel Chion's trilogy, *La Voix au cinéma* (1982), *Le Son au cinéma* (1985), and *La Toile trouvée* (1988), remains available only in French. His book *L'Audio-Vision* (1990) has been translated into English (by Claudia Gorbman) as *Audio-Vision* (New York: Columbia University Press, 1994). For an excellent study of sound art, see Brandon LaBelle, *Background Noise: Perspectives on Sound Art* (London: Continuum Press, 2007). For a rare and very illuminating essay on the practice of interactive sonic performance, see Julie Wilson-Bokowiec and Mark Alexander

Bokowiec, 'Kinaesonics: The Intertwining Relationship of Body and Sound', *Contemporary Music Review*, 25:1 (2006), 47–57.

6   Chion, *Audio-Vision*, 1994: 54

7   Rick Curnutte, 'Genre-Bender: An Interview With Andrew Repasky McElhinney', *The Film Journal*, 11 (January 2005), http://www.thefilmjournal.com/issue11/mcelhinney.html [accessed 31 October 2008]

8   Gilles Deleuze, *The Logic of Sensation*, trans. Daniel W. Smith (Minneapolis: University of Minnesota Press, 2004): 81–90

9   Quoted from Serge Cardinal, 'Radiophonic Performance and Abstract Machines: Recasting Arnheim's Art of Sound', *Liminalities: A Journal of Performance Studies*, 3:3 (November 2007), http://liminalities.net/3-3/cardinal.htm

10   Quoted from the composer's notes, sent to me in February 2008

11   For the composer's notes on the production, see his 'Corpo, Carne e Espírito: a digital oratorio', published online in the theory pages of Interaktionslabor, the media lab where the initial collaboration between Chagas and myself began. (http://interaktionslabor.de/lab08/theory.htm)

12   Cf. Johannes Birringer, 'Bodies of Color', *Performing Arts Journal* 87 (2007): 35–46

13   Rudolf von Arnheim, *Radio: An Art of Sound* (Salem: Ayer Company Publishers, 1986): 20

14   Cardinal, op. cit.: 21

15   For Lingis' provocative readings of 'splendor', see *Body Transformations*, pp.21–43.

16   Quoted from Martin Harrison, *In Camera: Francis Bacon. Photography, Film and the Practice of Painting* (New York: Thames & Hudson, 2005): 204, 216

SECTION 13

Theory and Theories; Thesis Proposals and Thesis Development; Explicit, Delayed Completion, Assembled and Inferred Knowledge; the Perspective from Research Students; Hockney's Secret Knowledge; 25 Questions

> We live in an age where the artist has forgotten that he can be a researcher. I see myself that way. I work intuitively. I follow my instincts. I don't mind if something fails.
>
> **David Hockney**

The fact that this book is concerned with the theoretical explanation of practical activity might seem to imply that theory is something that automatically follows practice. The relationship is not this straightforward and any assumed binary is prone to collapse: the two cannot be isolated in a way that locates one emphatically before the other. The codes through which practice is constructed are complex and the ways in which these codes are deciphered are never absolute. Performance cannot but leave spaces for spectators to fill in, in the act of watching; and likewise, ongoing practice is read by the reflecting practitioner in ways that will inevitably impact on the work as it grows. Indeed, the knowledge that practical work is being carried out within a research context can hardly fail to shape any work that is made before the event. Practice emerges as a result of choices made, so that any practice offered up as research is but one approach from an immeasurable trove. In the normative terms of research we are able to say that practice relates to the idea of prototypicality, where one's practice serves as a model for the work of others in one's field; but practice also relates to the employment of existing work, so that practice is shaped by work seen, just as one's own practice as research is informed by begged, borrowed and/or stolen ideas.

Research is also always a form of re-search: a drawing on one's previous experience and developing this into knowledge. Viewed in this way, practice as research is about developing practical work into knowledge by transposing the experience of what it is that one does into data and then subjecting this to the type of reflection, analysis and discipline that is involved in serious compositional study. A research report tells the story of how a researcher investigated a particular area. Thus a research report or thesis is likely to have a linear narrative structure with a beginning, middle and end. When joined together in this way, information becomes easier to comprehend and recall. (Nisbett and Wilson, 1977) This is not the same thing as 'merely' telling the story of one's practice, no matter how intelligent this act of telling might be. As Cohen and Cohen remind us, 'a successful piece of research doesn't conclusively settle an issue'; (Cohen and Cohen, 1990: 149) yet research demands the pursuit if not always the creation of new knowledge and this is unlikely to emerge through little more than a well-articulated narrative accompanied by extracts of practical work on an accompanying disk. At the very least we should expect to see some indication that researchers are able to look beyond their personal predilections and preferences towards an engagement with critical perspectives that challenge their own. This does not mean that the specificities of one's practice need to be diluted in order to accommodate generic notions. On the contrary, it is about researching practitioners engaging in reflective, analytical and theorised investigations that can address their concerns in ways that are rigorous, expansive and detailed. This involves utilising research discourse in ways that foreground practice without taking any of the integrity, substance and transferability out of research. Certain practitioners may feel that their experience (and this is often of an admittedly high level) is all that is needed in terms of data, so that their work functions as both the research practice and the researched into. The stark reality however is that data – the key information contained in and worked through the practice – is only brought into the realm of research through systematic enquiry that lays its own processes bare; and this is done with and through theory.

Theory provides us with an invaluable means of reading the activities of ourselves and others; of reflecting and communicating much of that which is done rather than merely accepting things as having happened. As Lyotard asked in his pared-down definition of art theory, why does this thing happen rather than something else? Why does something happen rather than nothing? (Lyotard, 1979: 17) At the same time we do well to recognise that theory can sometimes amount to no more than a self-satisfying attempt to justify the narrowness of the field in which much of this same activity takes place. At its worst then, the seeming clarity made possible through theoretically sustainable argument does little more than seek to legitimise tired techniques, applying the veneer of academic respectability to otherwise insignificant endeavour... insignificant at least within a research context.

Whilst it could be the case, as Susan Melrose has argued, that 'theory may, indeed, be counter-productive in the context of performance making', (Melrose, 1999: 39) the position taken in this book is clearly not designed to be read as a denial of theory. Neither is it premised on an anti-academic alliance with one of Sigmund Freud's repeated assertions that before the problem of the creative artist analysis must lay down its arms. Such alignment as exists here is closer to Borgdorff's response to the rhetorical question of how much theory artistic research needs. For Borgdorff the response is not 'Here is a theory that sheds light on artistic practice', but 'Here is art that invites us to think.' (Borgdorff, 2008: 96)

Study is theory, inasmuch as theory is at once a schema that explains practice and something that is embedded in the practice itself. In this way theory is practice at the same time as it stands slightly outside it. For our purposes theory and practice coalesce into praxis... practice informed by theory, theory informed by practice. The practical site of research becomes a laboratory, not in the neo-Grotowskian sense of a space for repeated exercises so much as a private/public place for trial and error. The distinction here between theory and theories is not to be glossed over. Theory implies a reflection on practice, a tracing of the processes that lead to the work. Theories suggest something entirely different. To apply certain selected theoretical models of study is to provide focus, but there is a danger that thinking about becomes dependent upon recognisably theoretical foci. Theories are useful, inevitable even, but their value lies in the ways that they can be used to open the ground for new practice. In and of themselves they have little value.

Research through practice, like any other research, necessitates an approach for carrying out the research. This approach is likely to be systematic, methodical and coherent: elements that we do not always associate with provocative performance practice. Furthermore, the approach will almost certainly need to be demonstrably appropriate within the context of the research question being asked. For practical enquiry to qualify as research, the approach will have to allow and even encourage questioning in an identifiably verifiable manner; more than this, the information gathered through practical work needs to adhere to certain aspects. The work is flawed at source if it has not been carried out in relation to something that has been framed as a question, and it needs to be the type of work – and a questioning of the work – that has as its intention the making of a contribution to knowledge, regardless of the size and scale of that contribution. The research has also to be of good quality, reliable and verifiable, using procedures that avoid the type of idiosyncrasies that deny replication, as the term is understood in performance circles. Because research takes place as a response to something that is seen to warrant investigation there is a need to understand, explain and act upon the information gathered through one's practice. Inasmuch as successful research makes explicit claims for the furthering of knowledge and the fostering of subject-specific understanding it is by definition a usually private activity towards a usually public outcome. This requires the keeping of records (anathema to most art and artists) in such a way that conclusions can be tested against information. Without this ability for the researcher's footsteps to be traced through enquiry to argument and from formulation to findings what results is unlikely to pass muster as research; for without the possibility of testing and interrogating findings we have nothing to rely on but trust. And whilst trust is a desirable commodity it needs first and always to be earned.

Practice-based research is research that is always potentially resistant to the boundaries of institution and discipline. Through its innately penetrative and flexible approach it serves as a barometer of performance initiatives at the same time as it registers shifts in academic expectation and acceptance. The consensus that new and progressive performance, like research, has to build on the already-known in ways that address and add to conceptual and critical clarity in a specific arena of investigation is common enough to need no elaboration here. This consensus brings with it an implicit demand for originality and dissemination. Originality will often reside in terms of techniques, viewpoints, methodological choices, application and/or aesthetics. Dissemination is different and, in the context of original creative practice, it is, and alarmingly often, regarded and/or treated as something of an add-on; as though the qualities contained in one's practical investigations, qualities that are generally driven by process, are shared with a subsequent public merely by dint of their having taken place. The crux of this is that detailed research needs to be matched by an equal detail in reporting, and this means attention to archiving in ways that make those same processes communicable, comprehensible and lasting. As Linda Candy puts it, 'In a doctoral thesis, claims of originality and contribution to knowledge may be demonstrated through creative outcomes.... Whilst the significance and context of the claims are described in words: a full understanding can only be obtained with direct reference to the outcomes.' (Candy, 2006)

For every academic practitioner who seeks through conference paper, article and book to define the nature of practice-based research there are many more who legislate against definition, arguing that to pin the work down flies in the face of subversive activity. These champions of that which is increasingly known as New Variant Research do much to move our understanding 'beyond the use of existing criteria that exists for qualitative research and toward an understanding of interdisciplinarity not as a patchwork of different disciplines and methodologies but as a loss, a shift, or a rupture where in absence, new courses of action unfold.' (Springgay et al., 2005: 898) An elegantly phrased position, but what exactly is it that is being identified as absent? We are subsequently informed that this is 'not a form of negation', so much as it is a 'space of active participation where one discovers that previous methodologies are not sufficient while simultaneously resisting the formation of specific criteria to replace them.' (Ibid.) But isn't this, potentially at least, replacing something historically present and visible (one's research methodology) with something that revels in its invisibility (one's research concept)? We know that the combining of a written thesis with practical work constitutes an intellectual innovation inasmuch as it attempts to combine the creative impulse with the traditional research criteria of systematic analysis, theorisation and dissemination through documentation; but this is not quite enough to make a case for widespread change without charter.

The ephemeral nature of practical work maintains an uneasy parity with the permanence of print. It remains a paradox that those of us who function as agents of the university system generally ask for innovative practice to be dissected via the most conventional forms of articulation available. This form, the standard written thesis (or essay, or accompanying description, or curatorial document) may be about to pass its sell-by-date; or so at least the doyens of practice as research would have us believe. Equally, the written word, valuable though it is, may well have maintained its place in the canon of postgraduate and professional research primarily as a means of exercising management and control over some of the excesses of practice. As all understanding and ergo all knowledge is interpretative, so the words we write are no more than our own received interpretations of the words we have read elsewhere. If research into, as and through practice is to move at a pace with its subject then the certainties of our own interpretative expectations have to be sacrificed to the mysteries of responses, desires, imaginings and interests that come with the territory of performance. This empowering of practice does not automatically herald the disenfranchising of text. On the contrary, just as contemporary directorial practice has moved on and away from the idea of finding the meaning and making it meaningful, so contemporary research has begun a shift from its equivalent position.

It is this practice-based centrality that is marking out the territory of new research. Models have been around for several years but these have tended to come from the study of art and design rather than literature: and the study of theatre, in Britain no less than anywhere else in the West, has remained joined at the hip to ideas of authorial ownership exemplified by the published word. A play, therefore, is rarely regarded as a blueprint for drama so much as the site of the drama itself. As Julian Meyrick sees it:

> Play texts are artworks that live at a remove from their ultimate
> meaning. Like schizophrenics, they are given over to permanent
> displacement of their identity. It is this remove, as much as the text
> itself, which is the substance of the drama…. Here we have another
> paradox: when a play is performed, its true meaning is discovered, even
> though that meaning is constructed in an entirely contingent way.
>
> (Meyrick, 2006: 272)

We might choose to challenge Meyrick's use of the phrase 'true meaning', preferring here the idea of 'probable purpose'; nevertheless, he articulates the sense many of us share about text as provocative instructions for actions rather than as something sacrosanct and complete.

What it is that is being communicated and to whom shifts from context to context, and the demands of professional academic practice-based research in performance differ in detail if not always in kind from the demands of PhD submission. The former stands or falls on a process of peer and peer-college review; the latter passes or fails through an entirely different process of internal and external examination.

A PhD thesis is designed to allow subsequent readers access to a collection of ideas and suggestions unified by a consistent train of thought. Insofar as that access is often limited, at least initially, to relatively expert readers the unification of ideas may well remain complex. Nevertheless, this complexity needs to be comprehensible and not least to the researcher him- or herself. Unless researchers know exactly what it is that they are committing themselves to, what they are seeking to understand and in what ways they are contributing to knowledge then their work is liable to be lacking in unity. Put simply, unless or until a researcher knows and is able to communicate through the submission what it is that the thesis is trying to say and do, rather than relying on the *viva* as an opportunity to add that which is lacking elsewhere, then readers will struggle to validate supporting arguments: readers and examiners need to know what proposition the evidence supports before they are able to determine the worth of that evidence.

A thesis then that does not move through a body of information in order to arrive at findings which are well defined, well supported and comprehensively focused is not quite a thesis, and in this regard a miss is as good as a mile. This is so because there are criteria which a thesis needs to meet in order to elevate it above the status of report. One of these is that a thesis, in order to be effective, needs to be in some ways persuasive. That is to say it needs to persuade its readers of two key and closely related elements: readers need to be persuaded as to the intellectual credibility of the researcher and they need to be persuaded as to the intellectual credibility of the work. This is not the same thing as being persuaded by the force of either argument or evidence contained in a thesis. It is perfectly acceptable and relatively common for examiners to disagree vehemently with a researcher's views and findings without this having any impact on the success or otherwise of a PhD submission. The persuasiveness of a thesis is about providing numerous and appropriately cogent examples that are strong enough to appease a critically informed and occasionally oppositional readership.

This is very difficult when one is using around 50 per cent of the usual word length for a thesis. Difficulty does not equate to impossibility, of course, but the demands made on any practical work submitted as part of the overall thesis are huge.

In her argument that conventional performance research documentation is the result of the invention of the printing press and little more, Caroline Rye writes:

> I'm sure that one of the reasons for the insistence, from some quarters,
> that writing can be the only reasonable form research can take,
> comes from the close association of the term research with that of
> dissemination and subsequently from a particularly modern notion of
> dissemination. Research prefigures dissemination and dissemination
> necessarily involves repetition, which has most widely been achieved
> for the past 550 years via mechanically reproducible writing.
>
> (Rye, 2003)

Rye makes a call for oral modes of communication, which would be 'more sympathetic and appropriate to the notion of practice as research in performance'. (Ibid.) Maybe so and maybe not, but what is most significant is Rye's seeming acknowledgement here that words, either spoken or written, are necessary if meaning and findings are to be effectively communicated... although it should be pointed out that Rye goes on to say that she is cautious of involving documentation in the practice-as-research debate, 'because it invokes the notion of repetitive dissemination and blinds us to the dissemination that already occurs at the level of the performance practice itself.' (Ibid.)

Well, certainly it does. Nevertheless, when Rye expresses surprise at the failure of some of her colleagues to acknowledge the 'productive power' of performances, she conflates retrievable documentation with adherence to the (old) demands of the (old-fashioned) academy rather than with the desire some of us (some of Rye's failing colleagues and Kershaw's illusory fools) have for written analysis because it adds to, contextualises, explains and develops the practical work, not because it is capable of being placed on a library shelf.

It is important to remind ourselves that ongoing professional research, where that research is through, in or for performance, is not automatically the same thing as a PhD. A PhD thesis is a definable entity, as Richard Braddock points out. Braddock suggests that a thesis is likely to develop in one of four ways: It is likely to be either:

> **Explicit**, stating its case in consecutive sentences, sections and examples;
> **Delayed-Completion**, begun in one section and completed later on in the work;
> **Assembled**, where ideas are scattered throughout the thesis; or
> **Inferred**, where readers are left to surmise their own understandings.
> (Braddock, 1981: 310–324)

In thesis terms these approaches are stated in the order in which they most commonly occur... or at least in the order in which they most commonly occur in successful cases. There are logical enough reasons why practical, creative performance interventions are likely to deal in inference rather than explication and to work in ways that flip Braddock's ordering on its head; but we do well to remember that the practice needs to fit the PhD requirements of thesis every bit as well as the PhD is being made to accommodate the constructive disruptions of practice.

An initial research question, aligned to an understanding of at least one's own methodological rationale, implies an engagement with theory that is firmly in place prior to registration. Such is not always the case and the academically phrased language of supposed theory, a name-dropping type of sound bite is all too often offered at the expense of clarity of expression and intent. The confusion of a rehearsed theoretical parlance with analysis is the Achilles Heel that many of us suffer from, from time to time, and peppering pages with words straight out of *The Beginners' Guide to Theory* is no substitute for clear thinking. Creative and practice-based activity is not antithetical to analytical engagement; and neither is it necessarily mystical. In some ways it is the overblown theoretical-sounding, blindly postmodern language of dissemination that shrouds culturally significant findings in obscure terminology. In fact, one of the purposes of a PhD in practice-based research is to explore ways in which students – as members of a community of scholars – can be encouraged to read and discuss their own creative practice through a systematic framework that can enhance rather than inhibit the developmental usefulness of their work.

The study of performance we are concerned with in this publication usually amounts to a schema that explains practice at the same time as being the practice itself. An essay is an attempt to see if something fits and in this it is no different to a PhD thesis. This, as readers will be well aware, is a trifle disingenuous; and yet the principle applies inasmuch as the ways in which a thesis differs from the investigative work undertaken for a less demanding essay is as much about scale and depth as any shift in the work's constituent elements.

Research can be applied to and through a diverse array of practices. In order to facilitate this flexibility, as well as seeking to ensure that such is not used to stymie development, a number of suggestions can be made. Some are generic, in that they are broadly applicable to all Humanities-driven PhD studies, others are specifically tailored towards students whose research processes and/or submissions incorporate practical elements. As the case studies of successful practice-based research submissions that have been used in this book reveal, the suggestions made here are not always regarded as important by those same researching practitioners who did so demonstrably well, either through challenging, subverting or directly ignoring them. Readers are, of course, invited to regard this as a deliberate and deliberately knowing strength of the book rather than as something that in its occasional contradiction exposes an inherent weakness. If the case studies provide a useful published snapshot of performance practice as research across a range of locations and approaches, they also serve as evidence that no regulations, guidelines or rules are ever quite watertight enough to halt the flow of art.

Periods of registration will often begin with, or at least include at an early stage, a statement of intent, or proposal. 'Intent' here is used to cover method and methodology as well as specific questions relating to research problems and their address. The proposed relationship between practice *per se* and its (almost exclusively) written elements is usefully explored here, not least because students and supervisors might need to discuss at this stage the desirability or otherwise of appointing external examiners at an earlier point than normal. Some useful comments on this can be found on the web pages of PARIP.

Equally importantly, a proposal is the foundation of a student's working relationship with a supervisor; as such, it forms something of a contract on both sides. A proposal will usually start with an explanation of the specific area in which the research will be located, alongside the providing of the key theoretical debates and/or practical challenges it intends to address. A proposal is likely to offer a brief review of the contribution the student intends to make to the field; to demonstrate an appropriate familiarity with and understanding of relevant academic literature and archive material and to demonstrate an awareness of the major lines of research already established in the chosen field. None of the above should pose any sort of problem to a serious candidate.

The proposal will probably address the extent to which the student's practice is intended to qualify as research and the extent to which it is likely to function as a means towards research. For example, is the practical work the object to be studied or is it the nature of the study? Early negotiation of this is important, as is its potential for reconsideration at various stages throughout the period of registration. It is important that fluidity and flexibility are not washed away in the search for a fixed idea of academic rigour; however, a student's research proposal should, wherever possible, be as focused and specific as possible. So, if the research is being entered into because of omissions in extant theoretical literature or in practice, it is useful to detail which of these gaps the particular research process is attempting to address (or fill); if the research is regarded by the student as a response to certain theoretical debates or shifts in thinking, then which aspects of these are going to be addressed... and, of course, *how* are they going to be addressed? A proposal is by its very nature predictive and although it is neither possible nor desirable to give an in-depth indication of what it is that one's research will discover, it can be helpful to include in the proposal an early idea of the contribution the research is likely to make. Because this carries within it an indication of the extent to which students feel that their research will be making an original contribution, and because this idea of originality remains one of the core elements of the PhD, it is logical to begin thinking in these terms at the outset.

With apologies for the prescriptive nature of that which is intended only as constructive provocation, the following is offered both as a place to start and as a structure to keep one's practice-based research on track.

1. What is the work about, why is it important and who is it for? More fully, what research questions are being addressed and how?

2. What is particularly timely or urgent about the research... why is it being addressed now and how is it being addressed elsewhere?

3. In what ways will this research develop thinking in the areas of academia and/or performance?

4. What defines the study (principally the practical study) as a research activity?

5. How are the parameters of the practical work being set?

6. Personal practice is always part of a wider community of work. What is the community within which this work functions and what useful light can this throw on the researcher's own work?

7. To what extent is the researcher's practical work dependent upon expertise or (performance) artistry? Is knowledge of the student's prior work important to the thesis and is it important to examiners?

8. Is the research in, on or for practice? What do these distinctions mean to the researcher and how will they impact on the ways in which the work develops, takes shape and develops its argument?

9. What is the relationship between potentially unseen process and probably seen performance?

10. What, if any, are the relationships and/or the tensions between the ephemerality of (live?) performance and the (recorded?) permanence of disseminated 'thesis'?

11. In terms of a contribution to knowledge, where does the claim for originality reside: is this in the making, in the made or in the manner of analysis?

12. The term 'research question' implies an answer and this can often prove to be a stumbling block, particularly during the early stages of registration. It is often useful to stress the idea of the research as something that comprises an address to a particular question, rather than an answer.

13. How (and why) might embodied performance knowledge be disseminated in print?

14. What are the notions of equivalence? What is the word equivalence of a performance and to what extent is this measured by the time and length of a performance?

15. What, why and how: what are you doing, who is it for and why is it important?

16. What are the practical resources needed and how able is the registering university to provide or support these?

17. What is the relationship between research and thesis? The research might be what matters most to the student, whereas it is the thesis that matters most to examiners, and also to subsequent readers. How is this potential imbalance being negotiated?

18. How clear and how clearly defined is the relationship between practical and written elements of the work?

19. What is it that makes practice imperative to the thesis?

20. What are the distinctions and potential overlaps between practice as research and practice as thesis?

21. Is the research fuelled by a particular theoretical approach? Why this approach, or these approaches? To what extent is the theoretical approach chosen by the researcher or demanded through the nature of the work? What is the relationship between 'practice' and 'theory'? Can the two be divided in the work? What is the order, timescale and relationship between doing 'practice' and writing 'theory'? Is the researcher making work in order to subsequently understand and communicate that work in print, or does the theoretical writing undertaken lead to further practical explorations?

22. Does the practice follow, lead, embody or create theory?

23. What is in it for the researcher and what is in it for the reader? What shifts analysis of the researcher's own processes away from something diary like and self absorbed? What particular challenges might arise from seeking to place the idiosyncratic, the personal and the experienced within an appropriate academic frame? What particular challenges come with trying to translate one's own private processes into something public and intellectually valid? Or is this an invidious binary… one, perhaps, that the thesis might be seeking to challenge?

What gives validity to the study of one's own practice? With the study of practice in a conventional sense, one is either engaged in non-participant observation, remaining in the margins of the work, or one is participating in the work one observes. How important is it that one understands the complexity of the relationship between doing and seeing, and developing cognisance of the fact that the act of watching is likely to alter what it is that one sees?

24. What are the research methods that will be used to conduct the research? A wide variety of research methods exist, so how will the researcher identify which are the most appropriate for the work?

25. What is the relationship between research methods and methodology? The terms are often used interchangeably, but they might not be by an examiner and they might not be by subsequent readers. We can usually say that methodology refers to an overriding system of research and that a research method is a particular action within that system. Stating the way in which any distinctions and overlaps apply in one's own work is a useful, even necessary discipline.

Apropos of this last point we can recognise that identifying the methodological approaches appropriate to a particular area of investigation is usually a major element of the process of research. The documentation of performance has no singular defining methodology and different researchers will choose to document their work in different ways. A distinction between research and documentation *per se*, however, between scholarship and reportage, is that in the case of research one's methodologies need to be at once clear and made known. This distinction continues inasmuch as researchers need also to separate methodology from method. For the purposes of this section I am taking methodology to refer to the theoretical framework that informs analysis and method to refer to the procedure(s) of gathering information for the study. In this way method is the how of one's research and methodology is the why. Richard Beardsworth urges caution in terms of a too-readily arrived at acceptance of this type of potentially reductive binary. In terms of method he notes that Derrida is careful to avoid using the word:

> because it carries connotations of a procedural form of judgement.
> A thinker with a method has already decided *how* to proceed, is
> unable to give him or herself up to the matter of thought in hand, is
> a functionary of the criteria which structure his or her conceptual
> gestures.
>
> (Beardsworth, 1996: 4)

When we hear the argument that performance is always already a theorising practice, which is able to produce and stand *as* the research thesis, rather than functioning as a supportive illustration, we are duty bound to ask how this is the case; to ask for some proof in support of the claim. Without that confirmation, the claim is little more than an assertion without evidence. At a time when academia is becoming more and more comfortable with the idea of accepting practice as thesis it is not perhaps surprising that the demands for evidential results in support of one's research are as easily sidelined as they increasingly are.

Susan Melrose has described what she sees as the 'emergent premise' in creative work, (Melrose, 2003) a premise Jane Edwards links to the idea of discarding 'the rational knowing and certainty of an "outcome" oriented system of research' (Edwards, 2006) at the same time as we have 'collectively avoided the delight of the inexplicable, the creative unknowing, the potentials that exist in the unformed parts of our informed ideas, even while recognising that these are fundamental to good practice'. (Ibid.) The implication is that practice-based research activity is hindered by our widespread privileging of theoretical writing, with all of the permanence and potential for dissemination that comes with the written word (read the *published* word). The point is well made, and there is, if we are honest, a tendency amongst many of us who teach, supervise and examine to reward the work of students that most closely resembles our own, as though the mirroring of our own ideas provided some prejudice-free badge of quality.

When practice is undertaken as part of a formally designed research programme any performance work created is not likely to be capable of either articulating or justifying its contribution to the fields of understanding and of knowledge. Despite the assertions we hear (and many of these are no more than assumptions dressed up as assurance), we have been offered little persuasive evidence that a performance or drama project can be possessed of the ability to communicate the rationale for its significance to a reasonably informed third party. In fact, we need a substantial written thesis, rather than a written account of the thesis-as-practice. This is in no small way as a response to the expert practitioner/expert spectator that Melrose so ably describes. If exploratory practice is left to speak for itself then perhaps the people it is able to speak to can only ever be experts in the field of practice, and this amounts to an act of exclusivity that seems at odds with the broadly inclusive ethos of practice-based research. One could argue that a formally written thesis requires a similarly expert reader to make sense of its findings. This may be true, at least in part, but the type of expertise required to work comprehensively through a thesis is not restricted to trained makers of performance or those vastly experienced in watching work of a particular type.

If communicating the knowledge from a PhD is usually regarded as communicating findings to one's peers, then the convention of scientists communicating theories through formulae which are understandable to other scientists would seem to place art at a disadvantage. There are key differences however, chief of which is the fact that scientific formulae are only ever one part of a thesis. Einstein's theory of relativity is not communicated through $E=mc^2$ and nothing else. As significant to the scientific formula/performance practice debate is the fact that scientific formulae function as an expression of the composition of a particular compound, the directions for preparing that compound or of a particular procedure which can be followed in order to obtain a desired result or determine a single concept. Performance simply does not achieve this... which is not to reduce the potency of what it *does* achieve. It comes down to fitness for purpose: and performance practice rarely fits the purpose of either distillation or diagram.

We are working at a time when everything appears to be up for grabs, and yet the thing we are grabbing at with most fervour has led to a Spartacus-moment where practice-based research is leading us from the slavery of intention to the freedom of reflexivity. One notable study of students' experiences of practice as research has been made by Nancy de Freitas. (de Freitas, 2007) The fact that de Freitas' study was into the experience of Art rather than Performance students does little to reduce its applicability to the debates we encounter in our field.

The research carried out by de Freitas was conducted at the University of Auckland, New Zealand and was designed to investigate postgraduate students' experiences of active documentation, of engaging in the types of reflection in action that are the inevitable mainstay of practice-based research. For the purposes of her study, de Freitas focused on the following aspects:

1: How students were using documentation as aspects of their creative practices.

2: The types of forms and processes that constitute these practical activities.

3: Questioning the perception students have of the role that documentation is playing in their creative research work.

4: The degree to which students regard documentation as having either a positive or negative aspect.

Some of de Freitas' students' responses are listed below. They are included here with the caveat that whilst we know some of the questions, we did not hear or see the ways they were asked, nor the ways they were phrased. Neither do we know the extent to which student responses were tailored to suit the expectations of those asking the questions. We need to be aware of this because raw data without interpretation sometimes tells us very little and because our attempts at interpretation are problematised by a lack of detailed information. What we do know is that de Freitas' study was carried out over several years and that her intention was to collect information on students' use of key practice-based research methods. At the time the questions were asked, all of the respondents were involved in projects that located their own creative practice as an integral element of their chosen research methodology. Students were told that the interviews formed part of de Freitas' ongoing research into reflexive documentation.

The following small sample is drawn from de Freitas' 2007 paper, 'Activating a Research Context in Art and Design Practice'. As a counter to my own conscious or unconscious skewing of de Freitas' results, readers are urged to seek out the original source material. Editorial corruption aside, the statements that follow are as written by de Freitas, with omissions but no (other) alterations on my part:

- Documenting a trial installation gave me the position of viewer for the first time.

- Documentation offered me a third-party view.

- The process brought me a realisation of the relational potential of the different perspectives and issues.

- The stopping/gathering/looking over a period of time changed my practice from a series of one-off experiments into a more complex, disciplined and interconnected approach.

- It has developed a consciousness about the way that I am living, not just the way I am making art. It's made me aware of wider implications.

- Making regular time for active/reflective documentation resulted in my valuing of things that might otherwise have seemed less significant.

- The processes of documentation revealed qualities in the work that were obscured when my focus was on the making.

- Later on in the process I was able to adapt ideas that would otherwise have been lost.

- On reflection I am able to identify key catalyst moments.

- I see some of the documentation processes becoming new works.

- The periodic suspension of work in order to reflect and document led me to challenge the hierarchy of outcomes over process.

- It allowed me to identify small steps as significant.

- I invested more of myself.

- I felt I could see more. I started to see my work with a different eye.

The context of this book has been an address to some of the debates around the need to define the role of practice as part the research process in performance studies and to explore the relationship between linguistic and non-linguistic components in the creation and articulation of a thesis. Drawing upon a range of writings and practices, the intention has been to produce a work that has some value within the field of practice-based research discussions and which has tried, with inevitably limited success, to offer as balanced a view as possible. As was touched upon in this book's early pages, that striving for balance may well have resulted in a schizophrenic quality where ideological positions have been set up, discarded and returned to, seemingly at will.

The original starting point was that practitioners' case studies would interrupt the book's various sections and in this way some of my own authorial certainties would be constructively challenged, perhaps taken forward and even undermined. Because the case studies were never going to be seen by me until very late on in the writing process, their inclusion amounted to the book's largest leap in the dark, an authorial risk, which I should say caused no real stress at all. This absence of stress was the result of two main factors. The first was that I had every confidence in the quality of those as-yet-unseen case studies. This qualitative gamble was premised on the belief that the inclusion of a range of practices, coming as they did from such a diverse group of people, could not fail to add considerable value to the book. Like the art historian Richard Shiff, 'I'm drawn to the chance illuminations that arbitrary sequences of documents provide': (Shiff, 1979: 83) my hope was that this would create something akin to the publication of a series of conference papers, made unique by the fact that the contributors would be highly unlikely to attend the same events or find their practices documented side by side in any other context. Put a little differently, the case studies function like performances at a festival, where their differences of agenda, intent and articulation do much to define an overarching idea.

The second reason was that, for those of us involved in performance, chance is deeply embedded in our professional lives. The best-laid performance plans rarely if ever amount to a route we can follow without the vagaries of creative practice forcing some sort of revision, re-think or re-adjustment and the choice between active and passive writing comes down to more than a decision to write that a particular person's idea is wrong-headed rather than suggesting that an idea might possibly be incorrect. The creeping norm in academic writing is to avoid revealing too much commitment to a particular idea, preferring instead to opt for a series of neat body swerves that put a little distance between the writer and the writing. We see this most notably in the reluctance to use the personal pronoun 'I' in ways that make one's writing read as personal. It is clear by this point that in its drive towards active writing this book has been fairly resistant to the use of phrases such as 'it can be argued that…', 'some approaches could be described as…' and 'it is therefore suggested that…'; this has resulted in a work that tries to adopt a personal position, even at those times when my stance has been unsure, impermanent and teetering on the edge of collapse. The strength of an overtly passive academic voice is that it can read at times as the desire to say something definitive, which also leaves room for doubt. It is to be hoped that doubt has been a constant feature of every section of this book and that where doubt has been silenced by authorial forays into bombast it has re-emerged through the insertion of case studies at those very points where my own seeming certainties have needed most to be undercut.

The inclusion of case studies was also a constant reminder to readers and writer that practice is always what matters most… although acknowledgement of this does not amount to a complete about-face. As Pavis sees it, 'certain observations and analyses require the theoretician to leave his protected shelter in order to test all his theories on the practical level. (Pavis, 1990: 41) Pavis sees it as significant, however, that the theoretician does not at this point become a 'practitioner or an artist, but remains a go-between, caught in the space between Page and Stage'. (Ibid.) Pavis suggests that researchers need to take some risks in order to test and refine their theoretical understanding, and this sometimes demands practice-based exploratory work, but reminds us that the 'study of theatre only has meaning if it is accompanied by or merges into practical work'. (Ibid.) The opposite also holds true, of course, insofar as practice only has real meaning in academic terms if it merges into theoretical discourse and dissemination.

Performance is as performance does, and the demands of university-sanctioned research are not always the same as the demands imposed on practice by either spectators or practitioners. Where performance prospers, ideas are exposed and confronted, worked through and worked out in ways that lead to awakened understanding. It is here where spectators enter into the realities of situations to the extent that development is asserted in the present; and it is here that performance proves its worth in terms of meaningful connections. A performance might amount to a thesis, in its broadest sense, but the rigours of academia ask for more than potential similarities wrought from commitment. As we saw at the start of this book, the word thesis is derived from Greek, where the word was related to the sense of a proposition. The meaning of the word has thus remained consistent with its ancient meaning, and it shares its etymological roots with hypothesis. A thesis then is always a blend of proposition, affirmation and/or assertion; it amounts to an assertion which can be examined to ascertain the quality of its truth value. In this way a thesis amounts to an open invitation to readers and/or spectators to consider and decide upon the reliability, reasonableness and validity of a particular argument. In this sense a thesis will always make some type of claim as to what is true, and it is this that leads to the terms 'truth claim' and 'truth value'. Neither truth claims nor truth values need to be 'true' in the everyday sense of the word. What matters is that the thesis will possess the capability in essence of being true, even when its findings are not.

We can look to David Hockney's (in)famous 2006 book *Secret Knowledge* for an example of this. In his book, Hockney makes the claim that the Old Masters were unable to paint many of the realistic images they have left us with using no more than observation, memory and imagination. Hockney's consistently maintained argument is that these artists used exactly the same method Hockney himself deploys when he wants to create realistic images. This amounts to the deployment of a projected image onto canvas and the subsequent tracing with paint of these projected images. Hockney links his nascent practice to the historical use of the camera obscura and camera lucida.

In Hockney's view, Renaissance artists inevitably traced projected images rather than using the methods of free-hand and brush that they (and history) have claimed. As a non-artist I have no particular axe to grind over Hockney's comments; neither have I any experiential way of gainsaying his argument. What *is* clear is that Hockney's thesis is based primarily on the fact that he could not accurately paint portraits from observation and recall; and so he feels nobody else could. Hockney's reasoning is clearly flawed at the outset insofar as it takes his own artistic talent as the benchmark for the ability or lack of ability of all other artists. Nevertheless, it does not matter so much that all of Hockney's investigative roads lead to the same conclusion nor even that all of his enquiries are possibly commenced from a spurious point. What matters is that he develops a thesis that possesses the capability to be true. In terms of the work's thesis value it does not matter a jot whether we agree with Hockney's findings, only that we can trace the line from research problem through to conclusion and that we find the writer's methodological processes reasonable, his data collection sound and his provocations worthy of interest. That many artists and critics disagree with Hockney's thesis has no bearing on its quality *as* a thesis.

This is significant inasmuch as it shows us not only what a thesis might be, but also what it might not. It is hard to envisage a work of art that satisfies the demands of being a proposition with intrinsic truth values, even when it demonstrates, as many artworks do, a serious concern for issues of truth. A concern for truth is not in and of itself the same thing as a thesis: a love affair is not a thesis; a statue is not a thesis; neither is a musical composition, poem, novel, scripted play or performance. And this has nothing to do with quality: Picasso's entire output does not amount to a thesis, although few would doubt its massive and perhaps unparalleled contribution to modern art; the peerless mass of Peter Brook's directed works do not amount to a thesis, neither do Grotowski's or Barba's. Their theoretical writings, however, might well be regarded as a series of outstanding theses, working as they do through the whys and wherefores of many years of process.

This is not about the elevation of articulation over practice, for such a belief would make a mockery of all that is at the heart of our subject. It is rather a simple recognition that a thesis makes particular demands that practice will seldom if ever be able to meet; just as practice makes demands that fall beyond the remit of all but the rarest written thesis. Practice may be many things, but practice as thesis is always something of a misnomer... which is why we avoid the term and rely instead on the equally inaccurate practice-based research. We do so despite the certain knowledge we have that practical research approaches have been with us since research began. A practical submission means practice as thesis: the sooner we acknowledge the fact that pinning the word 'practice' to research can be as much of an evasion as an avenue for genuine development, the sooner we can move towards ways of thinking, talking, writing and making work that deepen and develop our understanding of performance in a still-new century. The dramaturg and playwright David Lane puts things succinctly when he suggests that the potential advantage of scholar–practitioners above purely academic theorists 'is their opportunity to deploy theory through practice in the public domain, as a means to achieving greater clarity of expression in their own work or the work of their collaborators.' (Lane, 2009) Lane's words restore practical exploration to the heart of performance study as well as serving as a crucial reminder that public visibility is central to dissemination.

There are, it is clear, some major distinctions between practice as research and practice as thesis, which is not to suggest that part-practical submissions for drama, theatre and performance PhDs are not here to stay. The inevitability is that PhD submissions will continue to accommodate practical work and that the broadly fifty–fifty weighting that currently exists will swing in the direction of practice. In this sense, some of the half-cautions articulated in this book may well amount to a very small act of swimming against an overwhelmingly strong tide. Nevertheless, these reservations remain. The numerous alternative perspectives from scholars and practitioners whose views I hold in the highest regard casts a potential shadow on my judgement; and it would be remiss of me not to acknowledge this. Explanation of my own position, and of the way that this has at times become temporarily unfixed only to subsequently re-settle in an ever-shifting ground has been apparent in many sections and needs no reiteration here. What does need saying again is that the manner in which practice-based research has become, within little more than a decade, the default methodology for PhD study should herald a little concern.

That this concern and others will make little or no difference to the recruitment drive that defines the way many university departments regard PhD does not make them any the less reasonable. And it does not make them any the less a part of our subject's ongoing debate. When debate revolves around the cult of P-a-R, consideration morphs into acts of confirmation. And when argument is so willingly sacrificed to affirmation there is little space left for the type of questioning our discipline is predicated upon.

Clement Greenberg's concern was that art can be compromised by thinking. Our own might be that practice-based research is in danger of being compromised by the very fervour with which it is being embraced. What is needed is a different kind of support: not the evangelical/defensive one-size-fits-all we are currently seeing, so much as the considered, the fit-for-purpose and the bespoke.

Bibliography

Alleque, L., S. Jones, B. Kershaw and A. Piccini (eds) (2009) *Practice-as-Research in Performance and Screen* (Hampshire: Palgrave)

Allison, B. (1996) *Research Skills for Students* (London: Kogan Page)

American Education Research Association (2006) 'Standards for Reporting on Empirical Social Science Research in "AERA Publications"', http://www.aera.net/opportunities/

Anderson, H.H. (1959) *Creativity and its Cultivation* (New York: Harper)

Andrews, S. and R. Nelson (2003) 'Practice as Research: Regulations, Protocols and Guidelines', PALATINE, http://www.lancs.ac.uk/palatine/dev-awards/par-report.htm

Arendt, H. (1958) *The Human Condition* (Chicago: University of Chicago Press)

Arlander, A. (1999) *Keijut I–IV [Fairies I–IV]*, radio play written for the Finnish Broadcasting Company YLE (manuscript in the archive of the artist)

(2007) 'How to Turn Landscape into a Performance, How to Carry Out a Place?' in M. Niskala (ed.), *ANTI – Contemporary Art Festival 2002–2006: Time-Based and Site-Specific Contemporary Art* in Kuopio, Savonia University of Applied Sciences, Series D 2/2007, 49–61

(2008) 'Finding your way through the woods – experiences in artistic research', *Nordic Theatre Studies*, Vol. 20, 28–41

(2009) works distributed by AV-arkki, the Distribution Centre for Finnish Media Art, http://www.av-arkki.fi/web/index.php?id=35&artist=2064

Presentation of artistic work, http://www.harakka.fi/arlander/index.shtml

Arnott, J. (1981) 'An Introduction to Theatrical Scholarship', *Theatre Quarterly*, Vol. 10, No. 39: 29–42

Aronowitz, S. (1992) *The Politics of Identity: Class, Culture, Social Movements* (London & New York: Routledge)

Atwood, R. (2008) 'Rise in proportion of firsts to 13% renews inflation debate', *Times Higher Education*, 17 January 2008, http://www.timeshighereducation.co.uk/story.asp?storyCode=400190&sectioncode=26

Augé, M. (1995) *Non Places: An Anthology of Super-modernity* (London & New York: Verso)

Auslander, P. (1994) *Presence and Resistance* (Michigan: University of Michigan Press)

(1997) *From Acting to Performance. Essays in Modernism and Postmodernism* (London: Routledge)

(1999) *Liveness, Performance in a Mediatized Culture* (London & New York: Routledge)

(2006) 'The Performativity of Performance Documentation', *PAJ*, 84

Austin, J.L. (1975) *How to Do Things with Words* (Cambridge, MA: Harvard University Press)

Bachelard, G. (2003) *Tilan poetiikka* [*The Poetics of Space*] (Helsinki: Kustannusosakeyhtiö Nemo)

Bacon, J. (2003) 'Musings on documentation: performative self-ethnography as a methodological tool for documenting practice as research in performance', PARIP 2003 National Conference Proceedings, http://www.bristol.ac.uk/parip/bacon.htm

Bakhtin, M. (1994) *The Bakhtin Reader: Selected Writings of Bakhtin, Medvedev, Voloshinov* (London: Edward Arnold)

Baldwin, J. (1955) *Notes on a Native Son* (New York: Beacon Press)

Barba, E. (1995) *The Paper Canoe: A Guide to Theatre Anthropology*, trans. R. Fowler (London: Routledge)

Barba, E. and N. Savarese (1991) *A Dictionary of Theatre Anthropology: The Secret Art of the Performer* (London: Routledge)

Barker, H. (1997) *Arguments for a Theatre* (Manchester: Manchester University Press)

Barrett, E. and B. Bolt (2007) *Practice as Research: Approaches to Creative Arts Inquiry* (London: I.B. Tauris)

Barthes, R. (1977) *Image, Music, Text* (New York: Noonday)

Bateson, G. (2000) *Steps Towards an Ecology of Mind* (Chicago: University of Chicago Press)

Bauman, R. (1977) *Verbal Art as Performance* (Rowley, MA: Newbury House)

Bauman, Z. (1997) *Postmodernity and its Discontents* (Cambridge: Polity Press)

BBC News (2003) 'End of League Tables?' http://news.bbc.co.uk/1/hi/education/2891601.stm

Beardsworth, R. (1996) *Derrida and the Political* (London: Routledge)

Beasley, N. (2009) Transcript of personal interview, 2 April 2009

Belkin, A. (ed.) (2008) *Jewish Theatre: Tradition in Transition and Intercultural Vistas* (Israel: Tel Aviv University, Assaph Books)

Benjamin, W. (1973) *Illuminations*, ed. H. Arendt (London: Fontana)

Bennett, J.M. (1998) *Intercultural Communication: A Cultural Perspective* (USA: Intercultural Press)

Berger, J. (2005) *Here is Where We Meet: A Season in London* (London: artevents)

Bergson, H. (1946) *Stating the Problems: The Creative Mind: An Introduction to Metaphysics* (New York: The Wisdom Library)
(1994) *Matter and Memory* (New York: Zone Books)

Berry, C. (1982) *Voice and the Actor* (London: Harrap)

Bial, H. (2004) *The Performance Studies Reader* (London & New York: Routledge)

Biggs, M. (2002) 'The Rhetoric of Research' in D. Durling and J. Shackleton (eds), *Common Ground: Proceedings of the Design Research Society International Conference, Brunel University*, 111–118 (Stoke-on Trent: Staffordshire University Press)
(2003) 'The Role of "The Work" in Art and Design Research', http://www.bris.ac.uk/parip/biggs.htm

Bochner, A. and C. Ellis (2002) *Ethnographically Speaking: Autoethnography, Literature and Aesthetics* (Walnut Creek: Alta Mira Press)

Bodgan, R.C. and S.K. Biklen (2003) *Qualitative Research for Education: An introduction to theories and methods* (Boston: Allyn & Bacon)

Bogart, A. (2001) *A Director Prepares: Seven Essays on Art and Theatre* (New York & London: Routledge)

Bolt, B. (2006) 'A Non Standard Deviation: Handlability, Praxical Knowledge and Practice Led Research, Speculation and Innovation' in *Applying Practice Led Research in the Creative Industries* (Queensland: University of Technology) http://www.speculation2005.net

Borgdorff, H. (2004) 'The Conflict of the Faculties: On Theory, Practice and Research in Professional Arts Academies', unpublished manuscript (based on 'De strijd der faculteiten: over zin en onzin van orderzoek in de kunsten', *Boekmen* 58/59, Spring 2004, 191–196)

(2006) 'The Debate on Research in the Arts', Sensuous Knowledge 02, Focus on Artistic Research and Development, www.sensuousknowledge.org

(2008) *Artistic Research and Academia: an Uneasy Relationship* (Stockholm: Swedish Research Council): 82–97

Bourdieu, P. (1990) *The Logic of Practice* (Cambridge: Polity Press)

Brabazon, J. (ed.) (2005) *Albert Schweitzer: Essential Writings* (Maryknoll, NY: Orbis Books)

Braddock, R. (1981) 'The Frequency and Placement of Topic Sentences in Expository Prose' in G. Tate and E.P.J. Corbett (eds), *The Writing Teacher's Sourcebook* (New York: Oxford University Press)

Brady, S. and S. Jacobs (1994) *Mindful of Others: Teaching Children to Teach* (Olney, MD: Association for Childhood Education)

Brennan, T. (2000) *Exhausting Modernity: Grounds for a New Economy* (London & New York: Routledge)

British Broadcasting Corporation (1981) *The Lennon Tapes* (London: BBC)

Broadhurst, S. and J. Machon (2006) *Performance and Technology: Practices of Virtual Embodiment and Interactivity* (New York & Hampshire: Palgrave Macmillan)

Brohm, R. (1999) 'Bringing Polanyi onto the Theatre Stage: a Study on Polanyi Applied to Knowledge Management' in *Proceedings of the ISMICK Conference* (Rotterdam: Erasmus University): 57–69

Brown, R. and G. Alderman (2008) 'Is it time to unleash the watchdog to safeguard our degree standards', *Times Higher Education*, 17–23 July, No. 1,854: 24–25

Buber, M. (1996/1923) *I and Thou* (New York: Touchstone)

Butler, J. (2002) *What is Critique? An Essay on Foucault's Virtue*, http://www.law.berkely.edu/centers

Cabinet Office (2003) *Quality in Qualitative Evaluation: a Framework for Assessing Research Evidence* (London: National Centre for Social Research)

Cage, J. (1995) *Silence* (London: Marion Boyars)

Callens, J. (ed.) (2004) *The Wooster Group and Its Traditions* (Brussels: Peter Lang Press)

Calvino, I. (1993) *Six Memos for the Next Millennium* (Vintage Books)

Candy, L. (2006) http://www.creativityandcognition.com

Carasso, J.G. (1996) 'Identity and Dialogue' in J. O'Toole and K. Donelan, *Drama, Culture and Empowerment* (Brisbane: IDEA Publications)

Carter, P. (2004) *Material Thinking: The Theory and Practice of Creative Research* (Melbourne: Melbourne University Press)

Casey, E. (1998) *The Fate of Place: A Philosophical History* (Berkeley, Los Angeles & London: University of California Press)

Cixous, H. (1993) *Three Steps on the Ladder of Writing: Lectures at the University of California, Irvine* (New York: Columbia University Press)

Clark, L. (2007) 'The Best Results', http://news.bbc.co.uk/!/hi/education/7974661.stm

Clark, R. and R. Ivanic (1997) *The Politics of Writing* (London & New York: Routledge)

Classen, C., D. Howes and A. Synnott (1995) *Aroma: The Cultural History of Smell* (London: Routledge)

Cobussen, M. (2007) 'The Trojan Horse: Epistemological Explorations Concerning Practice-based Research', *Dutch Journal of Music Theory*, Vol. 12, No. 1: 18–33

Coffey, A. (1999) *The Ethnographic Self: Fieldwork and the Representation of Identity* (London: Sage)

Cohen-Cruz, J. (2004) 'The Problem Democracy Is Supposed to Solve: The Politics of Community-Based Performance' in D. Soyini Madison and J. Hamera (eds), *The Sage Book of Performance Studies* (London: Thousand Oaks)

Cohen-Cruz, J. and M. Schutzman (eds) (2006) *A Boal Companion: Dialogues on Theatre and Cultural Politics* (New York: Routledge)

Cohen, A. and L. Cohen (1990) *Early Education* (London: Paul Chapman Educational Publishing)

Cologni, E. (2006) 'Present-Memory: Liveness versus Documentation and the Audience's Memory Archive in Performance Art' in D. Meyer-Dynkgraphe, *Consciousness, Theatre, Literature and the Arts* (Newcastle: Cambridge Scholars Press)
(2009) *Mnemonic Present, Shifting Meaning*, texts by Andrighetto, Auslander, Blaker, Bell, Campitelli, Gotman, Jones, Lissoni, Suddendorf, Taylor (Vercelli: Mercurio Edizioni)

Conquergood, D. (2002) 'Performance Studies: Interventions and Radical Research', *The Drama Review*, Vol. 46, No. 1: 145–156

Corbin, A. (1994) *The Foul and The Fragrant: Odour and the Social Imagination* (London: Picador)

Cowan, J. (1998) *On Becoming an Innovative University Teacher: Reflection in Action* (London: SRHE & Open University Press)

Creswell, J.W. (2003) *Research Design: Qualitative, Quantitative, and Mixed Methods Approaches* (Thousand Oaks, CA: Sage)

CRIAD, 'Practice-based Research', http://www.rgu.ac.uk/subj/ats/r1.htm

Davies, C.A. (2008) *Reflexive Ethnography: A Guide to Researching Selves and Others*, 2nd edition (London: Routledge)

De Certeau, M. (1988) *The Practice of Everyday Life* (Berkeley, Los Angeles, London: University of California Press)

De Freitas, N. (2007) 'Activating a Research Context in Art and Design Practice', *International Journal for the Scholarship of Teaching and Learning*, Vol. 1, No. 2, http://www.georgiasouthern.edu/ijsotl

Deleuze, G. and F. Guattari (1984) *Anti-Oedipus: Capitalism and Schizophrenia* (London: Athlone Press)

(1988) *A Thousand Plateaus: Capitalism and Schizophrenia* (London: Athlone Press)

De Marinis, M. (1985) 'A Faithful Betrayal of Performance: Notes on the use of Video in Theatre', *New Theatre Quarterly*, Vol. 1, No. 4: 380–393

Denzin, N.K. (1978) *Of Grammatology* (Baltimore: Johns Hopkins University Press)

(1997) *Interpretive Ethnography: Ethnographic Practices for the 21st Century* (Thousand Oaks, CA: Sage)

(2003) *Performance Ethnography: Critical Pedagogy and the Politics of Culture* (Thousand Oaks, CA: Sage)

Denzin, N.K. and Y.S. Lincoln (eds) (2000) *Handbook of Qualitative Research* (London: Sage)

Derrida, J. (1978) *Of Grammatology*, trans. Gayatri Spivak (Baltimore: Johns Hopkins University Press, 1978)

(1981) *Positions* (Chicago: Chicago University Press)

(1988) *Memoires pour Paul de Man* (Paris: Galilee)

(1995) *Points* (Stanford: Stanford University Press)

DeVault, M. (1997) 'Personal writing in social research' in R. Hertz (ed.), *Reflexivity and voice* (Thousand Oaks, CA: Sage): 216–228

Díaz-Kommonen, L. (2004) 'Expressive artefacts and artefacts of expression', *Working Papers in Art and Design*, 3, http://www.herts.ac.uk/artdes1/research/papers/wpades/vol3/ldkfull.html

Dixon, S. (2007) *Digital Performance: a History of New Media in Theater, Dance, Performance Art, and Installation* (Cambridge, MA & London: The MIT Press)

Dogan, M. and R. Pahre (1990) *Creative Marginality: Innovation at the Intersections of Social Sciences* (Boulder, CO: Westview Press Inc.)

Donelan, K. (2004) 'Overlapping Spheres and Blurred Spaces: Mapping cultural Interactions in Drama and Theatre with Young People', *NJ* (Drama Australia Journal), Vol. 28, No. 1: 15–34

Duchamp, M. (1957) 'Session on the Creative Act, Convention of the American Federation of Arts, Houston, Texas' in Art Minimal & Conceptual Only, Maria Lewis, http://members.aol.com/mindwebart3/marcel.htm

Dundjerovié, A.S. (2009) *Robert Lepage Routledge Performance Practitioners* (London: Routledge)

Easterby-Smith, M. and M. Lyles (2003) *The Blackwell Handbook of Organizational Learning and Knowledge Management* (Cambridge, MA: Blackwell Publishing)

Edwards, B. (2008) 'Intuitive Ignorance', http://www.optik.tv/notes1

Edwards, J. (2006) 'Thresholds between Practice and Research: Thinking About Susan Melrose's Notion of the "Signature Practitioner"', http://www.voices.no/columnist/coledwards300106.html

Edwards, R. and R. Usher (2002) *Postmodernism and Education* (London & New York: Routledge)

Eisner, E.W. (1991) *The Enlightened Eye* (New York: Macmillan)
(1997) 'The promise and perils of alternative forms of data representation', *Educational Researcher*, Vol. 26, No. 6: 4–10

ELIA (2006) *Re:Searching in and through the Arts*, Proceedings of Research in and through the Arts conference, October 2005 (Berlin: Universität der Künste)

Elinor, G. (1996) 'Professional Doctorates in Creative Practice', *RADical: International Research Conference '94* (CD-ROM) (Aberdeen: Gray's School of Art, Robert Gordon University)

Ellis, C. (2004) *The Ethnographic I: A Methodological Novel about Autoethnography* (Walnut Creek: AltaMira Press)

Elwes, C. and R. Garrard (eds) (1980) *About Time* (London: ICA)

Engen, T. (1991) *Odor Sensation and Memory* (Westport: Praeger)

Etchells, T. (1999) *Certain Fragments: Contemporary Performance and Forced Entertainment* (London: Routledge)

Etherington, K. (2004) *Becoming a Reflexive Researcher: Using Our Selves in Research* (London: Jessica Kingsley Publisher)

Evans, M. (2000) 'Book Reviews: The Radical in Performance: Between Brecht and Baudrillard', *Studies in Theatre and Performance*, Vol. 20, No. 2: 121–122

Farquhar, M. (2000) 'Heather Woodbury: Introduction' in J. Bonney (ed.), *Extreme Exposure: An Anthology of Solo Performance Texts from the Twentieth Century* (New York: Theatre Communications Group)

Feron, V. (2009) *Five Years of Illegality: Time to Dismantle the Wall and Respect the Rights of Palestinians*, Oxfam International Report (Oxford: Oxfam GB)

Foley, J.M. (1995) *The Singer of Tales in Performance* (Bloomington and Indianapolis: Indiana University Press)

Foster, S. (1997) 'Dancing Bodies' in J.C. Desmond (ed.), *Meaning in Motion: New Cultural Studies in Dance* (Durham and London: Duke University Press): 235–257
(2003) 'Taken by Surprise: Improvisation in Dance and Mind' in A. Cooper Albright and D. Gere (eds), *Taken by Surprise: A Dance Improvisation Reader* (Middletown: Wesleyan University Press): 3–12

Foucault, M. (1969) *The Archaeology of Knowledge* (Paris: Editions Gallimard)
(1972) *The Archaeology of Knowledge* (New York: Pantheon)
(1980) *Power/Knowledge: Selected Interviews and Other Writings 1972–1977*, Colin Gordon (ed.) (London: Harvester)
(1988a) *Politics, Philosophy, Culture and Other Writings 1977–1984* (New York: Routledge)

(1988b) *Power/Knowledge: Selected Essays and Other Writings, 1972–1977* (Sussex: Harvester Press)

(1994) *The Order of Things* (New York: Vintage Books)

Frame, D. (ed.) (2003) *Michel de Montaigne: The Complete Works* (New York: Everyman's Library)

Frayling, C. (1993) 'Research in Art and Design', Royal College of Art Research Papers Series 1(1) (London: Royal College of Arts)

Frayling, C. et al. (eds) (1997) *Practice-based Doctorates in the Creative and Performing Arts and Design* (N.P. (UK): UK Council for Graduate Education)

Freeman, J. (2003) *Tracing the Footprints: Documenting the Process of Performance* (Maryland: University Press of America)

(2004) 'Performatised Secrets, Performatised Selves', *Contemporary Theatre Review*, Vol. 14, Issue 4: 54–67

(2006) 'First Insights: Fostering Creativity in University Performance', *Arts & Humanities in Higher Education*, Vol. 5, No. 1: 91–103

(2007a) *New Performance/New Writing* (Hampshire: Palgrave Macmillan)

(2007b) 'Making the Obscene Seen: Performance, Research and the Autoethnographical Drift', *Journal of Dramatic Theory and Criticism*, Vol. XXI, No. 2: 7–20

(2009) 'Socializing the Self: Autoethnographical Performance and the Social Signature' in S. Broadhurst and J. Machon (eds), *Sensualities/Textualities & Technologies: Writings of the Body in 21st Century Performance* (Hampshire: Palgrave Macmillan)

Freire, P. (2001) *Pedagogy of Freedom: Ethics, Democracy and Civic Courage* (USA: Rowman & Littlefield)

Funding Council for England (1999) http://www.niss.ac.uk/education/hefce/pub96/m14_96.html

Gadamer, H.G. (2004) *Hermeneutiikka: Ymmärtäminen tieteissä ja filosofiassa* (Tampere: Vastapaino)

Garner, R. (2008) 'It's Refreshing to Know that Exam Marks Can Go Down as Well as Up', http://www.journalisted.com/article?id=1688157

Garrick, J. and C. Rhodes (eds) (2000) *Research and Knowledge at Work* (London: Routledge)

Gasché, R. (1997) *The Tain of the Mirror, Derrida and the Philosophy of Reflection* (Harvard: Harvard University Press)

Geertz, C. (1973) *Thick Description: Towards an Interpretive Theory of Culture. In The Interpretations of Culture* (New York: Basic Books)

Gergen, M.M. and K.J. Gergen (2002) 'Ethnographic Representation as Relationship' in C. Ellis and A.P. Bochner (eds), *Ethnographically Speaking: Autoethnography, Literature, and Aesthetics* (Walnut Creek, CA: AltaMira Press): 11–33

Gibbons, M., C. Limoges, H. Nowotny, S. Schwartzman, P. Scott and M. Trow (1994) *The New Production of Knowledge: the Dynamics of Science and Research in Contemporary Societies* (California: Sage)

Gill, J. (2008) 'A matter of opinions', *Times Higher Education*, 11–17 December, No. 1,875: 30–35

Gioultsis, V.T. (2005) '"Me" and the "Other" – Intersocial Evaluation of the Quality of Living' (Aristotle University of Thessaloniki)

Glaser, B. and J. Holton (2004) 'Remodeling Grounded Theory', *Forum: QualitativeSocial Research*, Vol. 5, No. 2, Art. 4, http://www.qualitative-research.net/fqs-texte/2-04/2-04glaser-e.htm

Godin, B. (1998) 'Writing Performative History: The New New Atlantis?', *Social Studies of Science*, Vol. 28: 465–483

Goldberg, R. (2004) *Performance: Live Art Since the 60s* (London: Thames & Hudson)

Goleman, D. (1998) *Working with Emotional Intelligence* (London: Bloomsbury Press)

Graduate Jobs (2009) http://www.graduate-jobs.com/

Gray, C. and I. Pirie (1995) '"Artistic" research procedure: Research at the edge of chaos?' in *Proceedings of Design Interfaces Conference*, Vol. 3, European Academy of Design (Salford: University of Salford)

Gray, C. and J. Malins (2004) *Visualizing Research: A Guide to the Research Process in Art and Design* (Aldershot: Ashgate)

Greenberg, C. (1981) 'The State of Criticism: Art Criticism', *Parisian Review*, Vol. 48, No. 1: 42

Greenwood, H. (1991) *The British Journal of Photography Annual* (London: Booth Books)

Greiner, C. and P. Assumpção (2009) Hemispheric Institute of Performance and Politics, http://www.hemisphericinstitute.org/eng/encuentro/index.html

Grossberg, L. (1993) 'Cultural Studies and/in New Worlds', *Critical Studies in Mass Communication*, 10: 1–22

Grotowski, J. (1968) *Towards a Poor Theatre* (New York: Touchstone)

Guattari, F. (2000) *The Three Ecologies* (London: Athlone Press)

Guénoun, D. (2007) *Näyttämön filosofia* (Helsinki: Like)

Guerlac, S. (2006) *Thinking in Time: An Introduction To Henri Bergson* (Ithaca: Cornell University Press)

Hammersley, M. (2005) 'Countering the New Orthodoxy in Educational Research', *British Educational Research Journal*, 31: 139–156

Hannula, M., J. Suoranta and T. Vadén (2003) *Otsikko uusiksi: taiteellisen tutkimuksen suuntaviivat [Renew the Title: The Parameters of Artistic Research]* (Tampere: Juvenes Print) (eds) (2005) *Artistic Research: Theories, Methods, and Practices* (Gothenburg: University of Gothenburg) http://goart.gu.se/kf_publ/kf_publ.htm

Hassan, I. and S. Hassan (eds) (1983) *Innovation/Renovation* (Madison, WI: Wisconsin Press)

Heathcote, D., C. O'Neill and L. Johnson (eds) (1984) *Collected Writings on Education and Drama* (London: Hutchinson Education)

Heidegger, M. (1968) *What is Called Thinking* (New York: Harper & Row) (1977) *Basic Writings*, D. Farrell Krell (ed.) (San Francisco: Harper & Row) (2002) *The Origin of the Work of Art* (Cambridge: Cambridge University)

Heikkinen, H. (2001) 'Narratiivinen tutkimus – todellisuus kertomuksena' ['Narrative research – Reality as a Tale'] in J. Aaltola and R. Valli (eds), *Ikkunoita tutkimusmetodeihin II – näkökulmia aloittelevalle tutkijalle tutkimuksen teoreettisiin lähtökohtiin ja analyysimenetelmiin* [*Windows into Research Methods II – Perspectives on the Theoretical Starting Points and Methods of Analysis for Beginner Researchers*] (Jyväskylä: PS-Kustannus) 116–132

Heinämaa, S. (1996) *Ele, tyyli ja sukupuoli: Merleau-Pontyn ja Beauvoirin ruumiinfenomenologia ja sen merkitys sukupuolikysymykselle* [*Gesture, Style and Sex/Gender: Merleau-Ponty's and Beauvoir's Phenomenology of the Body and Its Meaning for the Sex/Gender Issue*] (Tampere: Gaudeamus)

(2000) *Ihmetys ja rakkaus: esseitä ruumiin ja sukupuolen fenomenologiasta* [*Wonder and Love: Essays on the Phenomenology of the Body and Gender*] (Jyväskylä: Gummerus)

Hermanis, A. (2008) 'Speaking About Violence', *PAJ: A Journal of Performance and Art*, September, Vol. XXX, No. 3: 8–10

Hertz, R. (ed.) (1997) *Reflexivity and Voice* (London: Sage)

HESA: Higher Education Statistics Agency (2008) Information Provision, http://www.hesa.ac.uk/index.php

Hessels, L. and H. van Lente (2008) 'Re-thinking new knowledge production: a literature review and a research agenda', *Research Policy*, Vol. 37: 740–760

Higher Education Funding Council for England (2002) The Research Assessment Exercise, Bristol: http://hefce.ac.uk/research/assessment

Hockey J. (2003) 'Practice-Based Research Degree Students in Art and Design: Identity and Adaptation', *Journal of Art & Design Education*, February, Vol. 22, No. 1: 82–91

Hockney, D. (2006) 'Secret Knowledge: Rediscovering the Lost Techniques of the Old Masters' (London: Studio Books)

Holmes, A. (2006) 'Reconciling Experimentum and Experientia: Ontology for Reflective Practice Research in New Media', *Speculation and Innovation: Applying Practice Led Research in the Creative Industries* (Queensland University of Technology) http://www.speculation2005.net

Holt, N.L. (2003) 'Representation, Legitimation, and Autoethnography: An Autoethnographic Writing Story', *International Journal of Qualitative Methods*, 2(1) Article 2, http://www.ualberta.ca/~iiqm/backissues/2_1/html/holt.html

Hooks, B. (1990) 'Yearning: Race, Gender and Cultural Politics' (Boston: South End)

Hubbard, R.S. and B.M. Power (1993) *The Art of Classroom Inquiry: A Handbook for Teacher Researchers* (Portsmouth, NH: Heinemann)

Huston, H. (1992) *The Actor's Instrument: Body, Theory, Stage* (Ann Arbor: University of Michigan Press)

Hutcheon, L. (1984) *Narcissistic Narrative: the metafictional paradox* (London & New York: Methuen)

(1988) *The Poetics of Postmodernism: History, Theory, Fiction* (New York & London: Routledge)

Ihde, D. (2002) *Bodies in Technology* (Minneapolis: University of Minneapolis Press)

Irigaray, L. (1985) *This Sex Which Is Not One* (New York: Columbia University Press)

Jarvis, P. (1999) *The Practitioner-Researcher: Developing Theory from Practice* (San Francisco: Jossey-Bass)

Jay, M. (1993) *Downcast Eyes: The Denigration of Vision in Twentieth-Century French Thought* (Berkeley: University of California Press)

Johnson, B.S. (1999) *The Unfortunates* (London: Picador Press)

Jones, A. (1998) *Body Art, Performing the Subject* (University of Minnesota Press)
(2006) *Self/Image* (London & New York: Routledge)

Jones, S. (2003) 'The Courage of Complementarity', keynote address: PARIP National Conference, 11–14 September 2003, http://www.bristol.ac.uk/parip/jones.htm

Kanafani, G. (2000) *Palestine's Children: Returning to Haifa and Other Stories* (USA: Lynne Rienner)

Kaye, N. (2006) *Multi-Media: Video, Installation, Performance* (London & New York: Routledge)

Kemp, M., (1990) *The Science of Art Optical Themes from Brunelleschi to Seurat* (New Haven and London: Yale University Press)

Kershaw, B. (2007) *Theatre Ecology* (London & New York: Routledge)

Kiljunen, S. and M. Hannula (2002) *Artistic Research* (Helsinki: Academy of Fine Arts)

Kinnunen, H.M. (2008) *Tarinat teatterin taiteellisessa prosessissa* (Helsinki: Teatterikorkeakoulu) www.helkamariakinnunen.fi

Knowles, A. (2009) 'Performance Drawings: Fluxus Long Weekend', *PAJ: A Journal of Performance and Art*, January 2009, Vol. XXXI, No. 1: 139–148

Kristeva, J. (1980) *Desire in Language: A Semiotic Approach to Literature and Art* (Columbia: Columbia University Press)

Kvale, S. (2004) 'The Social Construction of Validity' in N. Denzin and S. Lincoln (eds), *The Qualitative Inquiry Reader* (Thousand Oaks, CA: Sage Publications)

Laban, R. (1966) *Choreutics* (London: MacDonald & Evans)

Lakoff, G. and M. Johnson (1999) *Philosophy in the Flesh: The Embodied Mind and Its Challenge to Western Thought* (London: HarperCollins)

Lane, D. (2009) 'Professional Practice, Higher Education and Value', Research Seminar, Exeter University, 18 March 2009

Langellier, K. and E.E. Peterson (2004) *Storytelling in Daily Life: Performing Narrative* (Philadelphia: Temple University Press)
(2006) 'Shifting Contexts in Personal Performance' in D. Soyinyi Madison and J. Hamera (eds), *The Sage Handbook of Performance Studies* (London: Sage)

Lather, P. (1996) 'Troubling Clarity: The politics of accessible language', *Harvard Educational Review*, Vol. 66, No. 3: 525–545

Latour, B. (1993) *We Have Never Been Modern* (Cambridge: Harvard University Press)
(2007) 'A Plea for Earthly Sciences', keynote lecture for the annual meeting of the British Sociological Association, East London, April 2007, http://www.bruno-latour.fr/articles/article/102-BSA-GB.pdf

LeCompte, M.D. and J.J. Schensul (1999) *Designing and Conducting Ethnographic Research* (Walnut Creek, CA: Alta Mira Press)

Lepecki, A. (2006) *Exhausting Dance – performance and the politics of movement* (London & New York: Routledge)

Lester, S. (2004) 'Conceptualising the Practitioner Doctorate', *Studies in Higher Education*, 29(6): 757–770

Levinas, E. (1996) 'Martin Heidegger and Ontology', *Diacritics*, Vol. 26, No. 1: 11–32

Lincoln, Y.S. and N.K. Denzin (1994) 'The Fifth Moment' in N.K. Denzin and Y.S. Lincoln (eds), *Handbook of Qualitative Research* (London: Sage Publications): 575–585

Lyotard, J.F. (1979) *The Postmodern Condition* (Minneapolis: University of Minnesota Press)
(1984) *The Postmodern Condition: A Report on Knowledge* (Manchester: Manchester University Press)
(1991) *The Inhuman: Reflections on Time* (Oxford: Blackwell)

Maclean, M. (1988) *Narrative as Performance: The Baudelairean Experiment* (London: Routledge)

Macleod, K. (2000) 'The Functions of the Written Text in Practice-Based PhD Submissions' in *Working Papers in Art and Design*, 1

Macleod, K. and L. Holdridge (2006) *Thinking through Art: Reflections on Art as Research* (London: Routledge)

Madison, D.S. (2005) *Critical Ethnography: Methods, Ethics and Performance* (California: Sage)

Malfroy, J. and L. Yates (2003) 'Knowledge in Action: doctoral programmes forging new identities', *Journal of Higher Education Policy and Management*, Vol. 25, No. 2: 119–129

Marcus, J. (2002) 'Grade bandwagon runs wild', *Times Higher Education*, http://www.timeshighereducation.co.uk/story.asp?storyCode=170577&sectioncode=26

Marcus, L. (1994) *Auto/Biographical Discourses* (Manchester: Manchester University Press)

Margolis, J. (1978) *Philosophy Looks at the Arts: Contemporary Readings in Aesthetics* (Philadelphia: Temple University Press)

McAuley, G. (2002) 'How to Write about the performing body', *Real Time*, No. 47, February/March 2002: 38

McCammon, L.A. (2005) *Youth Theatre Journal*, Vol. 19, 2005: 5–6

McGinnis, D. and P. Roberts (1996) 'Qualitative characteristics of vivid memories attributed to real and imagined experiences', *American Journal of Psychology*, No. 109: 59–77

McKay, H. and B. Dudley (1996) *About Storytelling: A Practical Guide* (Sydney: Hale & Iremonger)

McNamara, B. (1996) *Step Right Up!* (Jackson: University Press of Mississippi)

McNiff, S. (2005) *Art-based Research* (London: Jessica Kingsley Publishing)

Melrose, S. (1999) 'Restaging "Theory" in the Postgraduate Performance Studies Workshop', *New Theatre Quarterly*, Vol. XV, Part 1, 1999: 39–44
(2002) 'Entertaining Other Options: Restaging "theory" in the age of practice as research', Inaugural Lecture, Middlesex University, http://www.sfmelrose.u-net.com/inaugural/

(2003) 'Who Knows – and Who Cares (About Performance Mastery)?', *Performance Arts International*, http://www.mdx.ac.uk/www/epai/virtuosity/performancemastery/

Merleau-Ponty, M. (1962) *Phenomenology of Perception* (London: Routledge & Kegan Paul Ltd)

(1968) *The Visible and the Invisible* (Evanston: Northwestern University Press)

Merlin, B. (2004) 'Practice as Research in Performance: A Personal Response', *NTQ*, 20:1, February 2004: 36–44

Meyer-Dinkgräfe, D. (2006) *International Conference Consciousness, Literature and the Arts* (Newcastle: Cambridge Scholars Press)

Meyrick, J. (2006) 'Cut and Paste: The Nature of Dramaturgical Development in the Theatre', *Theatre Research International*, 31:3: 270–282

Mock, R. and R. Way (2005) 'Pedagogies of Theatre (Arts) and Performance (Studies)', *Studies in Theatre and Performance*, Vol. 25, No. 3: 201–214

Mooney, Tony (2003) 'Inflation by Degress', http://www.guardian.co.uk/education/2003/mar/18/studentwork.highereducation

Moore, C. and K. Yamamoto (2000) *Beyond Words: Movement Observation and Analysis* (London: Routledge)

Moustakis, C. (1961) *Loneliness* (New Jersey: Prentice Hall)

(1972) *Loneliness and Love* (New Jersey: Prentice Hall)

Mroz, A. (2008) 'British Doctorates in the Dock', *Times Higher Education*, 4–10 December, No. 1,874: 23

Murray, S. and J. Keefe (2007) *Physical Theatres: A Critical Introduction* (London & New York: Routledge)

Neelands, J. and T. Goode (2001) *Structuring Drama Work* (2nd edition, Cambridge: Cambridge University Press)

Newman, M. (2008) 'Lecturer admonished to "find the excellence" and lift marks', *Times Higher Education*, 11–17 December, No. 1,875: 6

Nicholson, H. (2005) *Applied Drama: The Gift of Theatre* (London: Routledge)

Nisbett, R. and T.D. Wilson (1977) 'Telling More Than We Can Know: Verbal Reports on Mental Processes', *Psychological Review*, 84: 231–259

Novarina, V. (1993) 'Letter to the Actors', *Drama Review*, Vol. 37, No. 2 (T138), Summer: 95–118

Oakley, A. (2000) *Experiments in Knowing: Gender and Method in the Social Sciences* (Cambridge: Polity Press)

Office of National Statistics (2007) http://www.statistics.gov.uk/default.asp

O'Neill, C. (1995) *Drama Worlds: A Framework for Process Drama* (USA: Heinemann)

Organisation for Economic Co-operation and Development (2002) *The Frascati Manual* (Paris: OECD Press)

Owens, A. (1997) *The Development of Children's Thinking Skills Through Drama* (British Council Report)

Paavolainen, P. and A.K. Anu (eds) (1994) *Knowledge is a Matter of Doing: proceedings of the symposium Theatre and Dance Artist doing Research in Practice, Helsinki, 13–15 October 1994* (Helsinki: Theatre Academy)

Pakes, A. (2004) 'Art as Action or Art as Object? The Embodiment of Knowledge in Practice as Research', *Working Papers in Art and Design*, Vol. 3, http://www.herts.ac.uk/artdes1/research/papers/wpades/vol3/apfull.html

Park, C. (2005) 'New Variant PhD: The Changing Nature of the Doctorate in the UK', *Journal of Higher Education Policy and Management*, 27 (2)

Parviainen, J. (2007) 'Bodily knowledge: epistemological reflections on dance', choreography. net – a state of dance, http://choreograph.net/articles/bodily-knowledge-epistemological-reflections-on-dance

Pavis, P. (1990) 'Approaches to Theatre Studies' in *Assaph* C., 6: 23–42 (The Yolanda and David Katz Faculty of the Arts, Tel-Aviv University)

(2000) 'Theory and Practice in Theatre Studies in the University', *Studies in Theatre and Performance*, Vol. 20, No. 2: 68–86

Pearson, M. and M. Shanks (2000) Theatre/Archaeology (London & New York: Routledge)

Pelias, R.J. (2008) 'Performative Inquiry: Embodiment and Its Challenges' in J.G. Knowles and A.L. Cole (eds), *Handbook of the Arts in Qualitative Research* (London: Sage)

Phelan, P. (1993) *Unmarked: The Politics of Performance* (London & New York: Routledge)

Phillips, E.M. and D.S. Pugh (2000) *How to get a PhD: A handbook for students and their supervisor* (Milton Keynes: Open University Press)

Piccini, A. (2002) 'An Historiographic Perspective on Practice as Research', http://www.bris.ac.uk/parip/artexts.htm

(2004) 'An Historiographic Perspective on Practice as Research', *Studies in Theatre and Performance*, Vol. 23, No. 3: 191–207

Pike, K. (1954) *Language in Relation to a Unified Theory of the Structure of Human Behavior* (California: Summer Institute of Linguistics)

Pink, S. (2001) *Doing Visual Ethnography* (London: Sage)

Polanyi, M. (1983) *The Tacit Dimension* (Gloucester, MA: Peter Smith)

Polkinghorne, D.E. (1995) 'Narrative Configuration in Qualitative Analysis' in J.A. Hatch and R. Wisnievski (eds), *Life History and Narrative* (Washington, DC: Falmer)

Popper, K. (2002) *The Logic of Scientific Discovery* (London & New York: Routledge)

Powell, S. and E. Long (2005) 'Professional Doctorate Awards in the UK' (UK Council for Graduate Education) http://www.ukcge.ac.uk/filesup/ProfessDoc.pdf

Prose, F. (2002) *The Lives of the Muses: Nine Women & the Artists They Inspired* (London: Aurum Press)

Quick, A. (2007) *The Wooster Group Workbook* (New York & London: Routledge)

Rae, P. (2003) 're-invention: on the limits of reflective practice', PARIP National Conference, 11–14 September 2003, http://www.bris.ac.uk/parip/rae.htm

Rapaport, H. (1997) *Is There Truth in Art?* (Ithaca: Cornell University Press)

Reed-Dahanay, D.E. (ed.) (1997) *Auto/Ethnography: Rewriting the Self and the Social* (Oxford: Berg)

Rhode, E. (1976) *A History of the Cinema: From its Origins to 1970* (London: Allen Lane)

Richards, A. (1992) 'Performance as Research/Performance as Publication Position Paper presented to Australasian Drama Studies Association Executive Meeting' (Unpublished)

Richardson, L. (1990) *Writing Strategies: Reaching Diverse Audiences* (London: Sage Publications)

(1994) 'Writing: A Method of Inquiry' in N.K. Denzin and Y.S. Lincoln (eds), *Handbook of Qualitative Research* (London: Sage Publications): 516–527

Ricouer, P. (2003) *The Rule of Metaphor* (London: Routledge)

Riley, S.R. and L. Hunter (2009) *Mapping Landscapes for Performance as Research: Scholarly Acts and Creative Cartographies* (Hampshire: Palgrave)

Robinson, G. (2000) *The Creativity Imperative: Investing in the arts in the 21st Century* (London: The Arts Council of England)

Rouhiainen, L. (2003) *Living Transformative Lives: Finnish Freelance Dance Artists Brought into Dialogue with Merleau-Ponty's Phenomenology* (Helsinki: Theatre Academy)

Rubin, W. (ed.) (1977) *Cézanne: The Late Work* (New York: Museum of Modern Art)

Ryan, P. (2008) 'The Storyteller in Context: Storyteller Identity and Storytelling Experience', *Storytelling, Self, Society*, 4.2: 64–87

Rye, C. (2003) 'Video Writing: The Documentation Trap, or the Role of Documentation in the Practice as Research', http://humanitieslab.stanford.edu/ArchaeologyPerformance/admin/download.html?attachid=108605

Saastamoinen, M. (2005) 'Narratiivinen sosiaalipsykologia – teoriaa ja menetelmiä' ['Narrative Social Psychology – Theory and Methods'], http://www.uku.fi/⊠msaastam/narratiivi.htm

Said, E. (1978) *Orientalism* (New York: Vintage Books)

(1994) *The Politics of Dispossession* (New York: Vintage Books)

(2000) *The End of the Peace Process* (India: Penguin Books)

Sanders, A.F. (1988) *Michael Polanyi's Post Critical Epistemology, a Reconstruction of Some Aspects of Tacit Knowing* (Amsterdam: Rodopi Press)

Sauter, W. (2009) 'Theatre Research in the Nordic Countries (2000–2008)', *Theatre Research International*, Vol. 34, No. 1: 66–83

Schechner, R. (1988) *Performance Theory* (New York: Routledge)

(1992) 'A New Paradigm for Theatre in the Academy', *The Drama Review*, Vol. 36, No. 4: 7–10

(2002) 'My Art in Life: Interviewing Spalding Gray', *The Drama Review*, 46.4: 154–174

Schön, D.A. (1983) *The Reflective Practitioner: How Professionals Think in Action* (New York: Basic Books)

(1987) *Educating the Reflective Practitioner* (San Francisco: Jossey Bass)

Schratz, M. and R. Walker (1995) *Research as Social Change* (London: Routledge)

Scott, C., A. Brown, I. Lunt and L. Thorne (2004) *Professional Doctorates: Integrating Professional and Academic Knowledge* (London: Open University Press)

Scrivener, S. (2000) 'Reflection in and on Action and Practice in Creative-Production Doctoral Projects in Art and Design', *Working Papers in Art and Design*, 1, http://www.herts.ac.uk/artdes/research/papers/wpades/vol2/scrivenerfull.html
(2002) 'The Art Object Does Not Embody a Form of Knowledge', Working Wellcome Trust PhD Papers in Art and Design, http://www.herts.ac.uk/artdes1/research/papers/wpades/vol2/scrivenerfull.html

Scrivener, S. and P. Chapman (2004) 'The Practical Implications of Applying a Theory of Practice Based Research: A Case Study', *Working Papers in Art and Design*, Vol. 3, http://www.herts.ac.uk/artdes1/research/papers/wpades/vol3/ssfull.html

SCUDD (2009) Call for Papers (The Ends of PaR) Colloquium, 26 September 2009, Central School of Speech and Drama, http://www.cssd.ac.uk/

Seidman, S. and D. Wagner (eds) (1992) *Postmodern Social Theory* (Cambridge, MA: Blackwell)

Shaw, P. and M. Tennant (2001) *Arts Research Seminar Report: No. 3: Action Research in the Arts: Current and Future Uses* (Newcastle upon Tyne: University of Northumbria)

Shehadeh, R. (2008) *Palestinian Walks: Notes on a Vanishing Landscape* (London: Profile Books)

Shiff, R. (1979) *One-way Street and other Writings* (London: Verso)

Skjulstad, S., A. Aaberge and A. Morrison (2002) 'Researching performance, performing research' in A. Morrison (ed.) *Researching ICTs in Context* (Oslo: InterMedia/UniPub): 211–248, http://imweb.uio.no/konferanser/skikt-02/docs/Researching_ICTs_in_context-Ch10-Skjulstad-et.al.pdf

Sparkes, A.C. (2002) 'Autoethnography: Self-Indulgence or Something More?' in A.P. Bochner and C. Ellis (eds), *Ethnographically Speaking: Autoethnography, Literature, and Aesthetics* (Walnut Creek, CA: AltaMira Press): 209–232

Springgay, S., R.L. Irwin and S. Kind (2005) 'A/r/tography as living inquiry through art and text', *Qualitative Inquiry*, 11(6): 897–912

Spry, T. (2001) 'Performing Autoethnography: An Embodied Methodological Praxis', *Qualitative Inquiry*, Vol. 7, No. 6: 706–732

Stake, R. (1995) *The Art of Case Study Research* (Thousand Oaks, CA: Sage Publications)

Stanislavsky, K. and J. Benedetti (2008) *An Actor's Work: A Student's Diary*, trans. J. Benedetti (New York: Routledge)

States, B.O. (1987) *Great Reckonings in Little Rooms: On the Phenomenology of Theater* (Berkeley: University of California Press)

Stivale, C.J. (1998) *The Two-Fold Thought of Deleuze and Guattari: Intersections and Animations* (London & New York: Guilford Press)

Stoller, P. (1997) *Sensuous Scholarship* (Philadelphia: University of Pennsylvania)

Sturm, B.W. (2000) 'The "Storylistening" Trance Experience', *The Journal of American Folklore*, 113.449: 287–304

Sullivan, G. (2005) *Art Practice as Research: Inquiry in the Visual Arts* (California: Sage)

Swindells, J. (ed.) (1995) *The Uses of Autobiography* (London: Taylor & Francis)

Thompson, J. (2003) *Applied Theatre: Bewilderment and Beyond* (Oxford: Peter Lang Publishing)

(2006) *Digging Up Stories: Applied Theatre, Performance and War* (Manchester: Manchester University Press)

Thomson, P. (2000) 'Stop Press: The Intellectual Consequences of the Research Assessment Exercise', *Studies in Theatre and Performance*, Vol. 20, No. 2: 114–120

(2003) 'Notes and Queries: Practice as Research', *Studies in Theatre and Performance*, Vol. 22, No. 3: 159–180

Throop, J.C. (2003) 'Articulating Experience', *Anthropological Theory*, Vol. 3, No. 2: 219–24

Tierney, W.G. (2000) 'Undaunted Courage: Life History and the Postmodern Challenge' in N.K. Denzin and Y.S. Lincoln (eds), *Handbook of Qualitative Research* (Thousand Oaks, CA: Sage): 537–553

Torrance, E.P. (1981) *Creativity: Its educational implications* (Dubuque, IA: Kendall/Hunt)

Trimingham, M. (2002) 'A Methodology for Practice as Research', *Studies in Theatre and Performance*, Vol. 22, No. 1: 54–60

UCAS (2009) 'Helping Students into Higher Education', http://www.ucas.ac.uk/

UK Council for Graduate Education (2004) 'Professional Doctorate Awards in the UK', http://www.ukcge.ac.uk/ProfessionalDoctorates2002.pdf

Valery, P. (1970) 'Analects', in *Collected Works*, Vol. 14, trans. S. Gilbert (Princeton:, Princeton University Press): 26

Van Kerkhoven, M. (1993) *Silta ruumiin ja hengen välillä: tanssin ja teatterin rajamaasto [A Bridge Between The Body and Spirit: At the Borders of Dance and Theatre]* (Helsinki: Yliopistopaino)

Varto, J. (2000) *Uutta tietoa: Värityskirja tieteen filosofiaan* (Tampere: Tampereen yliopistopaino)

Vicario, B. (2005) *Il Tempo, il Mulino* (Rome: Ricerca)

Vroon, P. (1997) *Smell: The Secret Seducer* (New York: Farrar, Straus and Giroux)

Webster, L. and P. Mertova (2007) *Using Narrative Inquiry as a Research Method* (New York: Routledge)

Weiss, C. (1972) *Evaluating Action Programs: Readings in Social Action and Education* (Boston: Allyn & Bacon)

Weiss, G. (1999a) *Body Images: Embodiment and Corporeality* (New York & London: Routledge)

(1999b) 'Body Image Intercourse. A Corporeal Dialogue between Merleau-Ponty and Schilder', in D. Olkowski and J. Morley (eds), *Merleau-Ponty, Interiority and Exteriority, Psychic Life and the World* (Albany: State University of New York Press): 121–143

Wellcome Trust (2000) *Review of Wellcome Trust PhD Training: The Student Perspective* (London: Wellcome Trust)

Welton, M. (2003) 'Against Inclusivity: A Happy Heresy about Theory and Practice', *New Theatre Quarterly*, Vol. 19, No. 4: 347–351

Wenger, E. (1998) *Communities of Practice, Learning, Meaning, and Identity* (Cambridge, UK: Cambridge University Press)

Whelan, J.C. (2007) 'Practical creativity in process and live performance; Visual, Auditory and Kinesthetic elements of creative environments', http://people.brunel.ac.uk/bst/documents/johncwhelan.doc

Williams, B. (1973) *Problems of the Self* (Cambridge: Cambridge University Press)

Wilson, M. (2006) *Storytelling and Theatre* (Hampshire: Palgrave Macmillan)

Wittgenstein, L. (1968 [1953]) *Philosophical Investigations* (Oxford: Basil Blackwell)

Wolcott, H.F. (1999) *Ethnography: A Way of Seeing* (California: Alta Mira Press)

Yarwood, T. (2001) 'as<is & paradigm>paradox', PARIP Symposium, 10–11 November 2001, University of Bristol, http://www.bris.ac.uk/parip/sched.htm

Yates, L. (2005) *What is Quality in Educational Research?* (Milton Keynes: Open University Press)

Yin, R. (1993) *Applications of Case Study Research* (California: Sage)

Yuasa, Y., S. Nagatomo and M.S. Hull (1993) *The Body, Self-cultivation, and Ki-energy* (New York: SUNY Press)

Zarrilli, P.B. (2001) 'Negotiating Performance Epistemologies: Knowledges "about", "in" and "for"', *Studies in Theatre and Performance*, Vol. 21, No. 1: 31–46
(2007) *Kathakali Dance-Drama* (Oxford: Taylor & Francis)

Zinder, D. (1976) *The Surrealist Connection: an approach to a surrealist aesthetic of theater* (Michigan: UMI Research Press)

Zuesse, E.M. (1975) 'Meditation on Ritual', *Journal of the American Academy of Religion*, 43.3: 517–530

Zumthor, P. (1990) 'Oral Poetry: An Introduction', in W. Godzich and J. Schulte-Sasse (eds), *Theory and History of Literature*, Vol. 70 (Minneapolis: University of Minnesota)

Index